D0358425
This book belongs
to
Margaret
O'Farrell
Christmas 1982

PUBLISHED BY THE READER'S DIGEST ASSOCIATION LIMITED
LONDON NEW YORK MONTREAL SYDNEY CAPE TOWN

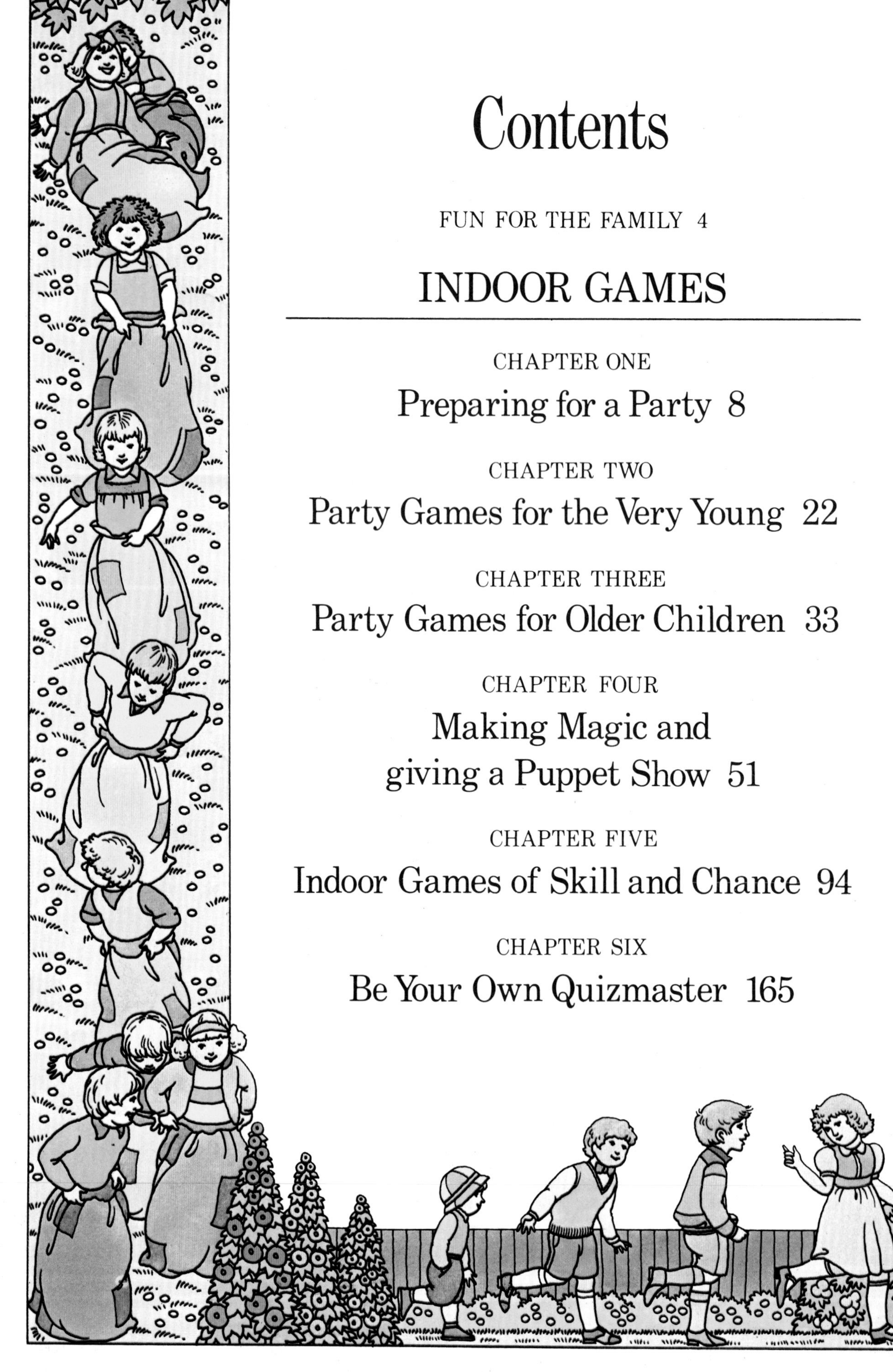

Contents

OUTDOOR GAMES

PARTY TREATS

Fun for the Family

This treasury of family games is designed to create a rich source of fun for a growing family. It gives information about games of every kind. Here are games that are robustly athletic and games that depend more on quick wits than on strength or physical ability. Here are teaching and learning activities, pastimes for rainy days, diversions to lighten the hours spent travelling, and games to play on holiday, whether at home, in the country or by the sea.

Some of the games have been favourites for centuries. The ancient Greeks, for example, played a game called Ostrakindra. Today it is still a favourite and is known in this country as Crusts and Crumbs.

The rules of such games have been handed down from generation to generation, and this book will help young parents to recall the favourite games of their childhood and so enable their own children to delight in them.

As a child grows up he will find some games exciting for a time, then he will pass these over for others that are more demanding on his developing mental and physical skills. Other games, such as draughts, chess and whist,

however, may inspire an interest that will last a lifetime. Teenagers and adults, therefore, will also find this book a source of information on those board, card and dice games for all ages that can be played competitively or as part of an evening's entertainment at home.

Organising a children's party can be an exhausting and worrying problem for parents. Some, indeed, have given up the struggle and hire professional party organisers and entertainers who choose and lead the games and also give a conjuring performance or a puppet show. Party organisers have contributed to this book. You can, with their help, organise your own children's party with confidence instead of foreboding.

As with traditional games, children's tastes in party games change as they grow older, and the most noticeable change occurs when they start school. The party games in this book, therefore, have been divided into two chapters—those for pre-school children and those for children aged from five to about ten years old.

The highlight of any children's party is the food, whether it is a sit-down tea or a garden barbecue. In the chapter Party Treats the recipes have been chosen to suit all ages, with something to satisfy even the fussiest young child.

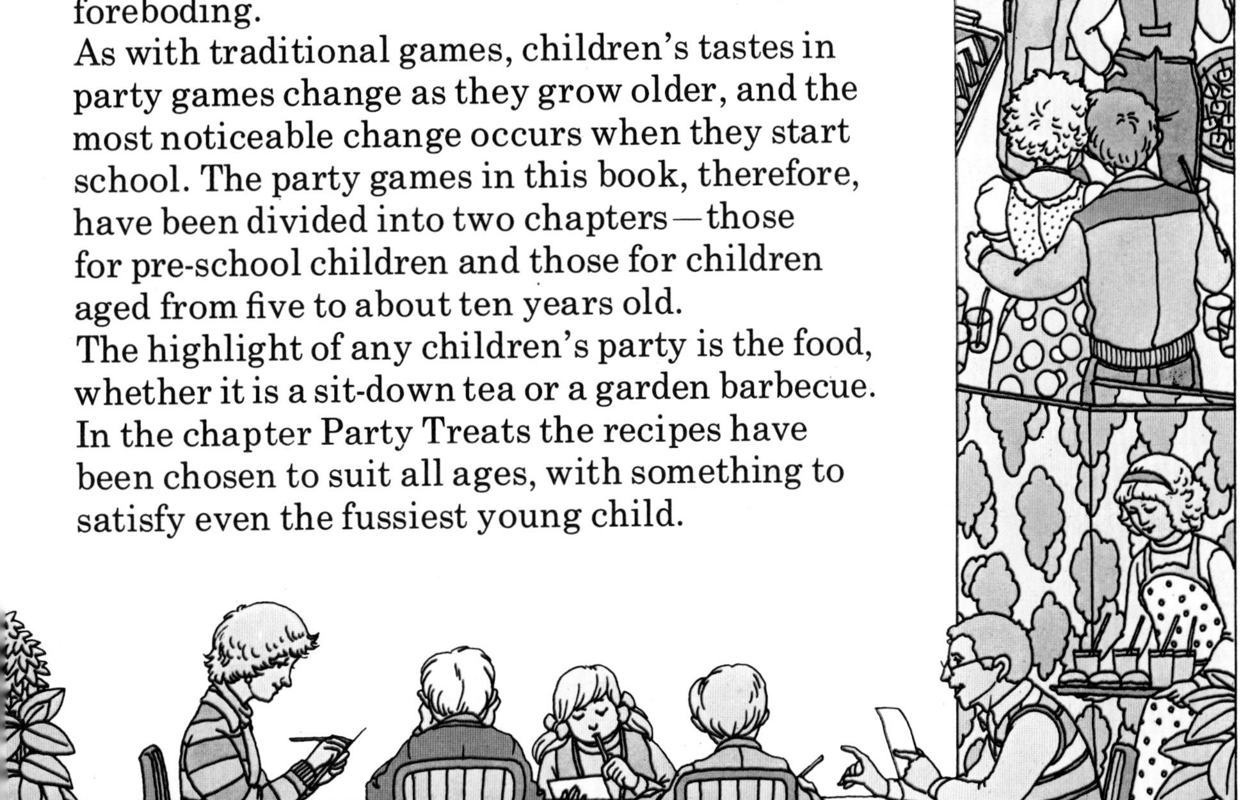

INDOOR GAMES

Making your parties go with a swing and finding things to do on rainy days and holidays

Chapter 1

Preparing for a Party

Deciding on the number of guests; Sending the invitations; Making the decorations; Organising jobs for your helpers

The fun should start from the moment someone says 'Let's have a party'. Sometimes the strain of arranging a party makes it easy for the organisers to lose sight of the reason it is being held in the first place; they should enjoy themselves as much as the guests. A party that is arranged with pleasure is a party that will be a success. As plans begin to take shape, pleasure will be overtaken by excitement, reaching a climax when the first ring is heard on the door bell. Finally, when the last guest has gone, filled with food and contentment, excitement subsides into the satisfaction of a job well done. That is the ideal. Let's find out how to achieve it.

The date is obviously the first thing you must consider. If you are giving a birthday party, for instance, it need not necessarily be held on the birthday itself. Sometimes it is better to hold the party on a different date which is more convenient—fitting in better with school times, for example.

If it is to be a Christmas party, it is a good idea to hold it after Boxing Day when the traditional family get-together is over. The same principle applies to all the festive days: Easter, Hallow-e'en, bank holidays. Time your party to allow for family activities. Whatever period you select, or whatever the reason for your party, fix a provisional date and then make a few enquiries around and about to make sure that it doesn't clash with anything else in your neighbourhood.

Settling the guest list

Once satisfied on the date, your next task will be to settle the guest list, quite often the trickiest part of all. The size of your house dictates the number of children you can invite and in most modern houses 20 is the maximum. But you have to remember that you may be in charge of the organisation, but the party is not being given by you. The host or hostess is one of your children, and children usually have very definite ideas about whom they want to be there. This can range from a couple of very close friends—and this would not be a party at all—to the entire strength of a school class with every boy and girl in your street added for good measure. This could strain the resources of Buckingham Palace. The best plan is to pare the list down to very close friends, those who have to be asked back, relatives, and then build on that.

Aiming for a mixture

You are sure to have some refusals for a variety of reasons—illness for example, or holidays away from home—so your invitation list can safely be a little larger than you think is your maximum. Nothing is more unfortunate than a sparsely attended party, even though for perfectly genuine reasons. Aim if you can for a mixture of guests. Inviting children from other schools can help to avoid exclusive groups being formed. Mixing the sexes is a good idea too unless, as is the case with some of the younger age groups, the child for whom the party is being given is utterly opposed to it.

Sending the invitations

Invitation cards should be sent out in time to give at least ten days' notice. Printed cards, which can be bought from any stationer, make the job easier, but you might like to give an original touch and design your own (see p. 12). People like to display the cards, which means they are not apt to get lost, and they can then easily check the date, time, address and telephone number of your home. Another point in favour of sending cards, instead of giving verbal invitations, is that they act as constant reminders and, even more important, they invariably include a request for a reply.

Invitations should never be given by word of mouth or over the telephone, even to the closest of friends. You may forget to give a vital piece of information in the general, informal chat or your guest can misunderstand some point such as the time or even the date. The telephone is useful, however, when party time draws near and some replies have not come in. A friendly check will let you know where you stand.

It is important to indicate on the invitation cards not only when the party is to begin but also when it is to end. This is most helpful to parents of younger children who will know precisely when to collect them; and the older children will not feel that they are overstaying their welcome. End your party on the hour rather than the half-hour. This is easier to remember and helps to prevent 'collectors' arriving too early or too late. Too early will disrupt the games and too late could mean your having to look after some small socialiser who has decided that the time to go home has long passed. So far as the length of your party is concerned it is better to make the party too short than too long, especially for the younger guests. As the old-time entertainers used to say: always leave them wanting more.

Getting together

The date has been fixed, the invitations have gone out, you are now committed. Your home is shortly to be invaded by young persons, pleasure bent, anxious to enjoy your food, drink and entertainment to the full and equally anxious to show that they are able to rise to social occasions. Whatever their age, at the early stages of the party this social pressure will result in embarrassment and they will show it in different ways. Some will be boisterous, some aggressive, some shy to the painful point of refusing to say a single word. The boys may knock things over, the girls may scream with laughter for no obvious reason. Possibly there might be no shortage of outspoken comments, on your house, the size of your sitting-room, the way it is decorated, the state of your garden if you have one. Whatever you may think at the time, these are signs that the party will go well; the guests are merely settling down. You can make things easier for them. Get your child, who is the real host, to answer the doorbell and welcome the guests. They immediately react when they see a familiar face.

Girls like to have somewhere private to take off their coats. If the party is in honour of your daughter, then her bedroom is the obvious place. Failing that, use your own bedroom and remember that even five-year-olds like to copy their mothers and look into the mirror to see how pretty they are and how smart their party dress is. Boys do not require such niceties. They are usually quite happy to leave their coats in the hall.

Throughout the party, the lavatory will be in constant use, at first because of excitement or nervousness, later as the result of party drinks. A cautionary note here; it is not unknown for very young revellers accidentally to lock themselves in. Keys are sometimes difficult to turn back, bolts difficult to slide. As a precaution, oil locks and bolts beforehand and make sure that they work easily and smoothly. This is much better than having to shout instructions through a locked door, which often fails to reduce the panic.

The decorations

In the party area, make sure that every non-essential item has been cleared away, especially ornaments which are liable to be knocked over and rugs which can be tripped over or stained by dripping drinks or falling sweets. It is best if the tea-table can be isolated from the play area. This is no problem if you have two living-rooms, but even in a modern open-plan house there is usually a dining alcove which can be separated from the main part of the room. The tea-table should be completely set before the guests arrive, apart from the food (see p. 222) which can be kept in the kitchen under paper napkins, foil and upturned plates.

After the play area has been cleared it will tend to look on the bare side when the first guests appear and there is room to spare. This bleakness is countered by the exciting sight of decorations and the sound of music.

Balloons are always the first symbols of festivity to float into mind and, really, it might be as well to let them float out again. They are a great distraction, they ask to be popped and even if moored to the ceiling they still lure would-be poppers, causing much clambering over chairs and tables and the general feeling that things are getting out of hand. Balloons are best confined to a cluster on the front door where they introduce the party spirit from the very first moment and also make it quite clear to arriving guests exactly where the party is. They can then be given to guests as they leave.

Streamers and coloured paper are just as effective as balloons, the more so if you use them in a definite style or theme. Just as in flower arranging, a little thought and attention can make all the difference. An effective idea is to concentrate on one colour, or variations of it. Red paper flowers, red real flowers, red streamers and some red bulbs in the lamps, for example, make a far greater impact than a random mixture of colours. You can continue the colour theme with red paper hats, red napkins, red paper carrier bags for the children to take home with their prizes or souvenirs (see p. 11). If you can't get red bags, white ones are just as good with a large disc of red paper stuck on each. You can suit your colour theme to the time of year, such as daffodils and yellow in spring, delphiniums and blue in midsummer.

If you prefer a variety of colour, you can turn your play area into an exciting impression of the interior of a circus tent by hanging strips of coloured crepe paper from the centre of the ceiling to the walls.

The music

Music has a most important part to play both in providing the right atmosphere and in some of the party games (see pp. 22 and 33). At the beginning of the party, when the guests are assembling, background music sets the mood, and covers up those embarrassing silences that can occur at even grown-up gatherings. Choose music that is familiar to your guests—and that means that you really cannot do better than selections from the 'Top Twenty'. As any listener to the radio knows, children of all ages are interested in the latest tunes. They make them feel at home in strange surroundings and the children are more than happy to comment on them. Your own taste may lie in the romantic, jazz or classical fields—but this is not your party.

Fancy-dress parties

Children love dressing up, so a fancy-dress party is always a popular idea, at least at the start. But there are snags. Bright, original and simple ideas are hard to come by. Many busy mothers simply have not the time to think them up, and in any case an unusual, clever costume is often extremely uncomfortable to wear and highly unsuitable for such party activities as playing games or sitting down to tea. The result is that you may find yourself with more than one Cinderella, several fairy queens, three Batmen and innumerable cowboys. This is a natural source of disappointment, embarrassment and jealousy, all of them emotions you can happily do without. Furthermore, not all your young guests will be coming by car and the experience of travelling by bus, train or simply walking down the street disguised, say, as Baron Frankenstein's monster, can lead the young guest to arrive in quite the wrong frame of mind.

Why not have a party within a party, when the children can use their own ingenuity in dressing up? Collect all the old, clean clothing you can find, both adults' and children's. Add some paper hats, masks, false noses, moustaches and beards, the sort of thing you can buy at carnival novelty shops. You will need to use two bedrooms as changing-rooms, one for the boys the other for the girls. Supervision in the changing-room is essential. Some children may grab the best things, others may be too shy to take anything or may have no idea what to select.

With children of seven or older you could suggest ideas for them, such as characters from TV programmes, fiction, pantomime or nursery rhymes. You should see that the proper items are available; fake fur for Muppets, a black hat for the wicked witch, an eye patch and a crutch for Long John Silver, holster, gun and large hat for a cowboy, and so on. For the younger ones it should be enough to suggest that they dress up as an old lady, a nurse or simply as a grown-up.

Usually, though, it is best to let the children think up their own ideas. Give help only if they are baffled by the whole thing. You can give small prizes if you like, but usually the fun is reward enough. In fact, rather than a few prizes for the best, a souvenir for everyone is a better idea.

If you have, or can borrow, a camera that takes instantly developed prints, ask the children to form a group in costume and to make the face they think best suited to what they are supposed to be. The resulting prints will make your party long remembered and will delight the parents when they are proudly carried home. You can do this only with a smaller number of guests or the cost will be too great. After this, make sure that the guests change back into their own clothes before the party continues, to ensure that they are ready for the next item on the programme.

Presents and prizes

Prizes are an essential party ingredient and they need not be a problem. The aim should be to make them souvenirs of a happy time rather than rewards for individual skill or objects of value on their own account. The more novel they are the better, and the cheapest article can give much pleasure if it is attractively wrapped in gaily coloured paper. There is no need to have a prize for every game; many of the games suggested in this book have neither winners nor losers, and the pleasure of playing is the thing. Even if you have to cheat a little, make sure that the prizes are evenly divided, for everyone should

CONTINUED ON PAGE 17

HOW TO MAKE YOUR OWN INVITATION CARDS

For a Birthday

A three-dimensional wish

Draw, decorate and cut out some daisy-like flowers. Make a tab for each flower by cutting a strip of paper about 10 millimetres wide. Make some tabs 20, 30 and one or two 40 millimetres long. Make two folds in each tab to form a Z-shape (see diagram). Glue one end of a tab to the back of a flower and the other end to the card. Because the tabs are varying lengths the flowers will stand out as if in a bunch. Draw stems held by a hand on the card.

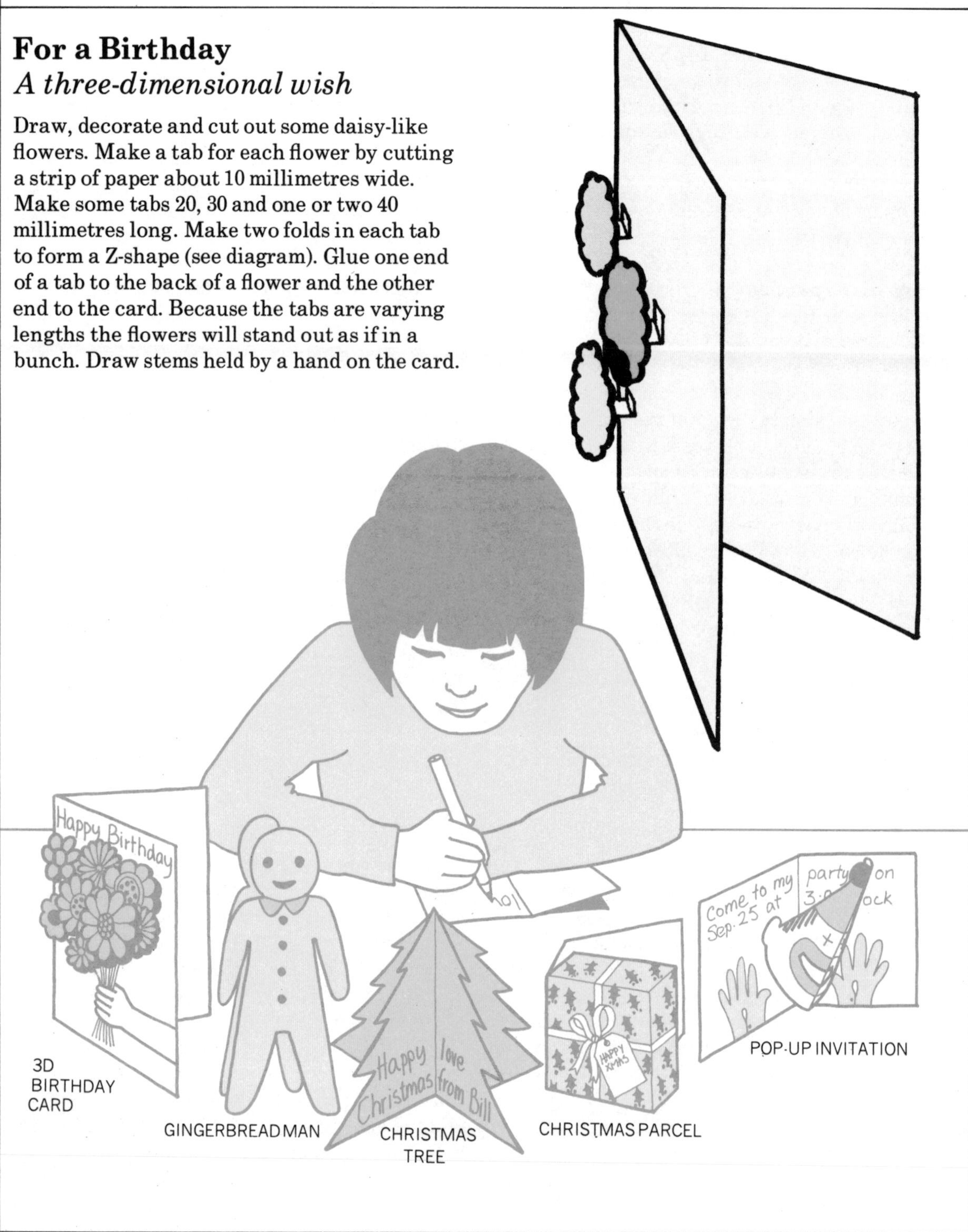

Gingerbread Man

He's a bit of a card

A young child can make this simple card. Fold the necessary number of cards. Use a gingerbread-man biscuit cutter as a stencil. On the front of each card trace round the outside of the cutter with a crayon. Draw in the eyes, mouth and some buttons.

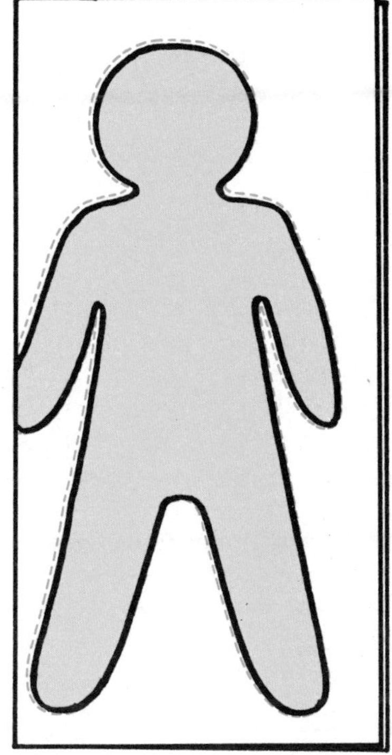

Christmas Parcel Card

A goodwill wish wrapped up to deceive the eye

A young child can trace this card from the diagram, cut and fold where marked, then colour the parcel. An older child might like to draw a larger card using the diagram as a guide. When the corners are cut the drawing looks like a parcel in three dimensions.

Christmas Tree

A card to stand up and stand out

This is a card that is simple to make, yet it will stand out among the others that your friends receive at Christmas.
First, fold two cards of the same size. Draw half the tree shape on each one as in diagram 1. Press the two sides of the card together and cut out the shape of the tree so that when it is opened it will look like the tree in diagram 2. Cut out a shape from the second card in the same way. Colour the tree and draw in some decorations, or give an added touch by pasting on some sequins and narrow strips of kitchen foil.
Cut a slit halfway up the fold of one tree (see diagram 2) and halfway down the fold of the other tree (see diagram 3). Slot one into the other and the tree will stand up.

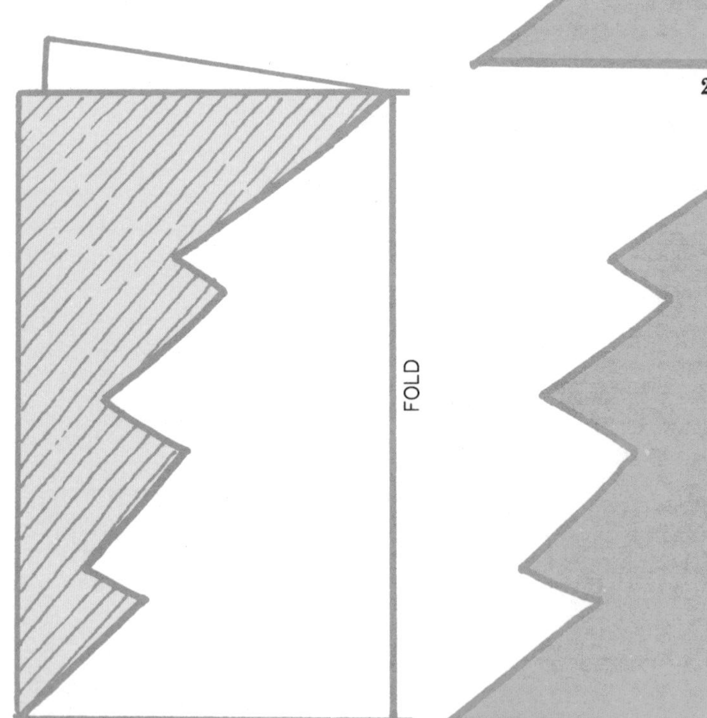

1 Draw the tree shape.

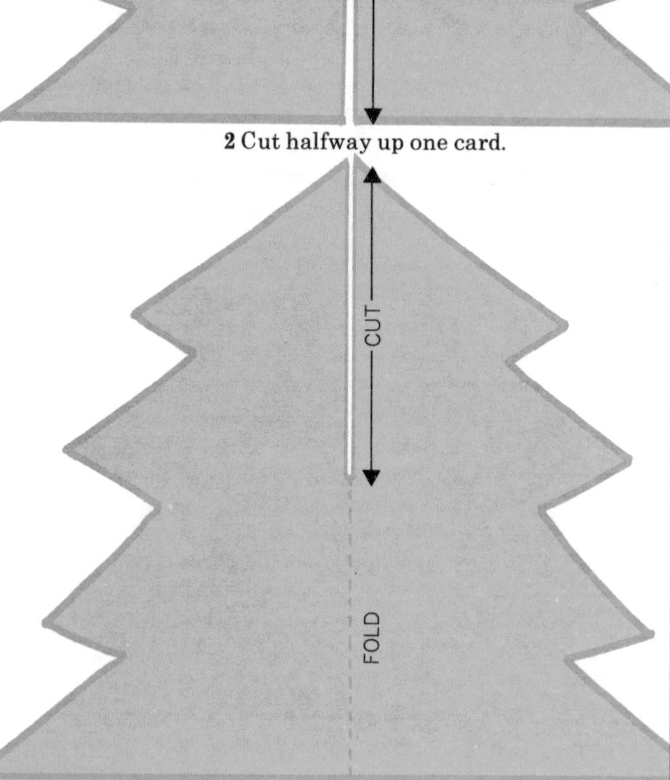

2 Cut halfway up one card.

3 Cut halfway down the other card.

Pop-up Invitation Card

A surprise that will make your friends jump

An unusual invitation or Christmas card can be absorbing for you to make and an exciting surprise for the friend who receives it. When the card is opened, the clown pops up. Fold a piece of paper and draw the half-face of a clown (see diagram 1). Trace if you are not confident that you can copy the face. Open up the paper to reveal the full shape of the clown's face and hat. Colour in the features (see diagram 2). Glue the tabs to the inside of a folded card (see diagram 3) and draw the hands (see diagram 4) on the card.

3 Glue the tabs to the card.

4 Draw hands on the card.

1 Draw the shape of the face.

2 Colour in the features.

Come to My Party – by balloon!

This invitation will give everybody a lift

A novel invitation almost guarantees the success of a party before it even begins. An invited guest receiving a formal, printed card might expect a formal, dull party—but when the invitation arrives by balloon, that could mean an exciting party full of surprises. Blow up the balloons, twisting the ends and keeping them inflated with clothes-pegs. Write the invitation with a felt-tip pen and leave to dry. Take the pegs off and put the invitation balloons in envelopes.

At the party, hang up balloons carrying messages such as 'Thanks for coming' and 'Welcome to my party'.

CONTINUED FROM PAGE 11

go home with about the same number of goodies. It adds to the excitement of the party if you put the prizes in a cardboard box, covered with coloured crepe paper and clearly marked 'Prizes'. You can do this either by using marking ink on a sheet of white paper which can then be stuck on the box with glue or sticky-tape—or you can cut the letters out in paper of a contrasting colour and stick them on the side of the box.

Suitable inexpensive prizes can be bought, such as badges, brooches, pencils, spinning tops, pens, bags of sweets and mirrors.

Gifts should be distributed at the end of the party, just before the guests collect their coats. This avoids losses, premature breakages and comparisons, which can be alarming.

Hiring a hall

It can happen that the only way to solve the problem of matching the size of the guest list to the accommodation available is to hire a hall. This is not so daunting as it sounds but it does reverse the problem. If you are giving the party at home you have to suit the guest list to the size of your house; if you are giving the party in a hall you have to suit the size of the hall to the size of the guest list.

Make sure, whatever you do, that the hall is not too large. In a large hall it is difficult to keep everyone together and to keep the party games going (see p. 43). The expanse of space encourages a lot of running about to no great purpose and if there is a stage this can be a challenge—children are fond of jumping off things and stages are often much higher than they look. What is more, if the hall is too large it has the effect of making the attendance seem sparse and the atmosphere chilly.

You should not have too much difficulty in finding a suitable hall. Local sports clubs are usually happy to hire out a room in the pavilion quite cheaply in the off season; halls can be hired from local councils, though these are often more expensive than, say, church halls. Best of all,perhaps, many restaurants have halls available for social functions with the added attraction that they look after the catering as well.

If you do hire a hall, it is important to make an extra effort to provide the personal touch. Your guests must be made to feel that the hall is an extension of your home. Welcoming notices, on the door and around the walls, help to give this impression. Flowers from your own garden, if you have one, family photographs prominently displayed, all combine to make your guests feel welcome.

Entertainment

The high spot of any party—if you can afford it—is a professional entertainer. He can offer any kind of programme you want: ventriloquism, Punch and Judy, film shows, magic, songs and jokes. Party entertainers are listed in the Yellow Pages under Entertainers and Entertainments, and it is as well to book early in the holiday seasons—they are in great demand. Entertainers, either whole-time or part-time professionals, are usually expert at their job of keeping children amused and enthralled. You should try to arrange a personal interview before booking so that you can discuss the party in detail and decide between you what the programme should be.

The best time for the show varies from party to party. For instance, if the guests are very young and shy it can be a good idea to open up with the entertainment to relax everyone and put them in the party mood. But usually the entertainment is best put on just before tea or as a grand finale before the gifts are handed out.

Helpers

To run a party successfully for more than half a dozen children you need some assistance. After all, you can't be everywhere at once and the aim of the party is not to reduce you to a state of near collapse.

Where do you find your helpers? The best place to look is your family. Let's begin with your mother or mother-in-law. She will work hard behind the scenes, and, every now and then she will slip you that cup of tea that makes all the difference. You, in turn, will be happy to drink her health at the end of the day when, without doubt, she will be helping with the washing up.

If the party is for your youngest child, older brothers and sisters may feel out of it. Recruit them. They will be invaluable in running the games, acting as 'cloakroom' attendants, helping to serve the tea and, in general, keeping an eye on how things are going. They will love being part of it all and they will enjoy making the party a success. You do not need too many helpers. They will get in each other's way and may even start a party of their own. Also, you may have to say a polite 'no thank you' to some volunteers. Mothers of guests, for example, will not make good helpers unless they are close friends. With the best will in the world, they will be preoccupied with their own children. Even if they don't show favouritism, other children may wonder why their own mothers are not there.

Similarly, it is best to avoid those well-meaning people who have theories about the care of children. They have an important part to play in society—but not at your party. You want your guests to have fun without the benefit of having their behaviour analysed, even by an expert.

As for you . . .

Having completed the arrangements, planned the food, the games and the entertainment, there is one more element that is most important to the success of the party. You.

The word 'discipline' is one that seems to run counter to the whole spirit of the party. But it doesn't. It is absolutely necessary in a successful party but it must be correctly applied. There is no point in acting like a sergeant major; that would only intimidate the shy without curbing the boisterous. The aim must be to establish an affectionate relationship with every child there. The children will then appreciate your firmness. They are the first to realise that disorderly behaviour—and you find it in the best-organised parties—gets in the way of everyone's pleasure. They don't like to waste time in pointless arguments about how a game should be played. They want to get on with the fun.

So be confident, be firm, treat your guests as equals. Never behave like an old-fashioned schoolmistress giving instructions beginning with the dread words 'Now children . . .' Above all, enjoy yourself. It's infectious.

GAMES THAT LINGER FROM THE PAST

Many of the games children play provide an insight into the rituals, customs and beliefs of people living many generations ago. Children are quick to imitate what they see and hear and fragments of folk dramas and customs have become part of their play in these traditional games.

Line games

Line games, such as Red Rover (see p. 210), are representative of contest. Usually there are two lines of players. In some games, by linking hands, players imply that they are of the same opinions or beliefs. Players on the opposing side are equally of shared opinions but these are different from those of the other side.

There is a clearly defined line separating the two sides and during play each side can advance as far as the dividing line to threaten the opposing side, but as soon as a foot is placed over that line the player is in enemy territory and can be taken prisoner. The game could represent attack for territorial gain: a foray into an adjacent village for the purposes of obtaining prisoners for sacrifice or for selecting partners for marriage.

Circle games

Circle games almost certainly have their origin in the rituals performed by people who were expressing the social customs of their region.

There are several distinct types of circle games. In the simplest form all the players taking part join hands in a circle and sing or dance, performing the same actions and singing the same words. No difference of opinion is expressed and there is no division of players into different groups. This form of circle dance or game probably commemorates a recurring festival or special event. The joining of hands in a circle signifies friendship.

In a second form of circle game the players dance around, joining hands sometimes in a circle and at other times in pairs. At times all the players sing the same words but the actions are carried out by couples called upon to do so by the rest of the players. In the remote past of folk drama this form of game is representative of courtship and marriage customs.

Courtship ritual is well illustrated by the game Nuts in May. The name is a corruption of 'Knots in May', which refers to garlands or 'knots' of May blossoms such as hawthorns. One child stands in the centre of a circle of players who hold hands and dance backwards and forwards, alternately reducing and enlarging the size of the circle. All the children sing these words:

Here we come gathering nuts in May,
Nuts in May, nuts in May.
Here we come gathering nuts in May
On a cold and frosty morning.

Who will you have for nuts in May,
Nuts in May, nuts in May?
Who will you have for nuts in May
On a cold and frosty morning?

We'll have . . . for nuts in May,
Nuts in May, nuts in May.
We'll have . . . for nuts in May
On a cold and frosty morning.

(During this verse the child in the centre chooses a partner from the circle.)

Who will you send to fetch him/her away,
To fetch him away, to fetch him away?
Who will you send to fetch him away
On a cold and frosty morning?

We'll send . . . to fetch him away,
To fetch him away, to fetch him away.
We'll send . . . to fetch him away
On a cold and frosty morning.

While the last verse is being sung, the children in the centre select a third to join them from the circle. All three then try to escape from the circle by trying to crawl between the children as they dance.

Trees were always a central sacred object in ancient marriage festivals, and there is no doubt that Here we go round the Mulberry Bush has its origins in a marriage dance performed around a sacred tree or bush.

The children join hands and dance around in a circle singing:

Here we go round the mulberry bush,
The mulberry bush, the mulberry bush,
Here we go round the mulberry bush
On a cold and frosty morning.

This is the way we wash our hands,
Wash our hands, wash our hands.
This is the way we wash our hands
On a cold and frosty morning.

During the second verse they mime the action of washing their hands. Then they hold hands again and repeat the first verse.

The action verse 'We wash our hands' is then changed to another action—wash our clothes, put on our shoes, go to school, play with our toys, comb our hair, brush our teeth, run on all fours, and so on.

Trees are also featured in games in which a line of players encircle a central figure in a spiralling movement. Tradition and ritual are closely bound up in this form of game. The central figure represents a tree.

Certain types of trees were held in great respect and veneration and it was customary to encircle them as an act of worship to propitiate the gods and to encourage them to send rain to ensure a bountiful harvest.

In another form of circle game the players forming the circle are stationary and the actions are carried out by one or two players. The circle of stationary players represents a village or town and the players perform in and around the circle. The spaces in between stationary players probably represent doorways or arches, or the walls of a town.

Arch games

Games in which part of the play sequence involves the making of an arch for the rest of the players to pass through, perhaps for one player to be taken 'prisoner' by the arms forming the arch, probably have their roots in the primitive rites surrounding foundation sacrifice and well worship.

The building of bridges and the construction of archways used to be accompanied by a foundation sacrifice. There is considerable superstition surrounding the building of London Bridge—the mortar for embedding the bricks was said to have been tempered with the blood of beasts and the stones themselves to have been spattered with the blood of children. On completion, the heads of executed prisoners were placed on the bridge and gateways. When the Tower of London was being built, reports mention that the blood of beasts was mixed into the mortar.

Some stories instance victims offered as foundation sacrifices being forced to enter a hole or space left in the building. The hapless victim was then walled in and buried alive.

The superstition surrounding the building of London Bridge is reflected in the game. Two children form the bridge with hands joined, arms outstretched and raised. The rest dance around and around passing under the bridge. They all sing:

London Bridge is falling down,
Falling down, falling down.
London Bridge is falling down,
My fair lady.

At the word 'lady', which is sung with considerable emphasis, the players forming the bridge bring their arms down and capture whoever is passing underneath. The captured player retires from the game and the rest dance around again singing:

Build it up with silver and gold,
Silver and gold, silver and gold.
Build it up with silver and gold,
My fair lady.

Then they repeat the first verse and another child is captured at the word 'lady'. The sequence is continued until only one player remains—and his fate is sealed unless he is very clever at timing his dashes through the bridge.

Oranges and Lemons is rich in elements of social history. Two players raise their clasped hands to form an arch. One of the players is Lemon and the other is Orange, but the names are kept secret from the rest of the players. The children run under the arch in a long line singing these words:

Oranges and lemons,
Say the bells of St Clement's.
You owe me five farthings,
Say the bells of St Martin's.
When will you pay me?
Say the bells of Old Bailey.
When I grow rich,
Say the bells of Shoreditch.
When will that be?
Say the bells of Stepney.
I do not know,
Says the big bell of Bow.

Then the two forming the arch say:

Here comes a candle to light you to bed,
Here comes a chopper to chop off your head.
Chop-chop-chop-chop . . .

At these words the arms of the arch come down and take a prisoner. The prisoner is then secretly asked whether he will be Orange or Lemon. After choosing, the captive stands behind whichever leader he has selected and puts his arms around the leader's waist.

The game continues until all players have been taken prisoner and are ranged behind the leader of their choice. The two teams then play a tug of war, which ends when one team has been pulled over a mark between them. Historians believe that the names Oranges and Lemons originally represented partisan colours and not fruits. They indicated support for the local baron whether or not that support was voluntarily given. In fact, an interesting feature of the game is that the players pass under an arch or 'yoke' which symbolises servitude. The power of the barons was absolute, and any of their retainers who refused to join their private armies when ordered to do so faced execution.

The lines 'Here comes a candle to light you to bed' and 'Here comes a chopper to chop off your head' are of particular interest. A criminal being led to his execution would have torches to light the way and the bells of the neighbourhood would be tolled. After execution the body would be quartered and the parts displayed on gateways or entrances to the town.

At one time in Siam, whenever a new city gate was being built, it was the custom for a number of officers to ambush and take prisoner the first four or eight persons who passed by. These unfortunate prisoners were then buried alive under the city gate-posts to serve as guardian angels. Later, human sacrifice was banned and animals were slaughtered instead. This practice then passed into a ritual which involved the capturing of animals, the owners of which could avoid the slaughter by paying money or some other form of forfeit.

Chapter 2

Party Games for the Very Young

Greeting the guests;
Getting the party going;
Choosing games to suit the ages of the children;
A ploy to get them to the tea-table

The final preparations have been made and the door bell rings. The party has begun. Take the young host or hostess with you to greet the guests. That is all part of the excitement.

Show the guests where to hang their coats and where to find the lavatory. Let them give their presents and admire the decorations and the cake, then get them started on the first game, Hunt the Thimble. This is an ideal party opener because as few as two or three children can play and the game can be interrupted when more guests arrive.

The game begins by one child going out of the room while a thimble is 'hidden'. With young children, it is advisable to leave it in sight as well as in reach. Even then, they are likely to take a long time finding it. The child outside is called in and the other children call out 'Cold', 'Warm', 'Hot' or 'Boiling', according to how close the hunter is to the thimble.

When all the guests have arrived, get the other games moving quickly. Children under school age cannot concentrate on one subject for long, so start a new game as soon as you spot signs that interest in one game is fading. Some of the games in this chapter may seem pointless to an adult or an older child, but time has shown that very young children love them. As teatime nears, start a game called Dead Lions. This is a complete confidence trick on your part. All the children lie down and must not move. If one moves he is out and can then go to the lavatory, wash his hands and sit down at the tea-table. Cleverly, eliminate two or three at a time so that there is a fairly orderly procession to the table.

But, before this ploy, try out these games that will get the party going.

Noah's Ark
A party opener

This can be an early ice-breaker at a party for the very young. The game leader calls the name of an animal and the players imitate its movement or the sound it makes. The best gets a prize.

Blind Man's Buff
A favourite that has stood the test of time

Players are scattered around a playing area. One is blindfolded and is turned around three times. The blind man then goes searching for the other players. They are not allowed to move their feet but may twist their bodies around to escape his touch. When the blind man finds another player he tries to identify him. If the blind man guesses correctly, the player whose name he guesses becomes the next blind man. If not, the blind man must catch someone else and try again.

In *Circle the Blind Man* the players walk in a circle around the blind man until he claps his hands three times. The players stop walking and the blind man points towards the rim of the circle. The player closest to the spot where he points enters the circle, and the blind man chases him. If the player is caught within two minutes he becomes the blind man; if not, the blind man tries again.

In *Blind Man's Staff* players walk in a circle around the blind man, who holds a stick. Players stop walking when the blind man points his stick towards one of them. The player nearest the stick takes hold of it and the blind man says 'Who's there?' In a disguised voice the player says 'It's me!' If the blind man guesses the player's name, they exchange places; if not, the blind man takes another turn.

In *Seated Blind Man's Buff* all the players except the blind man sit on chairs in a circle. The blind man sits on the lap of a player and tries to identify him without touching any part of his body. If the blind man guesses correctly, he changes places with the seated player. If the blind man does not guess correctly he takes another turn. If, after three turns, he has still not made a correct identification, the game leader chooses another player to be blind man.

Hat Duel
The winner keeps his topper

Two players wearing paper hats stand in the centre of the room. They are blindfolded and each has a balloon. At a signal, each player tries to knock the paper hat off his opponent's head with his balloon. To help them find each other, one player must keep calling out 'Here' and the other 'There'. The first player to knock off his opponent's hat is the winner.

The Baker's Shop
With the buns in the middle

Children stand in a circle, holding hands. Four stand in the middle, not holding hands. The party organiser stands in the circle and leads the circle round and round chanting: 'Four currant buns in the baker's shop, big and round with sugar on the top, along came (the name of a circle player selected by the organiser) with a penny one day, bought a

currant bun and took it away.'
The named child chooses one of those in the middle who then joins those in the circle. The rhyme is repeated and the organiser chooses a different player each time to 'buy a bun'.
When the four in the centre have joined the circle the game ends. Four different children can be chosen for a second game—but that is usually the limit before young children get bored and are ready to move on to the next game.

Reuben and Rachel

Somewhere a voice is calling

Two players, a boy and a girl, are chosen to be Reuben and Rachel. They stand in the centre of a circle of players. To begin, Reuben is blindfolded. He calls out 'Rachel' and the girl must immediately answer 'Here, Reuben'. With only the sound of her voice to guide him, Reuben has 2 minutes to try to touch Rachel. If he succeeds another girl becomes Rachel, if he fails another boy becomes Reuben.

Discus Throw

A game that never falls flat

Children are given paper plates and line up at one end of the room; a small square is marked off at the other end. The party organiser demonstrates how to throw a discus with the hand flat.
Each child is given three tries to throw his plate in the square. The child who comes closest to a bull's-eye wins.

High Dive

Steady hand makes a splash

Each child is given ten corks and a glass half filled with water. He puts the glass on the floor and with an arm outstretched shoulder high he tries to drop the corks one at a time into the glass. The child who manages to get the greatest number of corks into the glass is the winner.

Ring o' Roses

Still a foremost family favourite

In this old traditional game, and others that follow, the party organiser will need to lead the singing of pre-school children—but they will soon catch on!
The children walk around singing: 'Ring a ring o' roses, a pocket full of posies, a-tishoo, a-tishoo, we all fall down!' They all fall down and then sing: 'Fishes in the water, fishes in the sea, we all jump up now, one, two, three.' They stand up again and repeat the game until they show that they want to get on with another game.

Hidden Treasure

A game that calls for sharp eyes . . .

A small object, such as a short pencil, a matchstick, a marble, a lollypop, is shown to the children.
They then leave the room and the object is hidden where it can be seen without the children having to lift or disturb other objects. At a signal, the children come back and search for the object. As soon as any child sees it, he whispers to the organiser of the game where it is and then quietly takes a seat without telling any of the other children. The game comes to an end when all the children have found the object.
In *Magic Music,* one child is sent out of the room, while the others hide an object somewhere in the room in plain sight. The child returns and looks for it, while the others hum a song—softly when he is at a distance from the object and much louder when he approaches it.
In *Hot or Cold,* one child leaves the room while the others decide on some action which he must perform. This may be as simple as

picking up or touching any object in the room, or may involve his doing something either with the object or with other children. He might be expected to turn a light on and off, change a record, untie someone's shoelace, shake someone's hand, and so on. When the child comes back into the room, the others all begin to sing a song they have selected. They sing softly at first. When the child moves close to the spot where he is expected to perform his action, the group sings louder. When he moves away, the singing becomes quieter. In this way, by indicating whether he is 'hot' or 'cold' they help him find the object or person involved in the action he must perform, and also help him as he tries different actions.

When he finally succeeds in performing the required task, the whole group sings out as loud as possible.

Musical Bumps

A game to get the children jumping

When the music plays, everyone jumps up and down. When the music stops, everyone sits down as quickly as they can. The last one each time is told by the party organiser to go to the back of the room and continue in the game, to keep up his interest.

The game goes on until the players look ready to go on to the next.

Farmer in the Dell

. . . and the children love to join him

Everyone holds hands and forms a circle. One child goes in the middle. The others walk round chanting: 'The farmer's in the dell, The farmer's in the dell, ee, aye, add-i-oh, the farmer's in the dell. The farmer wants a wife, the farmer wants a wife, ee, aye, add-i-oh, the farmer wants a wife.'

Then they all stand still and the child in the centre chooses someone to be the wife, who joins him in the circle. They hold hands and walk round the opposite way to those in the circle and all begin the next verse: 'The wife wants a child.'

Another child is chosen and the next verse begins 'The child wants a nurse'. Then they sing 'The nurse wants a dog'. Finally they pat the dog singing 'We all pat the dog'.

Choose another child to be the farmer and repeat the game. It can be played several times without anyone getting tired.

Shot-put

Good throw bags the prize

A large paper shopping bag or balloon is blown up and tied tightly at the end. Each child stands on a line and throws it as far as he can The longest throw is the winner.

Dusty Bluebells

But the children know just what to do

Children stand in a circle holding hands, with one child in the centre. Those in the circle raise their clasped hands, forming arches. The child in the centre runs in and out of the circle, under the arches. All chant: 'In and out the dusty bluebells, in and out the dusty bluebells, in and out the dusty bluebells, who shall be my partner?'

The child in the centre then stands behind one of those in the circle and taps him on the shoulder while everyone chants: 'Pitter patter, pitter patter, on my shoulder. You shall be my partner.'

Then the child who had his shoulder tapped leads the other one in and out of the circle and the game goes on until only two children are left holding hands.

Then the children chant: 'The bluebells are dusty because they need some water. Let's all water them with our watering cans,' miming the action as they sing.

Cobbler, Cobbler

His task: To find the shoe

Children sit in a circle and one, blindfolded, stands in the middle. The children in the circle chant: 'Cobbler, cobbler, mend my shoe; get it done by half past two; half past two is much too late, get it done by half past eight; cobbler, cobbler tell me true, which of you has got my shoe.'

While they chant the rhyme they pass a shoe, behind their backs, around the circle. When the rhyme is finished, the player in the middle removes the blindfold and is allowed three guesses to find who has the shoe.
If he is right, the child who has the shoe goes into the middle.

Chinese Puzzle

Get yourself out of this one

One player volunteers to leave the room. The others join hands in a circle and, without letting go, form themselves into a complicated, twisted mass of bodies like a human Chinese puzzle. This is done by raising arms and ducking under, lifting feet over joined hands, climbing over or under each other. The players are drawn closer together until finally they become a tight knot, with heads, arms and feet protruding in different directions.
The player outside comes back and tries to unravel them and return them to a circle shape without loosening any of their hands. This game lets off a lot of steam.

Match Race

Always a non-striking success

Two teams are formed. Each member, except the two leaders, has a match, either one that has been used or one with the head removed. The first child in each team holds a matchbox. At a signal, the leaders give the matchboxes to the next child in their team. They open the boxes and put their matches inside. They then close the boxes and give them to the next in line. The first team to get all the matches in the box wins.

The game can be played in reverse with the players taking matches out of the boxes until the first children receive empty boxes.

Matchbox Race

The children have a nose for winning

The children form two teams, standing in a line with their hands behind their backs. The first in each line puts a matchbox cover on his nose. At a signal each passes the matchbox cover to the second player in his team, using noses only.

The first team to pass a cover to the end child wins.

Javelin Throw

Can you pick the winner?

A small circle is drawn on the floor. One child stands in the circle, turns around two or three times and hurls a cocktail stick towards a line. Each child has three throws and the longest throw is the winner.

Balloon Tap

Keeping up the excitement

Children have to keep tapping three or four balloons in the air to stop them touching the ground. This can be a team game, but for the very young a team of three should be the maximum. The winning team is the one that keeps one or more balloons in the air when other teams have dropped theirs.

Land, Sea or Shore

The way to take sides

Two children hold a long piece of string tightly on the floor. The others kneel on one side of it. Their side is the land, the string is the shore, the other side is the sea.

The party organiser rapidly calls out 'Land!' or 'Sea!' or 'Shore!' and the children must put both hands in the right position.

Children who get it wrong are eliminated and the last still in is the winner.

Soldiers

Stepping out in time

A chair is placed at each end of the room and when the music plays the children march like soldiers around them in single file.

Each time the music stops they are told either to march sideways, or backwards, or to skip, run, hop, jump like frogs or march on the spot.

Laughing Balloon

This makes them see the funny side

A balloon is tossed in the air and the children have to laugh. When it hits the ground they must stop laughing and keep perfectly straight faces. The best gets a prize.

Pass the Parcel

. . . But it's finders keepers

This game is a guaranteed winner at a party of children who have not yet started school. Before the party, prepare the parcel by wrapping a small present in the centre, then sealing each layer of paper with sticky-tape. Put a little gift in every second or third layer so that a number of children will receive one.

At the party the children sit in a circle and, as the music plays, they pass the parcel from one to another. When the music stops, the child with the parcel unwraps one layer, keeping any gift that he might find. An adult should start and stop the music so that the gifts are distributed as evenly as possible.

The game ends when the parcel is completely unwrapped and the final gift won.

To prevent chaos at the end, an adult or older

child should collect the unwrapped paper as the game goes along.

Pass the Penny
And the faster the better

This game is a variation of Pass the Parcel. Children sit or stand in a circle, and as the music is played a penny is passed as quickly as possible around the circle.
When the music stops, the child who is holding the penny is eliminated. The game is played until only one child remains. If no music is available, the leader may beat a drum, ring a bell, or blow a whistle to stop the action.

Nut Hunt
When the children play squirrel

The party organiser hides nuts, any kind will do, in every possible nook and cranny of the room—under cushions, in drawers, behind doors and curtains, in ash-trays, and on top of books.
Each child has a plastic dish or a cup and sets out in search of them. The children may hunt as individuals or divide up into small teams. The game ends after the search has continued for 5 minutes, and the child or the team with the most nuts is the winner.

Animal Pairs
A game for making friends

This game, which needs a little preparation before the party, helps children to get acquainted and form partnerships for some of the games to come. The party organiser cuts out pictures of animals from magazines and then cuts each picture in half.
Each child is given half a picture and then, at a signal, all scurry about to find their partners—which is done by matching halves to form a whole animal.
In *Animal Calls* each child is given a picture of an animal. Two of each animal are given out. These must be animals with familiar calls, such as a donkey (hee-haw), a dog (woof-woof), a cat (miaow). It's up to the party organiser to give examples of the various animal noises.
At a signal, the children make the sound of the animal shown on their pictures and, at the same time, listen for the other child who is making a similar sound. When the two find each other they remain partners for the next game.

Shoe Hunt
Softly, softly in stockinged feet

Each child takes off both shoes and places them in a large box in the centre of the room. While the organiser mixes up the shoes in the box, the children form a large circle around it
At a signal, they all run forward, find their own shoes and put them on. The first child to come to the leader with shoes on, and tied or buckled, wins the game.

Hide the Clock
Tick tock is the clue

All the children leave the room while the party organiser hides a loudly ticking alarm clock.
At a signal, the children return to the room and search for the clock. The first child to find it is the winner and is given the privilege of hiding the clock the next time.

Dog and Bone
Creepy crawly without a sound

The children sit on chairs in a semicircle. One child, the dog, sits blindfolded on the floor as far in front of the others as possible. Beside the dog is a book which is the bone. The party organiser points to a child in the semicircle who tries to creep or crawl silently

to the bone and take it back to his place without being heard by the dog. If the dog hears a child creeping up, he points in the direction of the sound and if the leader decides he is reasonably accurate, the dog keeps his role for another round.
If not, and the thief gets back to his chair without being pointed at, the thief becomes the dog for the next round.

Sixer

The sign to spoon the sweets

The children sit in a circle. Two plates are placed in the middle, one empty and one containing a pile of small sweets. A spoon is set beside the sweets. The children take it in turn to throw a dice and when a six is thrown shout 'Sixer!'
The child who threw the six takes the spoon and transfers the sweets one by one to the empty plate. The others continue throwing the dice until another six is thrown.
The new Sixer changes places with the previous one, who keeps all the sweets he managed to transfer.

What's the Time, Mr Wolf?

Lunch hour is rush hour

One child, Mr Wolf, walks around followed by the others who continually call out: 'What's the time, Mr Wolf?' The wolf says different times. Nothing happens until the wolf says: 'One o'clock, lunch time!' Then they all dash to the side of the room.
Anyone who is touched by the wolf before reaching a wall becomes the new wolf.

Grandma's Footsteps

To be followed with great care

A chosen leader walks slowly from one end of the room towards the other, followed by the other children. Every now and then the leader suddenly looks back and any children caught moving are sent back to the start. The child nearest to the leader when he reaches the end of the room becomes the new leader.

Grandpa's Clock

It's spring time for children

Children hold hands and form a line with an 'anchorman' at one end who stands in the middle of the room. The others walk round and round him, holding hands tightly, so that they wind up like a clock spring. They chant: 'Wind up the clock, tick tock, tick tock.' When they are 'wound up' they let go their hands and jump apart counting aloud up to 12.

Tom and Jerry

Playing cat and mouse

Children form a circle and one child is chosen as Jerry the mouse. He creeps around the outside of the circle and touches one of the children on the shoulder.
The one touched, Tom the cat, chases Jerry around the circle back to his place. If the mouse is touched, he carries on as before and the cat goes back to the circle. If not, the cat becomes the new mouse.

Changeover Race

When the slow can beat the swift

Children line up at one end of a hall or large room. When the party organiser blows a whistle they run towards the opposite end. Before they reach it the whistle is blown again and they turn around and race back. Every time the whistle goes they change direction. Anyone who reaches one end of the room is the winner.
The fastest runner does not necessarily win. Someone who is slow may be nearest one end when the whistle blows.

Nursery Mimes

Learning to suit the actions to the words

In this game the children sit on the floor facing the party organiser who recites some rhymes and mimes actions to fit them. The children copy the actions and repeat the rhymes. Here are some examples:

'Hickory, dickory, dock, the mouse ran up the clock'
(MIME RUNNING FEET WITH YOUR FINGERS)
'The clock struck one'
(SWING YOUR ARM LIKE A PENDULUM)
'The mouse ran down'
(CRAWLING FINGERS)
'Hickory, dickory, dock.'

'Little Miss Muffet, sat on a tuffet'
(CROUCH DOWN WITH HANDS SPREAD WIDE)
'Eating her curds and whey'
(MIME EATING)
'Along came a spider'
(HOLD HAND UP, WIGGLE FINGERS AND LOWER HAND SLOWLY)
'Who sat down beside her'
(CROUCH DOWN)
'And frightened Miss Muffet away'
(SWEEP ARM ACROSS BODY).

'Pat-a-cake, pat-a-cake, baker's man'
(PAT HAND ON WRIST)
'Bake me a cake as fast as you can'
(MOVE HANDS IN CIRCLES)
'Pat it'
(DO SO)
'and prick it'
(POKE WITH FINGER)
'and mark it with a B'
('DRAW' WITH FINGER)
'Put it in the oven for baby and me'
(PUSH HANDS FORWARD, POINT TO A CHILD AND YOURSELF).

Fish and Net

It's fun to be in the swim

Five children are chosen as the net and the others become the fish. The children who form the net join hands in a line. When the party organiser calls out 'Swim, fish, swim!' the players who make up the net move about the playing area with hands joined and try to capture as many fish as possible by surrounding them.

Fish who are caught become part of the net and the game continues until all the fish have been caught. The last five fish caught become the new net.

'Ride-a-cock-horse'
(PULL IMAGINARY REINS)
'To Banbury Cross'
(CROSS FOREARMS)
'To see a fine lady upon a white horse'
(PULL REINS)
'With rings on her fingers'
(WIGGLE FINGERS)
'and bells on her toes'
(POINT TO FEET)
'She shall have music wherever she goes'
(WAVE IMAGINARY BATON).

Other suitable rhymes are Little Jack Horner; Hey diddle, diddle; Little Polly Flinders; Sing a song of sixpence.

John Brown's baby
Some words are dropped

Everyone at the party can join in this jolly singing and miming game wherever they happen to be seated—so there is no rushing around to take up special positions.
To the tune of *John Brown's Body*, sing:

John Brown's baby has a cold upon his chest,
John Brown's baby has a cold upon his chest,
John Brown's baby has a cold upon his chest,
So we rubbed it with camphorated oil.
(Chorus)
Camphor-amphor-amphor-a-ted,
Camphor-amphor-amphor-a-ted,

CONTINUED ON PAGE 32

Stack the Beakers
Ready, steady . . . whoops!

This is a game for the very young, who can be so unsteady with their hands that they give everybody else a laugh. You need a set of coloured plastic stacking beakers, and a rubber ball. The children sit in a circle on the floor. You put the largest beaker in the centre. One child is given a beaker one size smaller and is asked to put it on the first beaker. The next child is given the next beaker in size and so on. The ball is balanced on the last and smallest beaker. If it stays in place all the children clap their hands.

Camphor-amphor-amphor-a-ted,
So we rubbed it with camphorated oil.

The children sing the verse a second time, but when they come to the word 'baby' they don't sing it—they cross their arms and pretend to rock a baby. The third time they sing the verse they leave out the word 'baby' as before and when they come to 'cold' they pretend to cough. Next time round they rub their chests instead of singing 'rubbed' and when they sing the verse for the last time, instead of singing 'camphorated oil' they hold their noses as if they don't like the smell. The chorus is sung between each verse without actions.

Heads and Shoulders
Tip-tap there they go

Players sit in a circle and, to the tune of 'There is a tavern in the town', they sing these words:

Heads and shoulders, knees and toes, knees and toes;
Heads and shoulders, knees and toes, knees and toes;
Eyes and ears and a mouth and a nose;
Heads and shoulders knees and toes, knees and toes.

As they sing, they tap their heads, shoulders, and so on. As the words are repeated, first the word 'heads' is left out then 'shoulders', then 'knees', and so on. Each time, however, the tapping is continued.

Mile Walk
They all go heel and toe

Children line up at one end of the room. At a signal they race across the room and back by placing the heel of one foot against the toe of the other at every step. The first child to complete two lengths of the room wins.

Chapter 3

Party Games for Older Children

Choosing the games beforehand;
When to start the music;
Team and individual games;
The time for tea;
Games to play in a hall

After children start school their tastes in party games change. They have become accustomed to being organised at school and, therefore, they take more readily to team games. They also enjoy competitions where they can show off their growing skills. Parents will find, however, that children's tastes keep changing. Games that were a riot at one birthday party may flop a year later. Before a party, run through the games in this chapter with your son or daughter and select those that promise to be most successful.

Just before the guests are due to arrive, put on some music. Let the young host or hostess answer the door to the guests and get the games going as soon as all of them arrive. When it is time for tea, avoid a stampede to the tea-table by forming everybody into a crocodile and leading them round the house, then bringing them back to the tea-table.

Profile Spotting

Party fun with the shadows

Guests arriving at a party stand sideways in front of a strong light which throws their shadows against a sheet of paper taped to a wall. The game leader outlines their silhouettes on the paper with a heavy black crayon or a soft pencil. He numbers each sheet on the front and writes the name of the

guest on the back of the sheet.
Later all the pictures are put up on the wall and everyone tries to guess who they are.
When everyone has written down his guesses, the leader reads the correct names and numbers.
Whoever has the highest number of correct identifications is the winner.

Baby-picture Contest
Trying to spot the changes

Each party guest is asked to bring a picture of himself as a baby. The pictures are numbered and displayed in a room. Guests try to guess the correct name to go with each picture and write the names on a piece of paper. After 3–5 minutes the young host or hostess collects the lists, and whoever has succeeded in correctly identifying the most photographs wins the game.

Guess Who
A game to get things going

This an ideal game for breaking the ice at the early stages of a party. Everyone has a picture of a well-known personality, pop star, sportsman and so on, pinned to his back without knowing who it is.
Each player then has to find out who the character is by asking questions of the others and without, of course, asking directly 'Who is it?' There is no winner. This game is strictly for laughs and for guests to get to know each other.

Musical Chairs
One of the oldest, one of the best

Musical Chairs is probably the oldest of party elimination games. At a party, play it only once, because young children who are eliminated tend to become bored and may disrupt the game by finding other diversions.
A number of chairs, one fewer than the number of players, are placed side by side facing in alternate directions. At a signal the players walk around the chairs to the accompaniment of a piano or music from a record-player. When the music stops, every player tries to find a seat. The player who cannot get a seat drops out of the game, a chair is removed and a new round begins.
The game continues until there are two players competing for one chair. The player who sits on it when the music stops is the winner.

One Too Few
And a player too many

Players line up side by side behind a starting line about 3 metres away from a heap of objects, such as pencils, spoons, items of clothing. There should be one object fewer than the number of players. At a signal, the players run forward and try to grab an object. The player who does not get an object is eliminated.
The game continues, with the leader taking away one object each time. The last remaining child is the winner.

Magic Carpets
Paper step by paper step

A number of newspapers or large sheets of cardboard, one fewer than the number of players, are scattered around on the floor. The music starts and the players march around the floor to the right in single file. When the music stops, each player must find a sheet of paper to stand on. The player who cannot find a 'magic carpet' is eliminated.
This game continues until only one player remains.
In *Prison,* a wide rectangle is marked on the floor with strips of paper. This is the prison. When the music starts, players either singly or in pairs walk around the floor in a circle,

passing through the prison each time around. When the music stops, any player or pair in the prison is eliminated. The game continues until only one player, or one pair, is left.

Fish-net Scramble
Angling to get a place

The fisherman stands in the centre of a circle of seated players and gives each the name of a fish. He then calls out the names of any two fish. The two children with these names quickly exchange places while the fisherman tries to get a seat for himself. Of the three, whoever does not find a seat becomes the fisherman for the next round.

At any time, the fisherman may call out 'Fish-net scramble!' and all the players, including the fisherman, scramble for new seats. The player who does not get one becomes the new fisherman.

In *Fruit Basket*, the players sit in a circle with one player in the centre. The centre player gives the name of a fruit to the circle players. He calls out 'All apples change places with all pears!', or something similar. While the two groups scramble to change places, he tries to get one of the seats for himself. If 'Fruit basket upset!' is called out, all the players must change seats. The player left out goes to the centre.

Pass-the-Orange
Fun for the foot-sure

Two teams sit facing each other on the floor. The first player in each line has an orange. At a signal, he places the orange between his feet which are close together and extended straight forward. Then, using only his feet, he transfers the orange to the top of the next player's feet. The orange is passed down the line and back again. If a player drops the orange he must pick it up with his feet before continuing. The first team to finish wins.

Squirrel and Nut
The high-speed runaround

Players sit on the floor in a circle, with their heads down, eyes closed and their hands cupped in front of them. One player, the squirrel, walks quietly around the inside of the circle. The squirrel holds a peanut which he drops into the hands of one of the players. The player who gets the nut jumps up and chases the squirrel once around the inside of the circle back to the empty spot. If the squirrel gets back without being touched, the player who received the nut becomes the new squirrel. If not, the old squirrel must continue.

Swat
A novel newspaper chase

In Swat, players sit in chairs in a circle facing inwards. A loosely rolled-up newspaper, tied with string or sticky-tape, is on a chair in the centre. The game leader chooses one player who takes the newspaper and walks around the inside of the circle.

Suddenly he hits another player across the legs with the newspaper. He then tries to put the newspaper back on the chair in the centre of the circle and return to his own seat, before his victim can grab the paper and return the blow.

If he succeeds he becomes the swatter again. If he is hit, the chaser becomes the swatter and proceeds as before.

Let's Go Fishing
—but watch out for sudden storms

A fisherman is selected and the rest of the players sit in chairs scattered around the room. Each is given a folded piece of paper giving the name of a sea creature. The fisherman walks around the room calling out the names of various fish or other sea creatures

such as whales, dolphins, limpets.
When a player hears the name of his creature, he gets up and walks behind the fisherman.
When most of the players have been called out of their seats, the fisherman shouts 'The ocean is stormy!'
At this, all the players must find new seats, including those who have not been caught.
The last player to find a seat becomes the new fisherman.

Who's Missing?
A game to test the memory

This is a game of observation. Players stand in a circle with one in the centre. He is given 5 seconds to memorise who is there, then he is blindfolded. Everybody changes places, except that one player quietly leaves the room.
The blindfold is then taken off the player in the centre and he is given 1 minute to name the missing player.
If he guesses right, the missing player is blindfolded. If not, the guesser takes another turn in the centre.

Up, Jenkins
Cash down on the table

Two teams sit on opposite sides of a table. The players on one side are given a 10p piece, which they pass about among themselves under the table. When the captain of the other team says 'Up, Jenkins!' the players in the team with the coin hold clenched fists up high. Then he says 'Down, Jenkins!' and they bring their hands down sharply on the table, palms flat, trying to keep the coin hidden. The players in the other team try to guess who has the coin.
This requires keen observation of the players' expressions and acute hearing to identify the source of the clinking sound made by the coin against the table.
A team guessing correctly gets one point.
After each guess, the coin goes to the other team and the roles are reversed.
The team which accumulates the most points after 5 minutes wins.

Find the Bell
Ding dong, right wrong

One player stands with eyes closed in the centre of a circle formed by the others. The centre player counts aloud to 20. At the same time, the other players pass a small bell around the circle, ringing it as it travels. When the centre player reaches 20, all the other players put their hands behind their backs.
The centre player opens his eyes and tries to guess who has the bell. If he guesses correctly, the player who holds the bell comes into the centre. If not, the centre player closes his eyes, counts to 20 and the game continues as before.

Ring on a String
After the count-down, a guess

Players sit in a circle holding a string which is long enough to reach around the entire circle, and which has a ring threaded on it. The ring is moved along the string from player to player in either direction. One player stands in the centre.
As the ring moves around the circle, the centre player closes his eyes and counts slowly to ten. Then he opens his eyes and guesses which player has the ring. If he guesses correctly, the two players switch roles.
After three incorrect guesses, the game leader chooses another child to stand in the centre and the game continues as before.

Simon Says
And it's the way he says it

One player is Simon. He faces the other players and orders them to carry out certain actions, such as 'Clap hands', 'Jump', 'Bow', 'Touch your head', 'Touch your toes', which he also carries out.

The other players instantly obey, but only if the order has been preceded by the words 'Simon says'.
If the words 'Simon says' are not used the players ignore the order. A player who ignores an order with 'Simon says', or performs an action that was not preceded by the words, is eliminated.
Simon has to try to confuse the players by giving his orders very quickly, with or without the key words. The last player to remain in the game is the winner.
With very young players it is wise for a grown-up to take the part of Simon.

Indian Chief
Tracking down the leader

A scout is chosen and goes out of the room. The other players, who are sitting in a circle, choose one of their number to be the Indian chief. The Indian chief leads the other players in a series of actions, such as clapping, stamping, waving or nodding heads.
The scout enters the room and stands in the centre of the circle. As the players in the circle continue to change from action to action, the scout tries to find out who is leading them.
The scout is given three guesses. If he is successful, the Indian chief becomes the new scout and a new chief is selected. If not, the old scout goes out and tries again.

Add an Action
And another . . . and another

The game begins when one member of a circle performs a simple action, such as clapping hands, stamping a foot, waving an arm in a circular motion. His neighbour on his right must perform this action and then add a different one of his own. The next player on the right must perform both these actions in the correct sequence, then add yet another. The game continues in this manner and players who cannot remember the previous actions, or the sequence in which they should be performed, drop out.
The last player to perform all the actions in the right sequence is the winner.

I Spy
A world-wide spell-binder

The game of I Spy is popular throughout the world with children as soon as they begin to spell—and it stays popular for years.
One player selects an object in the room and says 'I spy with my little eye something beginning with A'—or whatever is the first letter of the object.
The first player to identify the object selects a new object and the game is repeated.

Spot the Sounds
Tape your own quiz show

If you have a tape or cassette recorder, you can prepare some amusing quiz games. Before the party record a number of household noises such as:

Stirring a cup of tea; beating or whisking an egg; frying bacon; a vacuum cleaner; a food mixer; water running into a bath; scrubbing; opening a window; lighting the gas; scraping vegetables; brushing teeth.

After each recording allow a silent spell, then record the sound again. This will give players a chance to spot the sound and save you the trouble at the party of running the tape back to the correct spot. At the party give each player a piece of paper and a pencil. Play the recording of the first noise and the repeat. Switch off the recorder while the players are writing down what they think the sound is. Move on to the next sound. The player with the highest score wins.

In *Pop Quiz* record snippets from current popular music and give points for the correct name of each number and for the soloist or group playing it.

Mystery Shape
A puzzle in proportions

This game is a cross between I Spy and Twenty Questions. One player is asked to leave the room. The others sit in a circle on the floor and choose an object that the absent player will try to identify, when he is called back. Any object in the room may be chosen except items of clothing.
When the player returns, he is allowed to ask up to 15 questions about the mystery object's size or shape. When a player has guessed the object or used up his 15 questions, another contestant and another object are chosen. The game goes on until all players have had a turn. Those who guessed correctly may play elimination rounds until only one remains.

I See Blue
A contest in many colours

One player selects an object in the room and writes it down on a slip of paper, which is given to the game leader. The object should be visible to all players. The player who has chosen the object gives the others a colour clue, saying 'I see blue' (or whatever the colour of the object is).
One at a time, the players try to identify the object. It may be a piece of furniture, a section of a picture on the wall, or an article of clothing worn by any player.
The first player to guess the object selects a new object for the other players to guess.

Fizz
Fast and furious flows the fun

The fun in this game is to get it as fast-moving as possible. Players sit in a circle and count aloud from left to right, starting with the number one. When the number five or any multiple of five comes up, the word 'Fizz' is called out instead.
The first player calls out 'One!' the next 'Two!' and the game continues with 'Three!' 'Four!' 'Fizz!' 'Six!' 'Seven!' 'Eight!' 'Nine!' 'Fizz!' and so on. The game can be made a little more difficult if the player who says 'Fizz!' has to quickly stand up and sit down.
If the circle gets as far as the number 55 ('Fizz-Fizz!') the player bobs up and down twice. Any player who hesitates too long or who incorrectly calls out 'Fizz!' or a number is given a penalty point and starts the counting at 'One!' again.
After about 5 minutes the player with the fewest number of penalty points is the winner.
In a similar game called *Buzz,* any number which has a seven in it, or which is a multiple of seven (such as 14 or 21) the player whose turn it is calls out 'Buzz!' If the game progresses into the 70s, the counting changes to 'Buzz-one!' 'Buzz-two!' and so on.
Whenever a player makes a mistake he gets one penalty point and starts the counting from 'One!' again.
In *Fizz-Buzz* any five or multiple of five calls for a 'Fizz!' Any seven or multiple of seven calls for a 'Buzz!' A number that is a multiple of both five and seven, such as 35, would become 'Fizz-Buzz!'

Observation
Remembering things seen

A variety of objects are placed on a table. They may include such items as a pencil, a salt shaker, a slipper, a tumbler, a marble, a paper clip or an ash-tray. The players stand around the table for 1 or 2 minutes and try to memorise the objects.
Then the objects are covered with a sheet and the children write down as many as they can remember.
After 3 or 4 minutes, time is called and the player who has written correctly the greatest number of objects is the winner.
As a variation, two small prizes may be included among the objects. The winning player makes his choice of a prize and the runner-up receives the other.

Front and Back Race
Winning two ways

Select two teams and tell them to stand in two lines. On the floor beside the leaders are two empty plates and two plates full of matches. There should be the same number of matches in each plate and it should be more than double the number of members in each team.

When you say 'Go!' the leaders pick up the matches one at a time and pass them down their lines of players.

When the last member of each team gets a match he passes it back to the leaders behind the players' backs.

This means that, at the same time, matches will be going down the lines in front of the players and up the lines behind them.

When the matches are returned to the front of the lines the leaders put them in the empty plates.

The first team to get all its matches back is the winner.

Marble Golf
The fewest shots wins

Nine draughtsmen or similar objects are placed around the room to resemble a nine-hole golf course. Each has a number from 1 to 9, drawn in crayon on a piece of paper and taped or glued on. Some pieces of furniture may be used as obstacles or hazards.

The players each have one marble and, starting from the same spot, take turns trying to hit the 'holes' in order. The game may be scored on a hole-by-hole basis; the player who hits a hole in the fewest shots wins that hole. At the end of the game, the player who has won the most holes is the winner.

Another way of scoring is to keep a count of the total number of shots a player takes to complete the course—the lowest score winning.

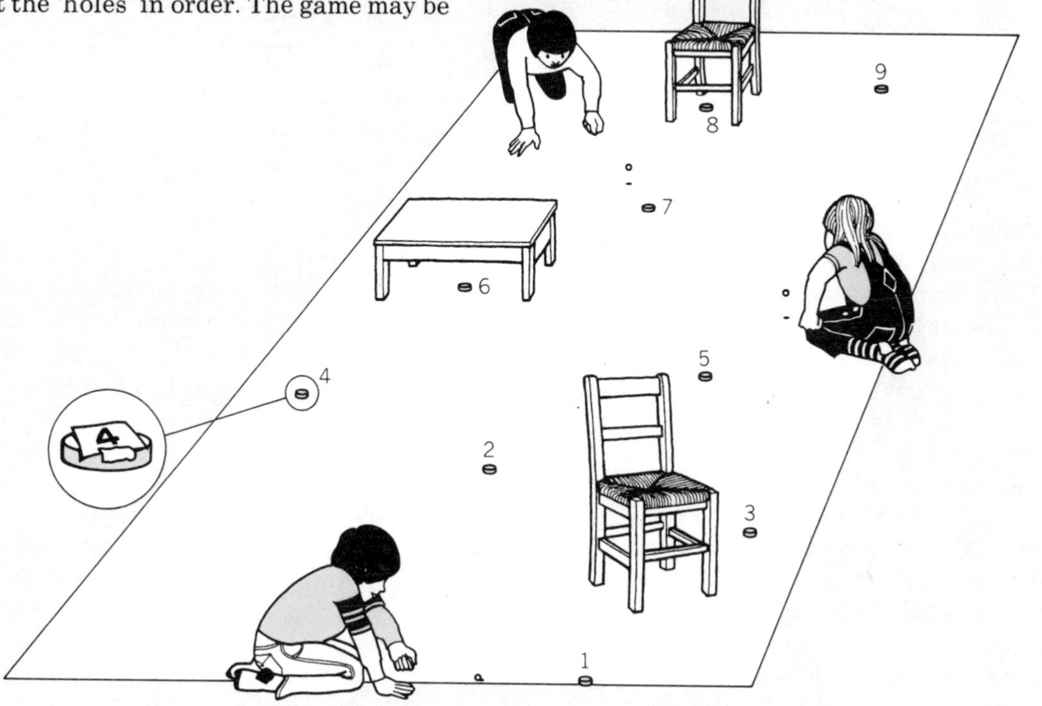

Coat and Hat Relay
A race for snappy dressers

After players divide into two equal teams each team leader is given a coat and a hat. At a signal, he puts on the hat and the coat, which he must button completely. Then he takes off the coat and hat and passes them to the next player in his line. The first team to complete the action wins.

Raisin Relay
Titbits come in threes

Every player in two equal teams is given a teaspoon. The teams line up and the first player in each line holds a small bowl of raisins.

At a signal, he turns and spoons up three raisins, which he feeds to the next player. Then the second player takes the bowl, turns, and feeds the next player three raisins in the same way. Finally, the last player must bring the bowl to the head of the line and feed the first player three raisins. The first team to complete the action wins.

The Artist's Game
Passing the word—in silence

A game leader sits in the centre of the room and players divide into teams of three or four. One player in each group, the artist, has a piece of paper and a pencil. The artists go to the leader who shows them a word he has printed on a piece of paper. It may be simple and direct, such as 'dog', 'house' or 'car' or may be more abstract, such as 'crime' or 'religion'. Each artist hurries back to his group and tries to draw a picture that conveys the meaning of the word. He may not write any letter or number and he must not speak or make any sound that would indicate what he is drawing. If the other players guess the word wrongly the artist does not speak but keeps drawing. They keep guessing until finally someone guesses the word. The first group to guess the word gets five points, the next three points and the last one point.

The game is played again with a new artist from each group. After everyone has had a chance to draw the secret word the team with the highest total is the winner.

Peanut Lift
The trick is in the pick-up

Peanuts are strewn on the floor. Each player is given two cocktail sticks and a small paper bag. At a signal, the players try to lift as many peanuts as they can with their cocktail sticks and drop them into their paper bags.

The trick is either to hold the sticks parallel and close together to lift the nut as if on a stretcher, or to press them against each side of a nut in chopstick fashion.

When all the peanuts have been gathered, the player with the greatest number is the winner.

Hanging Apples
Taking a bite at Hallow-e'en

This is a traditional Hallow-e'en game. Thread a large darning-needle with strong thread and run the thread through a button. Then, when the button is secured to one end of the thread, run the needle through an apple so that the apple rests on the button. Attach the thread to the ceiling, an overhead beam or fixture so that the apple dangles at about the height of a player's chin. Thread up other apples in the same way so that there is one for each player. Players line up in front of the apples with their hands behind their backs. At a signal, each player tries to eat the apple in front of him, keeping his hands behind his back.

In *Apple Turnover*, the apple is threaded in the same way but the thread has a loop large enough to go over a player's head. Two players, on their hands and knees, face each other. Each has an apple hanging from his neck. At

CONTINUED ON PAGE 42

Self-portrait

Face up to your features

Each player fixes a sheet of drawing paper in front of his face with sticky-tape.
Without being able to see what they are doing, the players draw their own eyes, nose, mouth, eyebrows and chin with a piece of wax crayon.
When all have finished their self-portraits they take the papers off and put them on display.
The players vote on who has done the best drawing.

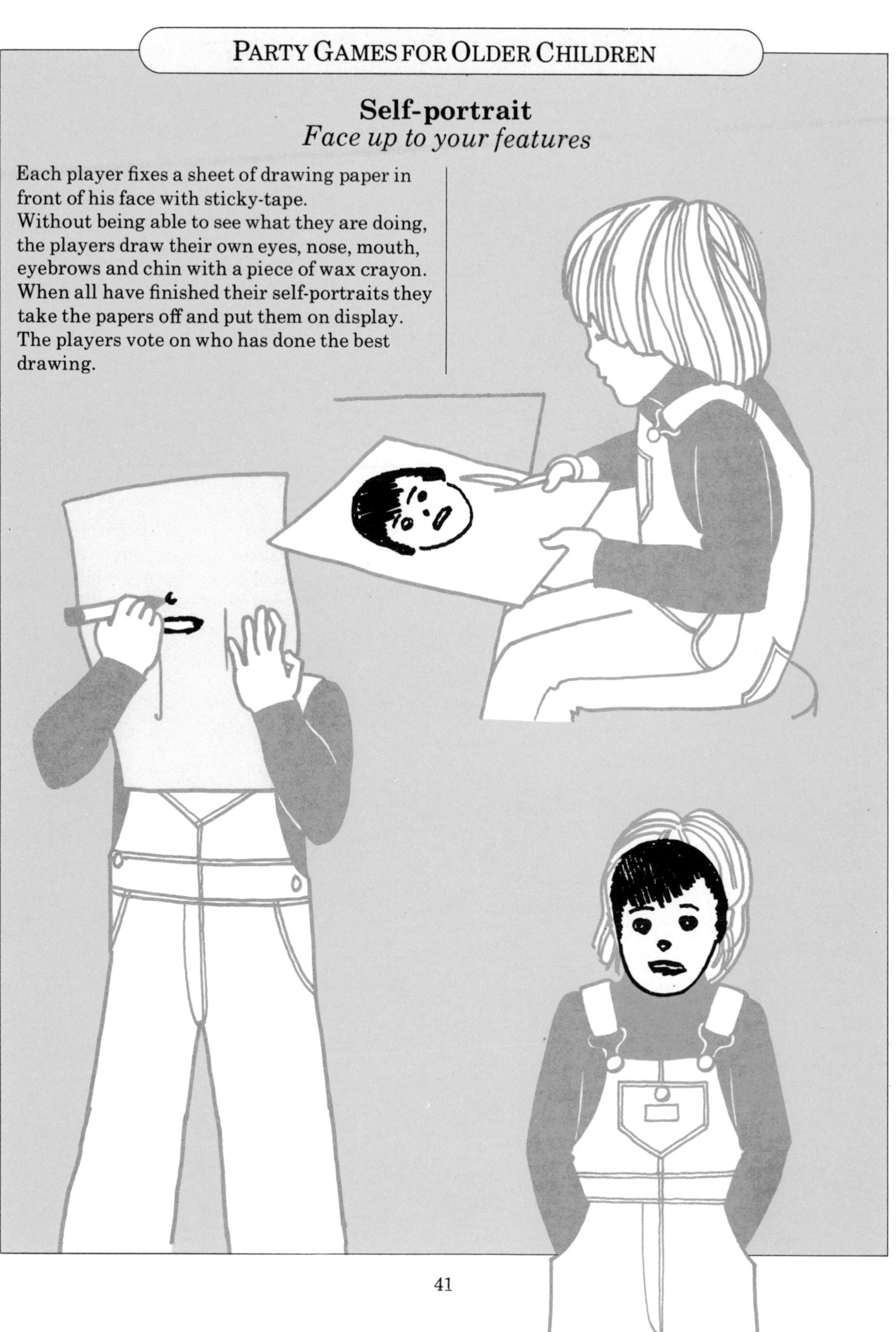

CONTINUED FROM PAGE 40
a signal each player tries to bite the apple hanging from his opponent's neck. The player who succeeds in getting the most bites after an agreed time wins. Contestants must remain on their hands and knees throughout the game.

Card Spelling Bee

Chance for children to show their skill

Each letter of the alphabet is written on two sets of cards and these are placed in two piles on a table about 3 metres in front of two equal teams. There are 26 cards in each pile and each card has a different letter on it. The cards are well shuffled. The game leader calls out a four or five-letter word. The first player in each team runs up and searches in his pile of cards for the first letter of the word. When he finds it, he races back and stands facing his team-mates holding that card across his chest. The next player finds the next letter of the word and so on. The first team to spell the word correctly wins a point.

The cards are then replaced and reshuffled. The players who have spelled the word go to the back of their lines. The leader then calls out another word. The first team to get an agreed number of points wins.

Peanut Hunt

The gathering goes gathering

Peanuts are scattered on the centre of the floor. Three or four players are blindfolded and are given a paper bag. At a signal, they get down on their hands and knees and grope for the peanuts. After 3 minutes, they remove their blindfolds and a count is made to see who has collected the most. The game can be played with any small objects, such as sweets.

In *Peanut Derby*, four or five players assemble at a starting line. On the floor, in front of each player, is a peanut. At a signal, each player gets down on hands and knees and pushes his peanut across the room to a finishing line—using only his nose. A player who touches a peanut with any other part of his body is disqualified.

When there are many players, several heats can be run to find the peanut-pushing champion.

Word-making Race

Making letters make sense

Prepare two sets of ten cards with a letter written on each. Choose letters that make it easy for the players to form words, such as ACDEEIORSY. The players form two teams and each player has a card. Each team has the same letters.

Using these letters, the players make up words of at least three letters and one player in each team lists the words on a piece of paper. After 5 minutes, the team with the greater number of correctly spelled words wins.

Knot Races

Never end in a tie

Divide the guests into two teams. Each team has a leader who is given a piece of thick string about 1 metre long. At a given signal the leaders tie a loose knot in their string. The string is then passed to each member of the team who also ties a knot in it. The last players take the knotted string back to the leaders who untie one knot. Each player then unties one knot. The first team to finish untying its knots is the winner.

Dressmaking

It's all in the paper

For this game you need several sheets of newspaper and some pins. Half the players are dressmakers, the remainder are their models. Each dressmaker is given an equal number of sheets of paper and an equal number of pins. At a given signal, the dressmakers have 5 minutes to 'dress' their models with the sheets of newspaper. The best design wins. They may tear holes in the paper to put arms through if they wish. Hats can be made as well as dresses.

How Many Beans?
A test to welcome the guests

Before the guests arrive a large glass bottle or other transparent container is filled with beans, marbles, large pebbles, or similar objects, which have been counted.
After examining the container carefully, the guests estimate how many objects are in the container and write the number along with their names on a slip of paper.
The player whose estimate comes closest is the winner.

Sweet in the Desert
Look—no hands!

Players stand in front of a table with their hands tied behind their backs. In front of each player is a paper plate on which is a sweet hidden in a heap of cornflakes.
At a signal each player tries to dig the sweet out of the cornflakes with his teeth. The first player to lift his head with the sweet wins.

Water Medley
How many swallows?

Each player has a straw, a teaspoon and a bowl filled with water. During the first 10 seconds, counted by a referee, the players use their straws to drink the water.
During the next 10 seconds, only spoons are used. The first to finish the water wins.

GAMES FOR A HALL OR GARDEN

These lively games for a large group of children can be played in a hall hired for a birthday or Christmas party, or they can be played in the garden. They are, however, too boisterous to be played in the home where there are any breakable treasures.

Jumble Relay
The object is to pass it on

Two piles of objects, such as old hats, books or pencils, are placed on a turning line, about 5 metres from a starting line. Two teams line up and, at a signal, the first players run to the turning line. Each picks up an object and runs back to the starting line where they pass on their objects to the second players, who in turn pass them down the line while the lead players take their places at the rear of their lines. When an object reaches the end of the line it is placed on the floor.
As soon as the second players pass on the objects they run to the turning line, pick up another object and run back to pass it on. As each player completes the action he goes to the end of his line.
The game ends when one team has picked up all its objects and rebuilt the pile behind the starting line.

Lemon Race
The answer is skilful spooning

Players line up, evenly spaced, behind a line marked on the floor, and face a turning line about 5 metres away. Each player is given a lemon and a tablespoon. Touching the lemons with their spoons only, they roll them to the turning line and back again.
The first player to complete the action is the winner.
If the contest is played as a relay, the first team to finish wins. Apples or potatoes may be substituted for lemons.

Stepping-stone Race

Bound for the winning post by hand and foot

Before this race each player is given two pieces of cardboard, measuring about 20 by 10 centimetres. These are the stepping stones. Players line up behind a starting line about 5 metres away from a turning line.

At a signal, each player places his pieces of cardboard on the ground, one in front of the other, and places one foot on the front piece and the other foot on the rear piece.

To move towards the turning line, he stands on one foot on the front piece and picks up the rear piece—moving it forwards for his next stepping stone.

All the players progress in this way and the winner is the first to return to the starting line. This method of this race can also be used in a team relay.

In *Sir Walter Raleigh,* players divide into pairs. At a signal, one player in each pair moves the pieces of cardboard forwards; the other walks only on the pieces as they are moved. Each pair travels to the turning line and back, when the roles are reversed. The first pair (or the first team, if the game is being played as a relay) to complete the action wins.

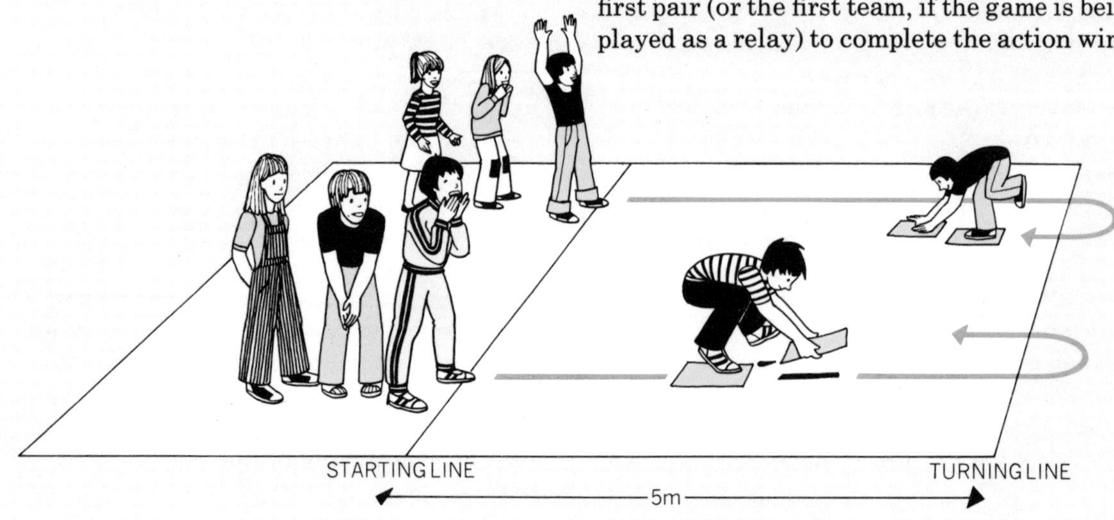

Forehead Fruit Relay

Just a face-to-face race

Teams divide into pairs and form up behind a starting line. The first two players in each team face each other and place an orange between their foreheads, holding it firmly without using their hands.

At a signal, they run to a turning line about 5 metres away and back. If they drop the orange they stop and replace it between their foreheads before continuing the race.

When they return to the starting line they may use their hands to set the orange between the foreheads of the next two in line. The race continues in this manner until one team completes the relay.

Balloon Basketball

Not so easy as it seems

A sheet of newspaper is taped to the wall at either end of the room to represent the baskets. Players form two equal teams, three or four in a side. One member of each team moves to the

centre and a coin is tossed to decide which has the balloon. The winner of the toss hits the balloon towards his team-mates.
The object of the game is for each team to try to hit the balloon towards the other team's basket. If the balloon touches the paper a goal is scored. After 5 minutes the team with the most goals is the winner.
In *Pop the Balloon* a goalie stands under each basket with a pin. As the balloon nears the basket, the goalie can either hit it away with his hand—or pop it with his pin.

Carton Tenpin

Boxing clever with a ball

Ten plastic or cardboard cartons are set up in a triangular pattern, like bowling pins—four in the back row, three in the second, two in the third and one at the front. The players stand about 5 metres away and try to knock down the cartons by rolling a ball. If a player knocks them all down he gets ten points, plus a bonus of five. If not, he has a second try and scores the number of cartons knocked down.

Skittle Bombardment

It's a knock-down knock-out

Two teams, with two balls each, stand on opposite sides of a centre line. Each team has a goal line about 5 metres behind the centre line. Four skittles, or cardboard cartons or plastic bottles, are placed, each about 1 metre apart, on the two goal lines. Each team tries to knock down its opponents' skittles with the balls while protecting its own.

Players may pass the balls from one to another but they may not step across the centre line. There are two ways to score: the first team to knock down all its opponents' skittles is the winner; or a team receives one point each time it knocks down a skittle (the skittles are put up again at once) and the team with more points after 5 minutes is the winner.

Hit the Deck

Start from the top to make a speedy run-down

Players form two equal teams of not more than 13 each. They line up facing each other. In between them are two card tables. On each table is a cardboard box with a pack of cards in it. The cards have been put into the boxes in complete disarray.
At a signal the first player in each line hurries to his team's box and tries to find a king of any suit. When he does find any king he runs to a corner of the room, places the card face up on the floor, hurries back and touches the next player in line.
This player now runs to his team's box and hunts for a queen of any suit. On finding it, he takes it to the same corner, places it face up beside the king and returns to the line.
The third player must find a jack and follow the same procedure as his team-mates before him. The game continues with each player hunting for the next card in sequence—regardless of suit. The first team to put down a complete run from king to ace, which is the low card, wins.
If there are too few players to make up two teams of 13 each, the game may be played by removing the kings, the queens and so on

Broom Hockey

Making a clean sweep of it

Players divide into two teams and stand in lines facing each other. Two chairs are placed at the ends of each line for goal posts. A rag and two brooms, with their handles facing the goals, are placed on the floor in the centre of the room.
One team numbers off in reverse order to the other so that, if eight are playing, the number 1 player is opposite number 4, number 2 opposite number 3 and so on.
The game leader calls out a number and the player in each team with that number runs forward and picks up the broom belonging to his team. Both players try to sweep the rag into the opposite goal. The first player to score a goal wins a point for his team.
When a goal is scored, the rag and brooms are put back in the centre of the room and new numbers are called. After 10 minutes the team with the most points is the winner.

until there are just enough cards in each box for each team.
As a variation, the players may be asked to find a sequence of cards in one particular suit.

Double-bounce
Success is in the basket

A wastepaper basket is placed against a wall and a line is marked on the floor about 3 metres away. From behind this line the first player tries to throw a rubber ball so that it bounces once on the floor and lands in the basket. One point is given for every ball that lands in the basket. Each player is given five tries. The highest score wins.

Broom, Potato and Plate
A test of speed and balance

Players form equal teams behind a starting line. A turning line, about 5 metres away, is marked by two chairs, one for each team. The first player in each team has a potato, a small broom and an unbreakable plate.
At a signal, each first player places the plate on top of his head and puts the potato between his knees. Then, waving the broom, each

Bottle-top Toss
Now you see it . . . now you don't

A target of five interlocking circles drawn on a large sheet of paper, each circle about 25 centimetres in diameter, is laid flat on the floor (see diagram). The circles and interlocked areas are numbered from 1 to 6.
The players stand on a line about 4 metres away and take turns to toss five bottle tops, one at a time, towards the target.
A player gets the appropriate number of points for each top that lands in a circle. If the top lands in an interlocked area he gets the higher score. If the top lands on the line between two circles, the player gets the higher score. The player with the most points wins.
In *Mystery Toss*, the same equipment is used but the numbers are covered. The game leader has a master chart showing the value of each circle. He keeps score, and when each player has had his turn the scores are added up. The highest wins.

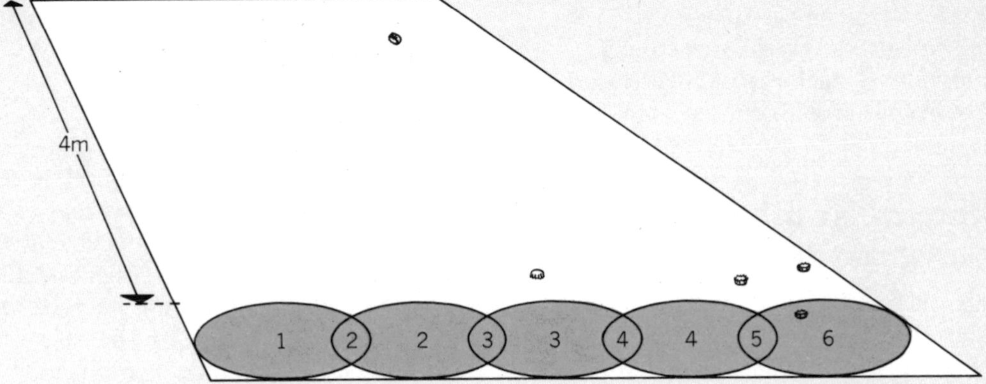

makes his way to the turning line, around the chair and back to the starting line to touch off the next player.

If any object is dropped, the player must pick it up and replace it before moving on. The first team to complete the action wins.

Numbers

Getting rid of a problem

Two boxes are placed on a turning line, about 7 metres from the starting line. Players divide into two equal teams and stand in single file. Every player has a folded card with a mathematical problem. The age of the contestants should govern the simplicity or complexity of the problem. Player number 1 in team A has the same problem to solve as player number 1 in team B. Player 2 in team A has the same problem as player 2 in team B, and so on.

A player may not open his card and begin solving his problem until his turn comes up. At a signal, the first two players on the starting line open their cards and each solves his problem. As soon as a player has written the solution to his problem he passes his pencil to the next player in line, who begins to solve his problem. The first player runs to the box and puts his card inside and then touches the next player and runs to the back of his line. The second player can then run to the box as soon as he has written his solution.

A team gets three points for finishing first and five points for each correct answer.

This game can also be played as a contest among individuals, each player receiving the same three or four problems.

Blackboard Numbers

The winner can sum it all up

Players divide into two equal teams and stand behind a line about 5 metres from a blackboard. At a signal, each lead player runs to the blackboard and writes a two or three-figure number. The second players follow, putting their two or three-figure numbers below those of the lead players. The game continues until the last players have their turn. Instead of putting down new numbers, the last players add up the lists. The first team with a correct total is the winner.

In the Hat

A game that's brim-full of fun

Players, each holding ten playing cards, form a circle. In the centre is a hat upside-down. Players try to flip their cards into the hat. A card that lands in the hat scores two points and one that lands on the brim or leans against the hat scores one.

The winner is the player with the most points.

Team Crawl

Coming first on all fours

Players line up in equal columns behind the starting line. The turning line is 10 metres away. At a signal, the first player in each team gets down on hands and knees and crawls towards the turning line. On reaching that line, the player crawls back to the starting line and touches the next player in the team, who repeats the action.

The game continues until the last player of one team is home.

Head Balance Relay

Steady up for the cup

The leading player of each team places a plastic cup on his head. At a signal, he walks or runs to a turning line about 7 metres away. He must balance the cup on his head without touching it with his hand. If the cup falls he replaces it before continuing the race. On returning to the starting line he passes the cup to the second player, and so on through the team. The winning team is the first to finish.

Fan Football

No point in making a hit

Goal lines are marked near opposite ends of a hall or large room and two equal teams stand between them. No child may move more than 1 metre from his place.

Each child has a piece of cardboard, and a table-tennis ball is thrown into the centre. Using their pieces of cardboard as fans, the children try to move the ball, from team-mate to team-mate, towards the opposing goal. The ball may only be fanned, not hit, and when it is sent over a goal line the scoring team gets six points.

Should a child hit the ball by mistake, his team is penalised one point. A goal scored by a hit does not count. After 10 minutes, the team with the most points wins.

Biscuit Race
Make a note to make it clear

Two teams line up behind a starting line. About 5 metres away, in front of each team, is a chair. The game leader stands between the chairs.
At a signal, the first players run to the chairs, sit down, and are given two dry biscuits each. They eat the biscuits and then try to whistle clearly. The crumbs will make it difficult, but they must not leave their chairs until they can whistle a clear note.
Having whistled, they run back to their lines and touch off the next players. The first team to complete the action wins.

Chair Ring Toss
It pays to throw a leg

A chair is placed upside-down on another chair. Each player has five quoits and stands about 3 metres from the chair to toss them underhand. A quoit 'ringing' a leg counts as five points, one landing on the seat one point. A player ringing all four legs during his five chances receives a bonus of 20 points.
The player with the most points after every player has had a turn wins the game.

Potato Scoop
Taking turns to chip in

Potatoes, in groups of three, are placed on the turning line, about 5 metres from the starting line. Players line up in equal columns behind the starting line, facing a group of potatoes. The first player in each team has a large spoon. At a signal, the first player runs forward and scoops up one potato with the spoon without touching it with hand or foot. He runs back with the potato on the spoon and places it on the ground at the starting line and returns for the second potato and then for the third. When all three potatoes are at the starting line, the first player passes the spoon to the second player who returns the potatoes, one by one, to their original positions on the turning line.
The game continues until every player has moved the potatoes back or forth, and the first team to complete the action wins.

Bag Pile Race
The back-to-front contest

Players form into two lines. Each team has an equal number of bean-bags at the back of its line. At a signal, the bean-bags are passed swiftly by hand from the back of the lines to the front. The players at the front of each line pile up the bags with only the bottom bag touching the ground.
Should the bags fall over, the player stacking them rearranges them, and the passing of bags must halt while the stack is rebuilt.
The first team to stack all its bean-bags wins the round, and the best out of five rounds wins the game.

Chapter 4

Making Magic and giving a Puppet Show

Preparing conjuring tricks to baffle young audiences; How to give a home puppet performance; Family fun in charades

A party becomes something special if it includes a conjuring act or a puppet show. All the following conjuring tricks—children like to call them 'magic'—are simple to perform after some preparation and practice. There are a number of tricks to enable a home conjuror to put on two or three performances without repeating his act.

A puppet show, equally, is easy to stage at home providing that the puppeteer first prepares a script that suits the age of the audience and keeps his act as brief as possible. A conjuring act or a puppet show need not, however, be just party pieces. Performances can be given as home entertainment to the family and friends at any time.

Since there is something of the actor in all of us, charades can be a party piece or part of an evening's home entertainment. Charades, however, require an understanding of words and are suitable only for older children.

Water into Wine
Vintage magic

The magician places four empty glasses on the table and says: 'Now I am going to turn water into wine.' He picks up a jug and pours water into the first glass: 'There's the water,' he says.

Then he says: 'Now for some wine from the same jug,' and the next glass is filled with a deep red liquid. 'Like some more water?' he asks, and pours some into the third glass. 'I think we'll finish with another drop of wine. I know there's more in this jug,' he says. And he fills the glass with red liquid.

The Secret You should be able to obtain from a chemist a chemical called potassium permanganate. It comes in powder form—dentists use it mixed with water for patients to rinse out their mouths. Put a small quantity in the second and fourth glasses. Enough to cover a 1p piece is sufficient.

Lifting Ten Matches

Time for a squeeze play

The magician challenges any player to lay ten matches on the table in such a way that they can all be picked up at the same time, using only one other match. When the players have tried and failed, he shows them how it is done.

The Secret Lay one match flat on the table, and lay nine other matches across it. They alternate, pointing in opposite directions, and the centre of each lies on top of the first match. Then place one other match across the top of the other nine matches, directly over the first match but pointing in the opposite direction. Using the thumb and forefinger of both hands, grip the ends of the two parallel matches and lift all the matches at once. As the magician claimed, only one extra match has been used to lift the ten.

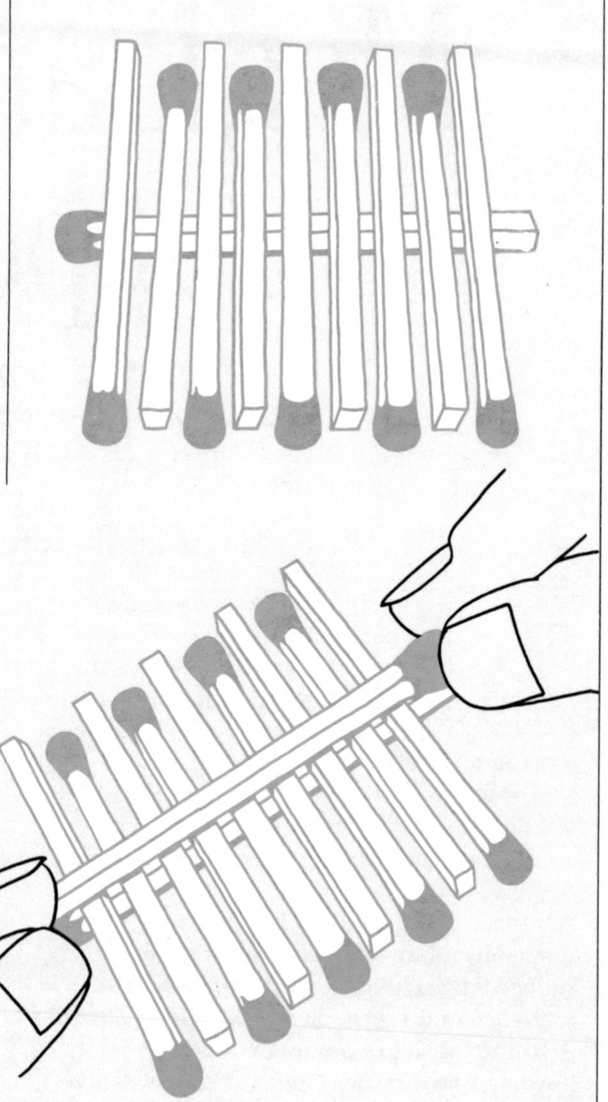

Linking Matches
Not easy to see through

The magician shows two matches, held between the thumb and forefinger of each hand. Bringing his hands together he presses the matches together and says 'One'. He moves his hands apart, then brings them together and says 'Two'. After the third move and his call of 'Three', the audience sees that one match has appeared to have passed through the other.

The Secret The matches are held head upwards for a good grip. As the magician moves his hands apart after the count of 'Two' he alters the position of his fingers on the right-hand match. He lets the match head slip over his fingertip so that it is gripped between his forefinger and his middle finger. He then says 'Three', lifts his thumb and passes the right-hand match over the other, immediately pressing his thumb back on the match. He reverses the action to separate the matches again. If the matches are then casually dropped on a table there is bound to be a curious watcher who wants to examine them.

This trick requires some practice so that the move is made smoothly. The trick is most effective when done slowly.

Mystic Ashes
Name of the game is the same

The magician asks members of the audience to name some famous people and he writes these names, one at a time, on slips of paper, folds them and puts them in a hat. He then asks a boy or girl to come forward and pick a slip out of the hat. The child is told to keep the slip folded. The magician puts the remaining slips in an ashtray and burns them. He studies the 'mystic ashes' and after a few seconds calls out the name of the person on the remaining slip.

The child who has drawn that slip unfolds it, announces that the magician is right and shows the slip to the audience.

The Secret When the magician is writing on the slips of paper he does not write down all the names suggested, only the first one. Therefore all the slips have the same name on them.

Black Magic
Dark doings of a magician

The magician and his assistant stand in front of the audience. The magician says he will leave the room and when he returns he will be able to name any object that the audience selected. When the magician returns, his assistant points to various objects. When the correct object is indicated the magician identifies it.

The Secret Before pointing to the correct object the assistant points to one that is black or nearly black.

In *Red, White and Blue*, the magician leaves the room three times, and three different objects are chosen for him to identify. The first time the assistant points to the secret object after pointing to a red article, the next time after a white article and the last time after a blue one.

Legs
Magically it stands to reason

When the magician leaves the room, his assistant tells the audience to select any object. When the magician comes back the assistant points to objects, each time asking if it is the selected one. Of course the magician says 'no' until the right object is indicated.

The Secret The first object the assistant points to contains the vital clue. If an object with legs is indicated by the assistant, then the magician knows that the correct article does have legs. The assistant then points to a number of articles without legs, such as ashtrays, lamps or pictures, and when next he indicates an object with legs the magician knows that is the correct object. If the audience selects an article without legs the assistant first points to an object without legs, then several with legs and, finally, the correct object.

Magic Spoon
Some pointers to mystification

The magician says that he has a magic spoon which can take a picture of anyone in the room. He also says that only he and his assistant can see the picture that appears on the bowl of the spoon. To prove it the magician sends his assistant out of the room and the audience selects one person to have his picture taken.
The magician holds his spoon up and pretends to take the picture. Then he places the spoon on the floor and calls his assistant back in. The assistant peers into the bowl and then identifies the correct person.
The Secret When the magician puts the spoon down on the floor, he points its handle in the general direction of, though not directly at, the correct person. That is clue number one. In addition, the magician sits in exactly the same pose as the chosen person. With these two clues, the assistant has no difficulty in selecting the right person.
If the magician has been asked to take his own picture, he lets his assistant know this by sitting with his legs crossed and pointing the handle of the spoon directly at the door.

Find the Matches
A trick that's bound to shake them

The audience is shown three matchboxes which are all shaken by the magician, but matches are heard to rattle in one only. The boxes are placed on a table alongside one another and their positions changed quickly. One of the audience is asked if he can tell the box with the matches in it. He fails. The magician shakes the boxes again and changes positions more slowly. The spectator still fails to find the box with the matches in it.
Finally, the magician makes a pencil mark on the box of matches. He changes positions again but the spectator still fails to find the right box.
The Secret The boxes the spectators see are all empty. A box half full of matches is under the performer's right sleeve attached by rubber bands to his arm near his wrist. When he wishes to show a box empty he shakes it with his left hand. To make the audience believe a box contains matches he shakes it with his right hand.

Car
Initially a certain winner

With the magician and his assistant looking on, the group selects three objects and places them in a row on the floor. The magician leaves the room and the group picks one of the three objects for him to guess. When the magician returns he immediately points to the correct article.
The Secret The clue is in the phrase the assistant uses to call the magician back. It is based on the word 'car'. If the phrase begins with a C (Come in), the magician knows that the correct object is the one on the left. If it begins with an A (All right), the object is the middle one. If it begins with an R (Ready), the chosen object is the one on the right.
In *Count the Letters*, several objects are placed on the floor, one of them having been chosen as the secret object. When the magician returns to the room the assistant points to the objects one by one and the magician selects the correct object. Again, the clue is in the first word the assistant says.
If that word has one letter, as in 'I think we're ready to start', then the first object the assistant points to is the one.
If the word has two letters, as in 'We can begin now', the second object pointed to is correct, and so on.

The Jumping Beads
Keep them on the hop

You need an assistant's wrist and two loops of beads, or string, of different colours; any contrasting colours will do. You place the loops around the wrist as shown. You hold the upper loop with the right hand and the lower loop with the left hand. Ask the audience which colour loop is around the wrist. Say 'Watch carefully'. Let go with the left hand and pull smartly with your right hand. The loops will change places. The trick can be done around a ruler instead of the wrist, with a spectator holding both ends.

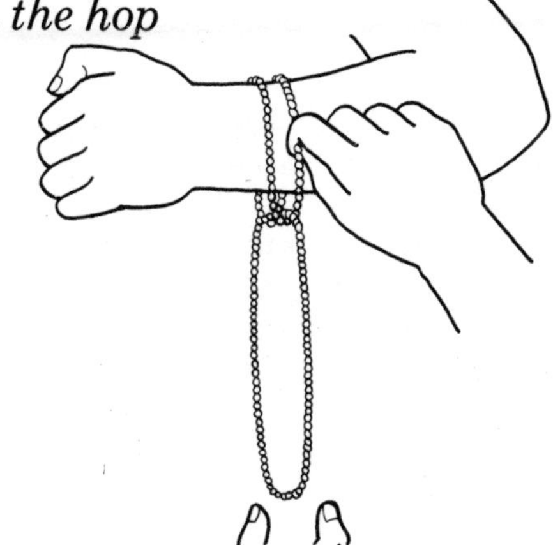

The Balancing Glass
The audience will fall for it

The magician holds a playing card in his right hand and places a plastic beaker on its edge. It falls off. He does it again and the beaker balances on the edge of the card.

The Secret Two cards are used. One is scored lengthways down the centre with a penknife and folded over.

The right-hand half of the face is glued to the back of the other card so that they both line up and both face the same way.

Both sides can be shown to the audience and look like one card—yet there is a strut that can be pulled out to support the beaker. The audience must be in front of the magician. Anyone at the side will be able to see how the trick is done.

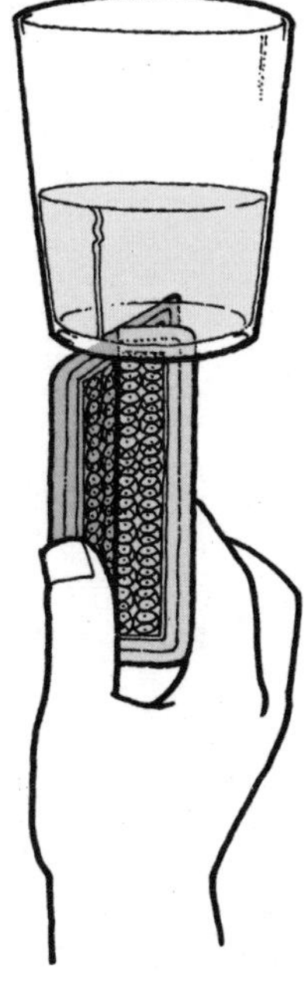

The Trick Bridge

Proving the power of the pleat

The magician takes a sheet of strong writing paper and places it over two plastic beakers set apart, forming a bridge between them. He tells the audience that he can place a third beaker upright on this bridge and challenges anyone to try it. When they do, they soon find out that the paper is not strong enough. Then the magician successfully performs the trick.

The Secret He takes the same sheet of paper and folds it several times lengthwise creating a pleatlike effect. This strengthens the paper and it is easily able to bear the weight of the beaker.

The Money Maker

It all depends on the way you look at it

The magician removes a folded piece of paper from an envelope. The envelope is shown to be empty. The paper is unfolded and also shown empty. It is re-folded and replaced in the envelope. He asks his audience to think 'Money, money, money'. Then he removes the paper from the envelope and when he unfolds it everyone sees it contains a 10p piece. 'Thanks very much,' says the magician, pocketing the coin.

The Secret Two equal squares of paper are used. They are folded into nine squares and the centre squares are glued together.
Then each sheet is folded back to back, a coin is placed in one side and the whole thing put into the envelope. When the magician takes the paper out of the envelope he unfolds the empty side and shows it to the audience—the audience of course cannot see the other side. Similarly, when he takes the paper out of the envelope again he shows and unfolds the side with the coin in it.

The Unburstable Balloon

A trick that goes with a bang

'I have a magic formula for sticking a pin into a balloon without bursting it,' says the magician. He blows up a balloon and slowly brings a pin to it. The balloon bursts and his audience laughs. 'Sorry, I forgot the magic spell,' says the magician.
He blows up another balloon and says 'Hi de hi, I won't stop, till this balloon, won't go pop'. This time he sticks a pin into the balloon and it doesn't burst.
'Now I'll do it without the spell,' he says, and the balloon bursts.

The Secret A small piece of sticky-tape is stuck to an *inflated* balloon. Then it is deflated and is used as the second balloon in the trick. The pin is pressed against the tape and the balloon won't burst. Next time the pin bursts the balloon.

Celebrity Squares

With a top star in the middle

The magician tears a piece of paper into nine squares and hands one square to a member of the audience to write down the name of his favourite television star. The magician turns his back so that he cannot see what is being written. He then asks other volunteers to write down their favourite TV stars on the remaining squares. The squares are shuffled and handed to the magician who holds them behind his back. He announces: 'I can detect writing by the feel of my fingers. I am now going to tell you the name of the favourite TV star named by my first volunteer.' And he does.

The Secret When the paper is torn there is only one piece that has a ragged edge all round—the centre one. This piece is given to the first volunteer.
When the pieces are given back the magician feels round the edges to find the one he wants.

The Powerful Breath

Magic secret of a glass-blower

The magician lights a candle and sets it behind a large bottle on a table. He blows against the bottle and the candle on the opposite side goes out. It looks as if the magician has blown directly through the bottle.

The Secret If the bottle is round, the magician's breath divides into two air currents that go directly around it and join on the other side to blow out the candle. With practice, this trick may be done with two or three bottles in a row.

The Magnetic Pencil

A trick that's hard to pin down

The magician holds up his right hand with the palm facing towards him. He places a pencil on the palm with his left hand and then grips his right wrist. The pencil appears to be stuck to

his right hand. The magician then turns his right palm to the audience who sees that he is keeping the pencil in place with his left forefinger and is gripping his right wrist with his thumb and other fingers. Then he does the trick again. But this time he takes his left hand away and the pencil still sticks to his right hand. He shows his right palm to the audience and the pencil is still there.
The Secret The pencil is faked. Two small pins are tacked into the centre of the pencil at a slight angle, painted flesh colour so that the audience will not notice them. The first part of the trick is done as explained. The second time, however, the second and third fingers of the right hand grip the pins.

Disappearing Pencil
The shape can be deceptive

The magician places a pencil under a handkerchief, holding it up so its shape can be seen. Suddenly, with the other hand, he pulls the handkerchief aside—and the pencil is gone.
The Secret The magician points his forefinger up under the handkerchief, making the audience think it is the pencil and at the same time he lets the pencil slip down his sleeve.

Where Did It Go?
Wanted: A right-hand man

The magician holds a small ball in his right hand. He then covers his hand with a large handkerchief and invites other players to reach in under the handkerchief to make sure that the ball is still there. As soon as the last person has felt the ball, the magician whips away the handkerchief and the ball has disappeared. He covers his hand with the handkerchief again and the other players reach under to make sure the ball is not there. After all the players have done this and agreed that his hand is empty, the magician again snatches away the cloth. This time, however, he has the ball in his hand.
The Secret The magician has a secret collaborator, who is the last person to reach under the handkerchief each time. The first time, he takes the ball away. It is small enough to be hidden in his hand. The second time he replaces it. Of course, the other players do not know that he is working with the magician.

The Travelling Ball
Threading through the air

The magician holds a table-tennis ball up in the air and suddenly it seems to travel mysteriously from one hand to the other.
The Secret This trick is done by tying the ends of a piece of black thread, 1 metre long, to form a loop. The magician holds the loop taut with his forefingers, both hands stretched out as far as the loop will permit. This forms a narrow track along which the ball glides easily. A table-tennis ball works well with this trick because it is light in weight and because its colour makes it easily visible to the audience. From a distance, the black thread will not be seen. Considerable practice is needed.

A Pencil from Nowhere
Something of a backhander

The magician shows his hand empty and says he wants a pencil to write something. Reaching into the air a pencil appears by magic in his hand.
The Secret A tiny rubber band is put around the right middle finger over the first joint. A small pencil is held under the band at the back of the hand. The magician looks in the air above his head, reaches slowly with the palm of his right hand facing the audience. Then he grabs with the fingers, bringing the pencil into view.
It can then be slipped from the rubber band and given to a spectator.

The Mysterious Ball

Practise to get the hang of it

The magician shows the audience the palm of his hand, which is empty. But then he reaches up in the air and a wooden ball suddenly appears at his fingertips.

The Secret A small tack is embedded in the ball. One end of a piece of thread is attached to the tack and the other end to a ring which the magician wears on his second finger. When he holds his palm up to the audience, the wooden ball hangs out of sight behind his hand. The magician throws his hand upwards and the ball swings up so he can catch it on his fingertips. With a little practice, this is a very deceptive illusion.

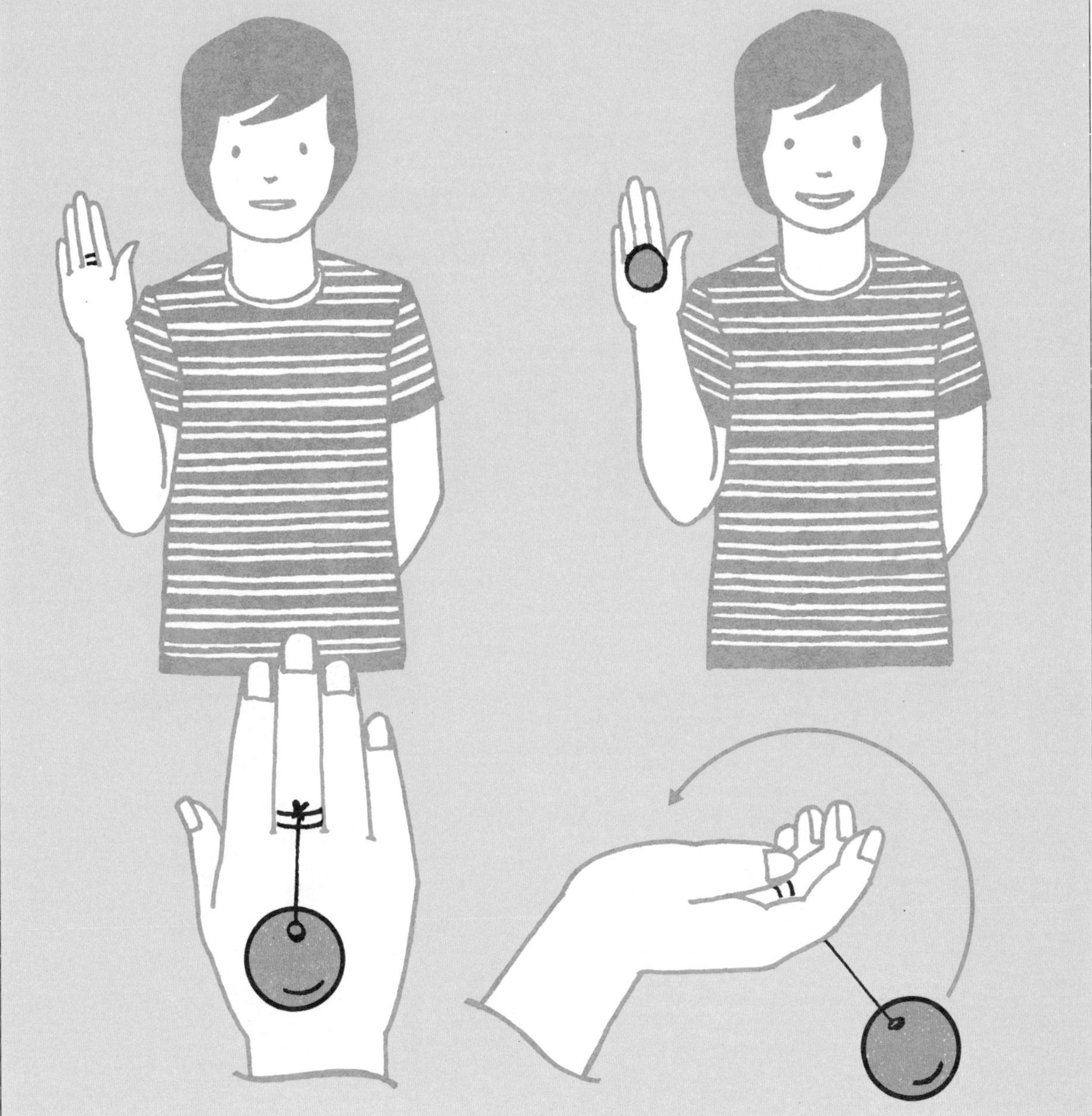

Disappearing Orange
It was only skin deep

The magician places an orange and a large coloured handkerchief or scarf on the table, saying that he is hungry and wants to eat an orange. He waves the handkerchief loosely in the air to show that it does not conceal anything and places it over the orange.
Then he says 'Come to think of it, I'd really rather have an apple. But that's all right, because . . . ' At this, he lifts up the handkerchief, crumples it and puts it in his pocket. Instead of an orange, an apple appears on the table.
The Secret The apple was there all the time, with a whole orange peel fitted around it (see diagram 1).
The trick is prepared by taking a thick-skinned orange and slitting the peel into four slices with a sharp knife, making certain to leave the rind joined at the top.
The magician sets the peel over a small apple.
The audience does not suspect because from a distance it is difficult to see the cuts in the skin. When the magician lifts the handkerchief, he squeezes off the orange peel (see diagram 2), crumpling it together with the handkerchief and placing it out of sight in his pocket. Spectators are unlikely to suspect that anything is in the handkerchief because all eyes are on the apple which has replaced the orange on the table.

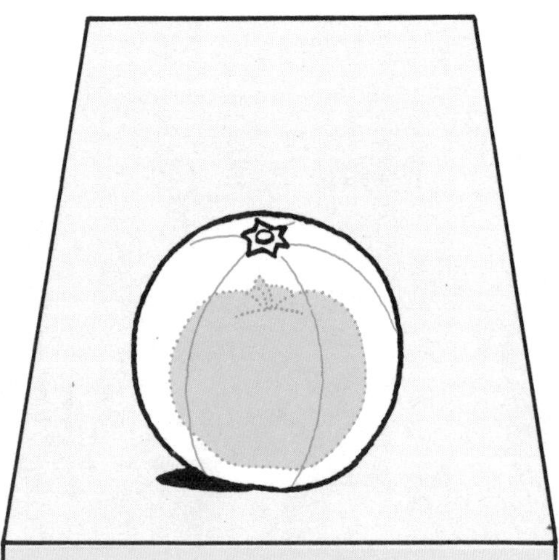

1 The audience sees only an orange, but an apple is hidden under the sliced skin.

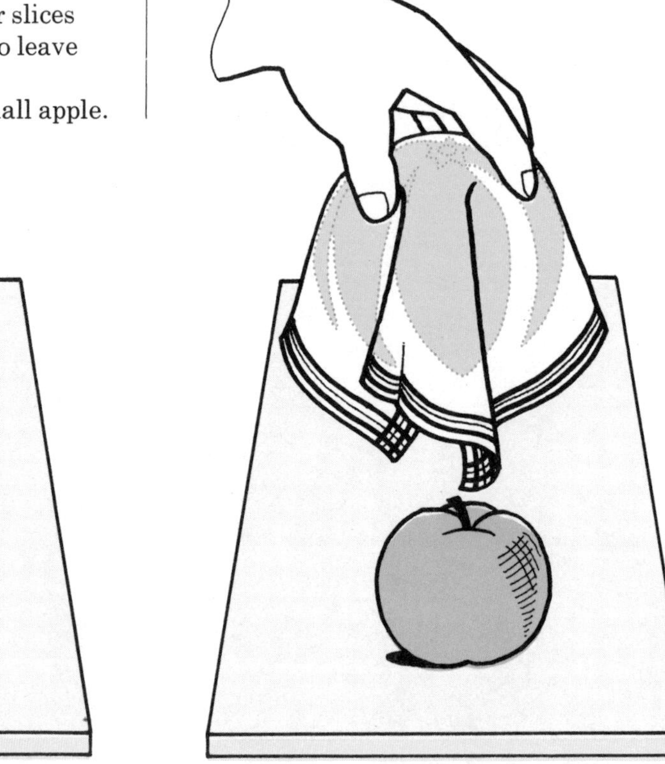

2 The audience sees only an apple because the orange skin is in the handkerchief.

Ring on a String

And an audience on tenterhooks

Allow your audience to examine a 2 metre length of string and a ring small enough to be concealed in a clenched fist. Ask a volunteer to thread the ring on the string and hold each end of the string tightly in each hand.
Then you issue the challenge: 'Can anyone get the ring off the string without breaking the string or our helper here letting go of the ends?' The answer to that is 'No', however hard anyone may try.
'Here's how it is done,' you say. Show them a pencil and a handkerchief, place the handkerchief over the ring and put the pencil and both your hands under it. After a few moments, slide your hands to the ends of the string and take it from the volunteer. 'Now,' you say, 'I am holding the string exactly as he was. But if he removes the handkerchief and the pencil he will release the ring—and I will still be holding on to each end.'
The volunteer removes the handkerchief and everyone can see that the pencil and ring are clinging to the string. He removes the pencil and the ring drops clear.
The Secret You have a second ring, hidden in your hand, which exactly matches the ring on the string. When you put your hands under the handkerchief you insert the pencil between the string and the second ring (see diagram). Then, when you slide your hands to the ends of the string and take it from the volunteer you conceal the first ring in one of your hands. The volunteer removes the pencil and the second ring drops off. All eyes are on him at this moment which allows you to remove the first ring and slip it in your pocket while the the string dangles from your other hand.

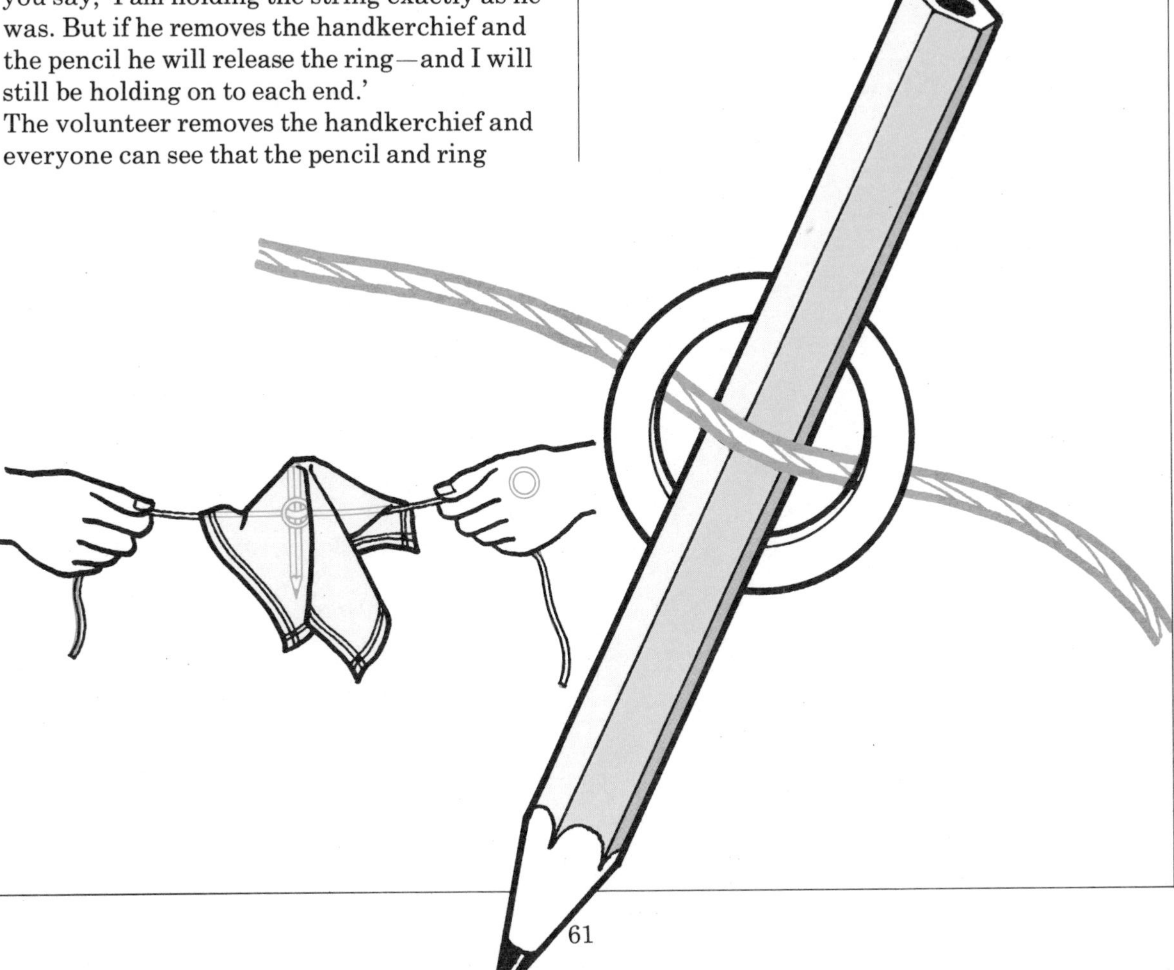

Tying up the Ring

The surprise is all tied up

You need a 1 metre length of string and a finger ring. Both ends of the string are tied to your wrists (see diagram 1). You take the ring and turn your back to the audience for a moment. When you face them again the ring is tied in a knot on the string.

The Secret Take up a loop in the centre of the string and push it through the ring (see diagram 2). Pass the loop under the string tied around the left wrist. Take the loop over the whole hand. Pass it through the string again on the underside of the wrist and finally over the hand again. Then pull and the ring is tied on the string (see diagram 3).

Tie the Knot

Folded arms avoid a hitch

The magician spreads out a large handkerchief or scarf. He challenges anyone to tie a knot in it by holding one corner of the handkerchief in one hand and the opposite corner in the other, but not letting go of either corner during the knotting. When a few have tried and failed, the magician shows how it is done.

The Secret He simply folds his arms across his chest, with one hand on top of one arm and one hand under the other arm. With his arms and hands in this position, he picks up the corners of the handkerchief. Then by uncrossing his arms and bringing his hands out to either side, he is able to make a knot in the handkerchief without letting go of either corner.

String Through the Neck

All fingers and thumbs

The magician takes a piece of string 1 metre long and makes a loop by knotting the ends together. He holds up the loop of string and explains that he is going to pass this cord right through his neck. He slips the string around his neck with the two ends of the loop stretched out in front of him.

Using his thumbs, the magician draws each end taut, as far from his neck as possible but with the two ends of the loop very close together. He says a magic word and pulls the loop sharply, apparently bringing it forward right through his neck. He is still holding the ends of the taut loop with his thumbs but the whole string is now in front of him.

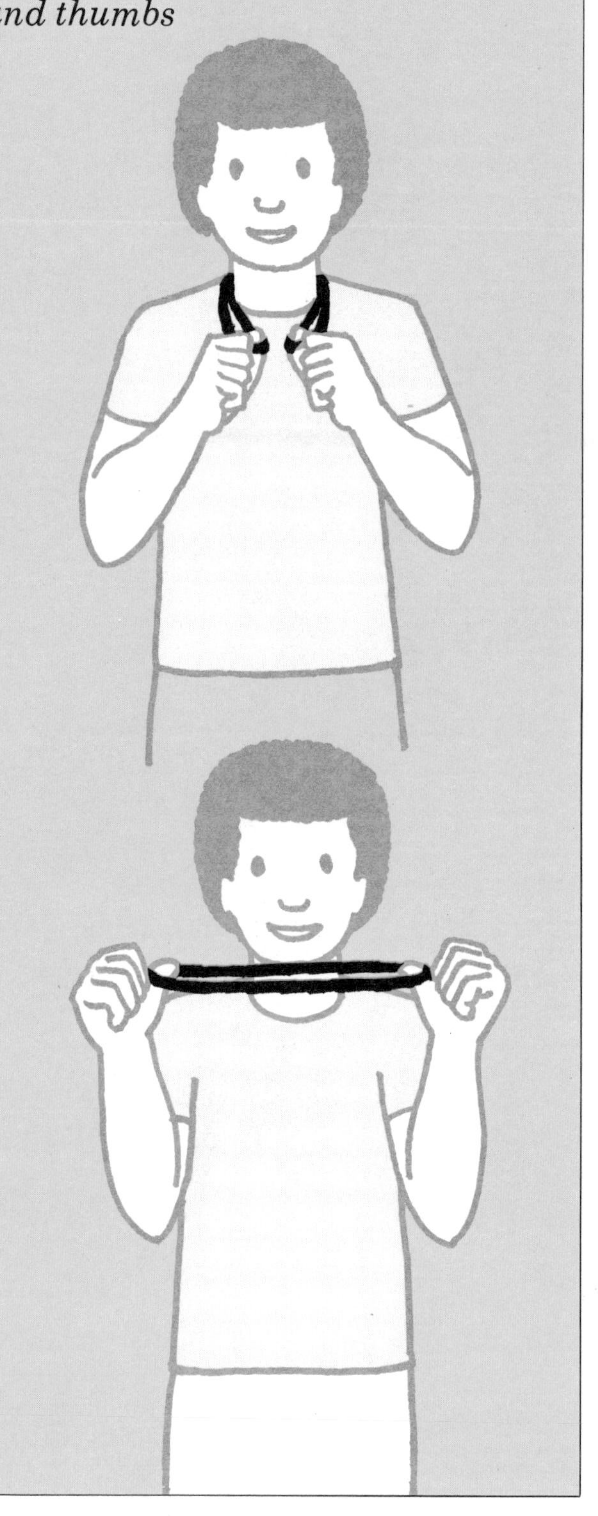

The Secret When the magician brings his hands together in front, he secretly slides his right forefinger into the right end of the loop and, still holding the left end with his left thumb, slips his right thumb through the left end of the loop. Then, all in one movement, he lets go of the right end completely and pulls the left end of the loop forward, straightening it out in front of him with both thumbs.

It happens so quickly that the audience isn't sure what has occurred but it looks as if the cord has gone through the magician's neck.

The Tie that Binds

How to make the freedom movement

The magician takes a large coloured handkerchief or scarf and wraps it around his left wrist, letting the ends cross. He places his right wrist over his left, with the fingers pointing towards the left elbow. He asks a volunteer to pull the ends of the handkerchief tight around his right wrist and tie a knot. The magician appears to be securely bound in the handkerchief, which is in a figure-eight shape. He turns his back and immediately is able to free himself.

The Secret The magician simply twists his right hand to the right and his left to the left so that the fingers come towards each other. This movement unties the figure-eight binding and frees both his hands.

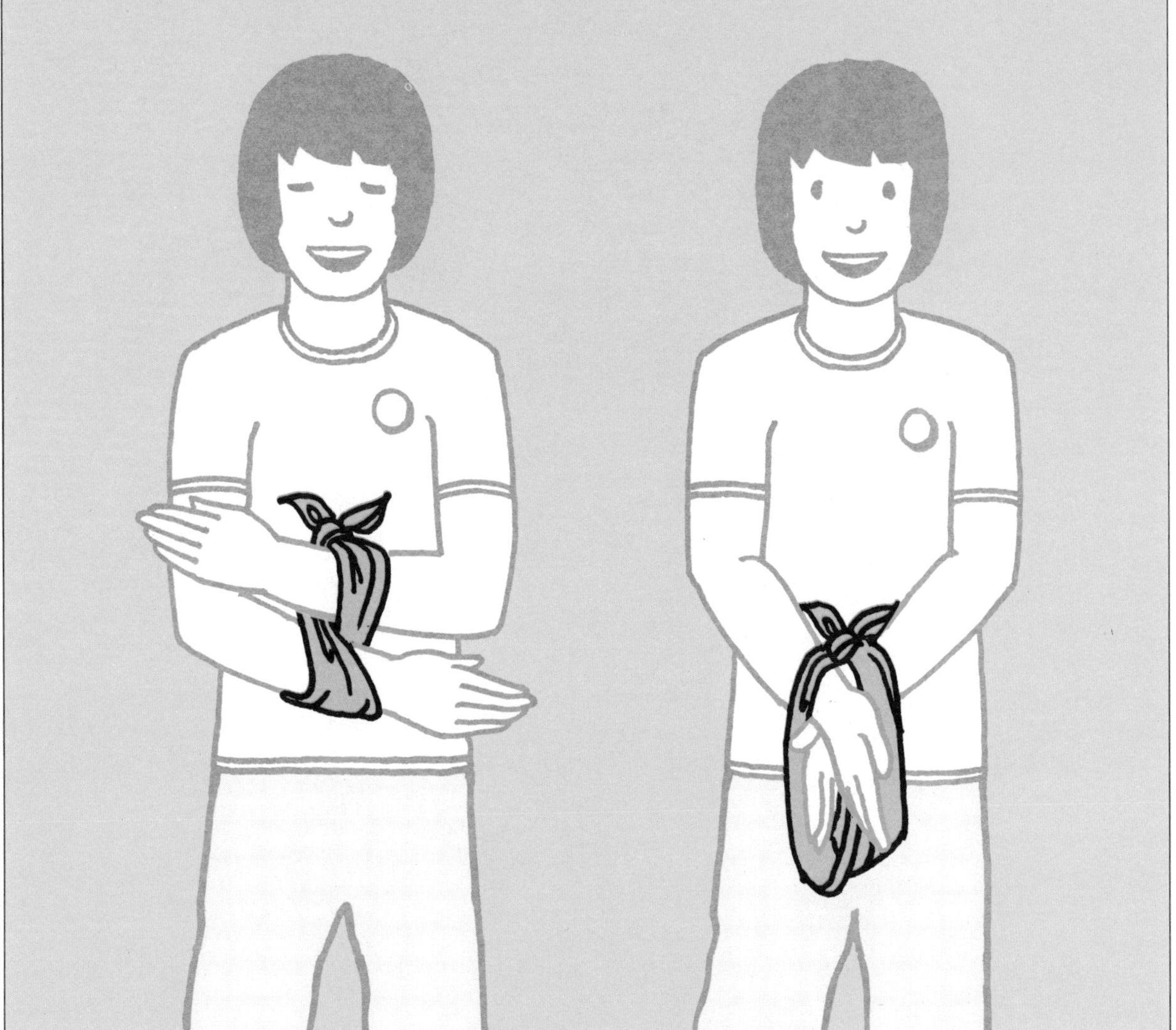

Captive Couples

This shouldn't end in a tie

The magician takes a cord about 1 metre long and ties the ends around the two wrists of one volunteer. He takes a second cord of equal length and ties one end to the wrist of another volunteer. He passes the free end of the second cord over and under the cord tying the first player's wrists and then ties the free end to the second player's other wrist.

The two players must free themselves without untying any knots, cutting the cords, or slipping them off their wrists.

After assuming all kinds of contortions, they will probably give up. Then the magician shows them how it's done.

The Secret One of the pair must take the cord of the other and pass it through the loop around one of his own wrists. He must pass it under the loop from the body side and not entangle it with his own cord while passing it through the loop. Then he pulls this cord far enough through the loop so that he can slip it over his own hand. As soon as this is done, the cords are no longer linked with each other and the two players are separated.

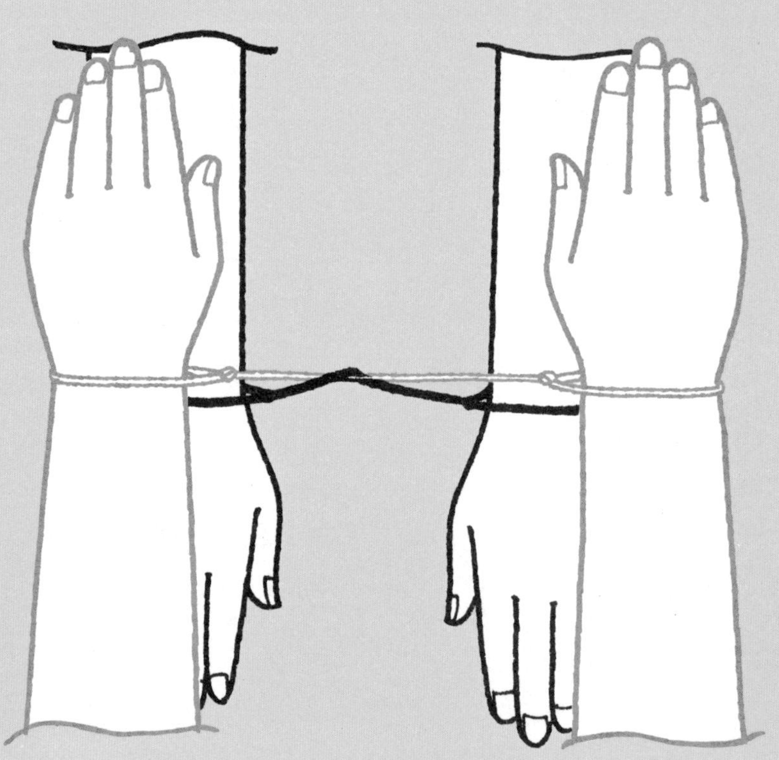

1 The magician ties the ends of a cord to the wrists of a volunteer. He loops a second cord over the first, then ties the ends to the wrists of a second volunteer.

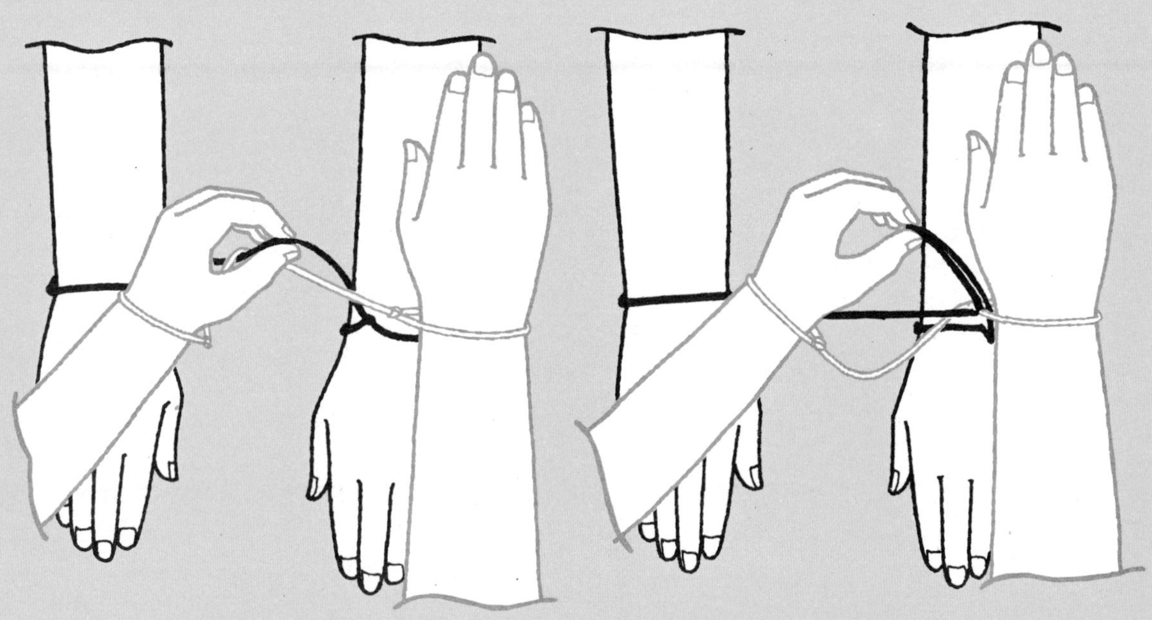

2 This is how to wriggle out of the problem. One volunteer takes the cord of the other and passes it through a loop on his own wrist.

3 He passes it under the loop from the body side, and must not entangle it with his own cord while passing it through the loop.

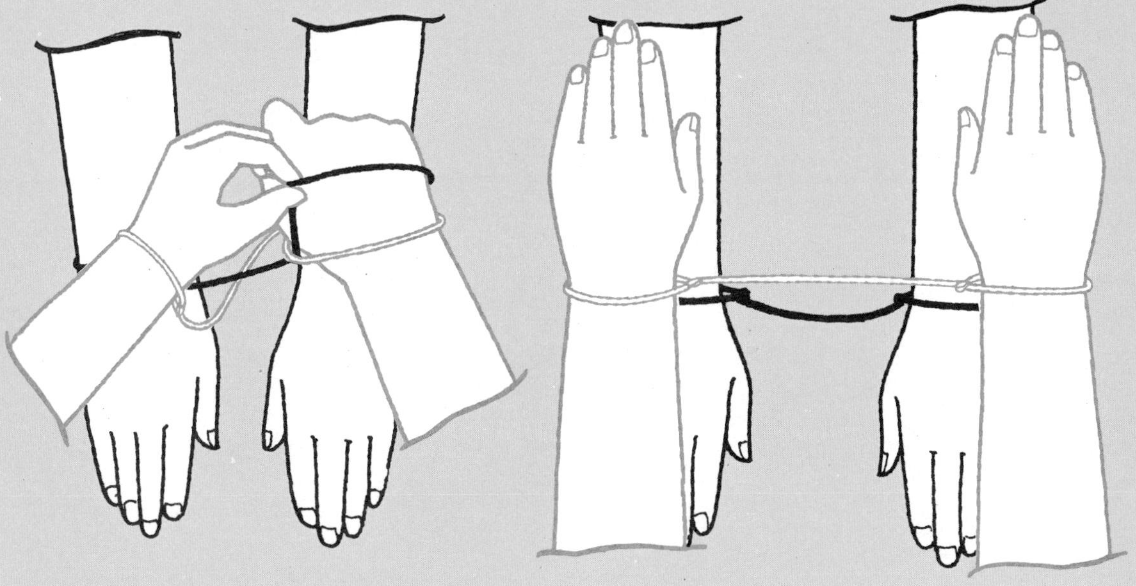

4 He then pulls this cord far enough through this loop so that he can slip it over his own hand.

5 When he achieves this, the cords are no longer linked with each other and the two players are separated.

The Strong Straw
The bend comes at the end

The magician challenges any member of the audience to lift an ordinary glass bottle using only a drinking straw. They try, but cannot. Then the magician shows how it is done.
The Secret He bends the straw near one end, so a short section of it is doubled back, and the magician pushes this part of the straw into the bottle. The short section is forced against the side of the bottle, pointing up, and acts as a lever which holds the straw firmly in place when the bottle is lifted. The magician lifts the bottle by raising the long end of the straw.

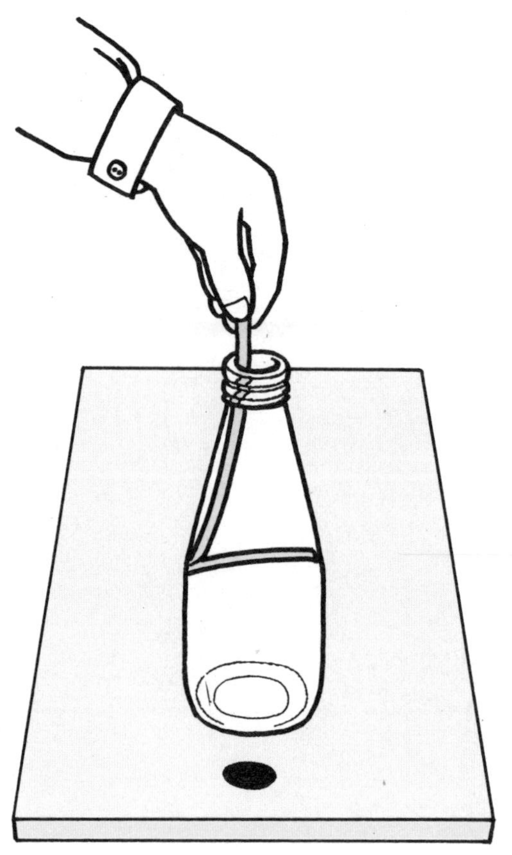

The Floating Needle
Just hold a candle to it

The magician drops a needle into a jar or bowl of water and it sinks to the bottom. He takes it out, wipes it with a cloth and permits another player to drop it into the jar. The needle again sinks to the bottom.
Then he takes the needle out of the water, wipes it and says a magic incantation. This time, when he puts it into the water, it floats.
The Secret While wiping the needle the second time, the magician replaces it with a similar needle which has been rubbed against a candle and has a wax coating. With the wax on it, the needle will float. The magician keeps the waxed needle hidden in the cloth that is used to wipe the first needle: he must practice beforehand so that he can secretly switch the needles without being detected.

The Rising Egg
The solution needs much more than a pinch of salt

The magician puts a hard-boiled egg into a tinted glass jar holding about 10 centimetres

of fresh water. The egg sinks directly to the bottom. He asks any member of the audience to pour a little more water into the jar. This is done, but the egg remains on the bottom. Now the magician pours some of the water out of the jar, saying that he will pour in more water and command the egg to rise from the bottom. He does this, mutters some mystic phrases and the egg obeys him, rising slowly, as if on command, to the surface of the water.
The Secret The jug from which the magician pours the second time contains a strong solution of salt water. Its density makes the egg rise. In preparing for this trick, the magician should experiment until he knows exactly what amount of salt is needed to make the trick work. Also, because salt water appears slightly cloudy, he should use a tinted glass jug to help conceal the trick from the audience.

The Educated Egg
A lesson in deception

In this trick the magician shows his audience a hard-boiled egg, which, he explains, understands English and will follow his instructions. He puts the egg into a glass jar filled with water and it begins to sink slowly. As the magician says magic words and commands it to stop, the egg slows up and then hangs suspended in the middle of the water. Then, the magician stirs the water with a wand saying 'Now, egg, sink'.
At once the egg obeys, dropping to the bottom of the jar.
The Secret The jar of water must first be prepared. In advance, the magician makes a strong solution of salt water filling the jar half way. Then, using a small funnel, he adds fresh water, a little at a time, trying not to disturb the salt water. The water is now in two layers, with the fresh water on top.
In the trick, the egg sinks through the fresh water and stops when it reaches the denser salt water. Stirring the water weakens the solution and the egg sinks to the bottom.

The Hindu Cane
When it taps, it tells

While the magician is out of the room the audience picks a word for him to guess. When the magician returns, his assistant stands in front of him and taps out with his magic 'Hindu cane', a walking-stick or a broomstick, an apparently meaningless pattern. As he taps, the assistant makes encouraging comments.
Suddenly the magician looks up from deep contemplation and says 'The cane tells me the magical word is . . .' and then tells the correct word.
The Secret Every vowel in the word is given by taps with the cane: one tap for A, two for E, three for I, four for O, five for U. Consonants, however, are given by the first letter of the first word in every sentence spoken by the assistant. Suppose the secret word is 'music'. The assistant might use the following signals:
'My feeling is that it may be difficult to communicate today.' There is the letter M.
Five taps of the cane for the letter U.
'Somehow, I think you feel the cane talking.' There is the letter S.
Three taps of the cane indicate the letter I.
'Come now, I'm sure you're getting it,' for the letter C.

Make It Odd or Even
Very simple but very tricky

The magician places a number of coins on a table top. He asks any player to take several coins in his hand and close his fist. Then the magician himself takes an odd number of coins and says 'I will add my coins to yours and, if you now have an odd number of coins, mine will make the total even. If you have an even number, adding mine to it will make the total odd'.
The player shows his coins and the magician shows his. It turns out just as he promised it would.
The Secret When the magician puts his coins

on the table they are, of course, an odd number. An odd number will always make an even number odd or an odd number even.

Although this trick is very simple, young boys and girls will rarely work it out unless it is repeated several times.

Draughts Challenge

Playing the numbers game

The magician puts eight draughtsmen in a row, white and black alternating. He challenges a volunteer to make four moves, using two men at a time, so that all the blacks will be together and all the whites will be together, still in a row. The magician puts numbered cards from 1 to 8 against each draughtsman and cards numbered 9 and 10 against blank spaces at the end of the row. When others have tried the trick and failed, the magician shows how it is done.

The Secret The magician moves men 2 and 3 to spaces 9 and 10; 5 and 6 to the places left by 2 and 3; 8 and 9 to the places left by 5 and 6; and 1 and 2 to the places left by 8 and 9.

He has moved all the men, making only four moves and moving two each time, so that now the whites are on one side and the blacks are on the other.

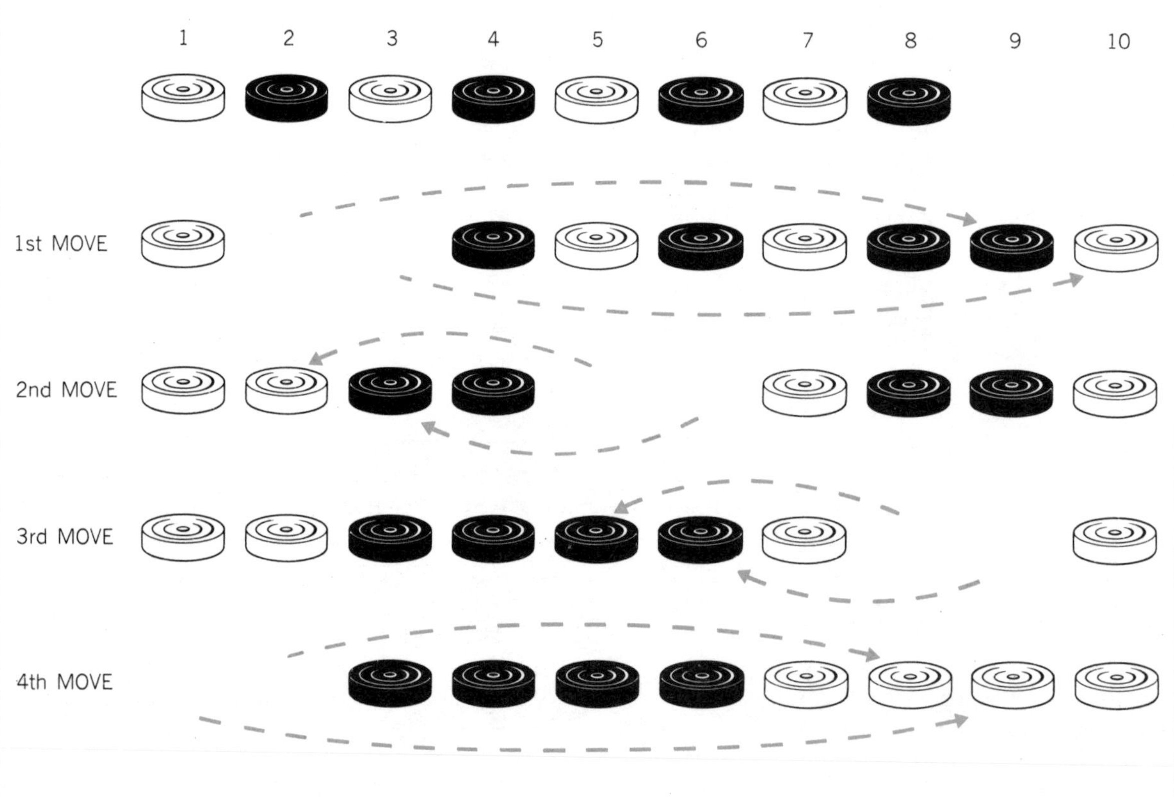

The Stubborn Napkin
—But damp rises to the challenge

The magician tightly twists a paper napkin so that it resembles a rope. The magician then invites volunteers to try to tear the twisted napkin in half by pulling directly by the ends. They will not be successful. Then the magician takes the twisted napkin and pulls it apart easily.

The Secret While the others are trying the trick, the magician wets his fingers in a glass of water. When he takes the napkin, he holds the centre and twists it tighter. By moistening the centre of the napkin, he weakens the paper and it tears easily when he pulls the ends.

Mystery Cities
Clues in ones and twos

The magician leaves the room and the audience selects a city for him to name. When the magician returns, his assistant begins rattling off the names of various cities. To each of these the magician shakes his head, but when the right city is named, the magician immediately nods.

The Secret If the audience has selected a one-word city, such as Paris or London, the assistant starts by naming several two-word cities such as New York, New Orleans, San Francisco. This is the clue the magician needs and he will identify the first one-word city after a string of two-word cities have been named. If, on the other hand, the audience has chosen a two-word city, the assistant will first name several one-word cities to give the magician the required clue.

Mystical Numbers
Digits add up to the clue

The magician leaves the room while the audience picks any number from 1 to 20. When he comes back his assistant calls out several numbers. When the correct one is called, the magician immediately identifies it.

The Secret The first number called by the assistant is the clue. If the assistant, for example, says 'Is it five?' the correct number will be the fifth one called. Another way of giving the clue—and one that is harder to detect—is that a two-digit number is called first and the magician adds up the digits to get the answer.

For example, if the assistant calls out 14, the magician adds the numbers 1 and 4 to get 5; thus the fifth number called will be the correct one.

This Row and that Row
Giving the hint in a few words—or none at all

Two rows of books are placed on the floor and the magician leaves the room while the audience chooses a book to be identified. When the magician returns, his assistant points at the books one by one until the magician identifies the correct one.

The Secret The upper row is designated 'this row'; the lower 'that row'. If the secret book is in the lower row, the assistant begins by pointing to the books in the upper row. As he points he asks 'This book?' When he reaches the lower row he switches and asks for each, 'That book?' But when he reaches the secret book, instead of saying 'that book' as is proper for the lower row, he says 'this book', giving the clue to the magician.

When the secret book is in the upper row, he says 'this book' for each until he reaches the one to be identified and then says 'that book'.

In *This One, That One*, the clue is much the same. Four books are laid out in a square. The book at the upper left is 'this', the one at the lower left, 'that'; the book at upper right, 'this one' and the book at lower right 'that one'. When questioning the magician, the assistant uses any words but the correct ones except when he is pointing to the secret book. When pointing to the books the assistant might say 'Could it be this one?' or 'Could

this be the book?' But if he is pointing to the secret book he uses the correct words. Thus if the secret book is the one on the upper right, the assistant will ask 'This one?'
The trick *Nine Books* is performed in a similar manner but the clue is given without speaking. Nine books are arranged in three even rows with one selected as the secret book. When the magician returns to the room the assistant points to various books.
The clue is in the way he points to the first book. If, for example, he touches it on the upper left-hand corner he is telling the magician that the secret book is on the top row, left; if he touches it in the middle, the book is in the centre of the middle row, and so on.

Loose Change

The magic formula sums it up

The magician tells the audience that he can tell not only a volunteer's age but also how much loose change is in the volunteer's pocket, provided it is less than £1.
The volunteer is told to write down the following:

His age: (say)	10
Double it:	20
Add 5:	25
Multiply by 50:	1250
Subtract 365:	885
Add amount of change in pocket: (say 65p)	950

The magician asks for the last figure and then adds 115 to it. In this example the result is 1065. The first two figures represent the volunteer's age, the last two the amount of change in his pocket. No matter what the volunteer's age or the amount of change he has under £1, the formula always works.

Number and Age

Calculation—not speculation

The magician picks any volunteer from the group. He tells him that through the use of a magic mathematical formula he will deduce both the volunteer's age and the last five digits of his telephone number.
The magician gives the volunteer a piece of paper and pencil and asks him to perform the following calculations. (Sample figures are used.)

Telephone number: (last five digits)	89858
Multiply by 2:	179716
Add 5:	179721
Multiply by 50:	8986050
Add age: (say) 11	8986061
Add 365:	8986426
Subtract 615:	8985811

The first five digits of the result are the last five digits of the volunteer's telephone number; the last two digits are his age. To add to the bafflement of the audience, the magician can ask the volunteer for the number he has reached after adding 365. The final step—subtracting 615—the magician does by himself.

Your Age, Sir!

How maths can be fun

The magician tells a volunteer from the audience that he can guess his age through the use of a secret mathematical formula.
The volunteer is told to list the following:

His age: (say)	11
Multiply by 3:	33
Add 6:	39

Divide by 3:	13

The magician then asks the volunteer for the last figure and subtracts 2: the result is the volunteer's age. It doesn't matter how old the volunteer is. The answer will be correct.
In *How Old Are You?* a volunteer's age is revealed through a different formula.

His age: (say)	12
Double it:	24
Add 1:	25
Multiply by 5:	125
Add 5:	130
Multiply by 10:	1300

Now the magician asks the child for the answer. The magician subtracts 100 from this figure, giving him 1200. Then he drops the last two digits and the result–12–is the volunteer's age.

Reverse the Numbers
For the seal of success

The magician writes a number on a slip of paper and seals it in an envelope. He tells the audience that a volunteer can write any three-digit number in descending order—i.e. 831, not 138—on a piece of paper and through a magic formula the resulting figure will match the one in the envelope.
The volunteer writes a number.

The number: (say)	742
Subtract the reverse of that number:	247
First result:	495
Add reverse of result:	594
Final total:	1089

The final total will always be 1089 so long as the number picked by the volunteer has three digits written in descending order.

Magic Numbers
Every year there's a change

The magician writes a number down on a piece of paper and places it in an envelope. Then he picks a member of the audience and tells him that by using a formula based upon the volunteer's age, date of birth and other information, the volunteer will reach a total the same as the number in the envelope.
This is a straight matter of addition as the sample figures show:

Year of birth:	1970
Year entered school:	1975
Age at the end of the current year:	9
Total years since starting school, at the end of the current year:	4
Total:	3958

When the magician opens the envelope he takes out the paper on which he had earlier written the number 3958, exactly the same number reached by the volunteer. The secret is that the sum of the numbers above will always total twice the year in which the trick is performed. Thus, if the trick is performed in 1980, the number the magician writes down is 3960 and the total reached by the volunteer will be the same.

Ashes to Ashes
Answer to a burning question

This trick will delight and mystify younger audiences—although older children may see through it because it involves some bluff on your part.

Hold a pack of playing cards face down in one hand and deal them face down on the table until a volunteer calls 'Stop!' Ask the volunteer to show the last card to the audience—making sure that you don't see it—and write the name, such as the four of hearts, on a piece of paper. Give the volunteer an empty ash-tray and tell him to burn the paper to ashes. When this is done you say 'Would everyone please concentrate hard on the name of the card'. While they are doing this, roll up one of your sleeves and rub the ashes on your bare arm. The audience will be astonished to see the message '4H' appear on your arm. 'The chosen card was the four of hearts,' you announce. And you are right.

The Secret Before the show you write '4H' on your arm with a pointed piece of soap. The ashes stick to the soap and the message appears. How do you know the four of hearts is the card? You 'force' it on the volunteer like this: put the four of hearts on the bottom of the pack you are dealing face down to the volunteer. Deal the cards swiftly from the top of the pack, but when he calls 'Stop!' deal him the four of hearts from the bottom. If you do it with practised efficiency, he will not notice your deception.

How Far?

Listen to what the man says

The magician places two coins on a table about 20 centimetres apart and puts another coin between them, but not exactly in the centre. He asks the other players to judge which two coins are the farthest apart. Usually, they will pick the middle coin and either the end coin on the right or the left. Then the magician tells them that they've all guessed wrong.

Using a ruler, he shows that it is the two end coins that are the farthest apart.

The Secret Of course it's all based on deliberately confusing the audience. By putting the centre coin down last, the magician implies that he is talking about the distance between the centre and one of the two ends; but this is not what he said, as the audience realises after it has been tricked.

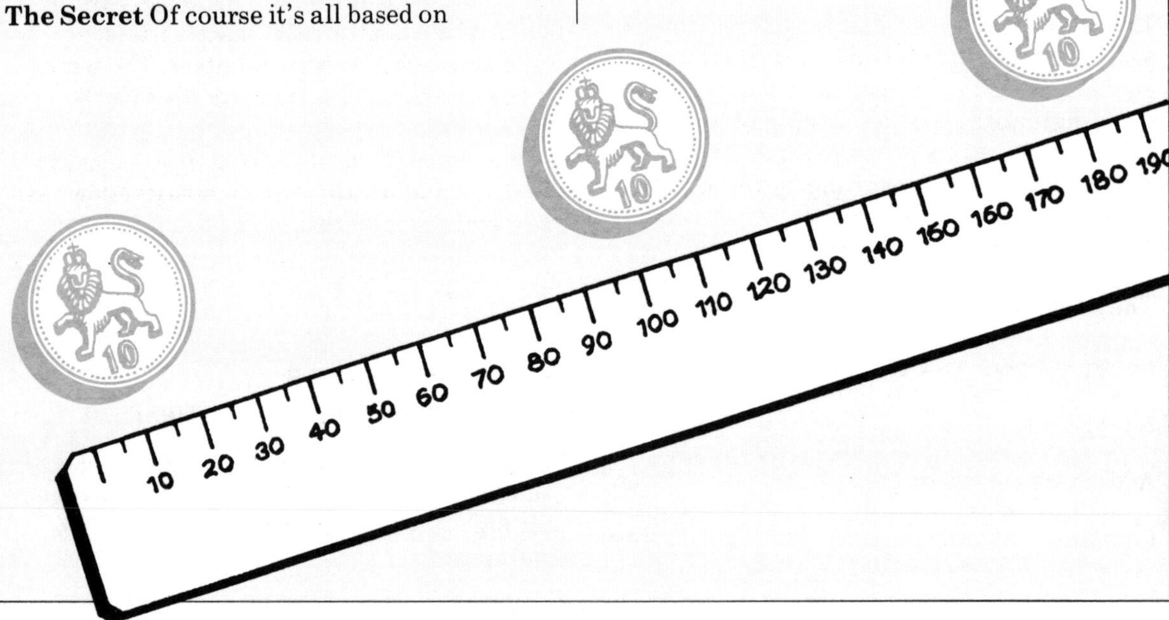

Get In Line

Small change is all that's needed

The magician lays out 12 coins in four horizontal rows and three vertical rows. 10p and 5p pieces must be placed exactly as shown in diagram. The magician challenges any member of the audience to see if he can make the first and third horizontal rows (from the top) all 10p pieces and the second and fourth horizontal rows all 5p pieces only touching one coin.

The Secret When the others have found the trick impossible the magician shows that it is really quite easy. He places his forefinger on the centre coin of the top row (a 5p) and slides it to the right around the other coins so it is just below the middle vertical row of coins. Then, touching only that 5p, he pushes the entire middle row up one place.

Move the Coins

A trick that's strikingly different

The magician takes two 10p pieces and a 5p and places them in a row touching each other with the 5p in the middle. The magician says he can move one of the 10p pieces from its place on the end of the line and put it between the other two coins while following these rules:

1 The 10p on the left may not be touched.
2 The 5p in the middle may be touched but not moved.
3 The 10p on the right may be both touched and moved.

The Secret Following these rules, it would seem impossible to carry out the trick, but the magician shows how it can be done. He puts the forefinger of his left hand on the 5p, which may be touched but not moved. He puts the forefinger of his right hand on the 10p on the right, which may be both touched and moved. He moves the 10p away slightly, then strikes the 5p with it. He holds the 5p in place with his finger. The force of the blow will knock away the 10p on the left.
The magician has now created a space between the 10p on the left and the 5p so that he can slide the other 10p between the two.

The Vanishing Coin

Shake, rattle . . . and palm

The magician places a coin in a wooden matchbox. He closes the box and shakes it to show that the coin is still there. When he opens the box, however, the coin has disappeared.

The Secret This trick depends on advance preparation. The magician has cut a narrow slit in one end of the matchbox drawer, close to the bottom.

When he shakes the box sideways, the coin rattles, proving it is still there. When he tilts the box slightly, with the slit down, the coin slides into his hand. A moment later he opens the box and it is empty.

Take the Coin

On the other hand, it's baffling

The magician holds a coin and switches it rapidly from hand to hand. Then he holds his clenched right hand forward and says 'Take the coin,' at the same time slapping it down on a table. The sound of the coin hitting the table can be heard clearly. Yet when someone reaches to take it, the coin is not there.

The Secret The magician has kept the coin in his left hand, which rests on the table at a distance from the right hand. When the right hand seems to slap the coin down, it is the left hand that actually clicks it against the table. The audience is not watching his left hand, all eyes are on his right hand at the time. There is astonishment when the magician lifts his right hand and the coin is not there.

The Disappearing Coin
But it is still there

Here is a simple trick but it calls for lots of practice so that your movements are deft and decisive. You need a handkerchief and a 5p piece. Spread the handkerchief flat on the table. Place the coin in the centre. Fold the handkerchief in two. Then fold the left corner over to the right side of the top corner and the right corner over to the left side of the top corner. Ask someone to feel that the coin is still there. Hold corner A in the left hand and corner B in the right hand. Pull the hands apart and upwards and the coin disappears.

The Secret The coin is still there. It is hidden in the folds of the handkerchief. So be careful when you put the handkerchief away. It is best to bunch it up and put it in your pocket.

1 Place a handkerchief flat on the table and put a 5p piece in the centre.

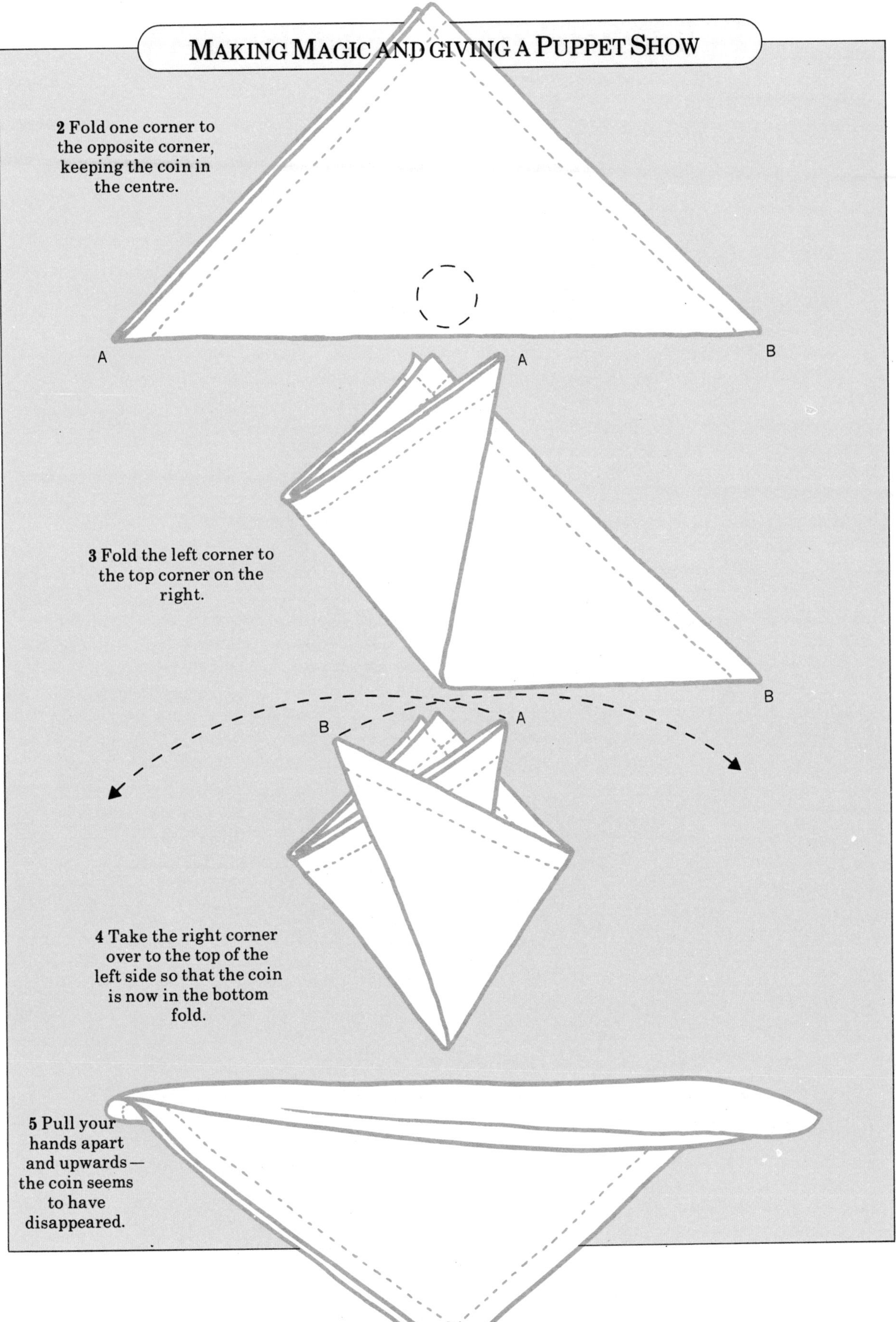

2 Fold one corner to the opposite corner, keeping the coin in the centre.

3 Fold the left corner to the top corner on the right.

4 Take the right corner over to the top of the left side so that the coin is now in the bottom fold.

5 Pull your hands apart and upwards — the coin seems to have disappeared.

Impossible Total
A puzzler for the tots

After closing his fist over an odd number of coins that add up to an even amount in value, the magician asks a member of the audience to guess whether the total he has is odd or even. No matter what the child says, the magician tells him, his answer will be wrong.
The Secret The trick depends on how the magician defines total. If the boy or girl guesses odd, the magician opens his fist to reveal, say, a 10p, a 5p and five pennies. Then he says 'Sorry, you're wrong. The total is 20p'. If, on the other hand, the child guesses even, the magician counts the number of coins—a total of seven—and again the child is wrong. This trick, of course, only works with small children and even they are very likely to catch on if it is repeated.

Heads or Tails?
The answer, of course, is neither

The magician tosses a coin into the air. He catches it in his right hand and slaps it on the back of his left hand. 'Heads or tails?' he asks. After someone guesses, the magician lifts his right hand to show that the coin has disappeared.
The Secret This is a sleight-of-hand trick. While pretending to catch the coin in his right hand, the magician holds the hand with the fingers straight up and the back of the hand towards the audience. Instead of catching the coin, he lets it drop into his coat sleeve. Then he closes his right hand and pretends to slap the coin on the back of his left hand. This trick requires careful practice.

Now You Have It
Pressing problem for a volunteer

A volunteer is given a penny, which he holds in the palm of his hand. The magician presses the volunteer's palm firmly with his left thumb and, at the same time, closes the volunteer's fingers over the coin with his right hand. The volunteer is certain that the coin is still in his hand. When he opens his hand, however, the coin is not there.
The Secret First, the magician has placed a small piece of double-sided sticky-tape on the ball of his left thumb. When the tape is pressed to the coin it sticks to it and lifts it away.
Secondly, by pressing the coin into the volunteer's palm, the magician creates a lingering physical effect. The volunteer cannot actually feel that the coin has been taken away and is extremely surprised when he sees it is missing.

What Date is It?
How to make an impression

A volunteer places a 10p piece date-side-up on a table. After the others have examined the coin the volunteer places a piece of writing paper over it. Although he has not seen the coin, the magician claims he can tell its date, without lifting the paper from its place.
The Secret By rubbing a well-sharpened pencil on the paper over the coin the magician makes an impression of the coin on the paper and is able to read the date without lifting the paper.

Slippery Coins
Sliding smoothly into place

The magician places two coins on opposite sides of the rim of a glass. He then challenges any member of the audience to remove them from the glass, using only the forefinger and thumb of one hand and moving both coins at the same time. After the volunteers have tried and failed, he shows how it is done.
The Secret He places his thumb over the coin on the left and his forefinger over the one on the right. He carefully tilts the coins over in an outwards direction, at the same time

pressing and holding them against the outer sides of the glass.
Then he slides the coins together along the outer edge of the rim so that they drop into his hand.

X-ray Eyes
Always one word ahead

'I have X-ray eyes,' you tell your audience. 'That means I can see through things.' You then proceed to prove it. Give each child a pencil, a piece of paper and an envelope and say 'Write any word you like, any word at all, on your piece of paper and seal it carefully in the envelope'. (If some can't write yet they can get assistance from someone who can.)
When this has been done, collect the envelopes, put them in a pile and hold the top one against your forehead. 'I can see an R,' you say, 'and a B and another B. The word is rabbit. Did anybody write rabbit?' A member of the audience says 'I did'. You take the paper out of the envelope, glance at it, nod with satisfaction, crumple it up and throw it into the wastepaper basket. You then move on to the other envelopes in turn and you are right each time.
The Secret You have a secret collaborator. Make sure that he does not allow his excitement about his important task to betray him. Before the show you tell him to be sure to write the word 'rabbit' on his piece of paper. When you collect the envelopes, collect his first, which means that it will be at the bottom of the pile. Take the first envelope, guess 'rabbit' though, of course, you have no idea what word is in it. Then open the envelope and glance at the word as if to check that you were right. You are now reading the word that was in the first envelope—'mouse', for example. You now know that someone wrote 'mouse', so when you pick up the second envelope you pretend to read 'mouse'. The writer will confirm it. Open the envelope as before and pretend to check –and now you know another word. Carry on like this until you have completed the pile—but make sure you crumple up each piece of paper when you have read it so that nobody will realise that you are working one word ahead all the time.

The Disappearing Ace
Mystery at the heart of the matter

The magician removes the ace of spades, ace of diamonds and the ace of clubs from a pack of cards and shows them in a fan shape to the audience, the ace of diamonds in the middle. He announces that he is going to make the ace of diamonds vanish. He puts the first ace at the bottom of the pack, the second in the middle, the third at the top. The magician then deals out the cards, face up. The ace of diamonds is not there. After a suitable pause, so that if necessary the pack can be examined, he produces it from his pocket.
The Secret The magician has not taken the ace of diamonds from the pack—it is already in his pocket. He has taken the ace of hearts instead and masked it by putting it behind the other two aces when he held up the fan so that it looked like the ace of diamonds.

Think a Card
The answer is in his pocket

After a member of the audience has shuffled a pack of cards, the magician deals the top three face up. He asks someone to think of any one of the three. The magician puts the three cards in his pocket and asks the volunteer to concentrate on the one he has chosen. He takes two of the cards from his pocket and puts them back in the pack, then asks the volunteer what card he had chosen.

When the volunteer tells him, the magician produces the third card from his pocket and it is the correct one.

The Secret Before starting the trick, the magician has put two cards in his pocket. When he deals the three cards he memorises them in order and puts them in his pocket, in the same order, beside the ones that are already there. The two cards he first removes from his pocket are the two he had put in beforehand. When the volunteer tells him the chosen card, it is easy to remember which of the three in his pocket it is.

The Four Robbers
The trick is helping them make their escape

The audience sees you remove some cards from the pack which you hold up in a fan and they turn out to be the four jacks. 'These jacks are four very successful robbers,' you say. 'The rest of the pack is a house they intend to rob. First, the four climb on to the roof.' You put the jacks on the top of the pack.

'One of them decides to stay on guard in the front garden.' Place the top card face up on the table beside the pack.

'The second robber opens the skylight and goes downstairs to the ground floor.' To demonstrate this, you place the next card from the top of the pack into the lower third of it.

'The next robber goes to the second floor to see what he can find.' You now place the next card from the top of the pack into the centre.

'The last crook goes to search the bedrooms.' Put the next top card into the upper third of the pack.

'While they are looking for jewellery and money the guard hears a police car in the distance and immediately warns his friends.' You riffle the pack by running your thumb from the bottom card to the top. 'The three robbers appear on the roof as if by magic, and they all join their friend and escape.' You place the three top cards of the pack face up on the table and the audience sees the three jacks beside the one that was on guard.

The Secret When, at the start of the trick, you are taking the jacks out of the pack you also take three other cards which you place behind the second jack from the left so that all four look like one card when you hold up the fan. When the fan is squared up and put on the pack, the first card is put face up on the table. This is a jack. The next three cards which are not jacks are the ones that are put into the pack. Be careful that you don't let the audience see their faces.

A Tricky Trick with Cards
A turn-up just for laughs

Ask someone to shuffle the pack, take out a card, look at it and tell him that he must remember it. Ask him to show it to his friends as you gather the rest and cut the pack in half. He puts his card on top of the face-down half and you put the rest of the cards on top. Square up the pack.

'I'm going to deal the cards face up and discover the card you chose,' you say. 'Don't tell me if you see it.' As the cards are dealt, the volunteer sees his chosen card go on the table with the others. 'The next card I turn over will be yours,' you say, and the volunteer will think you have gone wrong. You then pick up his card from the table and turn it over. This trick fools people because they think you are going to turn over the next card from the pack in your hand.

The Secret How do you know which card was

the one chosen? When the volunteer is showing everyone his card you have cut the rest of the pack. You glance at it and remember the card under the top pile. This is called the key card. When the volunteer replaces his chosen card on the face-down cards in your hand you put the others on top. The key card is now *above* the chosen card. When you deal them face up on the table the selected card is the one after the key card. Deal a few more but don't cover the chosen card before telling the volunteer you are going to turn over his card.

The One-way Pack
Every picture tells the story

The magician asks a volunteer to pick a card, look at it and then return it to the pack. He then tells the audience that he can identify the card chosen by the volunteer.
The Secret This trick can be done only with a pack with a picture on the back of each card instead of the usual symmetrical design. The magician arranges the cards so that the pictures all face in the same direction. He then shuffles the cards without changing the direction and holds them out fan-shaped to any member of the audience.
After a volunteer has picked a card, the magician unobtrusively turns the pack around so that when the card is replaced in the pack its picture will be facing in the opposite direction. Again the magician shuffles the pack and then, with a great show of concentration, searches for the secret card.
It is easy to find, because the picture on its back will be facing one way and all the rest of the cards will face the other.

Colour-changing Pack
A turn-up for red and black

The magician shows the audience a pack of cards with the joker in front. He riffles the end of the pack with his thumb and the audience sees only red cards. He then blows on the pack and riffles it again. This time they see only black cards. He blows on the pack again and riffles it once more. This time the cards are both red and black!
The Secret The magician prepares the pack in advance by separating the black cards from the red and then putting the pack together so that every odd card is black and every even card red. The edges of the cards are not flush: the red cards protrude slightly at the top and the black cards protrude at the bottom.
When the pack is first riffled, only the red cards show. Then, as the magician blows on the cards, he turns the pack around so that only the black cards show when he riffles them. The last time he riffles the pack, he pushes all the cards together—this time exposing both colours.
This trick demands dexterity and must be carefully practised. When it is performed, the pack must be held tightly.

The Columbus Card
The secret lies in the click

The magician fans out a pack of cards face down on the table and asks a volunteer to take any one and memorise it without letting the magician see what it is.
The magician gathers up the cards, cuts them and puts the top half on the table, keeping the rest in his hand.
The volunteer puts his card face down on top of the pile on the table, the magician adds his pile and squares them off. He runs his thumb down the pack, cuts it and shows the volunteer his card.
The Secret A card from another pack with the same pattern on the back is used. The border around the edge of the pattern is cut away and the card is glued, face inwards, to the back of a card from the pack the magician is using for the trick.
The magician makes sure that this faked card is on top of the pack when he gathers the cards up and that it is on top of the pile he puts on

the table. When he runs his thumb down the cards there will be a clicking sound when the faked card is reached. The mystery card will be the one before the fake.

The Falling Card
The catch is easily taped

A chosen card is shown to the audience and then placed on the top of the pack. The magician cuts the pack, placing the top half on a table with his right hand, holding the bottom half in his left hand.

The magician then throws the bottom half high in the air, thrusts out his right hand and catches the chosen card—presumed by all to be on the table—on the back of his right hand.

The Secret The magician has some double-sided sticky-tape on the back of his right hand. As he throws the cards high in the air and everyone is watching them, he presses the back of his right hand on the cards on the table. The top card, which is the chosen one, sticks to the back of his hand which he thrusts into the middle of the falling cards and pretends to catch the chosen one.

Magic Packs
It's all in the way they're stacked

The magician asks a volunteer to name any number between one and ten. He then goes through a pack of cards and takes out all four cards of that number. This leaves 48 cards. He deals these cards into six piles of eight cards each.

The magician then turns his back, or leaves the room, while the volunteer takes one card from near the centre of any pile. He shows this card to the audience, returns it to the top of the same pile and stacks the six piles in any order he wishes.

The magician returns to the room and goes through the pack of 48 cards, turning each card face up. In a short time he holds up the chosen card.

The Secret The pack has been stacked. In advance the magician places six picture cards at the top and the other six picture cards at the bottom. As a result, when he deals out the six piles of eight cards each, the top and the bottom card of each pile will be a picture card. The card that the volunteer picks from the centre of a pile, therefore, will never be a picture card.

When he returns this card to the top of one pile and places the piles one on top of another, this card must wind up between two picture cards. It is simple for the magician to find, since it is the only non-picture card between two picture cards. Unless, of course, the volunteer stacks the pack with the chosen card at the top of the other packs in which case the first card the magician turns up will be the chosen card, not a picture card.

Find the Card
You'll be right in the middle

The magician picks 21 cards from a pack of 52 and deals them out face up into three piles of seven cards each. While the magician's back is turned, a volunteer chooses any one of these cards, shows it to the audience and returns it anywhere in the same pile from which it came.

The magician turns around and asks the volunteer which pile the chosen card is in. He then puts all the cards together and deals them again into three piles.

He deals one card at a time to each pile until all 21 cards are dealt. Again he asks the volunteer who picked the original card to show him in which of the three piles his card appears.

He puts the cards together, deals three piles again—one card at a time to each pile—and asks the player for the last time which pile his card is in. This time the magician points to the chosen card.

The Secret Each time, before dealing out the cards, the magician puts the pile in which the chosen card appears between the other two

piles. In this manner, after he has dealt out the piles three times, the card will turn out to be the middle card in whichever pile the volunteer points to as the correct one.
All the magician has to do is go through this pile and hold up the fourth card.

Reverse the Card

The right is wrong way up

A member of the audience picks a card from a pack held out fan-shaped by the magician. The volunteer returns the card to any place in the pack, the magician looks through it and quickly identifies the mystery card.
The Secret The pack is rigged beforehand. The magician turns the bottom card so it is face up and all the others are face down. When he fans out the pack, he conceals the bottom card with his palm.
After the volunteer selects a card, the magician quietly turns the pack over so that the bottom card is now on top, face down, all the others being face up. When the volunteer returns the card to the pack the only card he can see is the one on top and he places the mystery card back in the pack face down, because he thinks all the cards face in that direction.
With flourishes of his hand and constant patter about the amazing nature of the trick, the magician looks through the pack knowing that the first card he comes to—after the top card—that faces in the opposite direction from the others will be the mystery one.

CURTAIN UP!—IT'S YOUR PUPPET SHOW

Puppets are man-made actors that, when operated by skilful puppeteers, are totally convincing creatures.
The most recognisable attribute of life is movement, and a puppet is given the appearance of life by the use of hands, or strings or rods. The means by which the puppet is made to move gives it a character and expression of its own.
There are several different kinds of puppets. Marionettes are operated by strings. The word marionette, meaning Little Mary, is of French origin and comes from religious puppet plays of the Middle Ages in which the Virgin Mary was represented by a puppet. In those days few people could read, books were very rare and religious plays were enacted by puppets in churches so that the people would come to know the Bible. Other types of puppet are worked by rods or by gloves.
Puppets, some in stone and amber, made in prehistoric times have been unearthed by archaeologists.
Long before the birth of Christ, the Egyptians were making puppets from terracotta, wood and other materials. Some of the wooden puppets were jointed, and the operators could move not only the arms and legs but mouths and noses too. Some puppets, dating back to AD 100, have been found in children's graves in Greece and Italy. These puppets were jointed and had wires attached to the head.
In the Middle Ages, puppets were very popular. People often acted with them and stories of battles, miracles and magic were staged, providing entertainment for rich and poor alike. In the 17th century the popular Italian puppet Punchinello made its appearance in France where it was known as Polichinelle. It crossed the Channel to England about 1660 and its name was shortened to Punch. Seaside Punch and Judy shows have been popular ever since. Punch is a glove puppet.
Puppets and marionettes can be bought from most toy shops, but they can also be made at home, some of them very easily. The simplest is probably the push puppet—a flat cut-out figure on stiff cardboard fixed to the ends of slats of wood. The theatre is a large, decorated cardboard box.
The 'actors' are pushed on to the stage through openings in the sides of the box.

Glove Puppets
Fun is always on hand

A wide variety of glove puppets, some based on those seen on television, are offered in shops. There are two ways to set your fingers and thumb to operate these puppets. Try both to find out which method seems the most comfortable. Put the puppet on your hand in the same way as a glove, with the palm on the face side. One way to operate the puppet is to crook your little and third fingers, putting the middle finger in one arm, the forefinger in the head and your thumb in the other arm. The second method is to put your little and third fingers in one arm, the forefinger and middle finger in the head and your thumb in the other arm. You can make a simple glove puppet by sewing together the forefinger, middle and third fingers of an old glove and painting a face on them. Paint sleeves and hands on the thumb and little finger.

Finger Puppets
Tiny shoes to fit the tips

Take a piece of stiff card and cut out the shape of the puppet, leaving two holes at the base of the card where the legs would start. Paint on the face, features and clothing. Make two little shoes out of Plasticine to fit your fingertips. Put your first and second fingers through the holes in the card, put the shoes on your fingertips and you are ready. By moving your fingers you can make the puppet walk, run, kneel and dance.

Ball Puppet

Just squeeze out the words

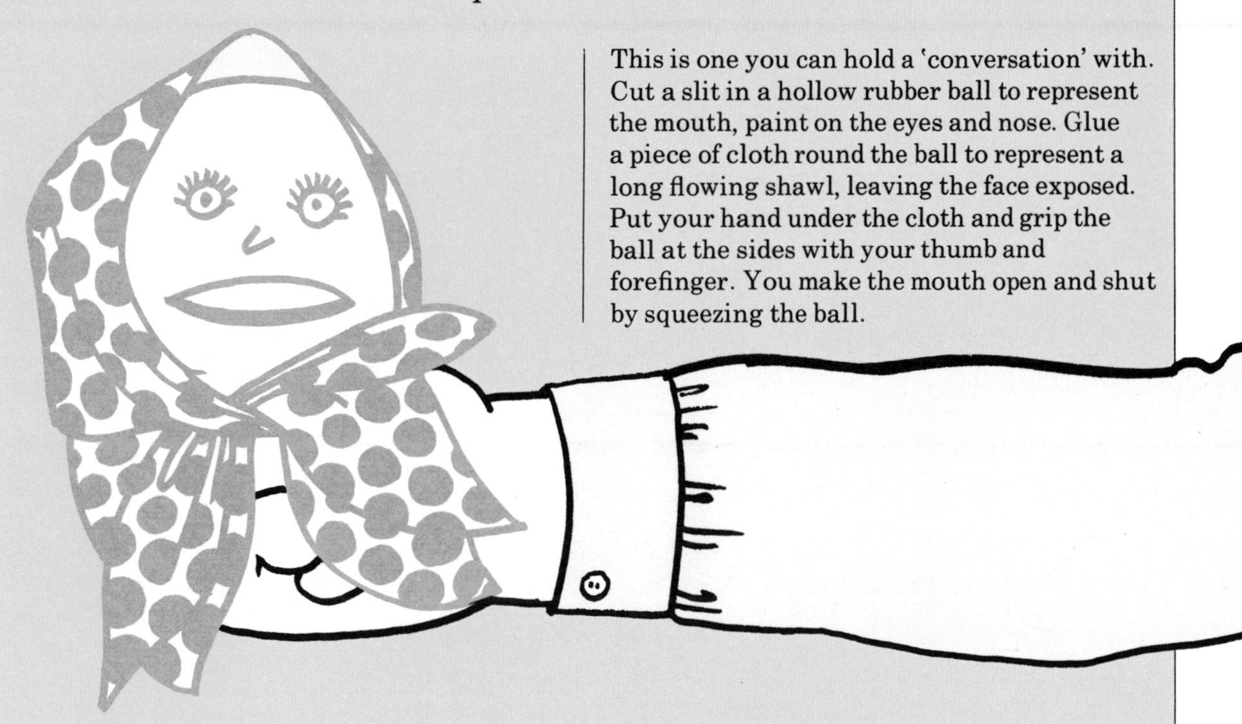

This is one you can hold a 'conversation' with. Cut a slit in a hollow rubber ball to represent the mouth, paint on the eyes and nose. Glue a piece of cloth round the ball to represent a long flowing shawl, leaving the face exposed. Put your hand under the cloth and grip the ball at the sides with your thumb and forefinger. You make the mouth open and shut by squeezing the ball.

The Marionette

When it's best to be big-headed

The string-operated puppet or marionette is the most difficult to make, but it offers the greatest range of expression.

The simplest form is the cut-out figure with one arm hinged at the elbow. It is operated by a string through the head and another through a hole in the hand of the moving arm. Because this simple marionette is so light, it is necessary to fix a small weight at the back of each leg near the foot. Use a small piece of lead or small washers.

An important thing to bear in mind is that the puppet's face is the biggest clue to its character. That is why, whenever possible, puppets have heads that are quite large.

The height of the head measured from the chin to the top of the head should be one-sixth of the puppet's whole body length. The facial expression should be exaggerated.

Living Marionettes

This is where YOU get into the act

These are not true marionettes because they are half-puppet, half-human.

You need a wooden frame approximately 1 metre square with two brackets, which act as 'feet', to make it stand erect. Screw two curtain hooks at each end of the top bar. Get some black material, 1 by 2 metres, and a length of curtain wire. Sew a pocket at the top for inserting the wire. Cut a vertical slit in the centre of the material about 60 centimetres long. To prevent fraying, tape the edges of the slit at the back of the material. Insert the curtain wire and hang on the hooks, using eye screws.

Use a piece of thin plywood or hardboard, 1 metre by 30 centimetres, to act as a stage and provide a sounding board for the feet of the marionette.

Cardboard and cloth are the basic materials

for the marionette. Its arms and legs are cloth tubes approximately 2 centimetres in diameter. Sew up one end, stuff loosely with cotton wool then sew up the other end. Hands are made from card or felt and sewn to the arms. Note that only three fingers are illustrated. This gives a neater-looking effect. The feet are made from wood. They are controlled by thick wires (clothes-hanger wire is ideal). Drill holes in the back of the feet so that the wires fit tightly. The legs are then tacked to the feet.
The body is made from stiff card, It can be covered with cloth material and padded slightly with cotton wool. However, a simpler idea is to paint it with poster paint. If the card is an unsuitable colour glue some white cartridge paper on it before painting. Cow gum is suitable. The arms and legs are sewn to the body. At the neck part of the card sew two black tapes, each about 30 centimetres long, the exact size depending on the operator's neck size. Sew Velcro to the free ends of the tapes so you can attach the tapes around your neck and the body of the marionette hangs close to you.
Place a cloth on a table so it hangs down to the floor and hides your legs and feet. The frame is set at the rear of the table. The plywood or hardboard stage is put in front of the frame. With the puppet attached to your neck, put your head and the puppet through the slit in the cloth on the frame. The wires

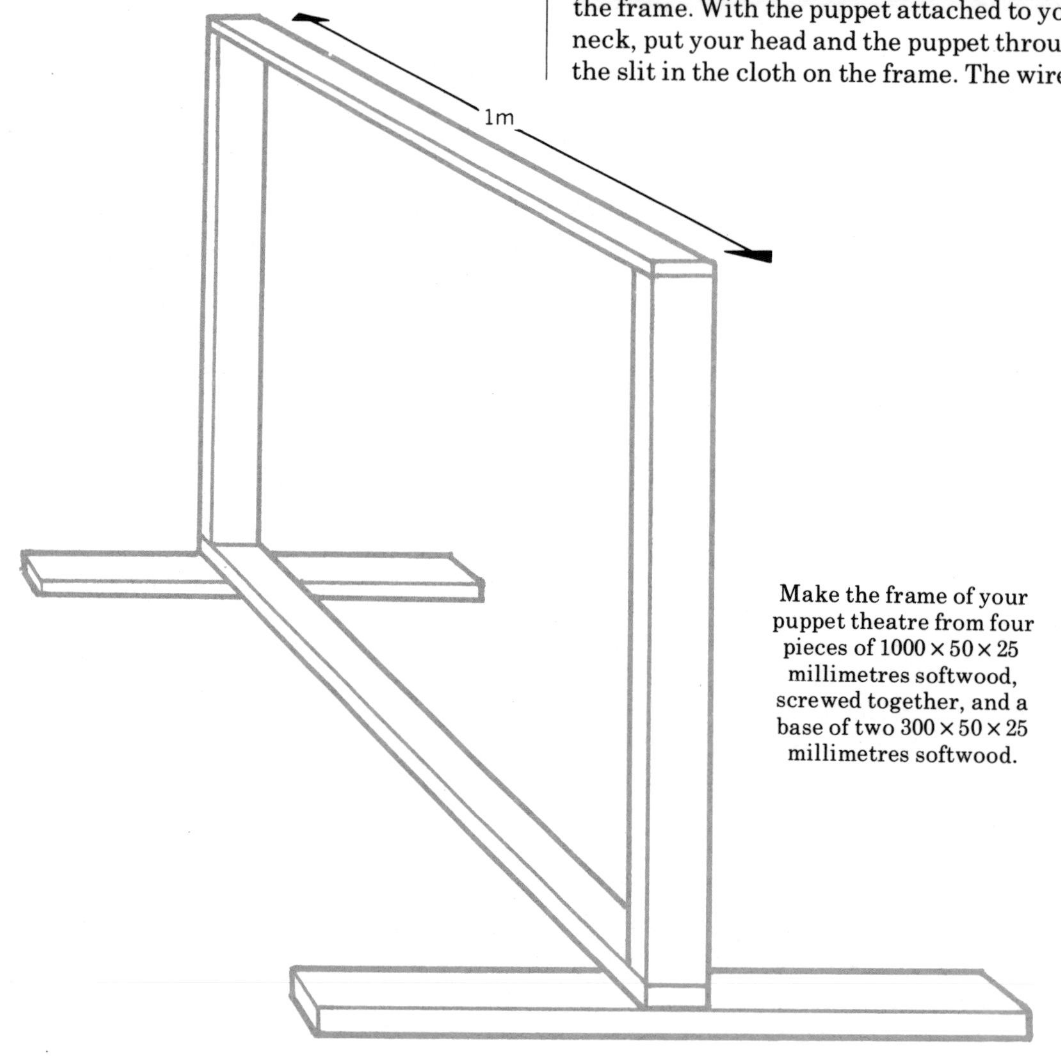

Make the frame of your puppet theatre from four pieces of 1000 × 50 × 25 millimetres softwood, screwed together, and a base of two 300 × 50 × 25 millimetres softwood.

from the feet go underneath the cloth.
By manipulating the wires you can make the marionette dance and carry out crazy antics, while you add to the fun by pulling funny faces.
Remember, the marionette is a fantasy creature and it is not enough to make it carry out realistic human movements. You will add greatly to the enjoyment of your young audience by making it do things which no human ever could. For example, when the puppet is dancing, it can do the splits in mid-air; in 'ballet' movements its feet can turn in all directions, and in the middle of the performance it can suddenly scratch itself under the arm with one of its feet.

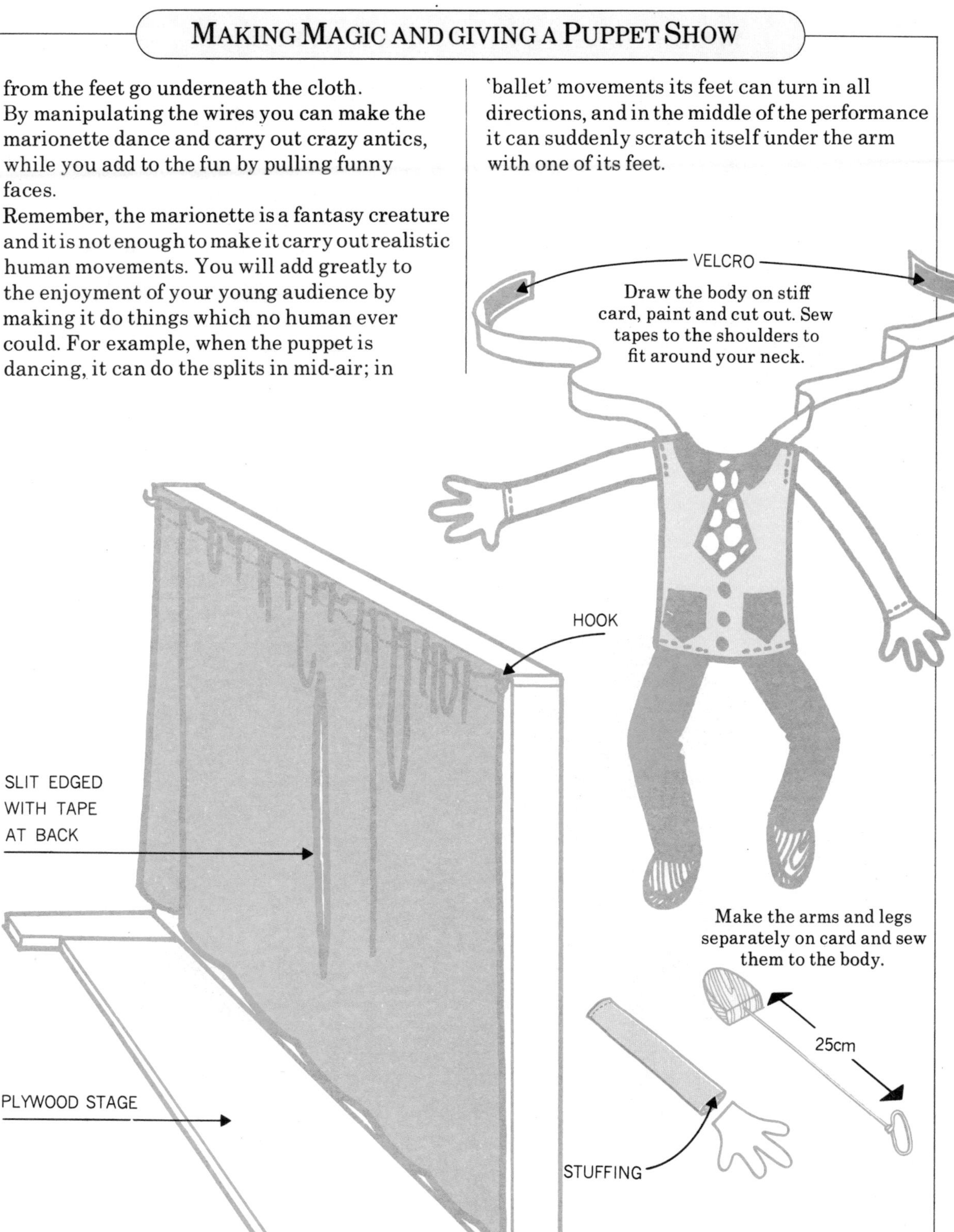

How to give a performance

Practice makes perfect

Whether they are made of glove or cardboard, and whether they are operated directly by hand or indirectly by strings, all marionettes and puppets are prominent citizens of the enchanted world of make-believe. You must join that world and take your audience with you. Constant practice is most important; you will be surprised by the skill you can reach as a puppeteer if you work at it. Rehearse in front of a mirror so that you can get an audience's view of your show and improve the movements. Remember you are the one who brings the puppet to life. Until you pick it up it is nothing more than a small, limp doll or a piece of painted card. Give your puppet a personality; make it mischievous, humorous, shy or all three. Provided you believe in it, your audience will believe in it too.

To present your 'living marionette' show, put your theatre near the edge of a table, place the puppet's tapes round your neck and then put your head and the puppet through the slit in the curtain.

The patter that brings your puppet alive

In a performance the patter of the puppeteer is as important as the actions of the puppet. This is an example of a simple script that will interest very young children because it involves them in the action. It is written for the glove puppet.

'I have a little friend to show you. Would you like to see him? He's very well behaved. He won't come out unless I tell him.'

Move the lid up a fraction with the puppet so that the audience gets a glimpse of him. A child is bound to call out 'I saw him' or 'There he is'. Keep the lid still.

'No, he is very good and he will not disobey me.'

Open the lid wider.

'There you are. Now come out and say Hallo to everybody.'

Bring the puppet out and hide his head in your coat or bent arm.

'He's shy. Would you all say Hallo to him?'

The children do this and the puppet looks at the audience and becomes lively, tickling your arm and nibbling your ear.

'Wave to everybody.'

He waves, and the children wave back.

'Who likes ice cream?'

Children raise their hands.

'He likes ice cream. Don't you?'

Puppet nods his head vigorously.

'I told him to have just one when he went to a party yesterday. How many did you have?'

The puppet hides his head then whispers in your ear.

'All right, tap on my arm to show how many you had.'

He taps and the audience counts.

'Eight! That's very greedy. You had better go back in your box. Wave goodbye to everybody.'

After putting him back in the box, raise the lid two or three times.

'He's asleep. Did you like my little friend?'

Hand Doll

Watch it while it talks

This is not strictly a puppet but a novel ventriloquist's doll.

First, you need a piece of stiff card with a strut on the back so that it stands up by itself. A calendar or a shop showcard is ideal. Cover the front with cartridge paper and draw and colour the body, arms and legs of a boy (see p. 92). The only other thing you need is a lipstick.

Set the card up on a table. Show your audience your hand and draw a mouth and eyes on it with the lipstick (see below). Place your hand above the neck of the boy on the card.

Now you can have a conversation with your hand! Simply move your finger and thumb to make the mouth open and close. You need not be an expert ventriloquist to operate this doll

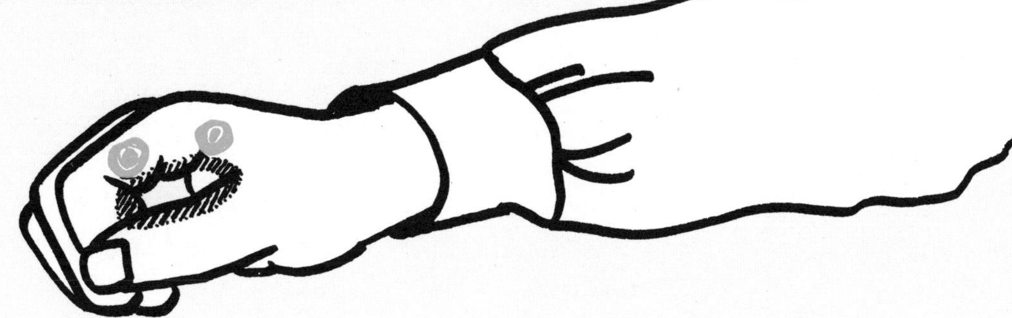

to good effect. When the doll talks, look at the doll. The audience will also look at the doll. If you can talk with the minimum mouth movement the illusion of the doll speaking will be perfect. But some successful ventriloquists make no attempt whatever to hide the fact that they are speaking when the doll is supposed to be talking. They use a different voice for the doll and look at it and animate it when it is supposed to be speaking. If you can finish your act with a song, so much the better.

CHARADES – EVERYBODY ON STAGE!

This has always been among the most popular of party games. It gives the players an opportunity to use their wits and to let them show their acting ability—and most people secretly believe that they can act as well as anyone.

The game is based on the sound of words and the best-known form of the game is played by two teams. One team chooses a word of any number of syllables and acts an impromptu play containing clues to that word. The other team tries to guess the word. Each syllable is acted separately, then the complete word is performed.

The plays can either be mimed or the spoken word can be used. If it is a play with dialogue, the syllable being acted must be included in the dialogue, and in the last part of the performance the complete word must be included.

For example, if the word chosen is 'catwalk', the word 'cat' must be spoken during the first act, the word 'walk' in the second and the complete word in the third.

If the play is to be mimed (acted without words) there are a number of signals the actor uses. He puts a number of fingers on his wrist to show the number of syllables in the word and then to show which one he is miming. If he is going to mime the whole word he makes a sweeping, circular movement with his hands. When the guessing starts he can show with a chopping movement that the correct word is a shorter form of the word guessed. If the correct word is a longer form, he makes a stretching movement.

In mimed charades, book titles, song titles, film titles, well-known sayings or famous names can be chosen. If the subject is a book title, the actor indicates this by pretending to read; if a song, he pretends to sing; if a film, he pretends to operate an old-fashioned movie-camera; if it is a saying, he holds up a finger of each hand to indicate inverted commas, and if it is a famous name he puts one hand inside his shirt in the well-known 'Napoleon' pose.

To show the number of words in the phrase to be guessed, the actor holds up an appropriate number of fingers and he uses the same method to show which word in the phrase he is acting. He holds up the thumb and forefinger of one hand to indicate a short word; to indicate that he is to mime a word that sounds like the correct one, he pulls his ear.

Here are some variations of the game.

Relay Charades
Where there's many a slip

This game needs a referee. The players form two equal teams and the referee writes out a list of subjects, in duplicate, on slips of paper, as many as there are players in each team. The first player in each team takes a slip and mimes the subject for his team. When the subject is correctly guessed another player takes a slip of paper, and so on. The first team to guess all the subjects wins.

Individual Charades
Solo for a single star

One player thinks of a subject and acts it for the others to guess. The player who guesses correctly is the next to act.

Individual Pass Charades
Fall in, the volunteers!

In this game one player writes a subject on a sheet of paper. Another player volunteers to act it. The player who thought it up may not, of course, take part in the guessing.

Circle Pass Charades
Acting in the ring

The players sit in a circle and each writes a subject on a piece of paper and passes it to his right. Then each player, in turn, steps into the circle and acts out what is written on his piece of paper. The player who succeeds in acting his subject so that it is guessed in the shortest time is the winner.

Speed Team Charades
The pressure is on

Players divide into two equal teams. Each team writes ten subjects on individual slips of paper and puts them into a container. The teams exchange containers and, simultaneously, one member of each takes a slip and acts the subject for his own team. When a team guesses correctly, a new player from that team acts out the next subject, and so on. The first team to complete all ten subjects is the winner.

Team Charades
Co-operation counts

For this one, players divide into three or more teams. Each team writes a subject on a slip of paper and passes it to another team. Each team in turn then briefly rehearses and puts on a 'team charade', with the entire group taking part. The team (or teams) that did not make up the charade does the guessing.

Chapter 5

Indoor Games of Skill and Chance

Fun with cards, dice and dominoes;
Learning to play draughts and chess;
Paper and pencil games for a rainy day

Just as outdoor games offer a physical challenge to a child, so many indoor games offer a mental challenge. Even a simple card game, such as Snap, is a stiff exercise in concentration and observation for a four-year-old child.

The pencil and paper games at the beginning of this chapter could be called 'Games for a Rainy Day'. They have been chosen to give children interest and stimulation if they become bored when kept indoors.

Some pencil and paper games could be selected for a quiet interlude at a party for older children, but choose only one or two, because the children will prefer more active games.

Other games, such as Tangram (see p. 108) and Patience (see p. 143), can help to while away the time for a convalescing child.

Many of the following games may be firm favourites for a time, but will then be discarded as a child grows older. Meanwhile, other games, such as Chess, Draughts or Whist, may develop into a lifelong interest.

Little equipment is needed for many hours of varied entertainment and mental stimulation for scores of games. You require only:

A pack of cards
A set of six dice
Dominoes
A chessboard and chessmen
A set of draughtsmen

Magic Square

The trick is in the centre

This first appears to be a really difficult game, and it is until you know the trick of it. Each player is given a piece of paper on which is drawn a square divided into nine smaller squares. The challenge is to write one number in each square, from 1 to 9, so that each line including the diagonals adds up to 15.

The trick is to start by writing number 5 in the middle square.

The difficulty now is to decide what to do with the high numbers, 8 and 9. The answer is that 9 must *not* go in any of the corner squares and 8 must go in either of the corner squares furthest away from 9.

Then it is easy to fill in the rest of the squares. If the players are baffled by this game after 10 minutes, the game leader can give clues which will keep the fun going.

1 How do you write a number in each square so that the lines and diagonals add up to 15? The trick is to start with 5 in the centre.

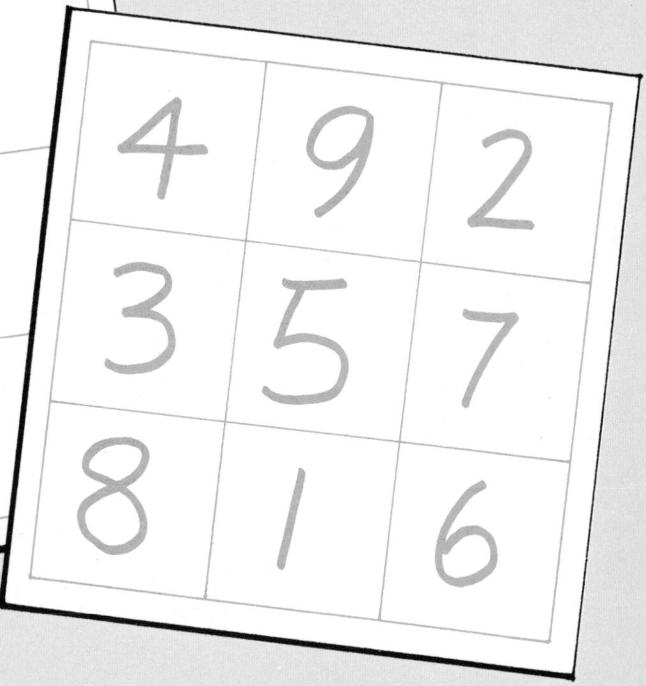

2 The second trick is to place the figure 9 in any centre square and the 8 in a corner. Other figures are added to make totals of 15.

Find the Fort

The lines must not be crossed

A small square with an opening in one side is drawn in the centre of a sheet of paper. The square is the fort and the opening is its gate. The numbers from 1 to 15 are then written at random all around the paper with a small circle around each number. The numbers represent outlying settlements under attack. The object of the game is to draw a line from each settlement—beginning with number 1 and then number 2, and so on—to the gate of the fort without touching or crossing the line from any other settlement. One penalty point is given for each line touched or crossed. This game is usually played between two players taking turns. The player with fewer penalty points when all settlements have been linked to the forts wins.

In *Pairing Numbers* a sheet is prepared with two sets of numbers from 1 to 15 written on it. No number should be near its paired number. The purpose of the game is to draw a line from each number to its pair—starting with number 1, then number 2, and so on—without crossing any other line. This game is generally played with two players taking turns. The first player who is unable to draw a line connecting two numbers without crossing another, loses.

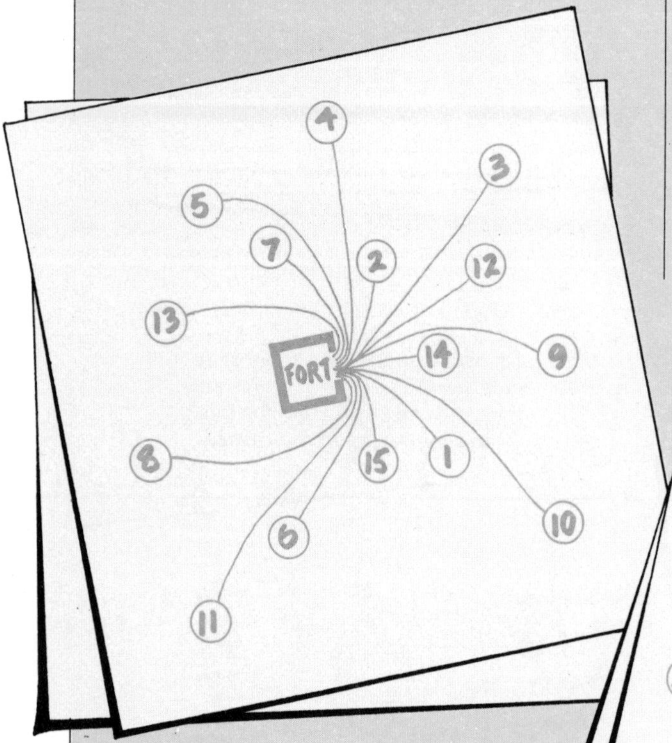

Find the Fort: This game looks easy when the lines are drawn like this, but a crafty player will draw a circuitous course home to make it difficult for his opponent's next move.

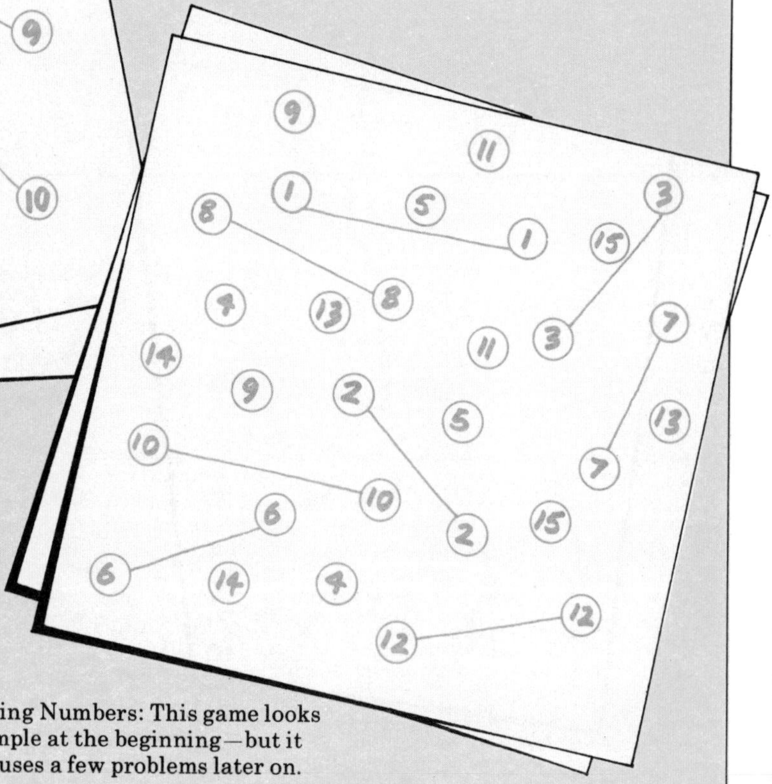

Pairing Numbers: This game looks simple at the beginning—but it causes a few problems later on.

Magic Circles
There's an easy way round

This is a more advanced version of Magic Square but the secret is similar. Each player is given a piece of paper on which are nine circles, three to a row. They have to write one of the nine even numbers from 2 to 18 in each circle so that each vertical and horizontal line and each diagonal adds up to 30. In this case the trick is to write the number 10 in the middle circle. Make sure that 18 is not in a corner circle and write 16 in either of the corners furthest away from 18.

Draw a Shape
Illustrating a sense of touch

A game leader blindfolds all players and places a piece of paper, a pencil and two cardboard cutout shapes in front of each. These shapes may be of any design, but it is wise to keep them relatively simple, such as a star, an aeroplane, a tree or a car. The two shapes must be identical for each player.
While blindfolded, the players are given one minute to feel the two cutouts. Then the game leader collects the shapes and takes off the blindfolds. The players try to draw from memory the two shapes. After 2 minutes the player whose drawings most resemble the cutouts is the winner.

What is it?
Children will love this one

Each player is given a large sheet of paper, a piece of chalk or a crayon and a slip of paper with the name of an animal on it. At a signal, each player draws the animal on the sheet of paper. The drawings are pinned on the wall and numbered. The players copy the numbers and write the animal beside each number. The player who identifies the greatest number of animals correctly is the winner. The player who drew the animal which was correctly identified by the most players is also considered to be a winner.

Initials
A game for designing players

Players write the initials of their first and last names on a sheet of paper. The two letters should cover a fairly large part of the sheets. Each player then does a drawing on the paper using his initials as a part of the design. When all the drawings are complete, the players vote for the drawing which uses the letters in the cleverest way.

Trick Crossword

A puzzle that shows its teeth

A blank crossword puzzle is drawn with four vertical and four horizontal squares. Players are told that the down clues all have the same answer and are given 5 minutes to solve the puzzle. The clues are:
Across: (1) insects; (5) what you see with; (6) to torment or tantalise; (7) comfort and relaxation.

Down: (1) what teeth do; (2) what fish do; (3) what dogs do; (4) what mosquitoes do. Here is a real clue to solving this trick crossword—answer the down clues first. Then read aloud the clues across.

The Solution The across answers are bees (Bs), eyes (Is), tease (Ts), and ease (Es). The down answers are all 'bite'.

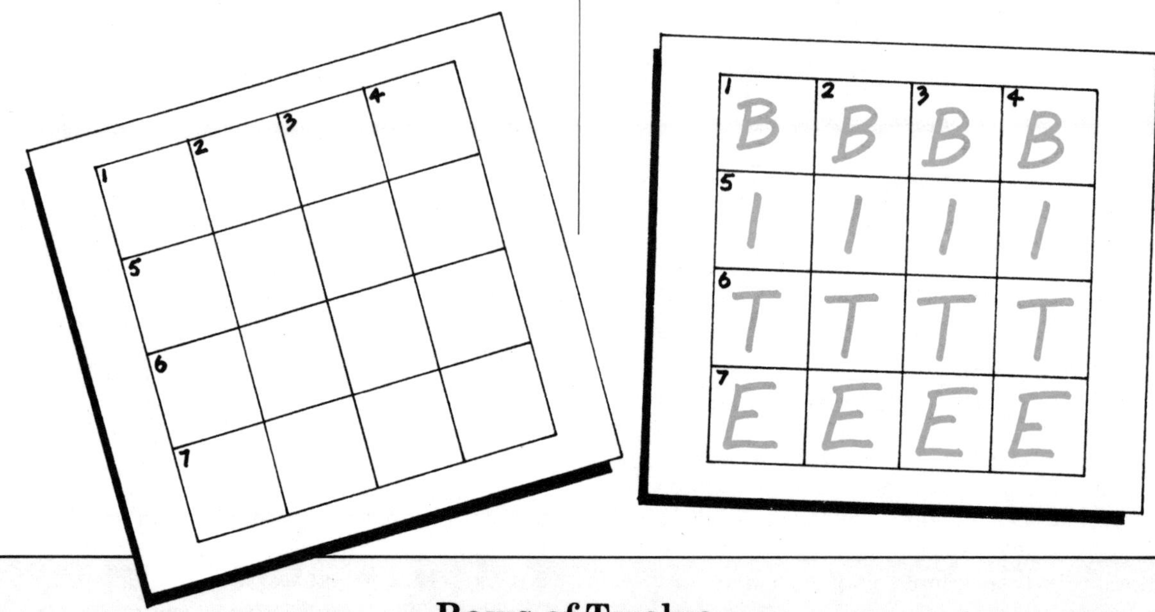

Rows of Twelve

Making dozens in circles

Seven circles are drawn. Players must fill them in with the numbers 1 to 7 so that each of the five rows of three circles (two horizontal, two diagonal and one vertical) adds up to 12. No number can be used in more than one circle and all seven numbers must be used.

The Solution The numbers in the two horizontal rows are 6, 1, 5 and 3, 7, 2. The numbers in the two diagonal rows are 6, 4, 2 and 5, 4, 3. The numbers in the one vertical row are 1, 4 and 7.

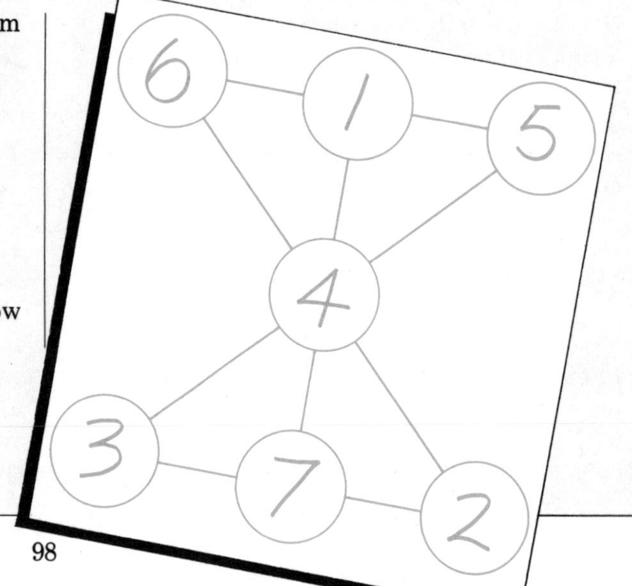

Stop the Tiger

The question-and-answer safari

On a blackboard, the game leader draws a lamb tied to a post with five ropes, a tiger creeping up to attack it and five fences which the tiger must cross to get to it.
Players divide into two teams, the lambs and the tigers. In turn, players from each team answer arithmetical problems put to them by the leader. When a lamb answers a problem correctly, he may erase one of the ropes tying the lamb to the post. When a tiger answers correctly, he may erase one of the fences. The lambs are trying to get rid of the ropes so that the lamb can escape. The tigers are trying to get rid of the fences so that the lamb can be captured.
This game may also be played by using questions on any subject such as sport, geography, history, spelling, and so on.

Target Arithmetic

Hit the problem—then solve it

The game leader draws a large target of four or five circles on the blackboard. An arithmetical problem is written in each with the simplest problem in the centre and the more difficult in the outer circles. Players stand behind a line, about 3 metres away, and take turns throwing a ball of clay at the target. The thrower must then solve the problem written in the circle in which the ball has landed. He gets one point for answering the problem correctly.
Once the problem is solved the leader rubs it out and writes another. After each player has had several turns, the player with the most points is the winner.

Blackboard Relay

Spelling out a win

Two teams stand behind a line about 5 metres from a blackboard. A question master calls out a word and the first player in each line runs to the blackboard, writes the word and runs back to the end of the line. The first player to complete the action wins a point for his team, provided he has spelled the word correctly. After each player has had a turn, the team with more points wins.
To make a change, the players can be asked to skip, crawl or walk backwards.

Building Words

Adding them up

The question master writes several three-letter words on the blackboard. Players write them down, one word to a line. At a signal, each player builds other words out of these base words by adding other letters.
Some examples are: ran—bran, grant, rant, cranberry, rancid; bar—barb, barber, bargain, barley.
After 5 minutes the player with the most words wins the contest.

Dots and Squares

Making a winning connection

Draw a rectangle of rows of dots—
13 horizontally and 12 vertically.
Two players take turns drawing lines which connect any two dots either vertically or horizontally, but not diagonally. The object of the game is for one player to complete as many small squares as he can, while trying to prevent his opponent from doing the same.
Whenever a player sees a place in the diagram where three sides of a square have been completed, he may draw in the fourth side and put his initial in the box. Whenever a player completes a square, he draws another line. Thus when the diagram is fairly well covered with lines he may find that he is able to complete several squares without stopping. For his last line he may then have to draw the third side of a square, giving his opponent the chance to fill in some boxes.
When all the lines have been drawn, the player with the most squares filled in and initialled is the winner.

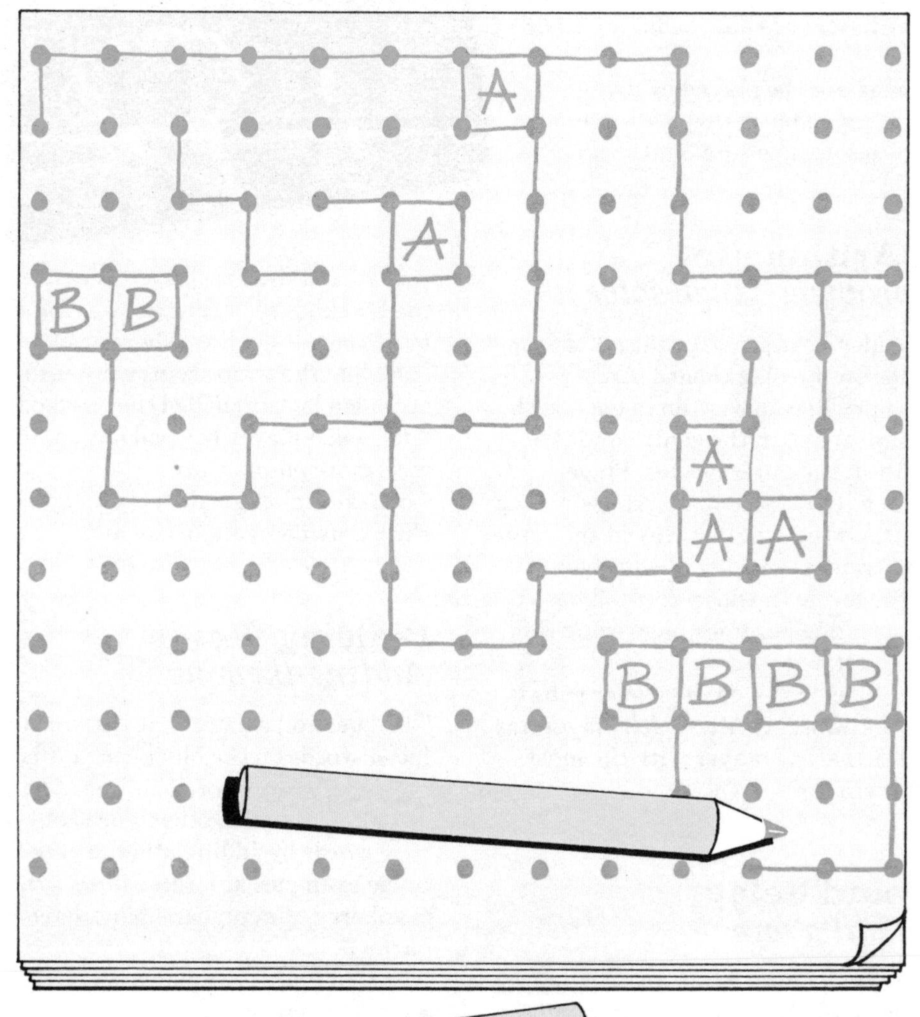

Progressive Artists
Pictorial consequences

This age-old game always produces some amusing surprises. Players are given a large sheet of paper and a pencil. Each draws a head, which can be human or animal, at the top of his paper. He then folds over the sheet so that the head is hidden but a bit of the neck still shows and passes the paper to the next player on the right. Each player then draws the body, including the arms, down to the waist and folds the paper over so that only the belt is showing. The papers are passed to the right again and the next players draw from the belt to the knees. These players fold the drawings for the last time and pass them to the players on the right, who finish the drawings by adding the lower parts of the legs and the feet. The completed drawings are unfolded and put on display and everyone gets a big laugh.

Roulette Wheel
Winning without looking

A large circle is drawn on a sheet of cardboard. The circle is divided into equal-sized segments and each segment is given a number. The circle is then fixed to a piece of plywood with a nail through the centre. The centre hole should be a little larger than the nail so the wheel will spin easily. Then, with his eyes closed, the first player spins the wheel and jabs a pencil down on it. He writes his initial in the segment where the pencil landed. There are two ways of scoring: A player may get credit for the numerical value of the segment and the first player to reach a set number of points is the winner. Or the player who initials the most segments is the winner. In scoring this second way, a player receives a point only if his pencil lands in a segment that has not been initialled already.

1 Draw a circle on a piece of card with a length of string tied to a pencil at one end and to a drawing pin at the other.

2 Cut out the circle, mark out and number equal segments. Nail the circle to a piece of plywood, so that it spins easily.

Non-stop Triangle
A many-sided problem

This is a good brain-teaser to try on your friends. You can look superior as they flounder in the attempt—but that is because you can see the solution at the bottom of the page. The problem is to draw three small triangles within a large triangle, without going over a line more than once or lifting the pencil. The secret lies in the starting point.

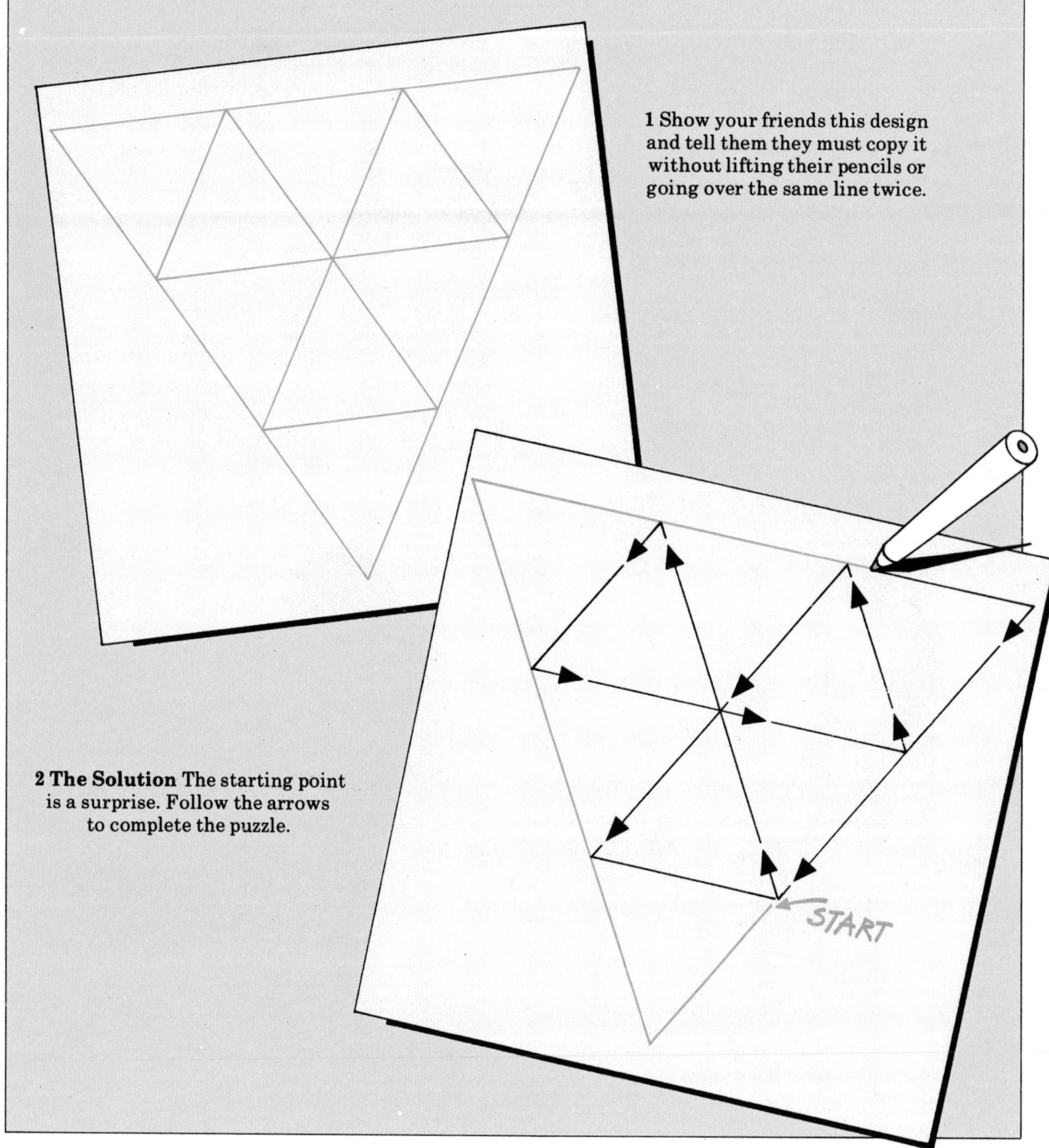

1 Show your friends this design and tell them they must copy it without lifting their pencils or going over the same line twice.

2 The Solution The starting point is a surprise. Follow the arrows to complete the puzzle.

Non-stop House
How soon can you build it?

Here is a brain-teaser similar to Non-stop Triangle on the facing page. After attempting the first puzzle your friends will realise there is a trick in finding the right starting point. Don't give them a clue—just let them flounder again. The rules are the same as for Non-stop Triangle. The house must be drawn in only one line without lifting the pencil.

1 This is the completed house. Now your friends must copy it without lifting their pencils or going over the same line twice.

2 The Solution It looks so simple when you know where to start. Follow the arrows and the house will be drawn.

Letter Jigsaw

Putting the alphabet together

A large letter is drawn on a sheet of paper and then cut up into several smaller pieces. Then an exact copy is made. Two players see who can correctly reassemble the letter in the shortest time. Several different letters may be prepared, with each jigsaw a separate contest; the player who wins the most contests wins the game.

For four and five-year-old children, it is advisable to indicate on the pieces the letter of the alphabet to be formed.

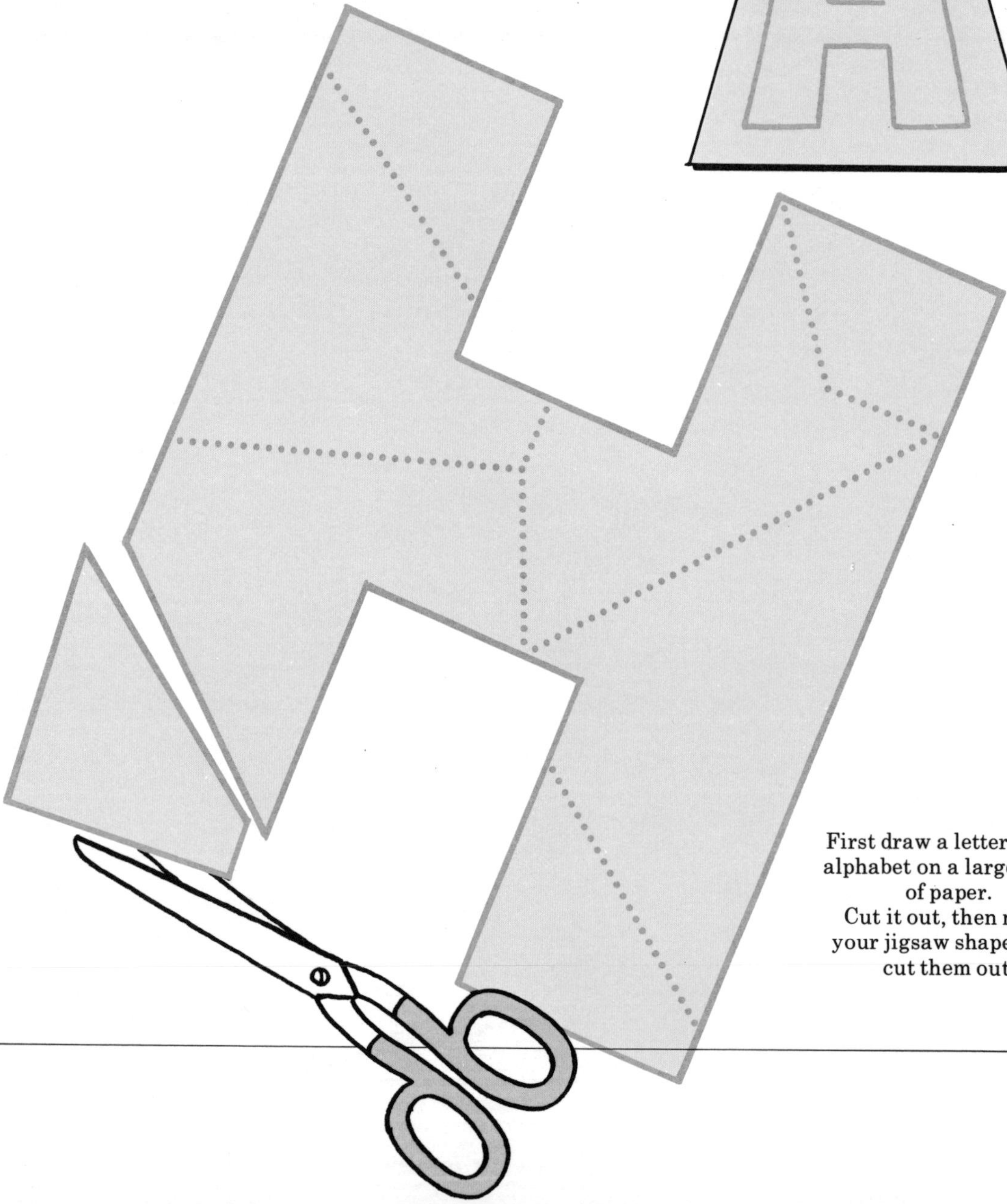

First draw a letter of the alphabet on a large piece of paper.
Cut it out, then mark your jigsaw shapes and cut them out.

Hit Every Dot
Dash from square to square

A large square, divided into 16 smaller squares, is drawn with a dot in the centre of each square. Players must then draw six straight lines, without lifting the pencil from the paper, that pass through each of the 16 black dots. You can solve the problem by starting at the point marked on the diagram and following the lines. Part of the secret is to let the lines travel outside the diagram when necessary.

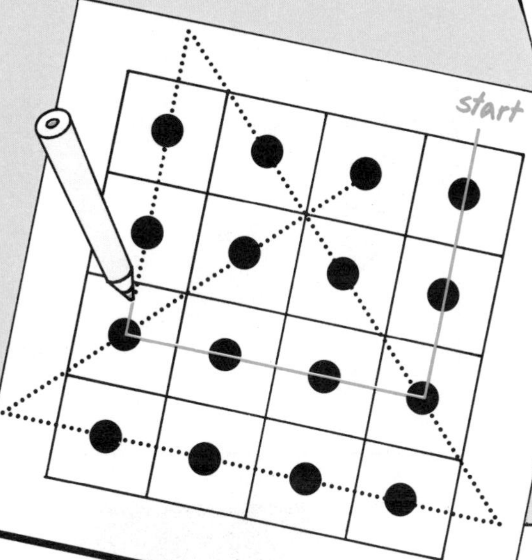

Guess a Size
Measure for measure

The game leader holds up various objects, one by one, and asks the players to write down a particular measurement for each item. The leader might ask, for example, the circumference of a tennis ball, the length of a book, the cubic capacity of a box, or the number of pints a jug would hold. When all the items have been shown, each player reveals his guesses. The player who comes closest to the correct answer for each object gets a point and the contestant with the most points wins. Two teams can compete, with team members discussing each item before giving an answer.

The team that comes closest for each item is awarded one point and the team with the higher score is the winner.

Memory Test
Getting it down on paper

This is a game for children who are proud that they can write a number of simple words. Pictures of objects such as a car, a flower, a tree, a house, a bus or a train are cut from newspapers or magazines. The players study the pictures for 2 minutes, then the pictures are taken away and the players write down as many of the objects as they can remember in a set time. The one who writes most wins.

Jigsaw Shapes
Racing to a fitting win

The game leader cuts out identical sets of cardboard shapes (squares, triangles and circles), each in a different colour. The shapes in each set are then cut into five or six pieces—the smaller the shapes, the more difficult the puzzle will be to complete.

A set of pieces is then given to each player. At a signal, the players fit the pieces together again into their original shapes. The first to complete the set of shapes wins.

Another way to play this game is for one group of players to prepare the shapes and another group to fit them together.

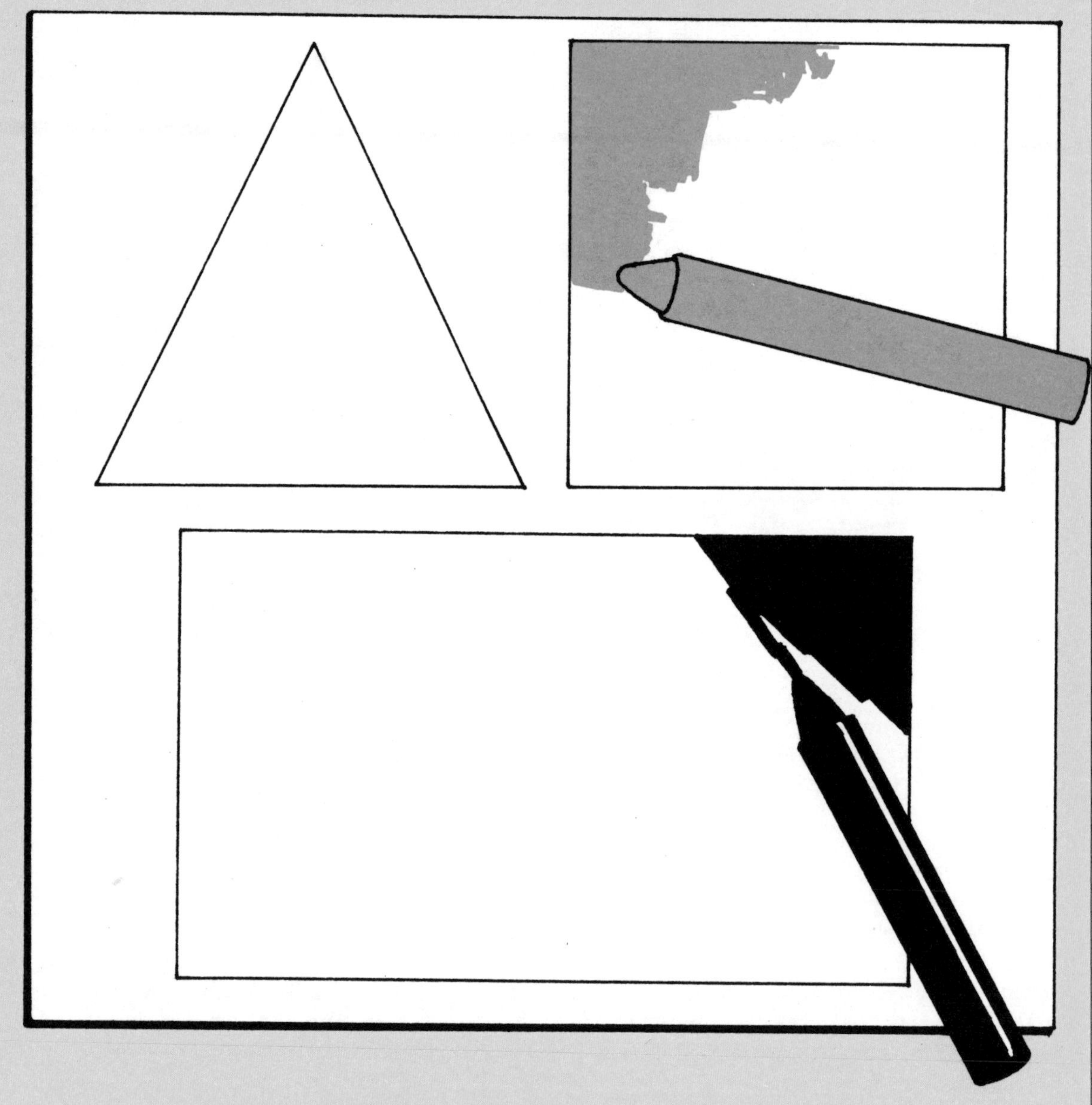

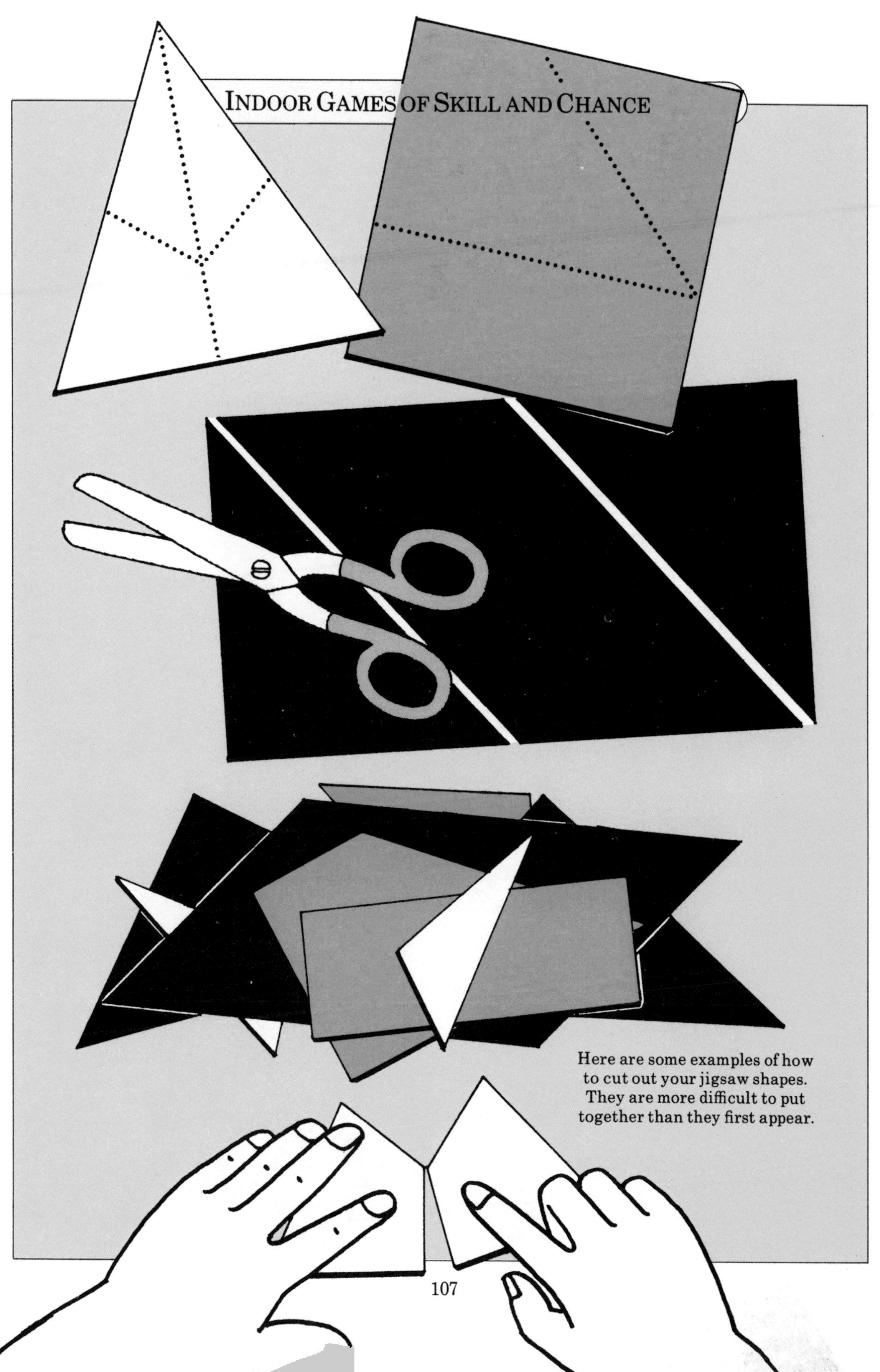

Here are some examples of how to cut out your jigsaw shapes. They are more difficult to put together than they first appear.

Tangram

Fitting the shapes to the figures

A tangram is a puzzle in which seven geometric shapes are used to construct various forms. The seven pieces are cut from a large square (see below) and all the pieces must be used when making a figure. The figures can represent animals, people, buildings, ships, numerals and letters of the alphabet. A wide range of geometric designs can be produced in symmetrical or asymmetrical forms.

The tangram originated in China and became very popular throughout Europe during the 19th century. It was described as 'scientific amusement for the old and the young, the grave and the gay, designed for centre table and fireside recreation'.

When Napoleon was in exile he spent many hours a day creating new designs and shapes.

A tangram is a puzzle as compelling as a jigsaw, but one which offers considerably more scope. The figures and shapes created with the seven pieces of the puzzle are seemingly endless. The puzzle can be enjoyed

The basic tangram square, showing how the seven geometric shapes should be marked out.

by all age groups either in individual play or in groups.

First, prepare several tangram puzzles. Draw each tangram on a card 10 centimetres square, using the diagram as a guide. Cut out the shapes and put each tangram in an envelope so that the pieces of one tangram are not mixed up with pieces from another.

Secondly, prepare three or four large tangram figures on separate cards. These figures are silhouettes of various objects that can be reproduced by using the seven pieces of the puzzle. You can make these silhouettes by tracing round the outline of the eight figures on these pages, ignoring the lines between the separate tangram pieces. Seen in outline, many of the figures will seem to the beginner to be impossible to reproduce with the seven pieces, but it can be done — as the complete figures illustrated here demonstrate.

Give each player an envelope containing the tangram pieces. The envelopes are opened at a signal and the first player to complete a figure is the winner.

After two or three rounds of this game, each player is asked to create a design of his own. The player who creates a design judged to be the most pleasing is the winner.

Matchstick Puzzles

Providing food for thought and fun for everyone

These puzzles require careful thought. If a large box of kitchen matches is used, several players can work together.

Puzzle No. 1. Arrange 17 matches as shown in diagram 1. Then remove five matches to make three squares (see diagram 2).

Puzzle No. 2. Arrange 12 matches as shown in diagram 1. Then move three matches so that there are only three squares (see diagram 2). All 12 matches are still used.

Puzzle No. 3. Arrange 24 matches to make nine squares, as shown in diagram 1. Take away eight matches and leave only two squares (see diagram 2).

Puzzle No. 4. Take six matches of equal length and make four triangles. The solution is to use three matches to make a base and then build a pyramid with the other three, as shown in the diagram.

Puzzle No. 5. Using nine matches, make three equal squares and two equal triangles, all connected. The solution is a tentlike structure illustrated in the diagram.

Puzzle No. 6. Using eight matches, form two squares and four triangles, as shown in the diagram.

Puzzle No. 7. Place six matches parallel to one another, with a space between each as in diagram 1. Then, without moving any of them, add five matches to make nine (see diagram 2).

Puzzle No. 8. Form three squares with 12 matches, as in diagram 1. Then take away any two matches and rearrange the others to leave two (see diagram 2).

PUZZLE NO 1

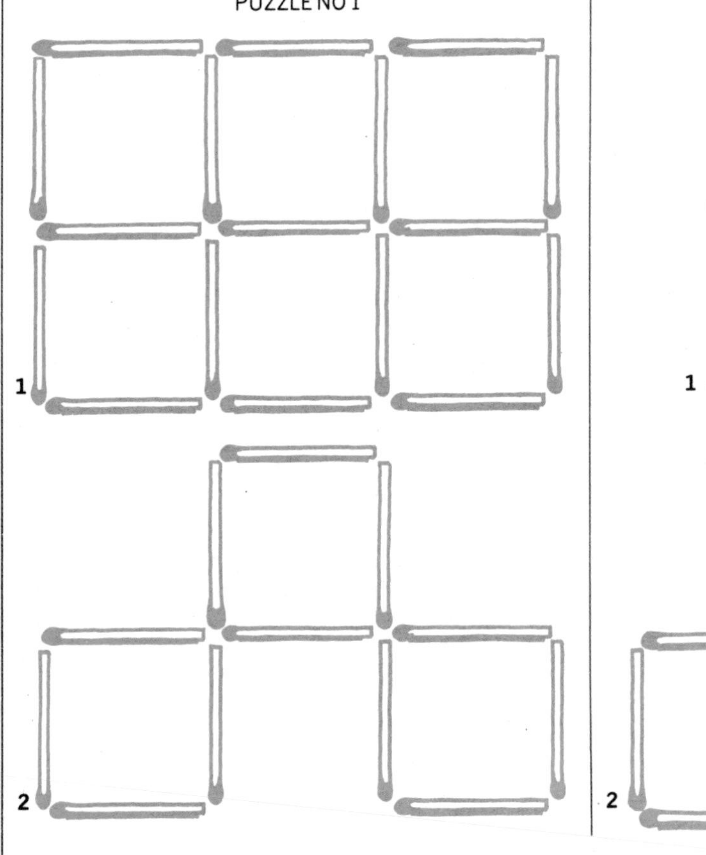

PUZZLE NO 2

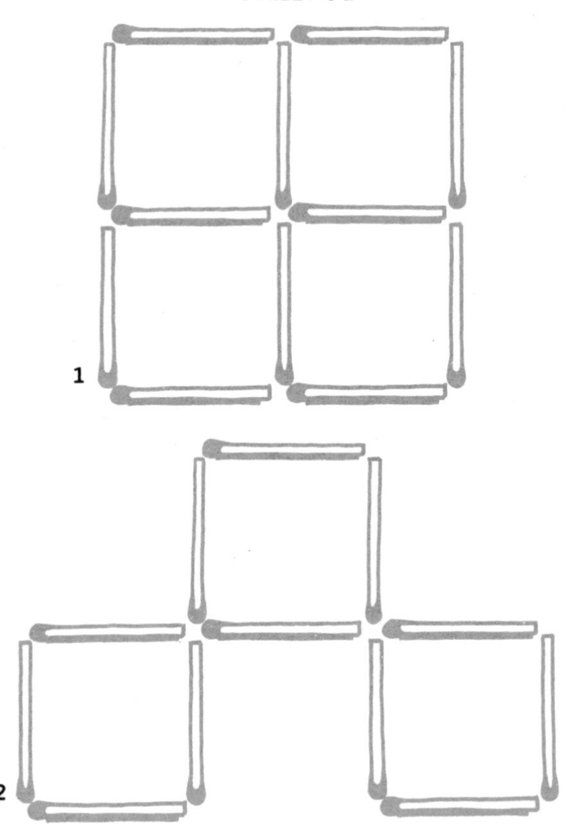

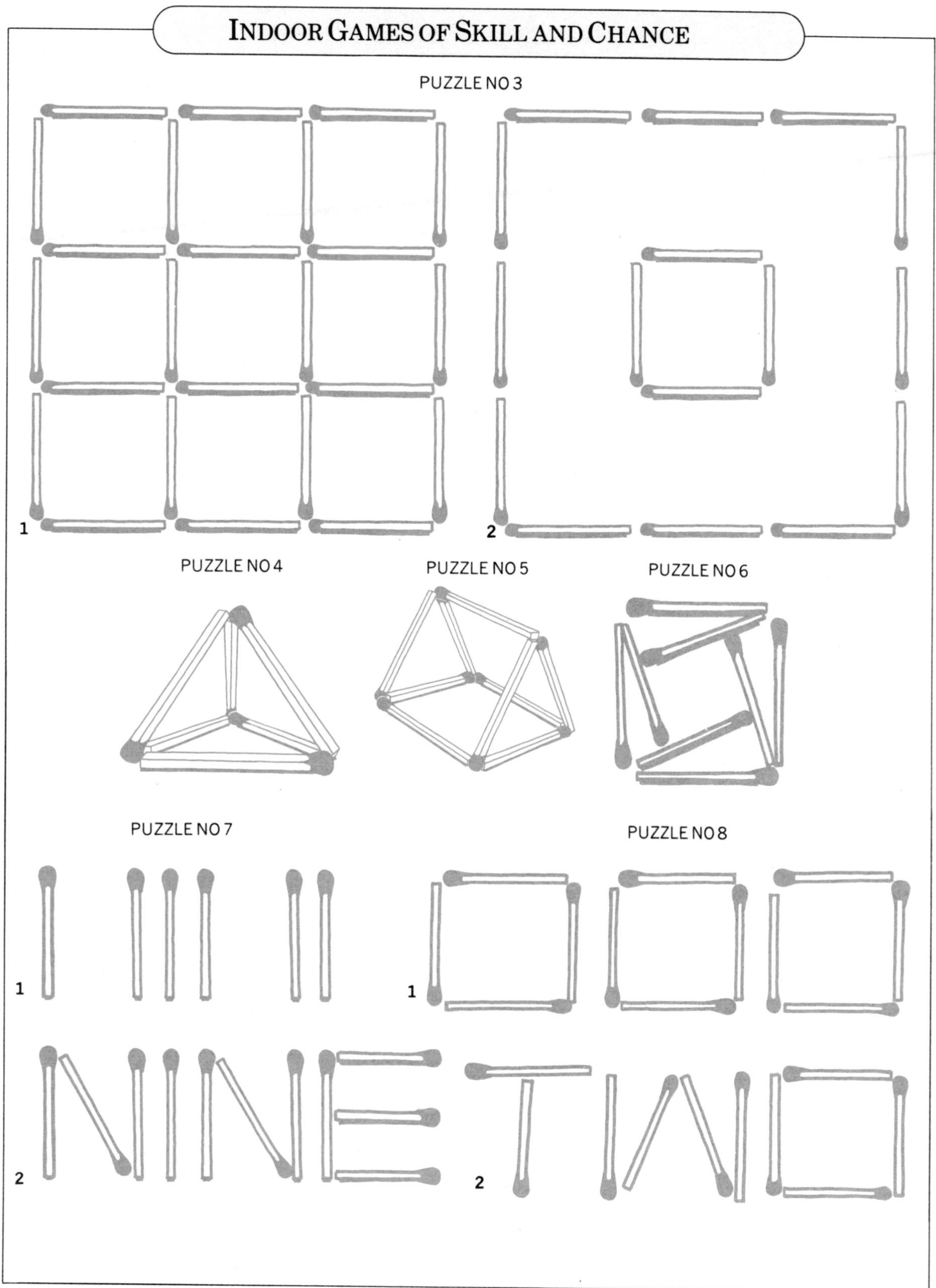
PUZZLE NO 3
1
2
PUZZLE NO 4
PUZZLE NO 5
PUZZLE NO 6
PUZZLE NO 7
1
2
PUZZLE NO 8
1
2

Noughts and Crosses

The game which nobody should ever lose

Although only nine squares are used in Noughts and Crosses, there are 15,120 different sequences for the first five moves of the game. There is no absolute formula for winning, but if you know the correct responses it is virtually impossible to lose. If you are O, the way to block any of the three basic opening moves, and force a draw, is to avoid the shaded squares shown below:

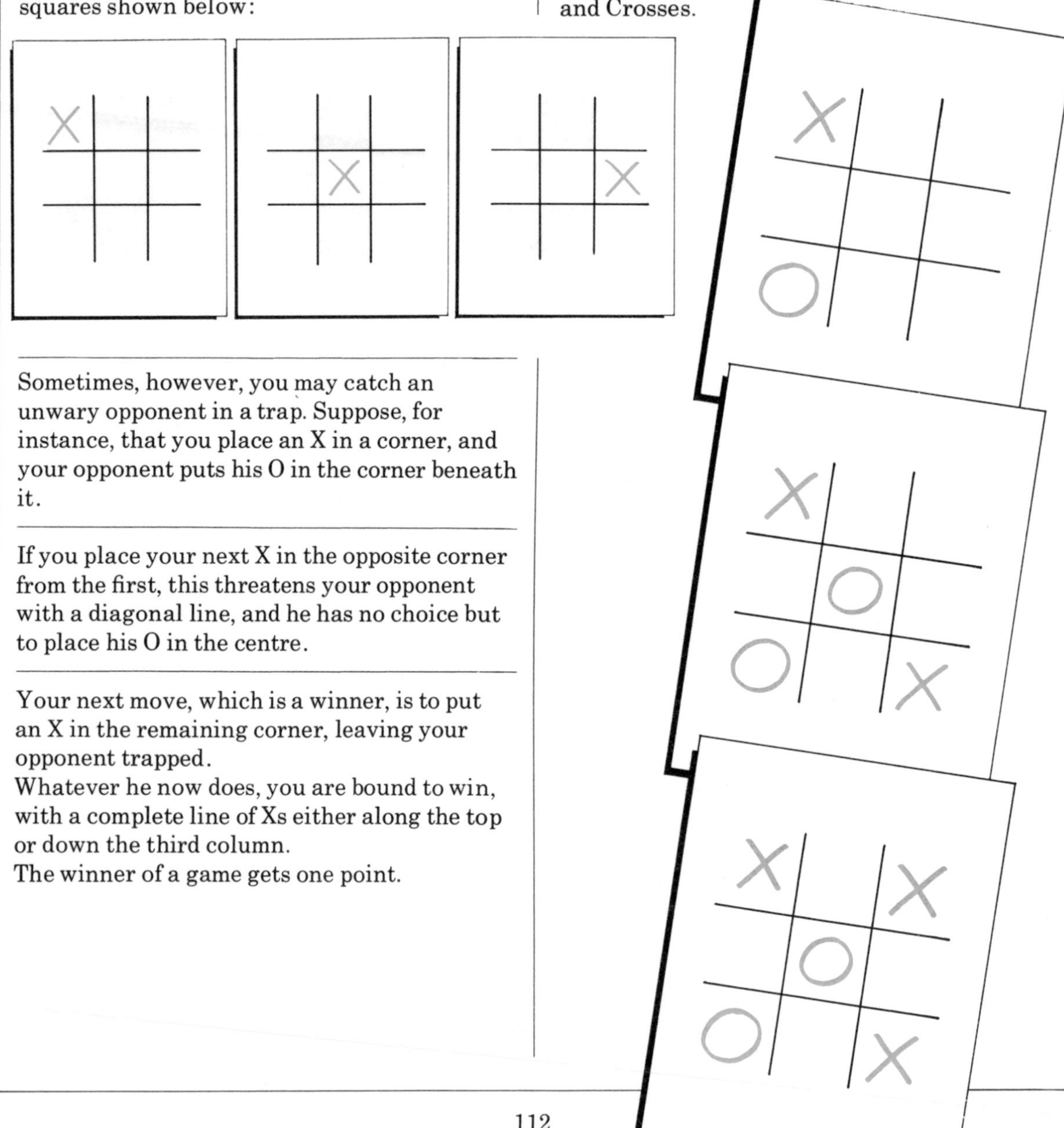

Sometimes, however, you may catch an unwary opponent in a trap. Suppose, for instance, that you place an X in a corner, and your opponent puts his O in the corner beneath it.

If you place your next X in the opposite corner from the first, this threatens your opponent with a diagonal line, and he has no choice but to place his O in the centre.

Your next move, which is a winner, is to put an X in the remaining corner, leaving your opponent trapped.
Whatever he now does, you are bound to win, with a complete line of Xs either along the top or down the third column.
The winner of a game gets one point.

Usually the game is played several times; the player with most points at the end is the winner. Since it is an advantage to go first, the loser of one game is usually allowed to make the first move in the next.
If you find you and your opponent are getting bogged down in a series of draws, try one or two variations, based on the idea of Noughts and Crosses.

Indoor Games of Skill and Chance

In *Gomuku*, a popular Japanese game, a grid is drawn with 19 vertical and 19 horizontal lines. One player chooses to use Os and the other player chooses Xs. They take turns drawing Xs or Os on the intersections of the lines. The first player to get five Xs or Os in a straight line is the winner.
In *Arithmetical Noughts and Crosses* the game leader draws a diagram on a blackboard. Players divide into two teams, the X team and the O team. In turn, players from each team answer arithmetical problems asked by the leader. When a player answers a question correctly, he writes an X or an O in one of the squares. If he gets the answer wrong, however, he cannot write anything. The first team to get an uninterrupted row horizontally, vertically or diagonally, wins.

Word Pyramid

Fill in the rows for a win

A pyramid design is drawn on sheets of paper and a copy handed to each player. At a signal, the players try to fill in the spaces horizontally with words that fit the number of boxes—a two-letter word for the top row, a three-letter word for the next row, and so on. The first player to complete the game wins.

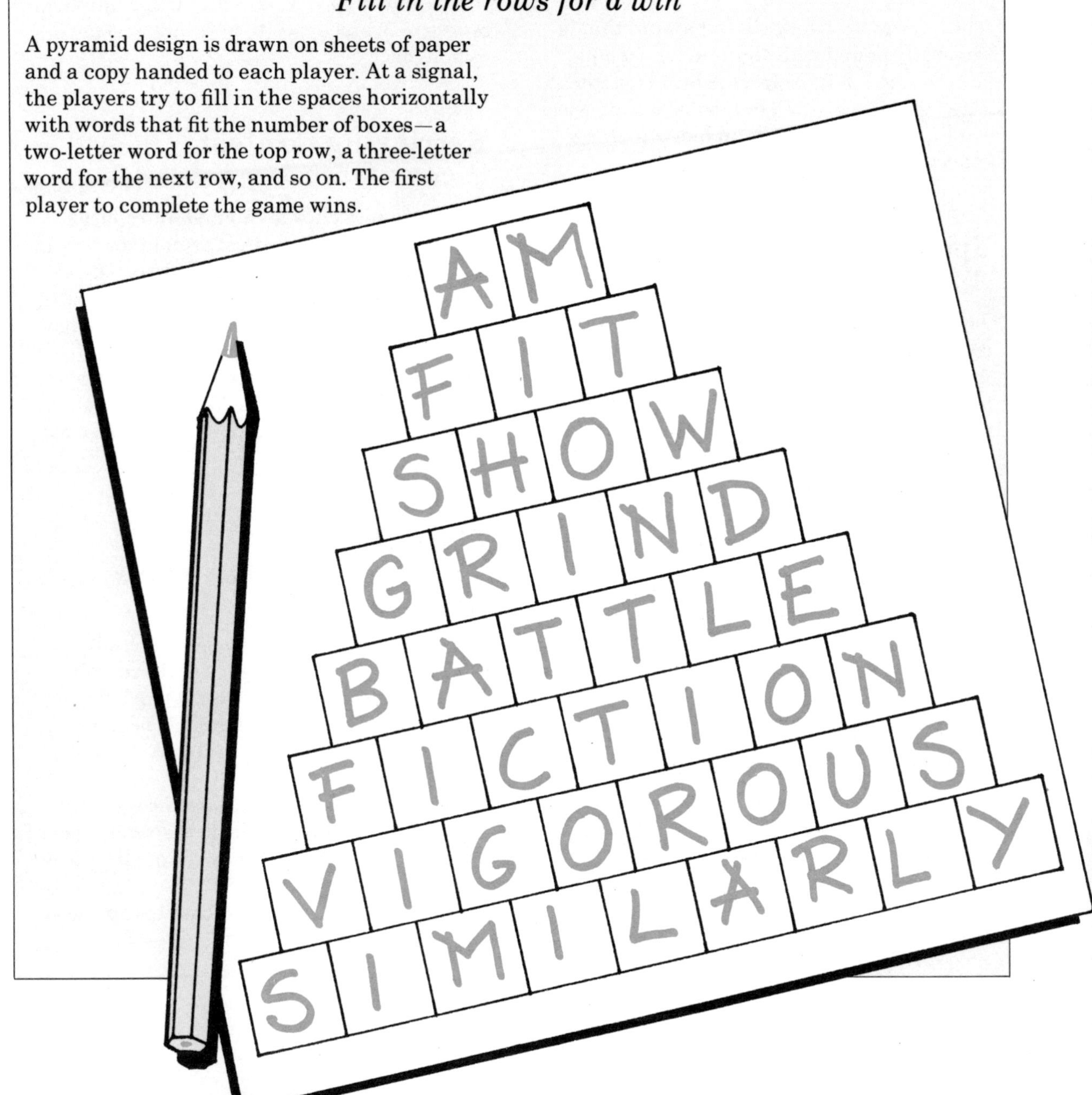

Begin-and-end Race
An A to Z challenge

Two players, or two equal teams, write down all the words they can think of that begin and end with letters called out by the question master. The player or team with most words, correctly spelled, after 5 minutes wins.

Matching Words
Make a quick strike

The question master calls out a word that is generally paired with another, for example bacon (eggs), salt (pepper) or bread (butter). The first player to call out the matching word wins a point. This can be an individual or a team game.

Spelling Bee
A sting for a loser

Two teams are formed and a question master reads out a word for the first player in team A to spell. If he is successful his team gets a point and the first player in the other team gets a new word to spell.

However, if the team A player cannot spell the word, the first player in team B has a chance to spell it and get a bonus point for his team. The question master then sets a new word for team B's first player.

When all the players in each team have had their chance, the team with most points is the winner.

Synonyms
The same is the game

The question master reads a list of words which the players write on a piece of paper. At a signal, the players write a synonym next to each word. Any word that is reasonably similar in meaning to the original word may be accepted. At the end of the game, players add up the total of the letters in their synonyms. The player with the highest total of letters, not words, wins.

In *Word Synonyms*, each player tries to think up as many synonyms for each word on the list as he can. The player with the largest number of acceptable synonyms wins.

Team Synonyms is played in the same way, except that players divide into equal teams, each team having the same list of words. Team members work together and the team with the highest total of synonyms wins.

These games may be varied by using antonyms, words with any opposite meaning, instead of synonyms.

Retrieving Contest
A game for indoor fishermen

A box of paper clips is emptied into a large pan of water. Players kneel around the pan and each is given a straight piece of wire which is bent at one end to form a hook. Wire coat-hangers can be straightened out to make these 'fishing rods'.

At a signal, the players try to pull out the paper clips with the hook. When all the clips have been retrieved, the player with the most is the winner.

Word Hunt
Catching up on your letters

Players are given a fairly long word containing two or three vowels, such as harvesting, which they print at the top of a sheet of paper. At a signal, each player writes down as many words of three letters or more, using only letters which are found in the key word.

No letter can be repeated more times in any word than it appears in the key word. Proper names, plurals or verb forms ending in 's' are not allowed.

The winner is the player who writes down the most words in 5 minutes.

Categories

Charting the best course

Players are given pencil and paper and each draws a chart that has five squares across and six squares down. Categories are then selected either by the players or the question master, for example: plants, trees, cities, food, birds. One category is written at the top of each vertical row. A six-letter word is then printed vertically beside the left-hand column (such as 'Charms' in the diagram).

At a signal, each player has to write a word in each square that begins with the letter outside the left-hand column and fits the category at the top. After 5 minutes, each player calls out the words he has written. Any correct word which no one else has written is worth two points. Duplicated words are worth one point. The player with the highest total wins.

This can be played as a team game in which team members decide on the words to be written. After 5 minutes the team with the higher total wins.

In *Exchange Categories*, players sit in a circle and make up a chart, using a key word and categories of their own choosing. They then pass their charts to the neighbour on the right. The first player to complete his chart wins.

Halma

Leaping to victory

Halma (the Greek for 'leap'), also known as Chinese Chequers, is played on a board with a six-point star design, obtainable at toy shops and stores. Coloured marbles are used. The object is to move all the marbles of one colour from one point of the star into the opposite point.

Players choose colours. If two are playing they take seats opposite each other and each player puts 15 marbles of a single colour into the point of the star in front of him and opposite his opponent's point.

If three or more are playing, ten marbles are used for each player instead of 15—each group of ten marbles being of the same colour. These marbles are grouped within any point of the star the player chooses.

Lots are drawn, or a coin tossed, to decide which player goes first. Players take alternate turns; with three or more people the turns move clockwise from the left of the person who goes first.

A player may move only one of his marbles at each turn and he may move it only one space forward into an open hole, unless a jump is possible. A player may jump any man in an adjoining hole—either his own marble or his opponent's—providing the hole beyond is open. Multiple jumps are possible when several marbles lie in alternate positions with open holes.

A player may not move backwards except in a series of multiple jumps which end ahead of the marble's starting point.

The first player to get all his marbles into the star point opposite his own wins the game.

DICE—THE EXCITEMENT OF THE THROW

The fascination of dice has persisted for thousands of years, from the days of prehistory when sheep's knuckle bones were used as aids to foretelling the future to modern times, when six-sided dice—precision made with dimensions accurate to 0·005 millimetres, but still colloquially known as 'the bones'—are used as an aid to winning or losing large sums of money. Dice was played by soldiers at the siege of Troy in 1184 BC. It was a popular pastime in ancient Rome, when six-sided dice made from crystal inlaid with gold were thrown from conical cups of carved ivory.
Some of the cups were fitted with crossbars to prevent anyone who felt that their luck needed a little illegal assistance from sliding the dice on to the table in a prearranged position. There is evidence that those Romans who were lower in the social scale also played the game—dice tables found in the Forum and the Coliseum were made not only of engraved marble but also of stone, with the divisions roughly scratched on them.

The Cheyenne Indians of North America played an interesting variation of the game using five plum stones. Three of the stones were marked with a cross on one side only, the other two were marked with a bear's paw, on one side only. The stones were placed in a basket, held aloft and shaken vigorously. The basket was then placed quickly on the ground and the combination of symbols determined the winner. It is interesting to speculate that the Cheyenne who came up with three crosses and two bear's paws hit the jackpot—and that the game could well have been the forerunner of the one-armed bandit slot machine.

Dice was particularly popular in England in the Middle Ages—especially in the army. In fact gambling was so prevalent that in the Crusades of 1190 the lower ranks were forbidden to play dice or any other kind of gambling game. This restriction did not apply to knights or chaplains—but if they lost more than a certain amount in one day they were heavily fined, which implies that it was not gambling of which the authorities disapproved but losing.

Dice developed through the centuries in two ways. First there evolved games in which the dice were used simply for gambling. Then they came to be used more and more as adjuncts to other games, a function they still fulfil today ranging from such simple nursery games as Snakes and Ladders to the more sophisticated Monopoly. In such games as these they are thrown by hand or from a cup, and the combinations of the spots on the uppermost faces of the dice determine the number of moves to be made.

The standard dice is marked with spots in patterns of different numbers on each side. The spots on opposite faces must always total seven.

The following games are fun for all ages.

Hearts Dice
For 4–6 players

In this game, letters spelling the word H-E-A-R-T-S are alloted to each face of the dice: H for 1, E for 2 and so on. Six dice are used, and each player needs a pencil and paper for scoring. To determine the order of play, each player throws the six dice; the highest total takes first throw and the others follow in the order of their totals.

Each player throws all six dice one at a time and scores according to the number of letters of the word HEARTS he can throw in their correct order. The scoring is as follows:

H= 5 points
H-E=10 points
H-E-A=15 points
H-E-A-R=20 points
H-E-A-R-T=25 points
H-E-A-R-T-S=35 points

'Wild' letters thrown between correct

letters are ignored for scoring purposes.
If no H is thrown, there is no score for that turn. If two or three letters of the same kind are thrown only one of them counts, but if three Hs are thrown, that player loses all his score to date and has to start again with nothing on his sheet. The winner is the player with the highest number of points after an agreed number of rounds.

Going to Boston
For 2–6 players

Three dice are used in this game and each player should have a pencil and paper to record his score.
Each player throws the three dice to determine the order of play, with the highest score going first followed by the others in their sequence.
The object of the game is to be first to reach 100 points, and this is how it is done. The leading player throws the three dice and sets aside the one showing the highest total. He then throws the other two dice and sets aside the higher of those. Finally he throws the remaining one and his score is the total number of spots showing on all three dice.
But there is more to it than that. If the first throw results in three of a kind (three ones, three fives, and so on) the player gets a bonus of 30 points. If his second throw produces two of a kind he gets another bonus, this time of 15

CONTINUED ON PAGE 118

Sequences
For 2 players

Each player uses three dice and a scorecard with numbered squares from 1 to 12 and 12 to 1 as shown in the diagram. The object of the game is to cross off the numbers in sequence from 1 to 12 and then from 12 back to 1, using the spots on the uppermost faces of the dice after each throw.
This is how the game is played. The first player throws the three dice and then studies the spots at his disposal. Suppose he has thrown 1, 2 and 4. He can cross off 1 and 2 straight away. Then he adds 1 and 2 which means that he can cross off 3. Then, keeping to sequence, he crosses off 4. Next he adds 4 and 1 and crosses off 5. Then he adds 2 and 4 and crosses off 6. Finally he adds 4, 2 and 1 and crosses off 7. This is a good score for one throw.
It is important to remember that the numbers must be crossed off in sequence, which means that if a player does not throw a 1 to start with he cannot cross off any number, and the other player takes his turn.
Throughout the game, if a player cannot make the next number in sequence he has to pass the dice to his opponent.
In *Everest* each number on the uppermost faces may be used only once. For example, if a player throws 1, 2 and 4 the numbers available to him are either 1, 2 and 4, or 3 (by adding 2 and 1) and 4 or 5 (by adding 4 and 1) and 2 or 6 (by adding 4 and 2) and 1 or 7 (by adding 1, 2 and 4). In this version the numbers need not be crossed off in sequence and the first player to complete his scorecard wins.

1	2	3	4	5	6	7	8	9	10	11	12
12	11	10	9	8	7	6	5	4	3	2	1

How to mark out the scorecard for Centennial or Everest.

Beetle
For 4–5 players

A specially prepared dice is needed for this game. Instead of spots on each face the letters B H L E F T are used. Each letter is the initial of a part of a beetle, B for body, H for head, L for leg, E for eye, F for feeler and T for tail. This can be done by sticking squares of paper on each face and marking the letters with a felt-tipped pen.
If you don't feel like doing this, you can use a standard dice—in which case you will need the accompanying diagram for reference.

Each player also needs a piece of paper and a pencil. The youngest player begins the game, then the play is clockwise
Each player gets one throw per turn and to start his beetle he must throw a B for body. If he throws a B he draws an oval shape on his piece of paper and his beetle has started to grow. In subsequent throws he draws in the rest of the parts. This applies to all the players. The first to complete a beetle is the winner.

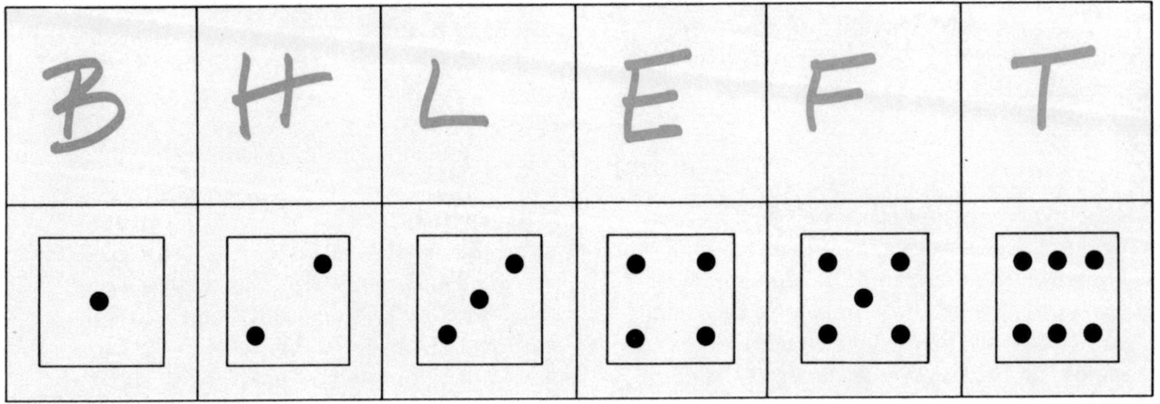

CONTINUED FROM PAGE 117
points. After his final throw—with the remaining single dice—he adds up the total spots showing on all three dice as before and adds it to his score.
This means that the best possible score for one turn would be 63 points, achieved like this: first throw, three sixes, bonus 30 points; second throw, with two dice, two sixes, bonus 15 points; third throw with one dice, one six. Total score: 30+15+6+6+6=63.

Ace in the Pot
For 2–6 players

Each player is given two counters and the object is to be the last to keep one of them. Two dice are used and the fun is fast and furious. The players sit round a table and throw for first go. The one with the highest total starts off and thereafter play proceeds clockwise.
The first player throws the two dice. If he throws a one he must put a counter into the middle of the table. If he throws two ones he has to put two counters into the middle.
If he throws a six he must pay a counter to the player on his left; two sixes means that he pays two counters to the player on his left.
If he throws a one and a six he must pay one counter into the middle and one to the player on his left. If, at this stage, he has only one counter he must put it in the middle.
A player who loses both counters is still not out of the game. While he is empty-handed he must pass the dice to his left. He is in the game, however, because at any time he may get a counter from the player on his right. In due course, one player will have the last counter but there is still more action to come.

He must throw the dice three times and if he throws a six he must pass the counter to the player on his left who throws the dice again. The first player to throw three times without throwing a six wins the counters in the middle of the table (sometimes called 'the kitty'), and everyone is ready for another round.
The final winner is the player with the most counters after an agreed number of rounds.

Centennial
For 4–6 players

Scoring in this game is based on various sequences of spots. You need a cup, six dice and a scorecard. The first player is chosen by throwing the dice to achieve the highest score. Then play continues clockwise.
Each player throws all six dice, then tries to arrange the spots into certain scoring sequences. Each sequence has a particular scoring value, as shown in the table below.

TABLE OF SCORE VALUES FOR SEQUENCES

Sequence	Score
1–2	5 points
1–2 1–2	10 points
1–2 1–2 1–2	15 points
1–2–3	10 points
1–2–3 1–2–3	20 points
1–2–3–4	15 points
1–2 1–2–3–4	20 points
1–2–3–4–5	20 points
1–2–3–4–5–6	25 points
6–6–6–6–6	30 points
6–6–6–6–6–6	60 points
1–1–1–1	Entire score for all turns wiped out and player returns to zero
1–1–1–1–1	
1–1–1–1–1–1	

When a player reaches a score of 100 or more he takes no further part. When all the players have reached the 100 barrier the highest total is the winner. For example, if four players finish with 120, 116, 110 and 100, then the player with 120 is the winner.

Twenty-one
For any number of players

Sometimes called Blackjack, this game requires a cup, two dice and a supply of counters.
The object is to achieve a total of 21 points or to come closest to 21. A score over 21 puts the player out of the game.
The first player is chosen by throwing the dice—the highest scorer starts and play continues clockwise.
Each player puts an agreed number of counters in the middle of the table to form the kitty.
Everyone gets one turn only in each game, but he may throw the dice as many times as he wishes.
Each time the dice are thrown, the player adds the number of spots showing on the uppermost face of each and keeps a running total. When this total reaches 14 or more he may use one dice only or continue with the two. If two dice are used he is liable to throw a high score, which could result in 'going bust' with a score of more than 21.
At the end of each game the player who has scored 21 points or who has come closest to 21 wins the kitty. If any players tie they throw the dice again until a winner emerges.

Chicago
For six players

This game requires a cup, two dice and a scorecard.
The youngest player begins the game and then all turns are taken in a clockwise direction.
There are 12 rounds in each game and each round has a 'key' number which is the number of the round. In round one the key number is one, in round four the key number is four and so on.
Each player has one throw of the dice in each round and to score points the key number of that round must be thrown. If neither of the two dice produce the key number there is no

score for the thrower in that round.
When a key number is thrown, its value is recorded on the player's scorecard. A player who throws a 4 with one of his dice in round 4, for example, records a score of 4 for that round. Key numbers of 6 or over can be made up by any combination of spots on the uppermost faces of the dice: 6 can be made up of 1 plus 5, 3 plus 3 and so on, and 10 can be made up of 5 plus 5, 6 plus 4 and so on.
At the end of this game there is still a chance for the apparent loser to emerge as winner. For after 12 rounds there is a play-off between those with the highest and the lowest scores; the higher score wins.

Jackpot
For 6–8 players

Avoid 'Snake Eyes' but welcome 'Box-cars'— you will soon see why in this game.
Jackpot requires two dice, a specially prepared sheet, as shown in the diagram, and an equal number of counters for each player.
A banker is chosen by throwing the dice for highest score.

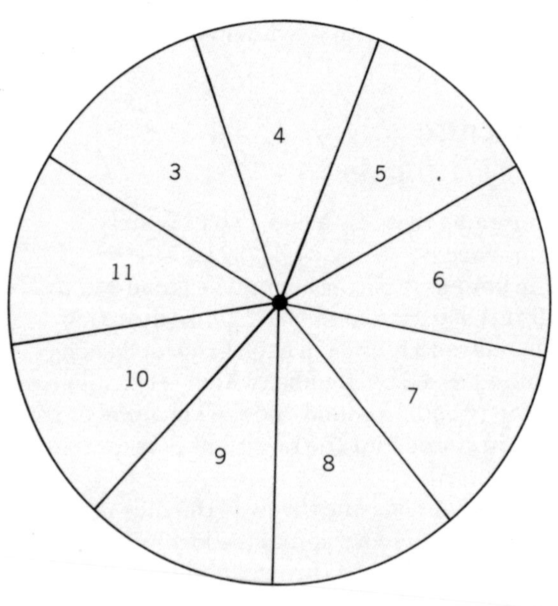

The player to the left of the banker throws the two dice and places a counter on the number on the sheet corresponding to the total he has thrown. The game continues clockwise, and subsequent players throw the dice and place counters on the corresponding numbers on the sheet.
When a number on the sheet has three counters on it the next player to throw that number collects the counters.
If a player throws two ones, or Snake Eyes, he must put a counter on every number that does not have three counters on it.
If he throws two sixes, or Box-cars, this counts as a Jackpot and all the counters on the sheet go to him.
The player to the left of the Jackpot winner begins the next round.

Round the Spot
For 4–8 players

This game is based on the formation of the spots on the dice. You can score only when they form a centre spot or a group round a centre spot.
You need three dice and a scorecard.
First, each player throws the dice and the one with the highest score starts the game. Play then continues in an anti-clockwise direction.
Each player has four turns of three throws each and only the ones, threes and fives count towards a score as follows: one is worth one point, three is worth two points (two spots 'round the spot'), five is worth four points (four spots 'round the spot').
If three twos, three fours or three sixes are thrown, the player doubles any score made during that turn. This throw counts as a bonus and is not included in the total of three throws allowed. The bonus score must be entered separately on the scorecard.
If a player throws another three of a kind during any later turn, he loses his bonus score.
The winner is the player with the highest score after four turns.

Crag
For 6–8 players,

This game requires a cup, three dice, a scorecard and a table showing the 13 categories and their value (see diagrams).
To determine the order of play, each player throws the three dice and the one with the highest score plays first. After that, play is in a clockwise direction.
Each turn, called a 'frame', entitles the player to two throws of the dice. The complete game consists of 13 frames, one frame for each category. The result of each frame is entered in the appropriate category on the scorecard. Players must fill in one category after each frame. If, after two throws, a player finds that he has no score to suit a vacant category he must put down '0'. In this case it is a good idea to put the '0' in the category with the lowest value.
After the first of his two throws, the player studies what he has thrown and how best he can improve it with his second throw. If he throws two of a kind, for example, he may decide to go for a Crag. He sets the pair aside and uses the remaining single dice for his second throw. The second throw could give him his Crag, or it could convert his two of a kind into three of a kind, or it could give him a thirteen, or it could fail to improve on his two of a kind. He then fills in the appropriate category. If he fails to improve, he is entitled to fill in his first throw, of two of a kind—for

SCORECARD FOR CRAG

CATEGORY	SCORE VALUE	PLAYER A	PLAYER B	PLAYER C
CRAG	50			
THIRTEEN	26			
HIGH STRAIGHT	20			
LOW STRAIGHT	20			
EVEN STRAIGHT	20			
ODD STRAIGHT	20			
THREE OF A KIND	25			
SIXES	Total of sixes			
FIVES	Total of fives			
FOURS	Total of fours			
THREES	Total of threes			
TWOS	Total of twos			
ONES	Total of ones			
TOTALS				

TABLE OF SCORE VALUES FOR CRAG

CRAG	Two of a kind plus another to total 13–(4+4)+5; (5+5)+3; (6+6)+1–scores 50 points
THIRTEEN	Sum of the spots on any three dice to total 13 scores 26 points
HIGH STRAIGHT	4–5–6 scores 20 points
LOW STRAIGHT	1–2–3 scores 20 points
EVEN STRAIGHT	2–4–6 scores 20 points
ODD STRAIGHT	1–3–5 scores 20 points
THREE OF A KIND	Any three of a kind scores 25 points
NUMBERS 1–6	The spots on the dice in the category chosen determine the score. Two fours equals eight and so on

example, two twos scoring four, two threes scoring six, and so on.
Every time he throws, he must keep an eye on the scorecard so that he knows what he wants. For instance, if he throws three of a kind but has already filled in that category, he will use all three dice for his second throw in an attempt to get something else. If he throws something he wants first time, he need not throw the second time—he simply fills in the category and passes on the dice.
After 13 frames have been completed, the player with the highest score wins.

Pig
For 4–6 players

The 'pig' is the one-spot, which brings trouble unless you throw two of them at the same time. This game requires two dice and a cup. A simple scorecard, as shown below, should be

INNINGS	PLAYERS' NAMES		
1st			
2nd			
3rd			
etc			

Bingo
For 6–8 players

A simple but exciting game of chance that requires two dice, a cup and an equal number of counters for each player, including the banker.
A banker is chosen by throwing the dice. The highest scorer becomes banker.
Each player makes a bet by placing a number of counters on the table in front of him. When all bets have been placed the banker puts an equal amount of counters in front of each of them.
The banker throws the dice first and notes his score. Then the player on his left throws them. If his score beats the banker he collects his bet and the banker's covering bet. If his throw is less, the banker scoops in the counters.
The banker then throws again, this time against the second player on his left and so on round the table. At the end of the round bets are placed again.
If the banker throws a double six he wins the bet outright and the player has no throw. If the player throws a double six the banker must pay double the player's bet.
After three rounds the job of banker passes to the player on his left.

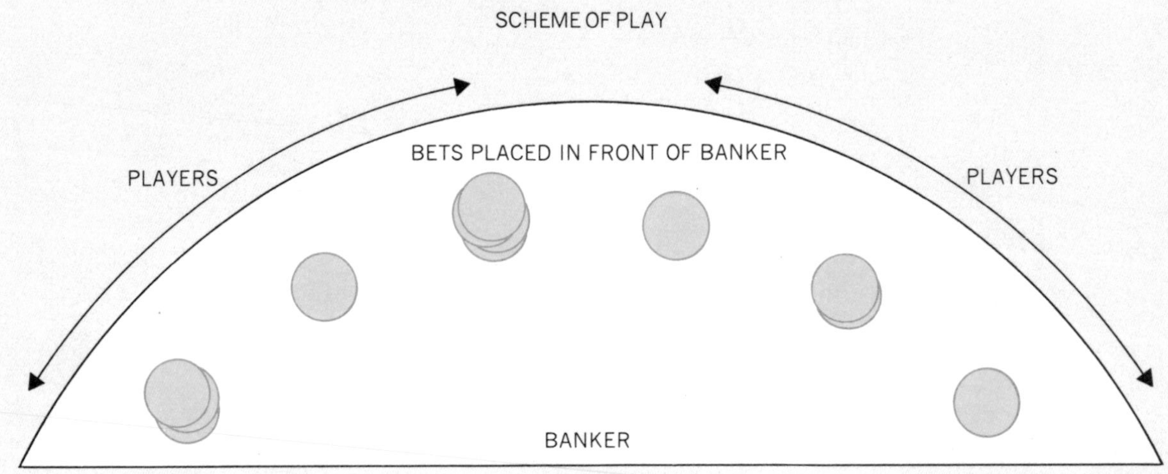

made to keep the running total of points scored by each player. In addition, each player needs paper and pencil to keep his own scores.
The dice are thrown to decide who plays first. The highest scorer wins, then play is clockwise. Each player throws the dice and totals the number of spots showing on the uppermost faces of each, making a note of the score. He may continue to throw the dice as many times as he wishes, making a note of all his scores in trying to reach a total of 100.

CONTINUED ON PAGE 124

Yacht

For 4–6 players

This game is more complicated than Crag but it is played in the same way. The differences are that in Yacht there are 12 categories instead of 13 and the categories use different formations. Five dice are used instead of three and each player gets three throws per turn instead of two. The game consists of 12 turns—one per category.
Another important difference is that each player may use only the result of his last throw. If he fails to improve on his first two throws that is bad luck, and he must put '0' on his card. As in Crag, he can stop throwing whenever he wants to.

SCORECARD FOR YACHT

CATEGORY	SCORE VALUE	PLAYER A	PLAYER B	PLAYER C
YACHT	50			
FOUR OF A KIND	Total spots			
FULL HOUSE	Total spots			
BIG STRAIGHT	30			
LITTLE STRAIGHT	15			
SIXES	Total of sixes			
FIVES	Total of fives			
FOURS	Total of fours			
THREES	Total of threes			
TWOS	Total of twos			
ONES	Total of ones			
CHOICE	Total spots			
TOTAL				

TABLE OF SCORE VALUES FOR YACHT

YACHT	Five of a kind scores 50 points
FOUR OF A KIND	Four of a kind scores the total number of spots shown
FULL HOUSE	Three of a kind play two of a kind, scores the total number of spots shown.
BIG STRAIGHT	1–2–3–4–5 or 2–3–4–5–6 scores 30 points
LITTLE STRAIGHT	1–2–3–4, 2–3–4–5 or 3–4–5–6 scores 15 points
NUMBERS 1–6	The spots on the dice in the number chosen determines the score. Two fours equals eight and so on.
CHOICE	If a player finishes a turn without being able–to fill in one of the above categories he may add up the total spots and insert it here under 'choice'

CONTINUED FROM PAGE 123

Should he throw a one his total score for that innings is wiped out and he must pass the dice to the next player. This also applies to the first throw. If he throws a one there is no score and the dice pass to the next player.

A player may choose to stop throwing at any time and pass the dice on to the next player. His total for that innings is marked on the combined scorecard. This total cannot be wiped out by a one in his next innings.

Each player continues to throw the dice, when he plays his innings, until he has achieved a total of 100 or more, depending on his last throw.

If a player throws two of a kind, he scores bonus points as follows:

1–1 is worth 25 points (the wipe-out does not apply in this case)
2–2 is worth 8 points
3–3 is worth 12 points
4–4 is worth 16 points
5–5 is worth 20 points
6–6 is worth 24 points

When all players have reached the 100 barrier, the one with the highest total wins.

Chuck-a-Luck
For 6–8 players

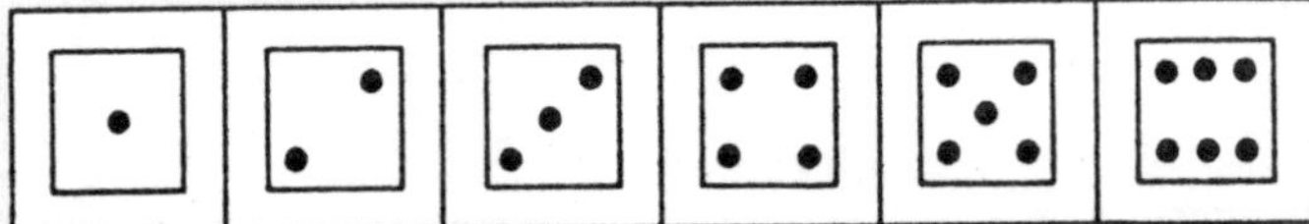

This is a simple form of roulette—and it's great fun. You need three dice, a cup and a paper playing area about 90 centimetres long, as shown in the diagram.

Each player is given an equal number of counters. A banker is chosen by throwing the dice for highest score.

Players bet as many counters as they wish on a number or numbers of their choice. When all bets have been placed the banker throws the three dice. Then he pays or collects according to the numbers he throws.

Any number that does not come up in his throw loses, and the banker collects all bets on those numbers.

If a number comes up once, he pays an amount equal to that staked on it; if it comes up twice, he pays double the stake; if it comes up three times, he pays three times the stake.

The banker changes after a number of rounds.

Dominoes
From China comes fascination in black and white

Domino pieces were designed in ancient China to represent all the throws with two dice. Consequently, Chinese dominoes had no blanks. The game as we know it today was not recorded in Britain until 1801, when it was described as a 'very childish game imported from France'.

The name is derived from the Spanish 'domino', a masquerade garment in black and white.

Early pieces were made of ebony with ivory faces and, although materials vary, domino pieces today are almost always black and white. The pieces are also known as 'bones', 'stones' or 'men'.

There are many variations of Dominoes but most games played with them share a common objective. This is to try to get rid of all one's own dominoes before an opponent or opponents can get rid of theirs.

In Dominoes, 'suit' and number mean the same thing. There are seven doubles: blank-blank; one-one; two-two; three-three; four-four; five-five and six-six. In addition, there are 21 dominoes with each end showing a different

denomination: for instance, six-five; four-one; three-blank. A domino with two different numbers belongs to two suits: a six-five, for example, belongs to both the six suit and the five suit. A double, since both ends are the same, belongs to one suit.
The dominoes are laid face down on the table and thoroughly mixed. Each player draws to determine who goes first, high winning, with the double six being highest. An appropriate number of dominoes is then drawn by each player to form his hand, the number varies depending on the game and the number of players. The remaining dominoes are kept face down in what is known as the 'boneyard'. A player conceals his hand from his opponents by standing his dominoes on end directly in front of him so that only he can see their values.

Matador
The lucky number is seven

As in Block Dominoes, all the dominoes are placed face down on the table. The players draw hands of seven each, if two are playing; five each when more than two play. Normally, the player holding the highest double opens, placing the double face up on the table as the foundation of a horizontal row.
Doubles are positioned end-to-end, and the other dominoes are placed at right-angles. Should no one hold a double, the highest two-suit domino is used to open play. Matador differs from other games in that the object is not to match suits but to make adjoining denominations add up to the value of seven. To play on a six-six, a player has to hold a domino one side of which is a one; in order to play upon a five, he has to have a domino showing a two, and so on.
The double blank is wild and is playable on any number. Dominoes with a face value of seven are also wild and may be played on any number. So there are six wild men—or 'Matadors'—in the game. Only the Matadors (or a double blank representing a seven-seven) may be played on a blank.
If a player cannot make a total of seven, he draws from the boneyard until he gets a domino that allows him to do so. However, the last two dominoes in the yard may not be taken. The first player to get rid of all his dominoes wins the total points held by his opponents. If the play is blocked all round, the low player wins the difference in points between him and his opponents.

Block Dominoes
When a player is stopped the call is 'go'

There are two players; each draws seven dominoes to form his hand. The winner of the draw for first play takes any domino from his hand and places it face up on the table. His opponent must follow suit; in other words, he must match with a number from his hand one of the ends of the domino on the board. For example, if the first domino is a five-five, any domino with a five at one end will do. Should the opponent hold, say, the five-one, he places it with the five end touching either end of the five-five. The first player then takes his second turn. Before him he sees two dominoes in a row; at one end of the row there is a five (the unplayed-on end of the five-five) and at the other end there is a one. Any domino with a five or a one at either end can now be played. When a double is played (in this case, a five-five), the next player, if he has two dominoes with a five on one end, may play a domino on each end.
The players take turns to build a row of dominoes across the table—the dominoes always linked by numbers of the same suit. If a player cannot follow suit, he calls out 'Go!' and his opponent can make another play. If the blocked player still cannot follow suit after this second play, he must again call 'Go!' continuing to do so for as long as he is blocked. When one player plays all his dominoes, the game ends. His opponent counts up the points on all the dominoes he still holds—the total

going to the winner as his score for that hand. In cases where both players are blocked, they each count up the points remaining in their hands. The one with the fewer points is the winner and collects the difference in points between the two hands. Fifty is generally set as the game-winning total. After each hand, the players draw new hands of seven from the boneyard and the loser of the previous hand begins play.

In *Draw Dominoes* the player who finds himself blocked must draw from the boneyard until he gets a playable domino. Two dominoes must stay in the boneyard; in other words, the drawing stops when only two bones remain in the yard.

Tiddley Wink is played by six to nine people. To start, each player draws three dominoes from the boneyard. No additional dominoes may be drawn. The first play is made by the player holding the highest double. Afterwards, each player must follow suit or pass, as in Block Dominoes. A domino may be placed only against the last domino played. When someone plays a double he may take another turn, if he can. The game continues until one of the players rids himself of his dominoes or play is blocked all round. The scoring is the same as in Matador.

All Fives

The formation is different but the skill is the same

This game is best played by two or three players, but it may be played by five. All aspects of the game are the same as in Block Dominoes. However, even when he can follow suit, a player may, instead, pass his turn and draw one domino from the boneyard to improve his hand. At the start in a two-player game, each draws seven dominoes; when more than two play, each draws five. The first move is made by the player holding the highest double, which he places face up on the table. Should no one have a double, the players take turns drawing from the boneyard until someone gets one.

All Fives differs from ordinary Dominoes in that points can be scored during the game. The initial double is built upon both at the ends and the sides, resulting in a cross formation with four ends, rather than the two of a simple horizontal row. However, all doubles after the first may be built upon only at their sides. Should a player place a domino that makes the outside numbers in all four arms of the cross total a sum divisible by five—such as 15, 20, 25—he receives that number of points.

The rule governing the matching of suits in ordinary dominoes also applies in All Fives—that is, a two can only be played on a two, a blank only on a blank, a six only on to a six, and so on.

As in Block Dominoes, the first player to get rid of all dominoes in his hand collects all the points still held by his opponent—but rounded off to the nearest five. For instance, if an opponent holds 13, 14, 16 or 17 points, the score is written as 15. If the play is blocked the low player subtracts his points from those of the high player—again rounding off his score to the nearest five. Points scored during play are added to those received for getting rid of all dominoes. Generally, the game is 100 points. After the game, the dominoes are collected, mixed and a new hand is drawn.

Sebastopol

Six the suit to follow

Four players; each draws seven dominoes from the boneyard. The opening play is made by the person holding the six-six. The person to his left is next and play continues clockwise around the table. After the six-six is set in place, the next four plays must also be of the six suit. A person not holding a domino of the six suit must pass his turn. The four plays are made end-to-end with the double and at right-angles on either side of the double—so that the initial formation is a four-pronged cross consisting of five dominoes of the six suit.

The game proceeds with the players following suit as in Block Dominoes, but building outwards upon the four arms of the cross. A player who first gets rid of his dominoes collects from the other players all points remaining in their hands. If all players are blocked, the one with fewest points collects the difference from each of his opponents.

Bergen
In quest of a scoring match

This is best played by two people but it is also a good game for three. The first play is decided by a draw, with the highest number winning. Each player starts with six dominoes drawn face down from the boneyard. When a player cannot follow suit he must draw from the boneyard until able to play. When the boneyard gets down to two bones, no more may be drawn. The dominoes are placed end-to-end in a horizontal line. Inside this line, the doubles are positioned at right-angles to the other dominoes. These inside doubles may only be played upon, horizontally, at their sides, not their ends. The object is to make the number at one end of the row match the number at the other end of the row. For doing this with a two-suit domino the player receives two points. He receives three points if he accomplishes a match by using a double from his hand or if he can make a match against a double already at the opposite end of the row. The first player to get rid of his dominoes scores one point; should play be blocked for everyone, the one with the fewest points remaining in his hand scores one point. In the latter case, though, the low player must not hold a double. If he does, the high player receives the point, providing that he also has no doubles. After each hand, the dominoes are mixed face down and the draw commences for a new hand. The winning total is 15 points.

THE FASCINATION OF CARD GAMES

Playing cards were introduced to Europe from China in the 13th century, but their origin is much earlier than that.

They evolved from the sacred arrows used by primitive man to foretell the future. A tribal soothsayer would cast the arrows on the ground and divine from the pattern they formed when they fell what the future held.

In the course of time the shafts of the arrows were decorated in various ways and the decorations were used in the fortune telling.

It was in this way that the decorations became indications of value and the next step was to use the decorations in guessing or gambling games.

Slim strips of oiled paper took the place of the arrows, one side showing the value, the other bearing a design in the shape of an arrow feather. The playing card was on its way.

Cards produced in China as early as the 11th century were decorated with figures bearing a striking resemblance to the figures on present-day picture cards.

The first card games in Europe were played in Italy. There were 36 cards in the earliest Italian pack, and from this game developed 'tarots' with a pack consisting of 78 cards in four suits, identified by emblems of cups or chalices, swords, money, and batons or clubs. In each suit there were four court cards, a king, queen, chevalier or knight, and a valet, and numerals 1–10. The additional cards were made up of a joker and 21 'atous' numbered 1–21. The tarot designs are still used in Italy and Spain.

In Germany the four suits are represented by hearts, acorns, bells and leaves in a pack of 32 cards.

Cards were introduced into Britain in the middle of the 15th century. The authorities at first frowned upon them, and in 1464 a regulation was made forbidding their import. Eventually, cards were reluctantly accepted, and the 52 card pack as we know it today was evolved in Britain and France. James I, however, also frowned on playing cards and imposed a tax on them.

Card Players' Terms and their Meanings

Ace A card with a single mark or spot. It counts as one (low) or as the card with the highest rank (high).
Chip in Contribute chips or counters to a pool.
Cut Take a stack of cards off the top of the deck. This is usually done by a player to the dealer's right, before the deal, as a safeguard against cheating.
Deal Distribute cards to players. Usually in a clockwise direction, one at a time to each player.
Denomination The number or face (king, queen and jack) on a card.
Deuce The two of any suit.
Discard To get rid of a card as part of the play.
Discard pile Cards disposed of and no longer required in play.
Picture cards or Court cards King, queen, jack of any suit.
Follow suit To play a card of the same suit as played by first player.
Foundation or Lay-out Formation of cards as laid out in Patience.
Go out When all cards have been played and no cards are left in the hand—usually when the object of the game, such as in Rummy, is to be the first to get rid of all cards to become the winner.
Hand The number of cards dealt to a player.
Joker A card that can represent any other card, as stipulated by a player.
Kitty or Pool or Pot Counters or chips or money contributed to by all the players—to be won by the winning player.
Lead Play the first card in a round of hands.
Meld Cards placed down on the table in combinations acceptable to earn points.
Pairs Two cards of the same denomination.
Pass When no suitable play is possible the opportunity to play a card is declined.
Run Three or four cards in sequence.
Stock A pile of cards in the centre of the table from which cards are drawn by players when their turns come round.
Suit The markings on a card determine the group to which it belongs. The four suits are spades, hearts, clubs and diamonds. Each suit is made up of 13 cards: Ace 2 3 4 5 6 7 8 9 10 jack, queen, king. A full deck of cards has 52 cards plus a joker.
Trick Cards played in turn by each player and won by the highest ranking card, or in some cases the last card.
Trump Highest ranking suit usually determined by a card turned over after the completed deal. Sometimes it is named by one of the players. In games where there is a trump suit the trump cards outrank other cards.
Wild A wild card enables its owner to declare it as any value of card that he decides.

CARD GAMES FOR YOUNGER PLAYERS

Card games such as Old Maid and Snap are great fun for young children and they can be a good introduction to adult card games such as Whist (see p. 136).

Old Maid
For 2–8 players

This is one of the most popular card games for children and in many cases is the first card game a child is taught to play. It combines the interest of collecting pairs with the excitement of trying to avoid being the 'Old Maid'.
Remove a queen from the pack, then shuffle the cards and deal them out one at a time to each player. To begin with, each player sorts his cards into pairs—two nines, two threes, and so on—and places his pairs face down on the table in front of him. The dealer then turns to the player on his left and holds up his cards in a fan so that their faces cannot be seen. The

player on the left takes one. If this card gives him a pair he places it face down on the table in front of him and is entitled to take another from the dealer. If it does not give him a pair he turns to the player on his left and proffers his hand in the same way. This continues round and round the table until all the cards are paired. But because one queen has been removed from the pack there will be one queen in play which cannot be paired, and the player left with it in his hand is the 'Old Maid'.

Naturally, if you have an odd queen in your hand you are most anxious to get rid of it, and much of the fun in the game comes from trying to bluff your left-hand neighbour into taking it. Sometimes this is done by raising it slightly above the level of the rest so that it is easier to pick, sometimes by moving it to the side of your hand in a very obvious way so as to make the other player think you don't want to lose it.

An often-played development of the game is to remove the queen of clubs and rule that all pairs must be of the same colour, red or black, such as the five of hearts and the five of diamonds, the jack of spades and the jack of clubs. This means that everyone knows from the start that the queen of spades is the 'Old Maid' because the matching black queen, the queen of clubs, has been removed and the excitement of trying to get rid of it causes great amusement.

Go and Fish
For 2–5 players

There is a lot of luck in this game but it is also a test of memory. The object is to collect the most pairs.

The pack is shuffled and six cards are dealt one at a time to each player. The remaining cards are placed face down in a stack in the middle of the table. Players hold their cards in a fan so that the others cannot see them. The player on the left of the dealer begins the game by asking the player on his left for a card which would make a pair with one of the cards in his hand. If the player on the left has the card he must hand it over, and the one who asked for it puts the pair he has formed face down on the table in front of him and may ask again.

If the player who is asked does not have the card he says 'Go and Fish', and the questioner must take a card from the top of the stack in the middle of the table. If by chance he gets the card he wanted from the stack he says 'I fished upon my wish', puts his pair on the table and is entitled to ask again.

If he does not get the card he wanted, it is the next player's turn.

Snap
For 3–6 players

This is a great favourite with the younger ones. It is fast, exciting and noisy. The object is to win all the cards.

The cards are dealt one at a time to each player. Shuffling is an unnecessary refinement and it does not matter if the deal is uneven.

The players put their cards face down in stacks in front of them. In order, going left, each player turns up his top card and puts it face up beside his stack. This is done at high speed and means that each player is building a second stack, this time face up. Whenever two players turn up a pair of matching cards—two kings, two fours, for instance—the first player to shout 'Snap' collects the face-up stack affected and puts them at the bottom of his face-down stack.

The game goes merrily on until someone has collected all the cards.

Lottery
For 5 or more players

This is a game for the quick-witted and could be described as Pontoon for the unsophisticated. Two packs of cards are needed and plastic counters to be used as 'stakes'. The counters are sold in sets by stores and toy shops. The first dealer deals one card from his pack face down to each player including himself. Each player then stakes a previously agreed number of counters on his card.

With up to eight players, the minimum number of counters staked by each player each time must be equal to the number of players—for example, if there are five players the stake must be five counters. With more than eight players, the minimum number of counters staked by each player each time must be eight. This means that there will be enough counters on the table each time for the winners to collect in the event of a shared win.

When the counters have been staked, the second dealer deals one card from his pack to each player face up. Then the fun begins.

Each player turns up his face-down card so that everybody can see all the cards. The cards are placed by each player in such a way as to make it clear which ones had been face down—say, face-down cards on the player's left.

If a player holds a face-down card that matches any face-up card in value he wins the counters staked by the holder of the face-up card.

If there is more than one winner, the counters are divided between them.

If the cards match in colour as well, the holder of the face-up card must hand over an extra counter to the holder of the face-down one.

If a player's face-down card matches his own face-up card he collects a counter from each of the other players and retains his own stake. Any counters which are not collected are left on the table and become an 'extra' to the new stake the player makes in the next deal. The game continues in this way until some heavy loser suggests something else.

Red and Black
For 2 players

The cards are not dealt in this game, they are divided between the two players in this way: One player takes the pack, face down, and holds up each card with its back to his opponent and the opponent has to guess if it is red or black. If he guesses correctly he gets the card, if he is wrong the player with the pack keeps it. Each player then puts his cards in a stack face down in front of him and the game proper begins.

The player who was the guesser places a card from his stack face up on the table. The other puts a card face up beside it and each plays in turn until a card appears that matches the original card in value. The player of the matching card collects the lot and play starts again.

The game continues until one of the players has all the cards.

Slap Jack
For 2–5 players

Quickness of the eye and hand is called for in this game. The object is to win all the cards.

The pack is shuffled and dealt one at a time to each player. It does not matter if the deal does not work out evenly. Each player places his cards in a stack face down in front of him.

The player on the dealer's left begins the game by placing one of his cards, as quickly as he can, face up in the middle of the table. The next player on his left quickly adds another and so on around the table. Whenever a jack appears the first player to slap his hand over it wins all the cards in the middle and places them face down under his stack.

If a player loses all his cards he stays in the game and tries to collect more cards by being the first to slap the jack.

War
For 2 players

In this game the value of the cards ranges from the ace down to the two. The object is to win all the cards.

After the shuffle the cards are dealt evenly between the two players and placed face down in two equal stacks. The players begin the game together. Each turns up his top card and places it face up beside his stack. The player with the higher card takes both and puts them face down under his stack. If the players turn up cards of equal value – then war breaks out. Both players say 'W' and turn up another card; 'A' and turn up another; 'R' and turn up a third. Then they call out 'War!' and turn up a fourth. The player who turns up the higher fourth card takes the lot and adds them face down to the bottom of his stack. If the fourth cards are equal the War game is played again until somebody wins. The game goes on until one player has all the cards.

In *Triple War* three players are each dealt 17 cards and the odd card is discarded. The three players turn up their top cards and the one with the high card takes all three, placing them at the bottom of his stack. If all three cards turned up have the same value, the players wage war as in War. If two cards match and the third card is higher, the holder of the third card wins all three. If the two matching cards are higher than the third, the players whose cards match wage war, the winner taking all the cards including the third player's card.

Go Boom
For 2–12 players

If more than six players take part, two packs are used. The object is to get rid of all your cards. The value of the cards ranges from the ace down to the two.

Each player is dealt seven cards one at a time and the remainder are placed in a stack face down in the middle of the table. Play begins with the player on the left of the dealer who leads any card. Each player must follow with a card of the same suit or the same value as the last one played.

If a player cannot do this he must draw cards one at a time from the stack in the middle until he gets a card he can play.

If he draws all the cards in the stack and still cannot play, the next player takes his turn. In this case, with the middle stack gone, each player must either play or pass. The player of the highest card of the suit which was led wins the trick and leads the next one.

When somebody gets rid of all his cards he says 'Boom'.

Bow to the King
For 2–5 players

This is a particularly charming game, involving a ritual of actions and words which must be followed. The object is to win all the cards.

The cards are shuffled and dealt one at a time to each player. It does not matter if the deal does not work out evenly. Each player makes a stack of his cards face down. The player on the dealer's left begins the game by placing the top card from his stack face up in the middle of the table. The next player on his left does the same, and so on. All the moves are made quickly.

This is how cards are won: When a king appears all the players must greet him with a bow and the first to do so wins the cards in the middle; when a queen appears they all say 'Good morning, Madam'; when a jack appears the players say 'How do you do, Sir?'; when an ace appears it is slapped. In each case the first player to follow the ritual wins the cards in the middle and puts them face down under his stack. Anyone who gives an incorrect greeting must forfeit a card to whoever played the last one. The game ends when somebody has won all the cards.

Stinker
For 2–6 players

This one is great fun and needs no card-playing skill. It is a matter of playing *with* cards not *at* cards.

Remove five cards from the pack and spread the rest over the table so that they overlap. The surface at the middle of the spread should be as even as possible because that is where you make a house with the five cards you removed from the pack. Do this by leaning two

of them together like a tent, add one more to each end and put the fifth on the top of these last two cards. The fun usually starts when the house is being built. It is not easy to do and it is best to play this game with an old pack because old cards are not so slippery. Once the house is up, players take turns to slide a card from the spread without making the house fall down.
The first to cause the house to fall is the 'Stinker'.

Flashlight
For 4–7 players

The object of this game is to be the first to collect seven cards all of the same suit.
After the pack is shuffled, seven cards are dealt one at a time to each player. The rest of the pack is not used. The cards are held in the shape of a fan so that other players cannot see them. The dealer begins the game by selecting a card he does not want and placing it face down on the table in front of the player on his left. Before that player may pick it up he too must choose a card from his hand and place it face down in front of the player on his left, and so on round the table. It is a game of continuous movement with the players quickly discarding and picking up cards. When a player collects seven cards of the same suit he calls out 'Flashlight!' and the game ends.

Authors
For 3–5 players

This is a game in which a good memory is a great help. The object is to collect the largest number of 'books', that is sets of four cards of the same denomination. The cards are shuffled and dealt two at a time to each player. All the cards are used and it does not matter if the deal does not work out evenly.
The player on the dealer's left begins. He asks any player around the table for a card that will help him to build up a set of four. For instance, if he holds a ten of diamonds, he asks for any of the other tens, and so on. If the player asked has the card he must hand it over, and the questioner has another turn. If he does not get the card he asked for, it is the turn of the next player on the left. When a player collects four cards of the same denomination he lays them face down on the table in front of him. This counts as a 'book'. When all the cards have been laid down the player with the most 'books' wins.

May I?
For 3–5 players

This is a game for very polite players, as you will see. The object is to collect sets of four cards of the same value. The cards are shuffled and dealt two at a time to each player. All the cards are used and it does not matter if the deal does not work out evenly. The players arrange their cards in a fan with those of the same value grouped together.
The player on the dealer's left begins the game by asking any other player for a card he wants. He must say 'May I have the two of diamonds?' (or whatever card he wants). If he does not use those exact words he must offer his cards so that the faces cannot be seen, and the other player chooses and keeps one of them.
If the other player has the card requested he must say 'Yes you may', and hand it over. If he gets the words wrong he must pay the same penalty as above.
The questioner accepts the card and says 'Thank you' and takes another turn. If he doesn't say 'Thank you' he must give the card back together with all others of the same value in his hand.
If the asked player hasn't the card requested he must say 'No you may not. You may have the —— of ——' (naming a card he wants to get rid of). Should the questioner hold a card of the named value he must accept it and say 'Thank you' and take another turn. (If he does not say 'Thank you' he must hand the card back together with all other cards he has of

the same value.) If he does not hold a card of the named value he must say 'No thank you' (or offer his cards as above), and it is the turn of the next player.
As soon as a player collects a set of four cards of the same value he lays them face down in front of him, and when all the cards have been laid down the player with the most sets is the winner.

Havana
For 4 or more players

This is a most amusing game of chance and certain preparations have to be made before play can start. First, all the players are given an equal number of plastic counters to bet with. Then a banker is chosen. The banker gives each player a previously prepared place card on which each square is large enough to take a counter—like this:

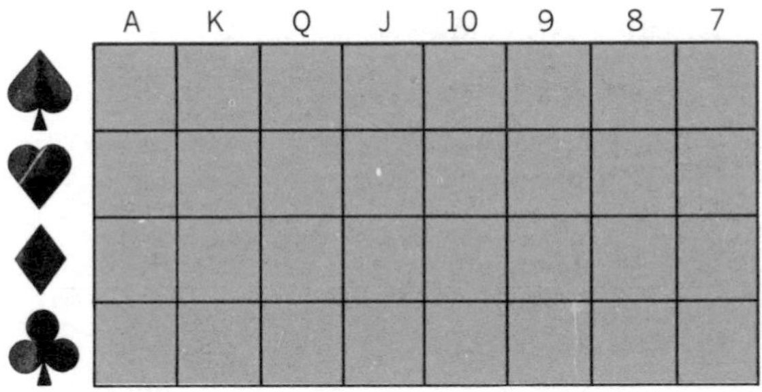

The banker then prepares the pack. He uses 33 cards, the ace, king, queen, jack, ten, nine, eight, seven of each suit—plus one joker. He shuffles and lays out four rows of eight cards face down in the same pattern as the place cards. This uses up 32 of his 33 cards and he puts the extra one face down on one side of the pattern he has made. Then he calls for bets to be placed.
Each square in the place cards represents a certain card—for instance, the top left square is the ace of spades, the bottom right square the seven of clubs, and so on. The players bet on the chance that the cards laid out by the dealer in the same pattern as the place cards will fall in the appropriate squares, and they place their counters accordingly. They may bet on single squares, they may put counters in a group on vertical columns or on horizontal rows.
When all bets have been placed, the banker turns up the extra card, the one he placed at the side of the pattern, and puts it on its appropriate square. For example, if the extra card turns out to be the seven of spades he puts it on the top right-hand square and pays out all bets which had been placed on that square. He then takes the card that was face down on that square and transfers it to its appropriate square and pays out all bets that were placed there. He continues in this way until he turns up the joker. This ends the game and the banker collects all the counters that are still on the place cards.
This is how he pays out the winning bets: On any single successful square he pays the amount staked. On a successful vertical column he pays four times the amount staked and on a successful horizontal row he pays eight times the amount staked. If it happens that the extra card, the 33rd card at the side of the pattern, turns out to be the joker, the banker collects all the counters staked without further ado.

Bango
For 2–10 players

As the name might suggest, this game is not dissimilar to Bingo and is just as much fun. Two packs of cards are needed, each with a different design on the back. Each player should have a number of plastic counters. One player is chosen to be caller, another to be dealer, each with a separate pack.
The dealer distributes five cards one at a time to each player who arranges them in a line, face up in front of him. The caller holds his pack face down and takes a card from the top. He calls out its suit and value and any player

who has that card in his face-up line places a counter on it. The first player to place a counter on all his face-up cards calls 'Bango' and is the winner.
All the cards are then reshuffled and another game starts.

Stop and Go
For 3–6 players

This game is a simple matter of following suit in sequence but as not all the cards are used it is not so easy as it seems. This is how the cards are dealt: For three players, 15 each; for four players, 12 each; for five players, nine each; for six players, eight each. The remainder are not used and are called the stop pile.
The player on the dealer's left begins by leading any card he wishes. The next player must follow with a card of the same suit in sequence upwards. The ace is the lowest in value.
In other words, if the card led is the six of spades, the next player must play the seven of spades. If he does not hold a suitable card he must say 'Pass' and it is the turn of the next player. The game continues until either there is no suitable card (because it is in the stop pile) or until someone plays a king.
In either case the player of the last card leads again and the game continues until one player has got rid of all his cards—and he is the winner.

Twenty-nine
For 2–8 players

It is a help to be good at simple mental arithmetic for this one. A standard pack is used but cards (the tens) are removed to make the pack divide evenly among the players. For two or four players use all 52 cards; for three players remove one ten; for five players remove two tens; for six or eight players remove four tens; for seven players remove three tens. The ace is low in this game which means that it counts as one, picture cards count as ten and the other cards are worth their face value.
The dealer shuffles the cards and distributes them one at a time to each player in a clockwise direction. The player on his left leads any card he wishes on the table in front of him and calls out its value. Thereafter, the aim of each player in turn is to play a card that will bring the total value of the cards played to 29 exactly. It is not necessary to follow suit.
The player whose turn it is must play if he has a card that makes a total of 29 or under, but he is not allowed to play a card that would bring the total to more than 29. In that case he says 'Pass', and it is the turn of the next person on his left.
The first player to bring the total to 29 wins the trick and leads again. The winner of each trick scores one point and the first to reach an agreed total of points is the winner.

Newmarket
For 3–8 players

For this fast and exciting game, ideal for a family gathering or a small party, you need a pack of cards plus an ace, king, queen and jack of different suits from another pack. These four cards are the horses and are placed in the centre of the table. Each player has an equal supply of counters.
The game begins with the betting. Each player may stake four counters any way he likes on the horses, all four on one, or one on each, and so on.
The object of the game is to play a card that matches any of the horses. Whoever plays such a card collects all the counters placed on the respective horse.
When the betting is over, the dealer distributes the cards one at a time to each player and to himself. He also deals an extra hand to himself just as if there was another player sitting beside him. It does not matter if the cards do not divide evenly.

All the players examine their hands and if the dealer decides to play his own hand—a decision he must make without looking at what the extra hand contains—he auctions his extra hand which goes to the player who bids the highest number of counters. The player who buys the extra hand discards his own. If the dealer decides to play his extra hand, he discards his own hand and there is no auction.
The game proper is started by the player on the dealer's left. He leads a card of any suit, but it must be the lowest card of that suit which he holds in his hand. The next highest card of that suit is played by whoever has it and so on until the ace—which in Newmarket is the highest card—is played. Whoever plays the ace restarts the game by leading another card which must be of a different suit and colour to the previous suit played. If he is unable to do this, the lead passes to the player on his left.
During the game, if nobody can play the next highest card to the last one played a 'stop' has been reached and the last person to play leads another card as above. A 'stop' is reached when the card needed is in the discarded hand or has been played already.
If someone gets rid of all his cards before any or all of the horses have been played he collects a counter from each of the other players and the round comes to an end. The uncollected bets remain on the horses and new bets are made before the next round begins. This greatly adds to the excitement as it is possible for quite a large number of counters to be placed on any particular horse.

Thumbs Down
For 3 or more players

This game is unusual in that the object is to find a loser, not a winner. If three are playing, only the four kings, four queens, four jacks and the ace of spades are used. For each additional player a further set is added, for example four tens or four threes. This means that after the cards have been dealt the player on the dealer's left will have one more than anybody else. The object of the game is to collect sets of four of a kind. The selected cards are shuffled and dealt, those not dealt are placed face down in a stack in the middle of the table.
The player on the dealer's left begins by passing a card he does not want, face down, to the player on his left. That player picks it up and decides what he wants to pass on. He may pass on the card he picked up unless it is the ace of spades. If he picks that card up he must keep it, he can only pass it on if it was in his hand in the first place. The game continues until one player has collected four of a kind and as soon as he does he makes the 'thumbs down' sign. The other players must immediately copy this sign and the last player to do so must pick up the top card from the stack in the middle and the value of that card decides the number of penalty points he has earned. These penalty points are noted down and the cards are dealt again. When a player has 25 or more penalty points the game ends and he is the loser.

Pig
For 3–6 players

From three to six children can play this game. A pack is prepared with four cards of a kind for each player. If there are five players the pack has 20 cards—four aces, four kings, four queens, four jacks and four tens. The pack is shuffled and dealt, each player receiving four cards.
The aim is to get four cards of a kind or to notice when some other player gets four of a kind. Each player looks at his own hand and passes an unwanted card, face down, to the player on his left. This continues until one player collects four cards of a kind. The successful player then stops passing and puts his forefinger on his nose. As soon as another player notices, he stops passing and also puts his finger on his nose. The last player to realise what is happening and to put his finger

on his nose is christened the 'pig'.
In *Donkey* any player who gets four of a kind instead of placing his finger on his nose simply places the cards face down on the table. As other players notice what he is doing, they do the same. The last player to put his cards on the table becomes the 'donkey'.

Seven of a Kind
For 3–5 players

Three, four or five players can play this game. For three players make a pack of 21 cards with seven cards in each of three suits (hearts, diamonds, spades); for four players, a pack of 28 cards with seven cards in each of the four suits; for five players a pack of 35 cards with nine cards in three of the suits and eight in the fourth. The pack is shuffled and seven cards are dealt to each player.
One at a time, each player passes a card to the player on his left and the first to collect seven cards of one suit wins.
Players quickly learn to keep those cards that look as if they might develop into useful suits, while passing along cards from other suits.

Earl of Coventry
For 3 or more players

After being shuffled and cut, the cards are dealt one at a time. Any number can play and the hands need not be equal.
The player to the dealer's left puts any card, face up, on the table announcing: 'There's as good an ace (or whatever it is) as can be.' If the player to his left has a card of the same denomination, he lays it down saying: 'There's one as good as he.' If he does not, the next player to the left has a chance to play.
Going around the table, the holder of the third card plays it, saying: 'There's the best of three.' The holder of the fourth card then plays, announcing: 'There's the Earl of Coventry.' The player of the fourth card then starts the game again. The game continues until a player gets rid of all his cards.

Concentration
For 2 or more players

This game tests alertness and memory. The cards are spread over the table face down and each player, in order left to right, turns up two cards. If they are the same, such as two fives or two jacks, he keeps them, making a pile in front of him. He then is given a second turn. If he does not turn up a pair he turns the cards face down again, leaving them in the same spot. The next player takes a turn and the action continues until all the cards have been collected.
The skill in the game is to remember what cards were turned up and where they are. This becomes easier as fewer cards are left. The winner is the player with most cards at the end.

CARD GAMES FOR ALL THE FAMILY

Card games are among the most absorbing of pastimes.
The games that follow can be played with great satisfaction by people of all ages. They are also designed to stimulate the developing mind, sharpen the wits and to achieve the satisfaction of competition in a quiet atmosphere.
Some of the games have given pleasure for centuries. Whist, for example, was developed in the early 17th century from games such as Ombre and Triumph. It derives its name from the Cornish *huist,* meaning 'silence'—due to the concentration demanded by the players.

Whist
A game of concentration

This is a game for four playing in two teams. The ace is high, having more value than any other card. The object is to win as many tricks as possible.

Players first cut for partners; the two highest play the two lowest. Partners sit opposite each other and cut for deal. The high card wins.
The dealer distributes the cards, clockwise, starting with the player on his left. He turns up the last card he deals to himself to determine the trump suit.
Players arrange their hands in suits, paying particular attention to the trump suit. The ace, king, queen, jack of trumps are called 'honours' and they figure in the scoring.
The player on the dealer's left leads any card he wishes and the game begins. The others play in turn, clockwise. They must follow suit, that is play a card of the suit that is led. If they haven't a card of the suit that is led they may trump if they wish. The winner of the trick is the one who plays the highest card of the suit led or the highest trump.

The dealer faces up the final card dealt to himself to determine the trump suit. The ace, king, queen, jack of trumps are called 'honours'.

The winner of the trick leads a card to continue the game until all 13 tricks have been won. Both teams then count their score. The first six tricks taken are called a 'book' and score no points. With every trick taken over six, a team scores a point. To these points the honours are added. If one team has held all of them, the ace, king, queen, jack of trumps, it scores four points. If it holds three, it scores two points and if the honours are divided equally no points are scored.
The cards are then shuffled and dealt again, by the player on the first dealer's left. The game goes on until an agreed total of points is reached.

The last card to be played was the ace of clubs. As the highest-ranking card of the suit that was led, it takes this trick. All players had clubs, so nobody could play a trump card.

Six tricks, each with a card from every player, make up what is called a 'book'. With diamonds the trump suit, the trick at the bottom right has been won because the player had no clubs and played the eight of diamonds.

Rummy

One of the most popular of all the card games

This is the basic and most popular form of the game. Two to six people may play. The ace is low, that is it counts as one.

The cards are shuffled. In the cut for deal, the low card wins: the next lowest gets first choice of seating position with respect to the dealer and the third lowest, second choice of seat, and so on.

The dealer distributes the cards, one at a time, clockwise, beginning with the player on his left or his opponent in a two-handed game. If two are playing, each receives ten cards, if three play, seven; if four or more, six. After the deal, the remainder of the pack is placed, face down, in the centre of the table as a stock; its top card is turned up beside it, beginning the discard pile.

The player on the dealer's left begins. He may draw either the top card from the stock or the face-up card. He adds this card to his hand and he inspects his hand for combinations called 'melds'—three or more cards of the same denomination or a sequence of three or more cards in the same suit, such as the ace, two and three of hearts. Such combinations are put on the table face up in front of the player. In addition to these melds, a player may put a single card on an opponent's meld. A fourth jack, for example, might be played on someone else's three jacks; a four or an eight of hearts on a five, six, seven of that suit. Only a single meld of any type is permitted per turn.

Once the player lays down his meld—or cannot play—he must discard one card from his hand on the discard pile. Each player draws either the top card from the stock or the top card from the discard pile. If the stock runs out, the discard pile is shuffled, placed face down as a new stock and the top card turned up.

When one player empties his hand by melding his last remaining cards or by melding and discarding his last card, play stops. The winner of the hand receives points for all the cards still held by his opponents—picture cards counting ten, aces one and the other cards their face value. The score is marked on a pad, the cards reshuffled and the deal passes to the left for the next hand. Game is usually set at 150 points.

Knock Rummy differs from standard Rummy in that a player avoids melding until he thinks he can catch his opponents holding a higher sum of points than he holds in unmatched cards. Suppose all cards in a player's hand except one, say a three of hearts, can be melded; he holds only three unmatched points. After his draw and discard, he knocks on the table, exposing his hand for others to see. If no other player holds as few points, the player who knocks collects from each opponent the difference between their unmatched points and his. Should someone else have fewer points, or an equal number, that player wins the hand—collecting points from the others, as described above, and a bonus of ten points from the knocker as well.

In *500 Rummy* a player may draw from the discard pile all the way down to a card that he intends to meld in the same turn. He must take all the cards above it as well. The discard pile must be arranged so that all cards are at least partly visible.

Remember, the card stopped at must be used as part of a meld in that same turn. It need not necessarily be used to make a new combination. It may be added to a sequence or combination already melded by the player, or it may be added to match another player's meld. In the last case, the card is melded face up among the player's own exposed cards—not with the other player's melded cards.

Thus, sequences can be continued by more than one player. For example, should someone meld a sequence of ace, two, three and four of hearts, someone else may meld the five, and still another person may lay down the six. Sequences may also run in descending numerical order. No card can be played until after the appearance of the card immediately before it in the series.

Besides being able to draw more than one card from the discard pile, the other big difference

In 500 Rummy, a player wanting to make a meld with the king in the discard pile must add all the cards on top of the king to his hand.

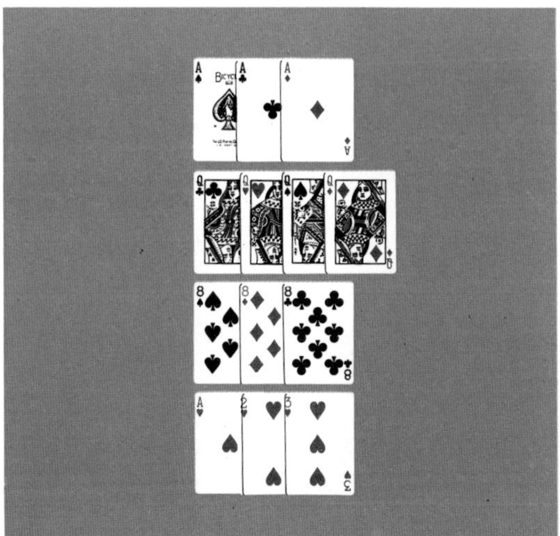

Each of these typical melds from a 500 Rummy hand carries a points value of its own. An account is kept on a scorecard, and the value of points is given below.

between 500 Rummy and Rummy is that, in 500 Rummy, points are awarded for the melds. A running account is kept on the score pad as players, in turn, lay down their melds. Each card of a combination is counted into the total as follows; ace is worth 15 unless melded in an ace, two, three sequence when it counts as one; picture cards are worth ten; all other cards are worth their numerical value. When ridding his hand of all cards a player calls out 'Rummy!', and play stops. The others are caught with cards in their hands, for which he collects points as valued above. The players still holding cards must subtract these points from the totals they have accumulated.

When more than four people play 500 Rummy, a double pack of 104 cards is used—each player receiving nine cards. When four or fewer play, one 52-card pack is used—with each player receiving seven cards in a four-handed game, eight cards in a three-handed game or nine cards when two play.

In *Michigan Rummy* a player may lay down as many melds as he wishes at any turn; also, if a card is discarded that will play upon a meld exposed on the table, the first player who notices may call out 'Stop!' He may then pick up the card, play it and receive points—without regard to following in turn.

Gin Rummy

Gin means trap in a game which gives hours of pleasure

A game for two, using a standard 52-card pack. Each player tries to arrange his hand into combinations and outscore his opponent. In counting, the ace equals one; picture cards equal ten each; the rest follow their numerical value. In the cut for deal, low card wins.

The dealer, beginning with his opponent, distributes the cards, one at a time, face down. In the most popular form of the game, he deals 11 cards to his opponent and ten to himself. He puts the remainder of the pack, face down, in the centre of the table as the stock.

The dealer's opponent starts by placing a card from his hand face up beside the stock (reducing the number of cards in his hand to ten). The dealer then either picks up the card played by his opponent or draws the top card from the stock. He discards one card, face up, on the pile of discards forming beside the stock. Only the top card may be taken from the discard pile and only this card should be visible.

Each player tries to arrange his cards into combinations. These are three of a kind, four of a kind or a numerical sequence of three or more cards of the same suit. If a player can arrange all his cards into combinations leaving one to discard, he calls 'Gin!' Then he exposes his hand on the table, winning a bonus of 20 points. He also receives points for every card not in a combination held by his opponent according to face value. Game is 100 points.

A player need not wait for a perfect Gin before exposing his cards. Any time his odd cards total ten points or less he may 'knock'—that is, rap the table and expose his hand. When a player knocks he is gambling that he holds fewer odd points than his opponent. If so he takes the difference. But his opponent may 'lay off', put odd cards into his combinations. For example, if the dealer knocks with three kings, three jacks, four, five, six of diamonds and an odd ace, and his opponent holds an odd king, an odd jack and a seven and eight of diamonds, he may put all these cards into the dealer's exposed hand, reducing the odd points in his hand. If the opponent's hand contains the same number, or fewer, odd points, he takes a bonus of ten from the player who knocked, as well as the difference in points.

In a variation of the game, hands of ten cards are dealt to each player. To begin the discard pile, the top card of the stock is turned up. If this card is a spade, the points totals for the hand are doubled. The denomination of the turned-up card sets a limit for knocking. For instance, if it is a six, a player must hold six or fewer points in odd cards in order to knock.

In *Around the Corner*, the ace may be either low or high, and may be used in around-the-corner sequences such as queen, king, ace, two, three, or king, ace, two. When a player knocks, the other may lay off cards as in Gin Rummy. All the cards in the discard pile may be inspected at any time. Odd aces in the hand are valued at 15 points. Game is 125 points.

Eights

Follow suit, follow number but don't forget what's wild

This game is played by two players or four in two teams. Each player or team attempts to be first to play all the cards in his hand.

Eights are wild. Other cards have their face value. The king is high, the ace low. The cards are shuffled and cut. The high card wins the deal.

The dealer distributes cards, one at a time, clockwise from his left. When two play, each receives seven cards; if there are four players each receives five cards. After the deal, the remaining cards are put face down on the table as a stock.

The top card of the stock is turned up as the 'starter'.

The player on the dealer's left begins by placing on top of the starter a card either of the same suit or of the same denomination.

Should the starter be the king of diamonds, any diamond or any other king can be played on it.

Since eights are wild cards, an eight may also be played. The player of the eight names the suit he wishes his card to represent.

The denominational value of the eight is that of the card on which it has been laid.

Here, in the game of Eights, the last card in the discard row is the two of spades. Another two, another spade or a wild eight may be played on it.

Play moves clockwise around the table. If a player has a card that can be played, he must play it. After playing, he may draw a single card from the top of the stock if he chooses. If he cannot play, he must draw from the stock until he gets a card that is playable. Once the stock is finished, anyone who cannot play forfeits his turn to the player on his left. The player (or team) to get rid of all cards first wins the hand. The winner collects points as follows: For each eight still held by opponents, 50 points; for each picture card, ten points; for each ace, one point; for all other cards, their numerical value. The winning total is usually set at 100 points. If the stock is finished and no one can play, the game ends in a 'block'. The hands are then put face up on the table and the player (or team) with the lowest number of points wins.

Pontoon
A skilful and amusing way to take a chance

This is a game for two to ten players using an ordinary 52-card pack. Each player tries to draw a hand with a higher points total than the dealer's without exceeding 21 points. Players are given counters or matchsticks with which to 'gamble'.

Ranking of cards: ace, either one or 11 points (at the option of the player), king, queen and jack, ten points each; the ten down to the two, worth their numerical value.

Cards are drawn from the top of the pack. The first player to receive an ace wins the deal. After the shuffle and cut, the dealer must 'bury' the top card of the pack face up at the bottom of the pack. An ace, a picture card or a ten may not be buried, they must be returned to the middle of the pack. If, after three tries, the dealer has not turned up a card that can be buried, he pays each player a counter, reshuffles and starts again. After he succeeds in burying a card, he deals the cards, one at a time, clockwise from his left. He gives each player, including himself, two cards—the first face down, the second face up.

In some groups, the rule is that players bet after examining their first card, which is kept face down on the table; in other places, the rule is that bets are made on the basis of the first two cards dealt. Players place their counters directly before them on the table as they bet. The dealer does not bet, since he is acting as banker, paying out or winning the

Pontoon (left, above) and five cards under 21 (right) win double the bet. The player (centre) sticks on 17 rather than risk exceeding 21 with his next card.

amount of each player's bet.

If any player draws an ace and a picture card for his first two cards, he turns his cards up and announces 'Pontoon'. In some groups a ten and an ace are also counted as a Pontoon. A player is always paid double his stake by the dealer for a Pontoon and he takes over the deal at the end of that round: shuffling, cutting, burying a card and acting as banker. If he wishes, however, he may sell the deal to the highest bidder.

After the dealer has dealt everyone two cards, each player, beginning with the one on the dealer's left, has the option of drawing one or more additional cards to add to his points total. These cards are dealt face up, one at a time, and are called 'twists'. After each twist the player decides whether to 'stick' with his hand or twist again. He may also 'buy' a card for a sum that is not more than his original stake. In this case the card is dealt face down and is a method of improving the player's original stake.

When a player decides to stick, the next player to his left may stick, twist or buy, and so on around the table. If a player exceeds 21 points—that is, goes 'bust'—he loses his bet to the dealer and folds his hand, which goes into the discard pile.

A player, other than the dealer, who receives paired cards in the first deal may turn up the face-down card and play two hands. He can receive twists on both cards from the dealer, the first on each card going face down. He

The pontoon dealer (the hand with a queen on the top) elects not to draw another card, but to call the players to show their cards.

All cards are face up. The dealer with 20 points (two queens) loses to 21 points (left), but beats 19 (top) and the hand that exceeded 21 points (right).

plays each hand separately.

When all the players have finished their betting, the dealer turns his two cards face up on the table and decides whether to stick or bust. If he sticks at 18 points, he collects the counters of those with scores of 18 and under, and pays out the bets of players with 19, 20 or 21 points. If the dealer goes over 21, he must pay all players who have totals of 21 or less. If the dealer has a Pontoon and no other player has one, he declares this and sweeps all bets from the board. Then all hands are discarded and a new deal follows.

In some places, the dealer collects double each player's stake for a Pontoon; in others, he collects exactly the amount bet from each player.

If a player keeps twisting or buying until he draws a hand of five cards totalling 21 points or less he wins double the amount of his bet. This is called a 'Five-card Trick'. A six-card hand under 21 wins triple the bet; seven cards, four times the bet, and so on. The highest progression would be the four aces (one point each), the four twos and three threes—11 cards totalling exactly 21 points; this would pay eight times the amount bet. If the dealer ends up with a hand exactly the same as another player or players, the dealer wins.

When the dealer reaches the buried card at the bottom of the pack, he collects all discards from the previous hands. Then follows the shuffle, the cut, the burying of the card and a new deal.

Fan Tan

In which the seven is the key to the action

This game is best played with three to six people. The ace is low. If three, five or six people are playing, one or more cards of one suit are removed from the pack to make the deal come out even. The 'end cards' are the ones removed; for example, the ace in a three-handed game, the ace and king in a five-handed game, the ace, two, king and queen in a six-handed game. The cards are shuffled and cut. In the cut for deal, the low card wins.

The dealer distributes the cards clockwise, one at a time, starting with the player on his left. Players discard one card a time into 12 piles—four horizontal rows and three vertical columns. The horizontal rows each consist of a

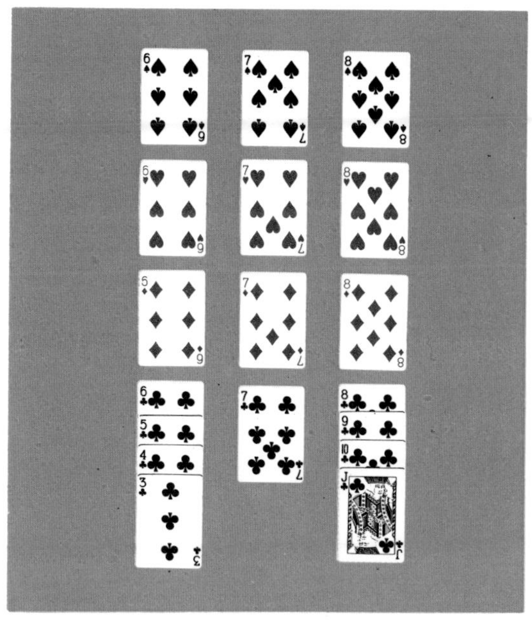

In Fan Tan, columns are laid out as above, with discards being placed on the sixes and eights in both numerical order and by following a suit.

single suit. The card that opens play is the seven. The four sevens eventually will be aligned in the central vertical column.
The player on the dealer's left goes first, discarding a seven of some suit if he has one. If he hasn't, play moves to the next person.
Once a seven is on the table, players have the option of discarding another seven under it or of building piles on either side of the seven (or sevens) already on the table.
The six of the same suit may be placed to the left of the first seven; the matching eight to its right. Then the remaining cards in the suit are discardable upon the six and the eight.
Discards must follow strictly in numerical order: At the left, beginning with the six, the order is descending—the five on top of the six, the four on top of the five, and so on, and at the right, beginning with the eight, the order is ascending—the nine on top of the eight, the ten on top of the nine. The order of the suits played is determined only by the sequence of the sevens laid down—changeable from game to game.
The first player to rid his hand of all cards is the winner. When scoring by points, the winner of the hand collects one point for each card still held by the other players. Fifty can be set as the winning score. If chips are used, a player pays one chip to the pot whenever he is unable to play a card. In addition to this pot, the winner collects a chip for each card still held by his opponents at the end of the hand.
In *Two-handed Fan Tan* the same rules apply except that hands for three players are dealt, with the extra hand forming a pack placed face down on the table. When a player cannot go, he draws from the top of the pack until the the pack yields a playable card.

Patience

When you're alone with time to spare and a pack of cards to hand

This is the most popular of the many variations of patience.
The ace is low, representing one.
After shuffling, the player deals a line of seven cards from left to right—the first card face up, the rest face down. Then he repeats the process but skipping the first card; he places a card face up on the second card from the left and cards face down on the remaining five. Again the deal is repeated—first card up, the remainder down—this time, beginning with the third column. The deal continues until space for only one card remains, which is laid face up on the seventh column. The resulting arrangement—the 'tableau'—has seven columns each with a face-up card. The columns contain one, two, three, four, five, six and seven cards respectively, 28 cards in all. The 24 remaining cards are held as a pack, face down, by the player.
The object is to extract the aces from the tableau—or from the pack—and place them beside the tableau, and build up the suits in ascending order on them. This is done by using the exposed cards.
A red card is put on a black card in descending order. For example, an exposed black two is

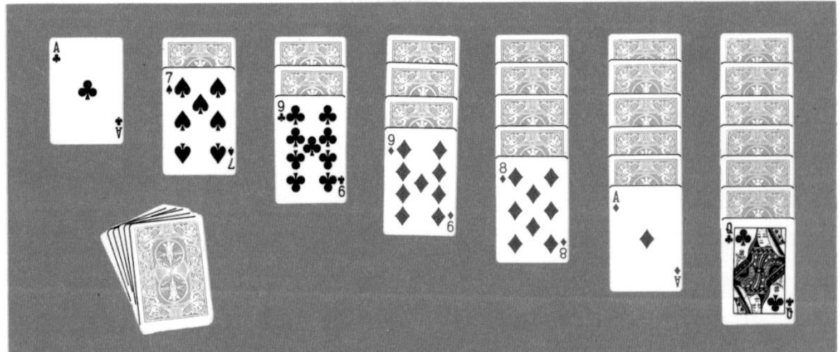

Before the start of play, the patience tableau contains 28 cards in seven piles of progressively larger size, each capped by a face-up card. The first pile consists of only one card, face up. The seventh pile of six cards face down, and one face up.

After the tableau is dealt, the remaining 24 cards are put aside as a stock to be turned up in threes. Above the tableau, suits are built up, starting with the ace. Within the tableau, the building alternates between red and black cards. As face-down cards are uncovered, they are turned up.

placed on a red three, a red jack on a black queen, and so on. When a face-up card is moved, the face-down card beneath it is turned up and can be played.

The cards can be moved in groups. If a black seven has a red six and a black five beneath it, for example, and a red eight appears the black seven may be moved, taking the other cards with it.

If an ace appears, it is moved to the side of the tableau; and as the two, three and so on of its suit appear, they can be built on it.

If a column is cleared leaving an empty space a king can be moved to fill the vacancy. Moves cannot be made from the middle of a column. The card to be moved must either be last in a column or alone, face up, at the top.

When the exposed cards cannot be moved, the player uses the pack he has kept after the first deal. He deals these in groups of three and plays the top card into the tableau or builds it on an ace. If he can use the top card the second is then available. If he can't use the top card, he deals another three and so on until he has gone through his pack.

If he goes through his pack without being able to use a card as described the game is over and he has lost. If he can build the four suits on the four aces he has won.

In *Clock Patience* the player tries to move every card into a clock formation before all four kings are turned up.

The ace counts as one o'clock, the two to the ten follow their numerical values, the jack is 11 o'clock, the queen 12 o'clock and the king goes in the centre.
The cards are dealt face down into 13 equal stacks of four cards each. Twelve stacks are arranged in the positions of the numerals of a clock. The 13th stack goes in the centre.
The player begins by turning up the top card of the centre stack. If this card is a seven, for example, he slides it face up beneath the pile of cards at the seven o'clock position. Then he turns up the top card of that pile and puts it face up at the bottom of the pile where it belongs, and so on. When a king appears, it goes beneath the centre stack; the top card is turned up and played just as any other card. When the fourth and final king is turned over, the game ends.

Dunk in the Ocean

Numbers are all-important, suits don't matter

This is a game for two to seven players, each using a standard 52-card pack.
Each player tries to get rid of 35 cards before any other player. The ace is low, the king is high. Each player deals 35 cards into five equal stacks, face up before him. The remaining 17 cards are kept face down in a stack called 'the dunk stack'.
The first player, picked by the toss of a coin, says 'Dunk!' At this signal, each player takes the top card from his own dunk stack and places it face up in the centre of the table. Then each player builds rapidly on all the centre cards—picking cards from the tops of his five upturned stacks. He builds without regard to suit; for instance, an eight of clubs may be laid on a seven of diamonds; a nine of spades on the eight of clubs; a ten of hearts on the nine; a jack of clubs on the ten, and so on. The sequence may also be built in descending order; six upon seven, five upon six, four upon three, and so on.
Turns need not be taken in any order—that is, players may lay a card on any pile when they see an opportunity. If two or more players put the same card on top of a pile, the first card that touches the pile remains. When no one is able to play a card from the top of his stacks, the centre cards are removed and the first player again calls 'Dunk!' and the game begins again.
The first player to get rid of all 35 cards in his face-up stacks is the winner.

Lift Smoke

When the trick is won, watch out for the draw

This is a game for four, five or six players. The ace is high, or counts as 11 points.
High card wins the cut for deal. The dealer distributes the cards, one at a time, clockwise from his left until each person, including himself, has six cards (five cards in a five-handed game, four if there are four players). The stock, made up of the remaining cards, is placed face down in the middle of the table. The dealer turns up the last card dealt to himself, indicating the suit that will be trumps.
Play begins with the person on the dealer's left, who leads any card from his hand. Play moves clockwise and the other players follow suit if possible. When unable to follow suit, a player must trump. If a player is void in the suit and void also in trumps, then he may play any card.
The highest card played of the suit led wins the trick if the trick is not trumped. When more than one trump card falls, the highest trump takes the trick. The winner of the trick draws a card from the top of the stock, then leads from his hand to open the next trick. Only the winner of the trick may draw from the stock. The winner of the game is the player who still holds a card or cards when the others have no cards left. If two or three players have a single card left they play a final trick and the player who takes this trick wins the game.

Bezique

A most sophisticated game, one for the connoisseur

This is a game for two players using a prepared pack of 64 cards containing two each of the ace, king, queen, jack, ten, nine, eight, seven of each suit.
Ranking of cards in descending order: ace, ten, king, queen, jack, nine, eight, seven.
OBJECT: Each player tries to be first to score a total of 1000 points. The game is based on the winning and losing of tricks, but the tricks themselves do not count in the scoring of points. Points are scored either by 'melding', that is by laying certain combinations of cards face up on the table, or by winning certain cards.
Here are the melds and their values:

CLASS I

A Marriage (king and queen, same suit)	20 points
A Royal Marriage (king and queen of trumps)	40 points
Trumps Sequence (trumps—ace, ten, king, queen, jack)	250 points

CLASS II

Bezique (jack of diamonds and queen of spades)	40 points
Double Bezique (both jacks of diamonds and queens of spades)	500 points

CLASS III

Four Aces (any suit)	100 points
Four Kings (any suit)	80 points
Four Queens (any suit)	60 points
Four Jacks (any suit)	40 points

The other methods of scoring points are:

Brisque (any ace or ten taken in the course of play)	10 points
Dix (any seven of trumps held in hand and placed on the table declared as a meld)	10 points
Last Trick	10 points

The game is played in two stages.
The first stage is played as follows:
The cards are shuffled and cut. The higher card wins the deal, according to the order of rank shown above. The dealer distributes three cards to his opponent, three to himself, two to his opponent, two to himself and a further three each. If the dealer makes a mistake, his opponent may call for a new deal. The remaining cards—'the talon pack'—are placed face down on the table. The top card is turned face up beside the talon pack to indicate trumps. If the trump card is a seven, the dealer receives ten points.
The opponent leads a card from his hand. In this stage of the game it is not necessary to follow suit. In other words, you may win a trick by trumping if you wish or lose a trick by 'throwing away' a card you don't want. The higher card of the suit led wins the trick, unless of course it is trumped. The winner of each trick has the option of melding, if he can. If he melds, he scores points according to the table above. Only one combination may be melded at a time. Then he draws a card from the talon pack, his opponent also draws a card from the talon pack and the winner of the trick leads a new card. If he cannot meld, he draws a card, his opponent draws a card and the winner leads a new card.
Scores are written down as they are made and are added up at the end of each hand. Once a meld has been placed on the table the cards in it can be used to form other melds *provided that* the new meld is in a different class *or* if the new meld is in the same class it has a higher points value. The same king or queen may

appear in only one 'marriage'.
The cards placed on the table as a meld remain part of a player's hand and can be used in the course of play as the player wishes.
If a player melds a false combination he must subtract the value of the true combination from his score. Then his opponent may instruct him to lead any card of the false combination to begin the next trick. If, however, the player hasn't already taken a card from the talon pack, he may correct his mistake without penalty.
When there is only one card left in the talon pack, the winner of the trick takes it and the loser takes the trump indicator.
With the talon pack gone, the second stage of play begins.
The players pick up their melds from the table and blend them into their hands. The winner of the previous trick leads. In this stage the players must follow suit. If they have no cards in the suit that is led, they must play trumps if they have any. They must overcall if possible, that is, play a higher card than the one that is led. Should two cards of the same rank fall on the same trick, the first one played wins the trick. If a player neglects to overcall when he holds a card that could take a trick, his opponent may require the game to be replayed from the point where the error was committed.
In this stage of the game points can be won only by taking an ace or a ten in any trick—plus the ten points for winning the last trick.
The points are added up after each hand and the game continues until someone reaches the target of 1000 points.

BOARD GAMES FOR ALL AGES

Board games fall into two categories: those, such as draughts and chess, that require a knowledge of the play and acquired skills, and those games, such as snakes and ladders and ludo, that require no skills and can therefore be enjoyed by young children. The excitement in these latter games comes from the element of chance involved in the throw of a dice. But, first to the games that require skill . . .

Draughts

A game popular since the time of the Pharaohs

Forms of draughts, also known as chequers were played in Egypt 3500 years ago. Draughts played according to rules similar to those of today entered Europe through Spain in the 16th century. It was first played in this country soon afterwards, and since then it has maintained its popularity with old and young alike.
Draughts is played by two people using a board which is divided into 64 squares, coloured alternately black and white. Sometimes the board may have other contrasting colours but they are still referred to as 'black' and 'white'. The players sit on opposite sides of the board which is placed so that the corner square on each player's left is black. They line up their men on the black squares of the three rows of squares nearest them.
The object of the game is to capture as many men as possible, and the game ends when one player has no men left. The game starts when the player with the black draughts moves one of his front men diagonally forward into an empty black square (see diagram 1, page 148). His opponent moves a front man in the same way. Each player moves in turn. An ordinary man can be moved only forwards.
During play, situations arise when one player is able to capture one or more of his opponent's men by jumping them. This occurs when a black square diagonally opposite one player's man is occupied by one of his opponent's men and there is an empty black square behind the opponent's man. The player must jump over the opponent's man and into the empty square, removing his opponent's man from the board (see diagram 2, page 148). One, two, or more

men may be taken in the same move if there are empty black squares diagonally in front and behind them. If there is the chance to capture a man the player must take that man.
Should a player overlook a possible jump his opponent may require any other man just moved to be replaced and the jump taken. Alternatively, the opponent may 'huff', or remove, the man failing to jump. If two or more jumping opportunities arise at one time a player must decide on one and be prepared for his second man to be huffed by his opponent.
When a player is able to move one of his men into a black square on his opponent's back line (see diagram 3) that man becomes a 'king', and is crowned by putting a man of the same colour, one of those captured by his opponent, on top of it. A king may move either forwards or backwards (see diagram 3) when it is taking other men or other kings. A king is not forced to take if there is the opportunity.
The game continues until one player captures all his opponent's men, removing them from the board, or traps them so that they cannot move.
The game may be considered a draw if only two pieces are left on the board, resulting in aimless shuffling from one square to another; or if only a few men remain on the board and it appears that neither player can win.

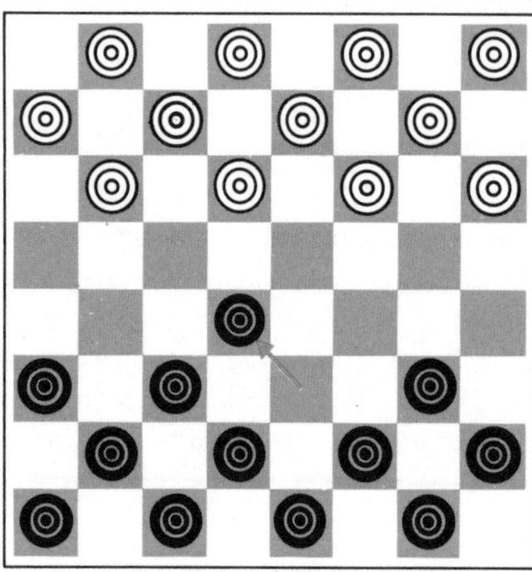

1 Black makes an opening move (arrowed) by advancing one of his men diagonally forward. White then makes a similar move, always keeping on the black squares.

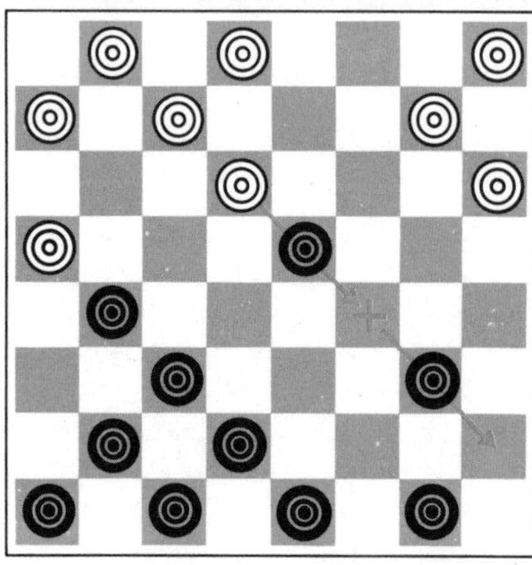

2 The object of draughts is to remove as many of your opponent's men as possible. Here, white executes a double jump, removing two of black's men in one move.

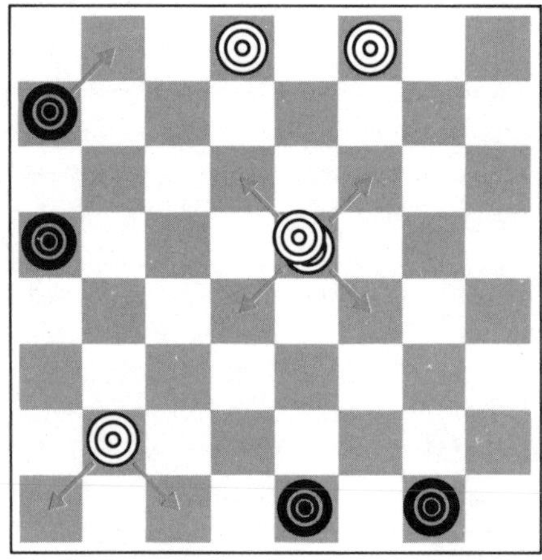

3 A player gains a 'king' by moving into his opponent's back row (single arrow). How a king may move (crossed arrows).

Chess

The game where it pays to start young

Chess is one of the oldest games in which one player pits his mind against that of another. It is believed to have originated in India about 1500 years ago, then spread to Persia, through the Middle East and, eventually, to Europe. Over the centuries chess has stimulated the minds of many famous British sovereigns, including Richard the Lionheart, Elizabeth I and Charles I.

In the 18th century it was a favourite game among aristocrats in fashionable clubs. It was also a popular tavern game among more humble enthusiasts as early as the Middle Ages. A reminder of this centuries-old interest can be seen today by inns called The Chequers, which usually have a sign consisting of a chess board outside. Although chess may appear a cool-headed game as two players crouch quietly over the board, it has aroused surprising passions. King Canute is said to have ordered the execution of a Danish noble in 1027 because the noble refused to allow him to replay a bad move.

In the Middle Ages parsons preached sermons against the wickedness of chess because the players appeared to be more absorbed in the game than in taking part in religious discussion.

Chess is a game that can be enjoyed by players of all ages, but if you want to become a first-class player you must start young. Unless you have learned to play chess before you are, say, ten years old, you have little chance of becoming a master player, let alone a world champion. The list of great players who learned chess at an early age is striking. Capablanca, the Cuban grandmaster who was world champion from 1921 to 1927, learned to play at the age of four. The American Sammy Reshevsky was able to play successfully against master players when he was eight years old.

The former world champion Bobby Fischer became a grandmaster at 15.

Whatever your age, this is where to begin . . .

How to set up the board Chess is played on a square board composed of 64 squares, coloured alternately black and white. It is played by two players; one has white pieces and the other black pieces. The player with the white pieces moves first, then the players move alternately. Each player has 16 pieces, or men, and these are arranged at the start as in diagram 1. The pieces are placed as if you, the reader, have the white pieces and all these are on the bottom two lines, or ranks.

On the bottom rank, from left to right, there are a Rook, which symbolises a tower or a castle and was known as a castle until this century; a Knight, a figure in the shape of a horse's head; a Bishop wearing a mitre; a Queen with a crown; a King with a larger crown; then again a Bishop, Knight and Rook. These three are known as the King's Bishop, King's Knight and King's Rook, and those on the left as the Queen's Bishop, Queen's Knight and Queen's Rook.

When setting up the board always place it so there is a white square in the right-hand corner. Make sure that the Queen is on a square of its own colour and that the King is on a square of an opposite colour. On the second rank there are eight men of the same shape. These are the pawns.

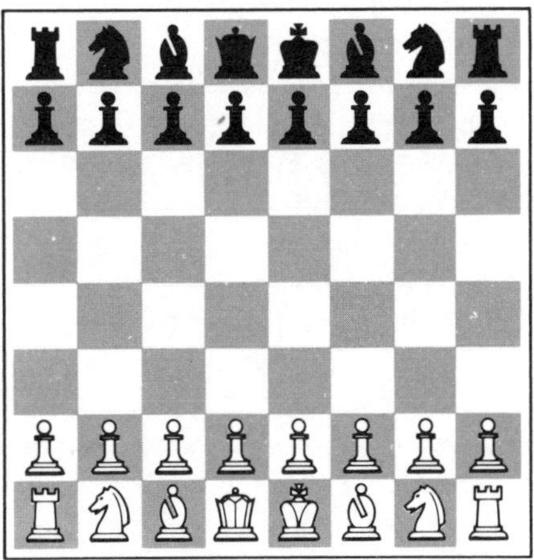

1 Setting out the pieces, a white square in your right-hand corner.

2 How the King moves: one square at a time, horizontally, vertically or diagonally.

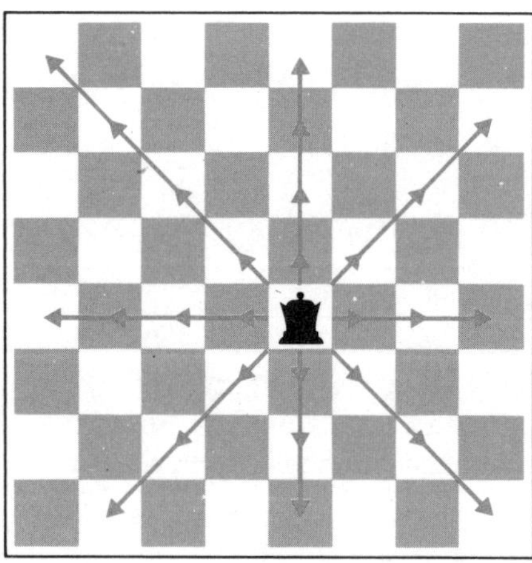

3 How the Queen moves: in any direction, capturing any piece in her path.

How the pieces move

The most important piece on the board is the King, but its powers of movement are limited. It can move only one square at a time as is shown in diagram 2.

The King moves in any direction, diagonally, vertically or horizontally, but it cannot go on to a square where it is attacked by the enemy. It captures enemy pieces by its moves and these, when so captured, are removed from the board and play no further part in the game. When an enemy piece attacks the King it is said to put it in check.

Next in importance to the King is the Queen, which is the most powerful piece on the board because it has the greatest field of action, as can be seen in diagram 3.

The Queen can move the whole length of the diagonal on which it is placed. It can also move the whole line horizontally, along the rank, or vertically, along the file (a file being a vertical line of squares). It captures anything in its path and must settle down on the square of the piece it captures. It can only capture an enemy piece and it cannot jump over a piece, either of its own colour or of the enemy.

The Bishop can only move along a diagonal as in diagram 4. It captures in its path along the diagonal and again must stop at the point of capture and is unable to jump over pieces. It must remain on the same colour square of its initial diagonal, so the White King's Bishop must travel on white squares only, while the White Queen's Bishop travels on black squares only.

The Rook is a powerful piece that ranks only beneath the Queen in strength. It cannot move along the diagonals but can move along both rank and file, that is it travels horizontally and vertically and captures opposing pieces along these lines.

Since the Rook likes wide open spaces it is most powerful in the endings when many exchanges have taken place and it can sweep up and down and across the open lines.

The Knight's move is at first glance a strange and complicated one, and it is the move the beginner finds most difficult to understand. It is comparatively slow-stepping since it moves only two squares and then one square more either to the left or the right, always moving away from the point of departure. It possesses one supreme virtue, that of being able to jump over any pieces.

The pawn's normal move is that of one square, always forward.

However, on its initial move the pawn can, if it likes, move two squares instead of one. It

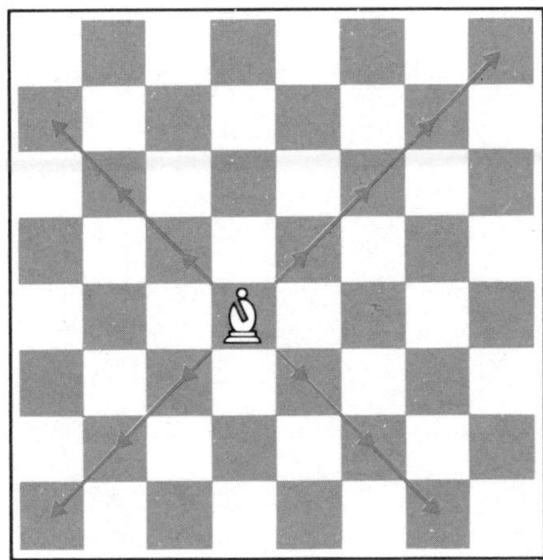

4 How the Bishop moves: along its own diagonal, either on white or black squares.

captures one square diagonally but, in order to make up for its initial two-square move, a capture known as *en passant* (in passing) can be put into operation.
Both these methods of capture are shown in diagram 8. When you examine the *en passant* capture you realise that it is really a capture made as though one side had merely moved the pawn one square.
The pawn has one remarkable advantage over all other pieces that makes it potentially the most valuable piece of all. Once it reaches the eighth rank it must be exchanged for another piece (of its own colour). That is to say, it is promoted to become a Queen, or a Rook, or a Bishop or a Knight, all of its own colour. It cannot remain as a pawn.
There is another type of move which concerns two pieces and yet is still classed as one move. This is known as castling, and is a joint move of the King and the Rook. In the case of Kingside castling you move the King two squares to the right and the Rook two squares to the left, all at the same time. In Queenside castling you move the King two squares to the left and the Rook three squares to the right. You cannot castle the King out of check. This means that you cannot castle when your King is in check. Nor can you castle across check; that is move your King across a square that is

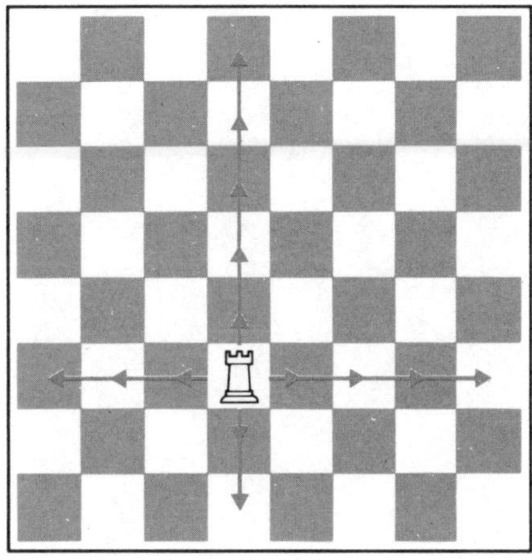

5 How the Rook moves: vertically or horizontally but never diagonally.

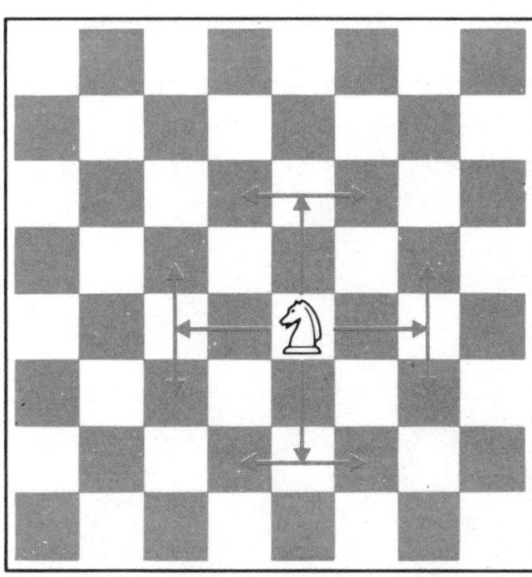

6 Knight moves two squares, then one right or left. **7** Pawn (below) moves one square forward, or two on first move.

8 How a pawn captures: by taking a piece one square diagonally, either directly or *en passant.*

9 Castling: the King moves two squares to the left or right, with corresponding Rook move.

attacked by an enemy piece. Since you are not allowed to place your own King in check, you are not allowed to castle your King into check. Finally, if you have already moved your King you cannot castle with it and, similarly, if you have moved a Rook you cannot castle with that Rook, but may on the other side if that Rook has not been moved.

How to record your moves

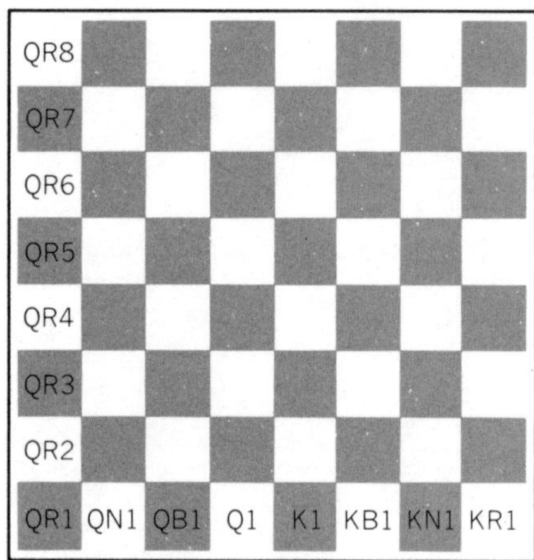

10 How White records the moves: seen from the bottom of the board looking upwards.

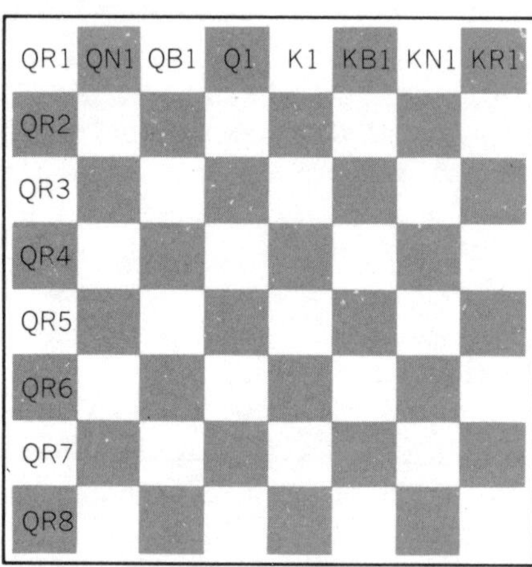

11 How Black records the moves: seen from the top looking downwards.

Chess has the advantage over most other games in that you can record the moves. In the descriptive notation which is used in English-speaking countries you indicate the piece you are using by its first letter, K for King, Q for Queen, B for Bishop, R for Rook and P for Pawn. The exception is the Knight which is commonly indicated by the letter N although at one time it was represented by Kt.

The squares also have a name and a figure as shown in diagrams 10 and 11.
The squares are numbered 1–8 according to their place in the file. They are also lettered according to the piece which was on the first square of that file at the beginning of the game. Thus, in diagram 10, which represents the board viewed from White's point of view, the first square of the most left-hand file is represented by QR1, since this is where the Queen's Rook is placed at the beginning of the game. The remaining squares on that file run from 2 to 8. A similar process is used for all the other files. Diagram 11 shows the board looked at from the Black point of view, and so you will find that Black's QR1 is White's QR8 and White's QR1 is Black's QR8.
To show how this works here is the start of a game. *1.* P-K4, which means that the pawn on the King's file advances two squares. Black replies *1.* . . . P-K4, and this means his King's pawn advances two squares. Then comes *2.* N-KB3 which means that the White Knight on KN1 goes to B3.
The actual process of moving is indicated by a dash and captures are shown by 'x'. Thus we have *1.* P-K4, P-Q4; *2.* PxP. If a pawn captures *en passant* this is indicated by the addition of the initial letters e.p.
Check is shown by the first two letters ch.
Castling on the Kingside is shown by 0-0 and on the Queenside by 0-0-0.

Starting at the end! It might appear illogical for a beginner to learn how to finish a chess game before learning how to start it. There are, however, good reasons for this. Towards the finish, or in the end game as it is called, there are fewer pieces on the board because of captures that have gone on earlier. A beginner can then see more clearly the problems and how to resolve them.
There are a number of ways a game can be finished but, undoubtedly, the most desirable is by checkmate, that is to say by placing the enemy King in check in such a position that it cannot get out of check. Whoever delivers checkmate, usually called 'mate', wins the game.
It is necessary at this stage to understand the meaning of 'check'. A King is put in check when an opposing piece threatens to capture it on the next move. The King, however, is never captured, meaning removed from the board. The player whose King is threatened can get out of check by a number of moves:
1 Capturing the threatening piece.
2 Interposing one of his own pieces between his King and the attacker (although this cannot be done if a Knight is checking the King).
3 Moving the King out of check. If none of these moves is possible it is mate, and the game is over. When a King is in check the player must make a move to get it out of check. He cannot ignore the situation and attempt another move.
The simplest example of mate can be shown where a player has two Rooks in the end game (see diagram 12).

12 A simple example of mate where one player has the advantage of two Rooks.

This goes: *1.* R-R4 ch, K-Q4; *2.* R-N5 ch, K-K3; *3.* R-R6 ch, K-B2; *4.* R-R6, K-K2 (or *4.* . . . K-B1; *5.* R-R7, K-K1; *6.* R-N8 mate); *5.* R-N7 ch, K-B1; *6.* R-N7, K-N1 (or K-K1) *7.* R-R8 mate.
Now go back to the position in diagram 12.

13 An easy mate with a King and a Queen against only a King.

14 Stalemate on Black's move: he cannot move except into check, so the game is drawn.

After *1.* R-R4 ch, Black can also play *1.* . . . K-Q6; and then comes *2.* R-N3 ch, K-K7; *3.* R-R2 ch, K-B8; *4.* R-QN2, K-K8; *5.* R-KN1 mate.

Another easy mate is made with the Queen (see diagram 13).

Just as you did with the two Rooks so, with the Queen, you follow the plan of limiting the area of the board on which the enemy King may be played.

1. Q-K4 ch, K-B4. Now, since you do not have another piece to help in the limiting process, you have to call in the assistance of your King. *2.* K-N2, K-Q3; *3.* K-B3, K-B4; *4.* Q-K5 ch, K-B3; *5.* K-B4, K-Q2; *6.* K-Q5, K-Q1; *7.* K-B6, K-B1 and now White gives mate by either *8.* Q-B7, or *8.* Q-K8.

There are other kinds of checkmate: by the King and one Rook, by the King and two Bishops and so on; but in fact the most common way in which one side wins is by the other resigning the game when his position is hopeless.

The game need not, however, end in a victory for either side. It can also end in a draw, in which case both sides score a halfpoint. Here the most usual finish is by agreement, both players thinking the position to be dead level. But there are other ways and the first, possibly the most interesting, is by stalemate. This occurs when the player who has to move finds he has no legal move (see diagram 14).

Here, if it were White to play, he could deliver mate by *1.* Q-B7, or by *1.* Q-B8, very much like the mates with the Queen already shown. But with Black to move we find that he has no move that avoids coming into check and, since it is illegal to place one's own King in check, the game is drawn by stalemate.

Stalemates are comparatively rare, but another way of bringing about the draw which quite often occurs is that involving a repetition of position. When a position recurs three times then that player whose move brings about this recurrence can claim a draw (see diagram 15).

In this position White's only chance of making progress consists in getting his King past the opposing King. So he plays *1.* K-R4, to which Black replies *1.* . . . K-R3. And not *1.* . . .K-B3; when White makes some progress with *2.* K-R5.

Then White plays *2.* K-N4, trying to get his King to B5. There follows *2.* . . . K-N3; when the same position occurs twice.

White plays *3.* K-R4, K-R3; *4.* K-N4, and now Black sees that if he plays *4.* . . . K-N3 the same position will have occurred three times. He therefore claims the draw by repetition of position, saying that with his next move (K-N3) the appropriate number of repetitions

15 Repetition: the game is drawn because there can only be a repetition of moves.

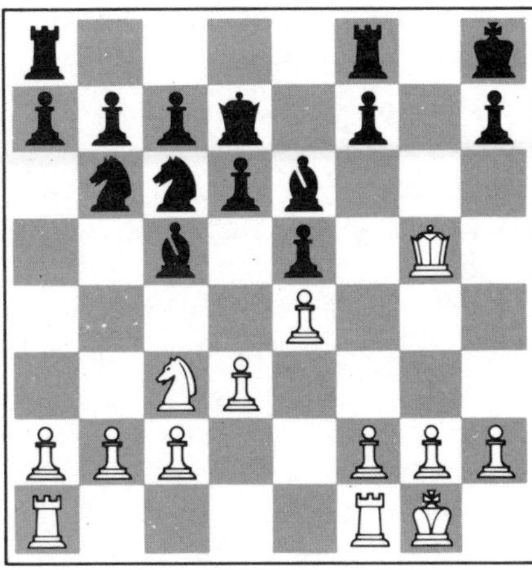

16 Perpetual check: one player can force a draw by repeating the same checking moves.

will have occurred.

Another method of reaching the draw which has something in common with that resulting from a repetition of position lies in perpetual check (see diagram 16).

In this position, if you count up the number of pieces (not including pawns) you find that Black has three more than White—two Bishops and a Knight. And yet White can force a draw by perpetual check as follows: *1.* Q-B6 ch, K-N1; *2.* Q-N5 ch, K-R1; *3.* Q-B6 ch, and so on.

The last method of gaining a draw, which is very rare indeed, is under the '50 moves' rule. This states that when 50 moves have been made without advancing a pawn or capturing a piece then the game is drawn. This is highly unlikely to occur with a beginner.

Equipped with a knowledge of these rules and a few further practical hints stemming from them you are ready to start play. One important hint is that when you castle you should either take hold of your King first or else take hold of both King and Rook simultaneously. Never touch the Rook first since a stickler for the letter of the law may insist that you then move the Rook alone.

Another rule is the '*j'adoube*' rule. When a piece is untidily placed, half on one square and half on another, you should say *j'adoube* (French for 'I adjust') and correct the position of the piece. Your opponent cannot then insist that you should move this piece.

Before you start a game you have to determine who shall move first by taking the White pieces. In a tournament all this is decided for you by a set of initial pairings, and in a match between teams each side has alternately Black and White.

If it is a friendly game then you must toss up for colour, either with a coin or else by holding a white pawn in one clenched fist and a black pawn in the other, and offering your opponent a choice of either hand.

Getting the feel of the game An 'opening' in chess is not a single move made by White, who always starts. It is a series of moves, initiated by White but also governed by Black's replies. In reliable openings, tested by masters over many decades, pieces are developed as quickly as possible so that the contestants have their armies strategically placed for the main battle, called the middle game. Two of these established openings are the Ruy Lopez and the Queen's Gambit. As a beginner, you can get a good understanding of chess and appreciate the feel of the game by playing the following examples of these two openings with a friend who is also keen to learn.

Play each opening right through, observing

the comments, then start again, with the player who was White taking the black pieces and the former Black playing White. Each player will then see the development of the pieces through the eyes of White and Black. Later, play the openings to a point where an alternative line of play is suggested, such as the third move for Black in the Ruy Lopez. Play these alternatives through both as White and Black.

By this time you and your opponent will have a good idea of how to tackle openings and will also have become familiar with the pieces and how they are moved. You are both now ready to play your first competitive game, but make the most of what you have already learned.

Start with the Ruy Lopez opening by playing: *1.* P-K4, P-K4; *2.* N-KB3, N-QB3; *3.* B-N5. Then carry on your own game. Note the moves of your game (see p. 152), then analyse the mistakes you think you have both made.

Start again so that each player has a turn as White and Black. Now play the Queen's Pawn opening in the same way. These two openings alone, and their innumerable forms of development, can absorb beginners for many exciting games, as they have done for generations of chess players.

When you feel ready to experiment further do not try wild openings of your own, but play some established openings. Begin, for instance, with these two openings:

Ruy Lopez This opening derives its name from an analysis published in the 16th century by a Spanish priest, Ruy Lopez, who was the leading Spanish player of his age. Its most important line is:

1. P-K4

This is a fine developing move that opens up diagonals for both Queen and Bishop and also uses a central pawn as a weapon of attack.

1. . . . P-K4

The remarks about White's move apply equally to Black.

2. N-KB3

By this move White develops his Knight and also attacks Black's pawn. He could also have developed his Bishop on B4, but in the early stages it is preferable to assist the slow-stepping Knight rather than the speedy Bishop.

2. . . . N-QB3

Black protects that attacked pawn and also develops a Knight.

3. B-N5

This is the move that marks the Ruy Lopez. White is threatening to take the Knight, then capture the pawn. Black can choose between many systems of defence. He can counter-attack by bringing out his other Knight, or he can defend by P-Q3, or he can continue developing his pieces by B-B4, or he can attack the Bishop by P-QR3.

3. . . . P-QR3

This is Black's most common move.

4. B-R4

White can also play BxN but he does not, in fact, win a pawn. For example: *4.* BxN, QPxB; *5.* NxP, Q-Q5, when Black wins back his pawn and has a good game.

4. . . . N-B3

Black develops the other Knight and imitates White by attacking the KP. Note that you do not have to say or write here *4.* . . . N-KB3 since the QN has already been developed and you will merely be wasting a useless symbol.

5. 0-0

White hurries to get his King castled away into safety on the flank. At the same time he brings his Rook nearer into action. You will observe that White does not bother to defend his KP.

5. . . . B-K2

Black could also take off the KP with complicated possibilities that lead to very lively play. But at this stage in your development as a player you would be wise to avoid such complications.

6. R-K1

White protects the KP and also further develops the Rook. If you contrast the position of the Rook now with its original position on KR1 you find that it now controls many more squares, and that is really what is meant by development.

6. . . . P-QN4

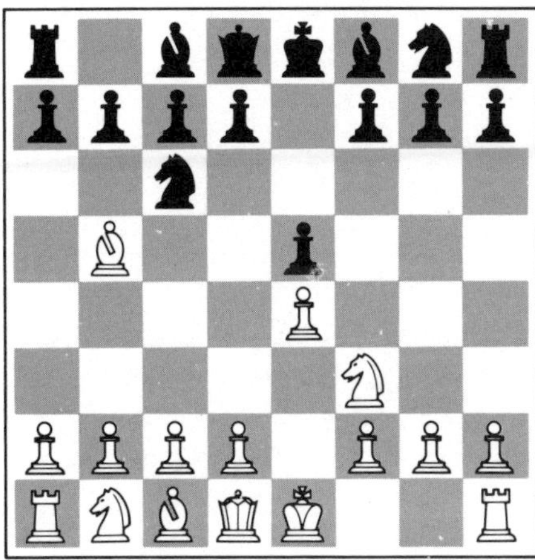

17 Ruy Lopez: the opening sequence after White's first move of P-K4.

18 Queen's Gambit: the sequence after White's first move of P-Q4.

Black now needs to chase the Bishop away since White was threatening to win the KP by *7.* BxN, QPxB; *8.* NxP, when *8.* . . . Q-Q5 is no longer effective on account of simply *9.* N-KB3.

7. B-N3 P-Q3

Black further protects his KP and allows his QB more breathing space.

8. P-B3

White gives the Bishop an escape hole on QB2 and prepares to advance his QP to Q4 with the further idea that if Black then plays PxP, White can reply with PxP presenting a serried array of pawns to attack Black.

8. . . . 0-0

Black breathes a sign of relief. In King's Pawn openings no side feels really safe with his King until it has been safely castled.

9. P-KR3

White would like to play P-Q4 at once but does not do so because he is frightened of allowing Black counterplay by B-N5.

9. . . . N-QR4

Black plays on the principle that the best defence is counter-attack.

10. B-B2

To the beginner this may appear odd and a little cowardly. Why does White allow the Bishop to cower behind the pawns? There are two reasons. First, this Bishop is a powerful part of White's attack and, secondly, it is surprising how quickly lines may be cleared to enable this piece to strike at Black's King.

10. . . . P-B4

An interesting move which shows Black is not content with passive defence. He sees that White plans to play P-Q4 and so prepares to make that move as dangerous as possible for White.

11. P-Q4 Q-B2

Now we see how useful Black's pawn move was. It allows the Black Queen to enter into the game.

At this stage, though text-books do go on to discuss what happens in the future of this opening, we have reached the middle-game. Black has adequately protected his central key-point on K4 and at the same time White has some pressure on a number of central points. Theory gives this position as about equal.

Queen's Gambit As the name implies, the Queen's Pawn is played first and not the King's Pawn as in the Ruy Lopez. Equally, it is a gambit. This means that it involves the sacrifice of a pawn in order to gain an advantage in position.

It begins as follows:

1. P-Q4 P-Q4

2. P-QB4

The point about this offer of a pawn is that it opens up lines of attack for White's pieces, especially for the KB. It has other points, too, and some of them are very important, as will be seen.

2. . . . P-K3

Black decides to maintain his pawn in the centre, where it is a vital point of defence. He could accept the pawn sacrifice by *2.* . . . PxP; but then, after *3.* N-KB3, N-KB3; *4.* P-K3, he should not try to retain his extra pawn by *4.* . . . P-QN4; since then, after *5.* P-QR4, P-B3; *6.* PxP, PxP; *7.* P-QN3, PxP; *8.* BxP ch, B-Q2; *9.* QxP, White regains his pawn with the better game.

So, after *1.* P-Q4, P-Q4; *2.* P-QB4, PxP; *3.* N-KB3, N-KB3; *4.* P-K3, Black should give back the pawn without a struggle by *4.* . . . P-K3.

3. N-QB3

White develops, and puts a little more pressure on the Black Q4 square. You will find throughout this fine opening that White continually tries to exert pressure on Black's Q4 and Black, just as vigorously, protects that point.

3. . . . N-KB3

4. B-N5

Another threat on Black's Q4. The threat is 5. BxN, QxB; 6. PxP, PxP; 7. NxP.

4. . . . B-K2

Black develops the Bishop and answers the threat of White's last move since now, after *5.* BxN, BxB; *6.* PxP, PxP, the Black Queen will still be protecting the QP.

5. P-K3

This is an essential move for White to allow the development of his KB and, thereafter, all the Kingside pieces.

5. . . . 0-0

A good aspect of this defence is that Black's King is castled into safety quite early. White, however, has excellent attacking chances on the Queen's wing.

6. N-B3 QN-Q2

Both sides develop their Knights, but if you look at and compare the Queenside position of either side you will find that Black has difficulty in developing his Queenside, particularly his QB.

7. R-B1

White places the Rook where eventually it can bring pressure to bear on Black's QB2.

7. . . . P-B3

Black tries to nullify that pressure.

8. B-Q3

At this point both sides can be satisfied with the progress in their development plans. White is preparing for an attack on either flank and Black has safely castled and developed his Kingside pieces.

But, Black's Queenside, in particular his QB, needs developing. He must, therefore, form a plan. This is how he does this:

8. . . . PxP

9. BxP

There is no need to write BxBP because if the Bishop had captured the RP you would have had to write BxP ch.

9. . . . N-Q4

10. BxB QxB

11. 0-0 NxN

12. RxN P-K4

The exchanges enable Black to make a freeing move that opens up a diagonal for the QB. Some of Black's aims have been achieved, but White has still some attacking chances.

Typical attacks The Queen and Bishop work very well together in an attack on the enemy King (see diagram 19).

In this position the defending Black Knight has been driven away from Black's KB3, to Q2. This has allowed the Queen to come to an attacking position on N4.

Now White plays *1.* B-R6, threatening mate on N7, and the only way that this mate can be avoided is by Black moving the NP. So there comes *1.* . . . P-KN3; *2.* BxR, and White wins the Rook for the Bishop.

This method of attack on the King is a very common one and is particularly formidable when the defending side has no minor piece (Bishop or Knight) protecting his King.

Another method of attack makes use of the 'pin' of a Knight by a Bishop to break up the pawn position in front of the King.

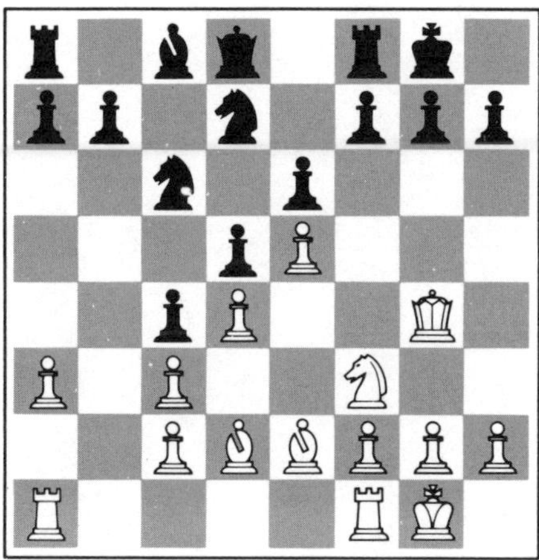

19 The Queen and a Bishop combine in an attack. White's next move is B-R6.

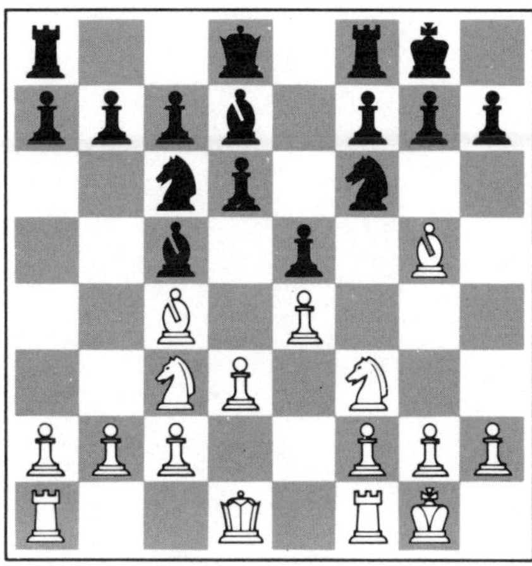

20 A pin: White's Bishop pins down the Knight, which cannot move or Black's Queen is lost.

21 The Queen and a Knight attack. The Knight seals off the King's escape routes.

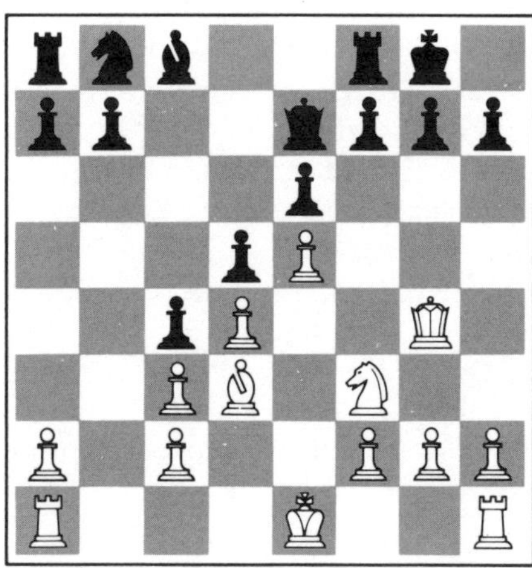

22 The Greek gift: the attacker (White) sacrifices a Bishop for a mating finish.

When a piece so attacks another piece that the attacked piece can only move at the cost of imperilling another piece of greater value the process is known as pinning. Thus, in diagram 20, the White Bishop on the KN file pins the Knight on the Queen. In other words if the Knight moves the Queen is lost. White plays *1.* N-Q5 and since this Knight cannot move without allowing the capture of the Queen, Black must allow White to play NxN ch, weakening Black's side.

The Queen and Knight also work well together in attack, and in diagram 21 the Knight acts as a sort of clamp to keep the enemy King in position and to seal off escape squares.

White plays *1.* QxP ch, KxQ; *2.* R-R1 mate.

Another position in which the defending side has no minor piece for the defence of the King allows the attacker to sacrifice a piece for a mating finish, This is known as the Greek gift or the Bishop sacrifice (see diagram 22).

Note that White has a pawn on K5 and that the Black KN should be posted on either KB3 or KB1. But this Knight has already been eliminated and White is able to play *1.* BxP ch, KxB; *2.* Q-R5 ch, K-N1; *3.* N-N5, after which

23 The scene is set for White to 'Queen' the pawn and go on to win the game.

24 A situation where both sides attempt to force a pawn through to win the game.

mate can only be averted by QxN, although White, with a Queen for two minor pieces, still has a won game.

The simplest, and at the same time the most common and the easiest type of ending, is the King and pawn ending. It is in fact essential for you to learn how to force a pawn through to the eighth rank and there promote it into a Queen. That is why pawns, though the weakest units on the board, are, potentially, the strongest, and that is why you must strive to win one.

One of the standard winning positions is shown in diagram 23.

The pawn is a 'passed' one, meaning that there is no enemy pawn that can impede its progress and, what is more, it is so placed that White has a number of moves in hand with which to manoeuvre.

The winning process is: *1.* P-Q5, K-K1; *2.* K-B7, K-K2; *3.* P-K6 ch, K-K1; *4.* P-Q7 ch and White makes a Queen next move.

Now go back to the position in diagram 23. After *1.* P-Q5, Black can also play *1.* . . . K-B1; when White wins by *2.* K-K7, advancing his pawn to the eighth rank by exactly the same process as he did when the enemy King went the other way.

Note, however, that if, after *1.* P-Q5, K-K1; White plays *2.* K-B6, K-Q1; *3.* P-Q6, K-B1; *4.* P-Q7 ch, K-Q1; *5.* K-Q6, no win is possible and there is a draw by stalemate.

That is one of the simpler forms of King and pawn endings. Nothing impeded the pawn and one merely had to march it up the board. Let us look at a position where you have to force a break-through to win, as in diagram 24.

Black plays *1.* . . . P-B5 ch; *2.* PxP ch, K-B4; *3.* K-B2, KxP; and Black has won his pawn back, converting it into a passed pawn in the process.

But it is no use trying to force it through to Queen as was done in the previous example, for example *4.* K-N2, P-N6; *5.* K-N1, K-B6; *6.* K-B1, P-N7 ch; *7.* K-N1, K-N6; and the game is a stalemate.

Yet there is a way of winning this ending. What one has to do is to abandon the pawn to be captured by the enemy King and run with one's own King to capture the remaining pawn. This is in fact the more usual way in which King and pawn endings are won.

So, return to the original position in diagram 24. Play should go *1.* . . . P-B5 ch; *2.* PxP ch, K-B4; *3.* K-B2, KxP; *4.* K-N2, K-Q5; *5.* K-N3, K-K5; *6.* KxP, KxP; *7.* K-B3, K-K6; cutting off the White King from the pawn. *8.* K-B2, K-K7; *9.* K-B3, P-B5; *10.* K-Q4, P-B6 and the pawn marches to the eighth rank where it is promoted to a Queen.

25 At this stage of the game the strength of the King is shown in attack and defence.

Simple and straightforward enough, but even in the closing stages Black might have gone astray if he had advanced his pawn regardless. Go back to the position where the Black pawn was still on B4, the Black King on K6 and the White King had just gone to B2. If 'then' Black plays *8.* ... P-B5; *9.* K-Q1, P-B6?? (queries indicate a bad move); then *10.* K-K1, P-B7 ch; *11.* K-B1, K-B6 stalemate.

The King in the ending In the opening and in the middle-game the King plays little part as it is vulnerable to attack and must in fact be protected at all costs against the onslaught of the enemy pieces. But, once the end game is reached, the King becomes a powerful piece and must be used as much as possible.

In diagram 25, if White tries to Queen his pawn straight away he will lose it, as in this example: *1.* P-QN4, K-B2: *2.* P-N5, K-K3; *3.* P-N6, K-Q3; *4.* P-N7, K-B2; and the pawn is lost.

The pawn is lost, not only because White failed to use his King but also because Black has used his King to the best advantage. So, the right way of playing this ending is to use the King as much as possible by *1.* K-B2, K-B2; *2.* K-K3, K-K3; *3.* K-Q4, K-Q3; *4.* K-B4, K-B3; *5.* P-N4, K-N3; *6.* P-N5, P-N3; *7.* K-N4, P-R3; *8.* P-N4, P-N4; *9.* K-B4, K-N2; *10.* K-B5, K-B2; *11.* P-N6 ch, K-N2; *12.* K-N5, K-N1; *13.* K-B6, K-B1; *14.* P-N6 ch, K-N1; *15.* K-N6, P-R4; *16.* PxP, P-N5; *17.* P-R6, P-N6; *18.* P-R7, PxP; *19.* P-R8=Q mate.

The value of the pieces It is important to have fixed in your mind the approximate relative value of the pieces and for this one can start off by taking the pawn as a single unit of valuation.

Bishops and Knights, which are usually termed minor pieces, are worth about three pawns. This means that the Bishop and the Knight are roughly equal in value. The Bishop is more valuable than the Knight when the diagonals are open, but when the board is cluttered, the Knight is better because of its ability to leap over obstacles. This in turn means that the Bishop is better in the endings, when one would normally expect many exchanges to have taken place. On the whole, therefore, the Bishop is slightly better than the Knight.

The Rook and the Queen, which are called the major pieces, are both better than the Bishop or the Knight and a rough estimate of the worth of the Rook is five pawns.

The Queen is worth considerably more than the Rook in view of its much larger scope of action. The Queen is worth about two Rooks.

Danger! Play Black with caution White, having the advantage of the first move, gets a chance to strike an early attacking blow. Black, therefore, must be careful in defence. What happens when he is not so careful is shown in the following game played at a chess congress.

Opening: Ruy Lopez.

1. P-K4	*P*-K4
2. N-KB3	*N*-QB3
3. B-N5	*P*-QR3
4. B-R4	

Now Black, instead of playing N-KB3, tries another sound line.

4. ...	P-Q3
5. N-B3	P-QN4

Black's move merely puts the enemy Bishop on a better diagonal. Instead he could have played *5.* ... B-Q2 or *5.* ... N-B3.

6. B-N3	B-N5

26 Isolated pawn: this pawn is weak because it cannot be supported by another pawn.

Black's incautious move soon leads to trouble. He should have hastened with his Kingside development with *6.* . . . B-K2.

7. P-KR3 B-R4

Black's move loses him the game. The essential move was *7.* . . . BxN.

8. NxP BxQ

9. BxP ch K-K2

10. N-Q5 mate.

On this occasion Black resigned on the 8th move without waiting for the checkmate.

Moral: Be extra careful when playing with the black pieces.

Pawn weaknesses As you play chess so you will discover that the thrifty saying 'Look after the pence and the pounds will look after themselves' has its equivalent in 'Look after the pawns and the game will look after itself'. To lose a pawn is to lose a potential Queen, so it follows that you must take special care to see they are all safe.

It pays to know what makes a pawn weak and to try to make sure that you do not, knowingly or otherwise, create a pawn weakness.

Pawn weaknesses fall into three main types and the first is the isolated pawn, which is shown in diagram 26.

Black's pawn on his K4 is isolated, meaning that it cannot be supported by another pawn. As a result it must be protected by the King.

27 Doubled pawn: both pawns lack power to advance in either attack or defence.

If it were Black's turn to move, he would at once lose a pawn. But, so weak is the isolated pawn, that even with White to move the isolated pawn goes, for example, *1.* K-Q6, and once again the Black King has to abandon the pawn to its fate.

The second pawn weakness is that of the doubled pawn (see diagram 27).

The doubled pawn is particularly disadvantageous when there are Knights on the board. Contrast the scope for action enjoyed by the Knights in this position. The Black Knight can go to three squares without being attacked by an enemy pawn. The White Knight has no fewer than eight squares and is, therefore, more than twice as powerful as Black's.

Another drawback of the doubled pawns is their immobility, their lack of power to advance either in attack or defence. So, whereas the White pawns can advance at will, the two doubled pawns are firmly tethered to their squares on the second and third rank and have no hope of ever moving.

In many ways the worst pawn weakness is that of the backward pawn.

A backward pawn is weak since it cannot be protected by another pawn, and it is also weak because it allows enemy pieces to settle down in these gaps and to dominate the board.

28 Backward pawn: this pawn is weak because it cannot be protected by another pawn.

Look at the position in diagram 28 and you find there are two backward pawns, the one on White's Q2 and the other on KN3. Both of these points can only be protected by White's King or his pieces. In addition, the Black Knights have been allowed to adopt such a dominant position that neither of White's pieces can move.

How to become a better player In the opening, concentrate on developing your pieces as quickly as possible. Try to control the centre but do not make many pawn moves. As a general rule those openings are best that demand the fewest pawn moves.

In the middle-game always try to get your pieces working together. You will find that this is best done by centralising them. This applies particularly to the Knights and Rooks which lose much of their field of action when they are away from the centre and near the edge of the board. Don't play from move to move but try to form a settled plan. The player who drifts from move to move without forming a plan is doomed to be a weak player all his or her life.

This last piece of advice also applies to the endings. Remember to make the utmost use of your King when the end game is reached.

Learn and practise mating processes. Don't be frightened of the end game and regard it as some mysterious and perhaps boring aspect of chess which can only be comprehended by a giant mathematical intellect.

Encourage your friends to learn chess and form a club at school, which should meet at least twice a week. Organise competitions which will be fun and excellent preparation for the time you join a local chess club.

Above all, enjoy playing chess. The more you enjoy it the greater likelihood that you will improve your play.

Table Tennis

The championship trail starts at home

Table Tennis is established at international standards as a game of great skill, but it can still be great fun when played at home on an ordinary table.

The standard table measures 2·7 × 1·5 metres and stands 0·75 metres high. The net is 150 millimetres high.

Simple table-tennis sets consisting of a net with a pair of clamps for fixing it to the table, two bats and a ball, can be bought at toy shops. For domestic use, simply clamp the net across the middle of the table and the game can begin. The bats are made of wood faced with rubber, cork or sandpaper and the ball is invariably made of celluloid.

It is a game for two players (singles) or four (doubles). It is suitable for both boys and girls. In singles, players toss a coin to win service. The server palms the ball into the air with one hand and hits it with the bat so that it bounces once on his side of the net and once on his opponent's side. If it doesn't bounce correctly it counts as a 'fault' and you lose the point. The opponent returns it by hitting it with his bat so that it bounces once on the side of the server who then attempts to hit it back in the same way. Anyone who misses the ball altogether, or hits it so that it doesn't bounce on the other side of the net or hits it into the net loses the point and the ball is served again. Each service lasts for five consecutive points, then it changes to the other player. If a service hits the net on the way across and bounces on the other side it counts as a 'let'. No points are scored and the service must be played again. If it hits the net and does not bounce on the other side of the table it counts as a 'fault' and the server loses the point.

The first player to reach 21 points wins the game but he must have a clear lead of at least two points. In other words, if the game reaches a score of 20–20 it continues until one player has a lead of two clear points, such as 22–20, 23–21, 24–22.

In doubles the method of striking the ball and scoring is the same. The difference is that the players on each side play the ball alternately. The same player in one team cannot play the ball twice in succession.

The service alternates between the teams after every five points and also alternates between the players in each team.

Most of the star players hold the bat in the same way as a tennis racket, but young players and beginners usually find it easier to use what is called the 'pen-holder' grip (see illustration). This makes control of the ball much easier and the ball can still be hit quite hard. It might not look as spectacular as the tennis-racket grip but it is very effective, and when a young player becomes expert with it and graduates to a full-size table he can always change his style without losing the accuracy which made him the terror of the dining-table.

Beginners may find it best to use the pen-holder grip, holding the handle with the thumb and forefinger.

When serving, the ball must land on the server's side, go over the net and land in the receiver's court.

Be Your own Quizmaster

Test your wits and your knowledge – then try out these brain-teasers on your friends

You would have to be very bright and knowledgeable to answer all the questions in this chapter correctly.

See how you get on, however, and write down your score and the date. In a few months, try again. Allowing for some answers you have remembered, you will find that your score improves as your general knowledge grows.

There are many trick questions, so don't jump at what seems to be the obvious answer.

You can also use the quizzes for competitions between two teams.

Choose one or two of the quizzes as an interlude between more boisterous games at a party. All the quizzes can help to while away a tedious car journey. You could also get out a dictionary or encyclopaedia and make up your own quiz.

The answers begin on p. 174.

Watch this Space

Ten questions to set your brain cells orbiting

We are already living in the Space Age, but have you caught up with it? Some of these questions may look simple, but be careful!

1 The earth turns on its axis once every 24 hours. *True or False?*

2 A light-year is equivalent to 100,000 ordinary years. *True or false?*

3 The sun is running out of fuel at a rate of about 4 million tonnes per second. *True or false?*

4 An astronaut in orbit is weightless because he is outside the reach of the earth's gravitation. *True or false?*

5 An astronaut on the moon weighs only about one-sixth of what he does on earth, because the moon is only about one-sixth the mass of the earth. *True or false?*

6 An Apollo spacecraft travelling at 32,000 kilometres per hour would take nearly 500 years to reach the nearest star outside our solar system. *True or false?*

7 It is possible to send up a satellite in such a way that it will remain permanently poised above the same spot on the earth's surface. *True or false?*

8 So far as history records, the Greek philosopher Aristotle was the first man to suggest that the heavier an object is, the faster it falls. *True or false?*

9 The 16th-century astronomer Copernicus was the first man to suggest that the earth goes around the sun. *True or false?*

10 In 1066, William the Conqueror's invasion of Britain was heralded by the sudden appearance of a brilliant new 'Star in the East'. *True or false?*

Quibble Quiz
Ask a silly question . . .

A quiz not to be taken too seriously. Some people might think that a high score is a sign of a twisted mind.

1 What colour is a black box?

2 On what part of a main road would you be likely to see a number of children riding up and down?

3 If a lot of railway workers are RUN over, what is CUT back?

4 What word is spelt incorrectly in this sentence?

5 Why is the road vehicle called a semi-trailer clearly pronounced?

6 What famous sailor in history sets forth the first of every month from July to November inclusive?

7 What Socialist theme was expressed by the Locomotives on Highways Act, passed by Parliament in 1865?

8 What is WHO?

9 Why should a pedestrian who has just been knocked over by a car be badly in need of a tonic?

10 What pastry should you avoid if you don't want to be upset?

11 Which country would you visit if you were going to Die?

12 If only right were wrong what would be left?

Don't Quote Me
When you use famous sayings—get them right!

The passages which follow include some of the more common misquotations in the English language. If you can correct only half of them it will be a commendable performance.

1 And they sewed fig leaves together and made themselves clothing. (*Genesis* 3:7)

2 Lead on, Macduff. (Shakespeare's *Macbeth,* Act 7 Scene 1)

3 The quality of mercy is not strained, it droppeth as the gentle rain from heaven upon the earth beneath. (Shakespeare's *The Merchant of Venice,* Act 4 Scene 1)

4 Power corrupts, absolute power corrupts absolutely. (Lord Acton)

5 To gild the lily. (Shakespeare's *King John,* Act 4 Scene 1)

6 Water, water everywhere, and not a drop to drink. (S. T. Coleridge, *The Rhyme of the Ancient Mariner*)

7 Many a mickle makes a muckle. (Cervantes' *Don Quixote*)

8 Money is the root of all evil. (*1 Timothy* 6:10)

9 Genius is one per cent inspiration, and ninety-nine per cent hard work. (Thomas Alva Edison)

10 There, but for the grace of God, go I. (John Bradford)

11 Fresh fields and pastures new. (John Milton, *Lycidas*)

12 A little knowledge is a dangerous thing. (Alexander Pope, *Essay on Criticism*)

13 I must go down to the seas again. (John Masefield, *Sea Fever*)

14 A darned long road to home. (J. R. Lowell, *The Biglow Papers*)

15 Big fleas have little fleas upon their backs to bite 'em. (Augustus de Morgan)

One and One Make One
Linking words to make new words

The 20 four-letter words given below can be paired off to produce ten eight-letter words, all of which are quite commonly used in speech and writing. For instance, OVER+RATE would make OVERRATE, though that combination might be inadvisable, since it could well leave you at the end with some four-letter words without partners. How many of the ten eight-letter words can you discover?

ABLE	OWED
ACRE	PLEA
BEST	PORT
DISC	RAIN
FLAG	RANT
HAND	RATE
JUST	READ
MASS	REST
MODE	SING
OVER	SOME

Don't Believe It
Be a detective—get at the truth

We are tempted to accept without question most of what we read in print: we tend to think that simply because it *is* in print, it must be right. But it can be very wrong indeed. Take the following unhappy tale, for instance. Should we sympathise with the writer's misfortunes, or dismiss him as a self-confessed liar?

'The first train this morning must be late,' I remarked to the porter at the station. I was waiting for the branch-line train which shuttles ceaselessly throughout the day between Exe and Wye.

'It left an hour ago,' exclaimed the porter. 'It will be another hour before it is back here and leaves again. The trip takes an hour each way, you know.'

I kicked myself. Of course! British Summer Time had started last night, and I had failed to put my watch back. That is how I came to be late.

Now I should have to wait another 30 minutes for the bus which plies between the two towns. It, too, turns around and sets off back again as soon as it arrives at its destination.

The bus journey takes 1½ hours each way, so that, plus the 30 minutes wait, plus the hour I had lost already, meant that I was 3 hours late arriving at Wye, where I had an appointment to view some property. I might as well have waited for the next train, which would have got me there earlier.

'The place is too big for me since the death of my wife eight months ago,' explained the ageing owner, when eventually I arrived. 'And the design is a bit odd in some ways. You see, my poor widow suffered from pyromania—you know, a morbid fear of fire; that is why every room and passage in the place has two doors opening off it.

'But all to no avail! While alone in the house one night last winter, she dreamt the place was on fire, leapt out of bed, dived straight through the bedroom window, and was dead by the time our neighbour, awakened by her scream, reached her.

'It is the only window in the house lacking an inside shutter.

'You see, burglars were another of her fears. That is why six of the house's ten windows have outside shutters, though the four downstairs are the only ones with shutters both inside and out. Why she should have chosen a window when there are three outside doors to the house I shall never know, but then . . .'

So he rambled on, with sad anecdotes to account for every architectural feature.

That meant that I got back to the bus stop just in time to see the 5.30 bus tootling off in the direction of Exe.

I, therefore, had to wait for the 6 o'clock train home.

What a day! But then, of course, it was Friday the 13th.

The writer of this chapter of misfortunes is a liar. How many absurdities did you spot while reading his sad tale?

There are at least 12.

Drawing the Line

Think before you put pencil to paper

Here are three simple puzzles which require only pencil and paper—though, on second thoughts, they are perhaps not quite so simple as you might imagine.

1 What is the smallest number of straight lines that can be drawn if diagram 1 must be divided into eight triangles?

2 Can you trace out diagram 2 without lifting pencil from paper, without crossing any previously drawn line, and without at any time going against the direction of the arrows?

3 By drawing lines from one dot to another in diagram 3, is it possible to mark out a perfect square which contains as many dots within it as there are dots left outside it?

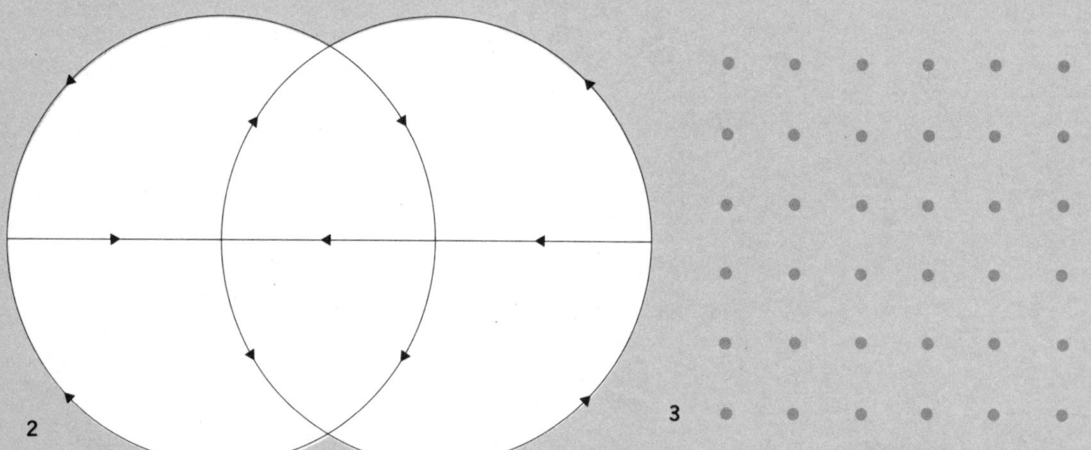

Grand Tour
Discover the hidden cities

By following the lines from letter to letter in the diagram here, it is possible to spell out the names of various cities in the world—more than you might at first imagine, for you are allowed to retrace your steps if that helps. For instance, starting from P in the bottom line, you could go north to R, east to A, north-west to I, then south-east back to A—which would give you PRAIA (capital of the Cape Verde Islands). But don't be alarmed—the other names are all better known than that one. There are at least 11 other cities concealed. How many of them can you find?

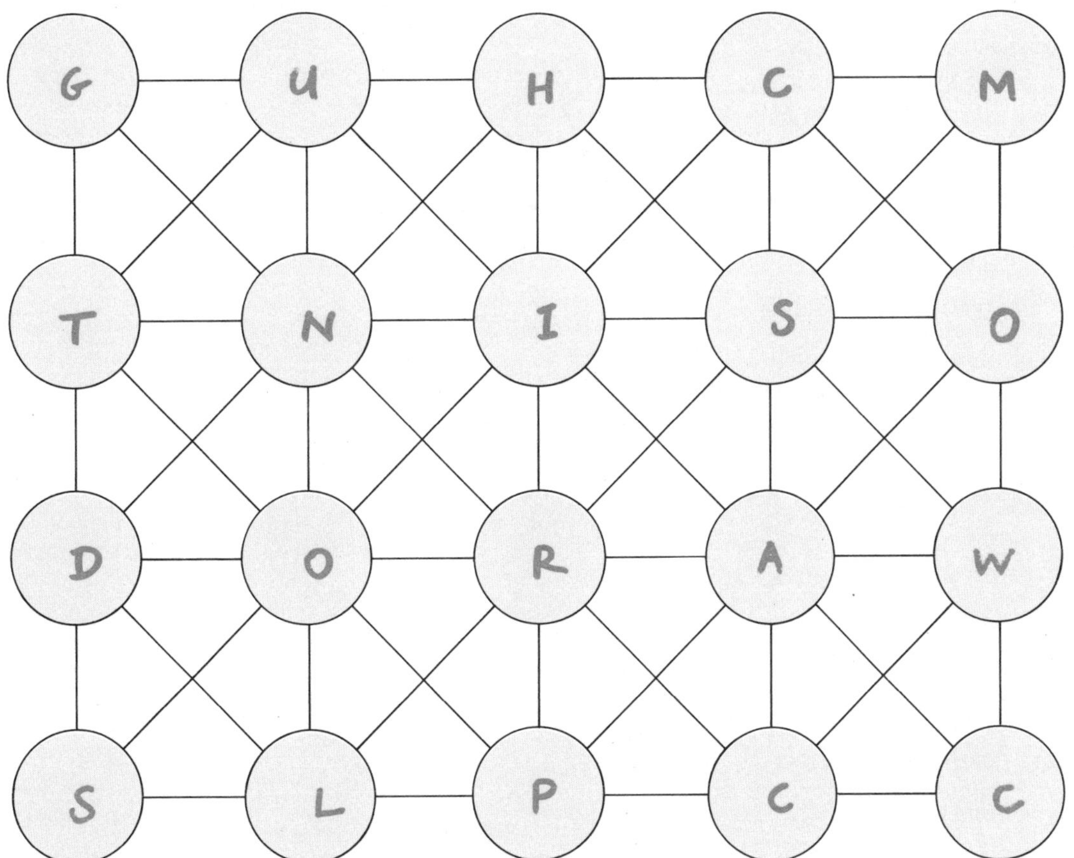

Hidden Animals
Finding out what's inside

An explorer from South America recently reported that he discovered, basking in the sun, a boa constrictor with a vastly distended stomach. On killing the reptile, he found the bulge represented a whole wild boar, which is not really surprising, because if you look at the spelling, a BOA *constRictor* always has a BOAR in it. For that matter, it also contains a BAT and an ANT, which makes it quite omnivorous. It also contains BACON and an ACTOR, but these words don't count because they are not animals. CRAB doesn't count either because, in this case, the letters appear in the wrong order.
The following ten species are similarly

omnivorous. Between them they contain more than 30 other creatures (the appropriate letters always appearing in the correct order) though some would certainly take some swallowing. How many can you discover?

1 BEAGLE
2 CHAMELEON
3 CORMORANT
4 CURASSOW
5 GRASSHOPPER
6 HARVEST MOUSE
7 HEDGEHOG
8 SEDGE-WARBLER
9 STONECHAT
10 WATER-HEN

Any Relation?
Sorting out the family

Bob, Tim, Jack, Mary, Anne and Janet are the names of Mrs. Watson's only grandchildren. Mary, Anne, Jack and Tim each have one brother and one sister.
What relationship is:

(a) Jack to Mary?
(b) Bob to Anne?
(c) Janet to Tim?

A Question of Identity
Track down the missing scientist

Can you identify an

IMAGINATIVE
DARING
RESPECTED
COURAGEOUS
SCIENTIST

To do so it is necessary to underline two consecutive letters in each of the five words above. When the ten underlined letters are then read together, they will spell out the Christian name and surname of the person to whom this description applies.

Awkward Letters
Would you believe they're part of a word?

Some combinations of letters look so awkward that it is hard to imagine they could ever form part of an English word. For instance, look at the group WKW. Standing in that order, those three letters look so unpronounceable that it may come as a surprise to learn that you have just read them. They actually appear in the title to this puzzle, for they form part of the word aWKWard.
Here are 15 other awkward-looking combinations. See if, for each of them, you can find an ordinary English word (unhyphenated) in which the group occurs.

1 AZO
2 BNA
3 CUU
4 DYB
5 HHO
6 HTN
7 KFA
8 LFP
9 RTZ
10 UOI
11 WOS
12 WYE
13 XOP
14 YMN
15 ZAA

Masquerade
Familiar people, unfamiliar names

For one reason or another, all the well-known people listed below changed their names. Some are now dead, some still living, so to make identification just a little easier, they are listed in chronological order. By what names are they now better known?

1 Siddhartha Gautama
2 Simon Bar-jona

3 Lucius Domitius Ahenobarbus
4 Jean François Marie Arouet
5 Mary Anne Evans
6 Charles Lutwidge Dodgson
7 Helen Porter Mitchell
8 George Saxe-Coburg-Gotha
9 Vladimir Ilyich Ulyanov
10 Joseph Vissarionovich Djugashvili
11 Lev Davidovich Bronstein
12 Margaret Gertrude Macleod (*née* Zelle)
13 Israel Balin
14 Lady Mallowan (*née* Miller)
15 Karol Wojtyla
16 Philip Schleswig-Holstein-Sonderbörg-Glucksburg
17 Cassius Clay
18 Priscilla White

Beauty Contest
Who was the winner?

'I notice,' said the chairman of judges, casting his eye over the five girls lined up on the stage, 'that there are more blondes than brunettes left in the finals.'
'And more brown eyes than blue,' remarked the second judge. 'But I'm voting for the blue-eyed girl standing next to one of the girls in a white costume.'
'But how can one distinguish between the two twins?' complained the third judge. 'Apart from the fact that they are not standing together, and that they are wearing differently coloured costumes, they are absolutely identical. To settle it I'll vote for the brunette at the end of the line.'
'The two redheads standing next to one another are very pretty,' said the chairman, 'but my vote will go to that blue-eyed brunette with the winsome smile.'
Here is the order in which the girls were standing before the three judges: Ann, Bunny, Chloe, Diane and Eve. What was the colour of hair, and the colour of eyes of each girl, and who won?
And, by the way, what were the names of the identical twins?

Jealousy
How did the couples cross the river?

A very ancient puzzle tells of two married couples who wished to cross a river in a rowing boat that would hold only two people, but so jealous were the men that no wife was ever to be left in the company of another man unless her own husband were present. They solved their problem in five trips thus: (1) First couple crossed (2) Husband returned (3) Both husbands crossed (4) Husband of remaining wife returned (5) Second couple crossed.
But what if there were three couples with only the same two-person boat, similarly resolved that no wife should be left in male company unless her husband were present? Could they all cross the river, and if so what would have to be the minimum number of trips?
No tricks, like suggesting that someone should swim, or that they should tie a rope to the boat and pull it across. The problem must be solved fairly, as in the original case.

The Geography Test
Finding the answers—without the questions

In their geography examination, Willie, Wally, Wendy, and Win each got half of the four questions right. Here are their answers:

WILLIE'S ANSWERS
Q1 Holland
Q2 Italy
Q3 Germany
Q4 Sweden

WALLY'S ANSWERS
Q1 Holland
Q2 Austria
Q3 France
Q4 Sweden

WENDY'S ANSWERS
Q1 Belgium
Q2 Austria

Q3 France
Q4 Norway

WIN'S ANSWERS
Q1 Holland
Q2 Austria
Q3 Germany
Q4 Denmark

There is no need for you to know your geography. In fact, you don't even have to know what the questions were, in order to work out the right answers to each question. What were the correct answers?

Bird-watching Holiday

How many hidden birds can you spot?

Dear Ed,

Starting early we took it easily, and at the Bell Inn, Eton, we picked up Jack Dawling and Ernest. One chatted a lot, so time passed swiftly, but rain on the motorway was a grave nuisance. After lunch I decided to hand over the wheel and steal an hour's sleep, before reaching Ullswater at midnight in gale-force winds.

Next morning on to Scotland, where our hotel is in as fine a glen as I have seen, with rushing stream at the bottom of a steep lovers' lane. It is all that is now left of an old mill, but it is now renovated, and very smart inside—no other one for miles around! Eric rows, though awkwardly, leaving Anne to doze in the stern. Excellent food—no good for taking off inches from the waist or keeping wide awake. Nothing is wanting, except perhaps regular kilts and pipers.

Love from all,
Ardelle

P.S. *I haven't forgotten that it is a bird-watching holiday.*
So far we have spotted 30 different kinds, and I have mentioned them all in this letter. You will, for instance, find 'redstart' in the first three words if you look hard enough. Since we *have spotted 30, see how many* you *can spot.*

Avowal

Juggling with vowels

The ancient Greeks had to learn seven vowels—thank goodness English has only five, but they are quite enough to create trouble sometimes. Here are a few teasers to see if you know them really well.

1 What is the shortest word in the English language which contains all the five different vowels (A E I O U) somewhere in its spelling?
2 What is the shortest English word containing all the five vowels in their correct alphabetical order (with consonants in between them of course)?
3 What is the shortest English word containing all the five vowels in *reverse* alphabetical order?
4 The Hawaiian word hooiaoia boasts a consecutive string of 7 vowels. No English word can match that, though the word *Hawaiian* itself has four. Can you think of an all-too-familiar English word containing a consecutive string of five vowels?
5 And what about the longest English word that contains no vowels at all?

Oceans of Knowledge

Thirteen questions about the Seven Seas

More than two-thirds of the earth's surface is covered by water, but how much do you know about the sea, ships, sea creatures, and the seashore? Here are some questions that will enable you to find out.

1 Can you name the traditional Seven Seas?
2 The average temperature of the world's oceans is 3·8°C, which is rather cold for bathing. If you don't want to shiver, what part of the earth would you visit in order to enjoy the warmest bathe in the sea?
3 Brackish water means water that is: (a) Stagnant? (b) Brownish? (c) Salty? (d) Evil-smelling?
4 How many masts must a ship have? Be careful!

5 Ratlines are ropes used for mooring a ship to the wharf, and get their name from the fact that they are the means by which rats usually find their way on to a vessel. *True or false?*
6 The name 'Blue Peter' has become widely known since it was given to a television programme for children, but what does it signify on a ship?
7 Chronometers (portable clocks of great precision) were invented in the 18th century because old-fashioned clocks were useless on board ship. Why were they useless?
8 Everyone knows that Nelson lost an arm and an eye in battle, but which arm, and which eye?
9 By what title is the Lord of the Isles better known?
10 How many limbs has a crab?
11 Which can fly faster, a sea-eagle or a sea-canary?
12 If, while fishing on the Norfolk coast, you managed to land a sturgeon, where in London should you send it to?
13 If you own a house fronting the sea, your property is normally regarded as extending to: (a) The beginning of the sand? (b) High-water mark? (c) Low-water mark? (d) A stone's throw from the last blade of grass?

Shades of Meaning

Make your language more colourful

Below are ten lists of words. For each list there is some colour which, when applied to each of its words, produces some other well-known word, description or expression.
How many of the appropriate colours can you discover?

1 Sugar, Paper, Shirt
2 Elephant, Panther, Salmon
3 Cheese, Sleeves, Fingers
4 Back, Streak, Peril
5 Fever, Runner, Pimpernel
6 Board, Mail, List
7 Feather, Collar, Wash
8 Print, Bell, Bottle
9 Beard, Owl, Hound
10 Carpet, Letter, Skin

Name Chain

Find the links so that they hang together

Here is a list of 12 names:

ARTHUR	REBECCA
DONALD	SAMUEL
DORIS	SID
ERNEST	THOMAS
LIONEL	TONY
LORNA	YVONNE

At present they are in alphabetical order. Can you rearrange the 12 names into a single chain, in which the last letter of each name is the same as the first letter of the name following it? For example, *DoriS SiD DonalD* could be the start of such a chain—but be careful, because you may find that such a start could produce difficulties later on in the list.

Prove your Point

Think clearly—and carry conviction

Finding the right arguments with which to prove your point is not always that easy, especially if you want to prove your point in a truly logical fashion. Consider, for instance, these five statements:

1 No expensive thing is popular
2 Some popular things are unavailable
3 Only popular things are worth having
4 Some available things are expensive
5 Some things worth having are cheap

Which of these statements do you need in order to prove conclusively that *some available things are not worth having?*

Postal Code
Break the mystery cipher

Postmasters claim to be past-masters not only at reading bad handwriting, but also at unscrambling confused addresses. But if you were a postmaster, what would you make of writing that was *intentionally* cryptic? Like this, for example:

shaft Avenue,
B, er, er, er,
HANTS.

From this encoded inscription, can you derive a full address consisting of two initials, surname, house number, street, town, and county? Be warned, this is a tricky one!

ANSWERS

Watch this Space

1 *False.* The earth revolves in 23 hours 56 minutes 4·09 seconds, but because of its movement around the sun, it takes nearly another 4 minutes before the sun again appears overhead.
2 *False.* A light-year is not a period of time, but a measure of distance (approximately 9·6 million million kilometres).
3 *True.* This is the rate at which it is fusing hydrogen into helium. But don't worry; it has enough hydrogen to last for several thousand million years to come.
4 *False.* It is the earth's gravity which *holds* him in orbit, the same as it holds the moon in orbit. He feels weightless because the earth's gravity is exactly balanced by the centrifugal pull of his swinging orbit.
5 *False.* The moon's mass is only 1/80th that of the earth. Because the moon is smaller, a lunar walker is much closer to the centre of gravity than an earth walker, so his weight is less—only one-sixth of that of an earth walker.
6 *False.* It would take about 148,000 years for it to reach *Centauri Proxima,* the sun's nearest neighbour.
7 *True.* At a height of about 42,000 kilometres the speed of an orbiting satellite exactly matches the earth's rotation, so always remains above the same spot. Our round-the-world TV pictures are relayed by just such satellites.
8 *True.* Aristotle *did* suggest just that—but he was wrong. In a vacuum—where there is no air to check their progress—all objects, whether a feather or a tonne of lead, fall at the same speed.
9 *False.* It was first suggested by the Greek astronomer Aristarchus of Samos about 250 BC.
10 *True.* Halley's comet—the most brilliant of all comets—appeared in that year, and is actually depicted on the Bayeux tapestry. There is no astronomical evidence to support the appearance of any similar phenomenon at the time of Christ's birth.

Quibble Quiz

1 Red. The famous 'black box' which automatically records details of a plane's flight is usually painted bright red, for easy identification in the wreckage should the plane crash.
2 A roundabout.
3 Trades Union Congress. RUN is the NUR turned *over*, and CUT is the TUC turned *back*.
4 The word 'incorrectly'.
5 Because it is articulated.
6 Jason (leader of the Argonauts) whose name J-A-S-O-N 'sets forth' the first letters of the months July, August, September, October, November.
7 The theme of 'Keep the Red Flag flying'. The act required mechanically propelled vehicles to be preceded always by a man carrying a red warning flag.
8 World Health Organisation.
9 Because he is run down.
10 A turnover.
11 France. Die is a town 180 kilometres due north of Marseilles.
12 Right. If only the right-hand side were wrong, it follows that the left-hand side would not be wrong, and would therefore be right.

Don't Quote Me

1 . . . made themselves aprons. (According to the Authorised Version. The *New English Bible* gives 'loincloths'.)
2 Lay on, Macduff.
3 . . . upon the place beneath.
4 Power tends to corrupt . . .
5 To gild refined gold, to paint the lily.
6 . . . nor any drop to drink.
7 Many a pickle makes a mickle. ('Mickle' and 'Muckle' would be absurd, since both words mean the same thing.)
8 The love of money is the root of all evil.
9 . . . and ninety-nine per cent perspiration.
10 But for the grace of God, there goes John Bradford.
11 Fresh woods . . .
12 A little learning . . .
13 I must down to the seas again.
14 A darned long row to hoe.
15 Great fleas have little fleas . . .

One and One Make One

BESTOWED, DISCOVER, FLAGRANT, HANDSOME, MASSACRE, MODERATE, PLEASING, PORTABLE, READJUST, RESTRAIN. (You really should have discovered DISCOVER. It happens to be the very last word in the instructions to the puzzle.)

Don't Believe It

1 For the start of BST you put a watch forward, not back.
2 Believing an adjusted watch would result in being an hour early, not late.
3 The writer should have arrived 2 hours late, not 3. (1 hour late at station PLUS 30 minutes wait, PLUS $1\frac{1}{2}$ hour bus journey, LESS 1 hour the train would have taken anyway.)
4 The next train to Wye would have arrived at the same time as the bus, not earlier.
5 Had the owner had a widow he would have been dead.
6 Eight months before BST commences is summer, not winter.
7 Pyromania is not fear of fire, but an irrational impulse to start fires.
8 If the wife died instantly, who knows what she dreamed?
9 With two door-faces to each inner enclosure, and 3 door-faces outside, the house would have had an odd number of door-faces, which is impossible since each door must have two sides.
10 If nine of the ten windows have inner shutters, and six have outer shutters, at least five (not four) must have both.
11 If a shuttling bus (on a $1\frac{1}{2}$ hour run) leaves Exe 30 minutes before a shuttling train (on a 1 hour run), as it did in the morning, at no time during the day will a train leave Wye 30 minutes after a bus.
12 BST invariably begins on a Sunday morning, never on a Friday.

Drawing the Line

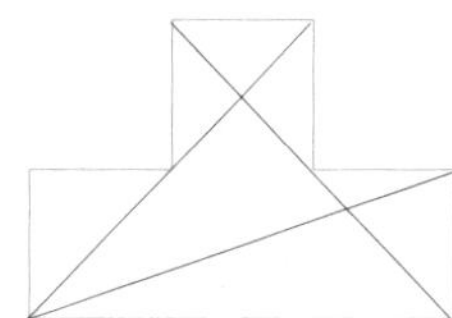

1 Three straight lines do the trick

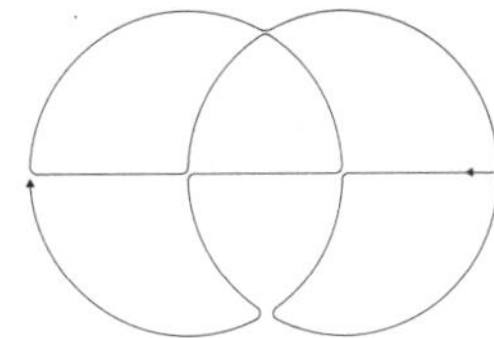

2 This is the way your pencil should go

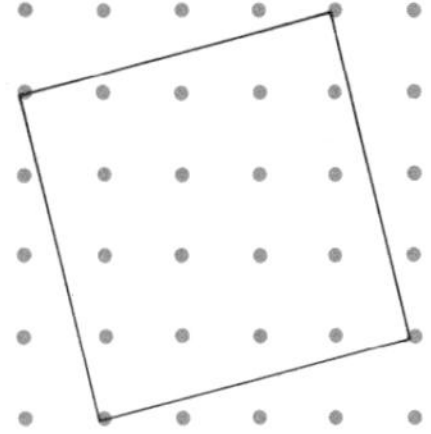

3 Join up four of the dots this way

Grand Tour

ACCRA, CAIRO, CARACAS, LONDON, MOSCOW, OSLO, PARIS, TORONTO, TUNIS, WARSAW, WASHINGTON. The island of CAPRI also happens to be in the puzzle.

Hidden Animals

1 Bee, Eagle.
2 Camel, Hen.
3 Coot, Cat, Man, Rat, Ant.
4 Crow, Cow, Ass, Sow.
5 Gaper, Gar, Groper, Ass, Asp, Ape.
6 Hare, Hart, Emu.
7 Hog, Dog.
8 Seal, Sable, Eel, Deer, Dab.
9 Stoat, Neat, Cat.
10 Wren, Tern.

Any Relation?

(a) Cousin. (b) Brother. (c) Sister. The children must belong to two families comprising (1) Bob, Mary, Anne, and (2) Tim, Jack, Janet.

A Question of Identity

The letters to be underlined are MA, RI, EC, UR, IE, which spell out the name MARIE CURIE.

Awkward Letters

1 rAZOr
2 thumBNAil
3 vaCUUm
4 laDYBird
5 witHHOld
6 ligHTNing
7 breaKFAst
8 haLFPenny
9 quaRTZ
10 qUOIt
11 tWOSome
12 laWYEr
13 saXOPhone
14 hYMN
15 baZAAr

Masquerade

1 Buddha **2** Peter (the Apostle) **3** The Emperor Nero **4** Voltaire **5** George Eliot **6** Lewis Carroll **7** Nellie Melba (the name being derived from Melbourne, near where she was born) **8** George Windsor, then King George V (the Royal Family's name being changed to Windsor by proclamation on July 17, 1917) **9** Lenin **10** Stalin **11** Trotsky **12** Mata Hari **13** Irving Berlin **14** Agatha Christie **15** Pope John Paul II **16** Philip Mountbatten (assumed his mother's maiden name in 1947 before being created Duke of Edinburgh) **17** Muhammad Ali **18** Cilla Black

Beauty Contest

Name	Ann	Bunny	Chloe	Diane	Eve
Hair	Brunette	Blonde	Redhead	Redhead	Blonde
Eyes	Blue	Brown	Blue	Brown	Brown

Ann, with the votes of both the chairman and the third judge, was the winner. Bunny and Eve are the twins.

Jealousy

1 Any two wives cross **2** One returns **3** Both available wives cross **4** One wife returns and stays with her husband **5** Other two husbands cross **6** One couple returns **7** Both available husbands cross **8** Third wife returns **9** Any two wives cross **10** Husband of remaining wife returns **11** Final couple crosses (steps 10 and 11 could be accomplished by one woman returning to fetch the remaining wife, but in no way can the trips be reduced to less than 11, so why be so ungallant as to fatigue the poor exhausted women further?)

The Geography Test

The only possible set of answers which would mean that each child got exactly two right and two wrong is: Q1, Belgium. Q2, Austria. Q3, Germany. Q4, Sweden.

Bird-watching Holiday

1 deaR ED STARTing **2** tooK IT Easily **3** belL INN ETon **4** JACK DAWling **5** dawlinG AND ERnest **6** erneST ONE CHATted **7** SWIFTly **8** gRAVE Nuisance **9** hanD OVEr **10** sTEAL **11** reachinG ULLswater **12** midNIGHT IN GALE **13** finE A GLEn **14** wiTH RUSHing **15** steeP LOVERs' **16** nOW Left **17** buT IT **18** noW RENovated **19** sMART INside **20** otHER ONe **21** eriC ROWs **22** thougH AWKwardly **23** leavinG ANNE To **24** sTERN **25** offF INCHes **26** waiST OR Keeping **27** iS WANting **28** reguLAR Kilts **29** kiltS AND PIPERS **30** froM ALL ARDelle

Avowal

1 SEQUOIA (the giant redwood tree of California) **2** FACETIOUS (beats ABSTEMIOUS by one letter)
3 SUBCONTINENTAL (beats UNCOMPLIMENTARY by one letter, UNCONTINENTAL would beat both, but is not given in most authoritative dictionaries) **4** QUEUEING (you see what we meant by 'familiar') **5** RHYTHMS

Oceans of Knowledge

1 In order of size they are: South Pacific, North Pacific, Indian, North Atlantic, South Atlantic, Antarctic, Arctic **2** The Persian Gulf where, in summer, the surface temperature of the sea rises to about 32°C
3 Salty **4** Three. Anything with fewer masts is, strictly speaking, a boat **5** *False*. Ratlines are the rope 'rungs' across the shrouds, used by ratings as ladders **6** The Blue Peter is a blue flag with a white square in the middle, which is hoisted to announce that a moored vessel will soon be sailing **7** Because accurate clocks were needed as navigational aids, and existing ones did not keep time well enough on a rocking, rolling ship **8** Right arm, right eye
9 HRH The Prince of Wales **10** Ten **11** The sea-eagle. A sea-canary can't fly at all. It is another name for the white whale **12** Buckingham Palace. Though you may be given permission to keep it, all sturgeon in British waters are the property of the sovereign **13** High-water mark—at least for the purpose of defining trespass.

Shades of Meaning

1 Brown **2** Pink **3** Green **4** Yellow **5** Scarlet
6 Black **7** White **8** Blue **9** Grey **10** Red

Name Chain

TONY, YVONNE, ERNEST, THOMAS, SID, DONALD, DORIS, SAMUEL, LIONEL, LORNA, ARTHUR, REBECCA.

Prove your Point

Statements **1**, **3**, and **4**. If (**4**) *some* available things are expensive, and (**1**) *no* expensive thing is popular, then some available things are *not* popular. Then, since (**3**) *only* popular things are worth having, it follows that some available things are *not* worth having. (Statements **2** and **5** can contribute nothing at all to your argument.)

Postal Code

A. B. Withers, 3 Undershaft Avenue, Andover, HANTS. (A 'B', with 'ers' three, under 'shaft Avenue', and over 'HANTS'.)

OUTDOOR GAMES

Old-established favourites and exciting new ideas for groups of children of all ages

Games for the Garden

Games for a summer party outdoors;
The skills in playing marbles and jacks;
Playing touch, quoits and croquet

Today, many town and suburban gardens have a playing space too small for some of the games loved by children in the past. The following games can be played in the restricted space of the average garden. If you have a large garden, the scope is much wider. Then children can also play games described in the next chapter, 'Games for Open Spaces'.

Apple Ducking
Traditional and great fun

This is a traditional Hallow-e'en game, but it can become messy indoors. It is, therefore, better played as a garden game. Players gather around a large tub of water in which several apples are floating. They compete either one at a time or all at once, to try to get one of the floating apples out of the water without using hands. To do this, they duck their heads into the water and try to bite the apple. If all the players duck at the same time, the winner is the first to get an apple out of the tub.
If the players take turns, to determine the winner they should be timed. Have a number of towels on hand!

Bear in the Cage
Much pushing and shoving

The bear stands in a cage formed by the hunters who join hands at arm's length in a circle around him. The bear tries to break free, the hunters must keep their hands joined, must not hold on to the bear and they must not move their feet. When the bear escapes or the hunters break the rules, a new bear is chosen.
Prison Break is a team version with the same rules. Two circles are formed and each circle

sends one of its members to be a prisoner in the other. The first to break out wins a point for his circle which sends over another prisoner. The team with the most points after an agreed time is the winner.

Back-to-Back
Locking out the runner

One player, the runner, stands in the middle of the playing area while the others scatter around in pairs. Each player stands back-to-back with his partner, their elbows hooked. The runner calls out 'Everybody change!' The players separate and try to lock arms with new partners. The runner seeks a partner for himself and, if he succeeds, the player left over becomes the new runner.

Run Around the Circle
Fast fun for the young ones

Players form a large circle facing inwards. One player, the runner, stands inside. The runner moves around then suddenly stands between any two players. These race around the outside of the circle in opposite directions. The one who returns first to the starting point fills the vacant place. The other becomes the new runner.

Toss the Cap
Players have their ups and downs

Two teams stand facing each other on lines about 2 metres apart. One player, the cap tosser, stands between them. About 7 metres behind each team is a base line. One team is the 'ups', the other the 'downs'.
The cap tosser throws his cap in the air. If it falls right-side up, the ups turn and run towards their base line with the downs chasing them. If the cap falls upside-down, the downs run towards their base line with the ups in pursuit. When a player is touched he joins the opposing team and the game continues until one team has no players left.

Fox and Farmer
A game of cunning and speed

One player is the fox, another the farmer. All the rest form a circle facing inwards with their arms outstretched sideways, their hands resting on one another's shoulders.
At a signal, the farmer chases the fox. To escape, the fox takes any route around the circle, weaving in and out among the players. The farmer must follow the fox's exact route. If the fox is touched, the farmer chooses one of the players in the circle to become a new farmer while he becomes the fox. Should the fox elude the farmer for 2 minutes a new fox and farmer are chosen.

Obstacle Race
Just to make life difficult

A referee sets up an obstacle course, made up of tins, boxes or similar markers, along a 10 metre track. Players line up in single file behind a starting line.
At a signal, the first player runs down the course, circling around the obstacles, each in its turn. Upon reaching the turning line, 10 metres away, he returns down the track, circling the obstacles in reverse order. When the first contestant has completed the run, the second moves out, then the third and so on. Each contestant is timed by the referee and the one to complete the course in the shortest time wins the race.

Three Jolly Workmen
Words traditional, action timeless

Players form two equal teams, workmen and employers, and stand behind two goal lines about 12 metres apart. The workmen select a trade or job that they can mime and go up to

the employers. The sides then chant this traditional dialogue:
Workmen: 'We're three (or the number in the team) jolly workmen come to do some work.'
Employers: 'What work can you do?'
Workmen: 'Anything to please you.'
Employers: 'Pray let us see you do it.'
The workers then mime the trade they have chosen. When one of the employers guesses correctly what it is, the workers rush back to their goal line chased by the employers. If a worker is touched before crossing the line, the workers and employers change roles.

Piggy
Five hits scoop the pool

A saucer is placed on the floor and a line is marked about 3 metres away. Each player is given five marbles.
The players take turns shooting their marbles from the line at the saucer. If a player hits the saucer, he continues to shoot. If he misses, the next player takes a turn. The first player to hit the saucer with all five of his marbles wins the game.

Cut and thrust in the ancient game of Marbles

Marbles developed as a children's game from bowls, which were originally made of marble. Marbles was at one time played with nuts or small stones, or anything that could be rolled along the ground. It was a popular pavement game but it can be played on any smooth surface.
Marbles is a game of attack. In most versions, the object is to win as many of an opponent's marbles as possible by hitting them with one of your own. Sometimes all marbles are kept by the winner, sometimes the marbles are returned at the end of the game, the winner being satisfied with the honour of victory.
The marble used to shoot with, called the Taw, is a prized possession. It is usually an Alley, a large marble, once made of coloured alabaster but now of coloured glass. Alleys are seldom used in games where the Taw itself is at risk. In such cases, the prudent player uses a marble of much less value such as a smaller glass version of the Alley.
The method of shooting the marble is to get down on one knee, and balance the marble on the first finger of one hand with the thumb. The knuckles are rested on the ground and the marble is shot by flicking it away with the thumb.

Bossout
A pavement version of the game of bowls

Sometimes known as Boss and Span, this game is the simplest form of marbles. Two players take part, each with an agreed equal number of marbles. The first player shoots a marble to any distance he likes. The other then shoots at it.
If he hits the target marble or gets close enough to it to span the distance with the thumb and little finger of one hand he wins it. It is then his turn to shoot a target marble. If he does not get close enough to span the distance he leaves his marble where it lies and it becomes the target marble for the first player to shoot at, taking aim from the spot where his original target marble lay. The game continues until one player has won all the marbles.
Long Taw is played in exactly the same way except that spanning is not allowed. The target marble must be hit if the shooter is to win it.

Roll 'em Through
All the points are boxed in

Five rectangular holes of different sizes are made along one side of a cardboard box, which is then placed on a smooth surface about 3 metres from a shooting line. Each hole has a

points value from one for the largest to five for the smallest.
Players take turns to kneel at the line and try to shoot five marbles into the holes.
The player with the highest number of points wins.

Shooting the Ring

And aiming for a quick knock-out

A circle about 2.5 metres in diameter is marked on a smooth surface. Each player lays one marble on the rim of the circle, spaced evenly.
A shooting line is drawn about 1·8 metres from the circle. Every player has a shooter, a jumbo-sized marble.
Players first decide the order of play by rolling their shooters from the line towards the centre of the circle. The player whose shooter lands closest to the centre takes the first turn; the next closest takes the second, and so on.
The first player aims his shot from the shooting line. Subsequent shots are taken from the point where the shooter stops. The first player tries to hit one of the marbles on the circle's rim and knock it outside the circle.
If he succeeds and his shooter also falls outside the circle, he wins the marble he hit and continues to shoot.
If he fails, he adds a marble from his own stock to the rim of the circle and gives way to the next player. If his shooter remains in the circle he must leave it there and use another shooter for his next turn. The game goes on until all marbles in the circle have been won, and the player with the most is the winner.

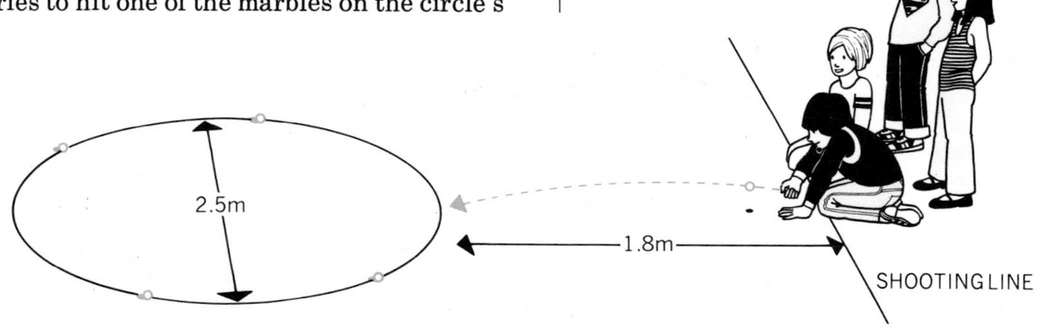

Ringers

When 13 can be lucky for the skilful shooter

A circle about 3 metres in diameter is marked on a smooth surface. Two straight lines are also drawn 3 metres apart from each other. One is the 'lag' line, the other the 'pitch' line. Thirteen marbles are placed, about 7 centimetres apart, in the form of a cross in the centre of the circle. Before the game begins the players decide the order of play by kneeling in turn at the pitch line and shooting their shooter marbles towards the lag line. The player whose shooter comes to rest closest to the lag line will take the first shot, the next closest is the second to play, and so on. The purpose of the game is to knock the marbles forming the cross out of the circle.

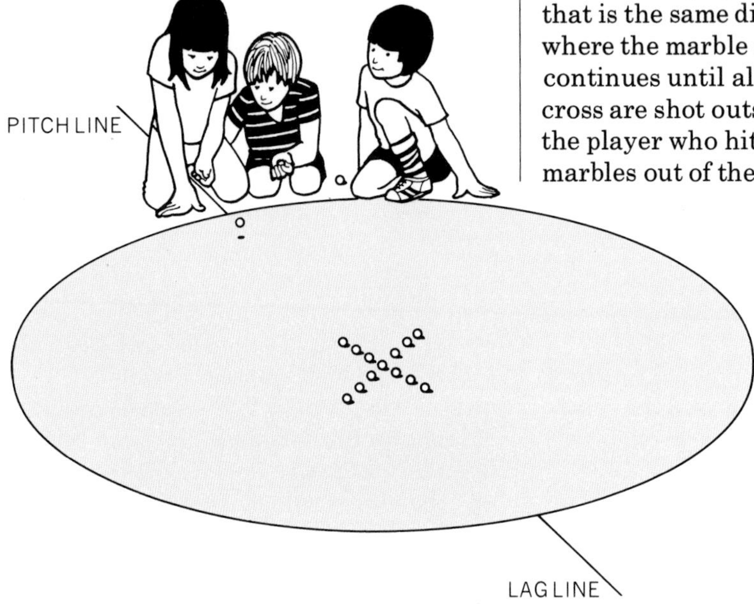

The first player takes his shot and if he knocks one of the target marbles out he shoots again. If, however, his shooter comes to rest either inside or outside the circle without knocking one of the target marbles out, the next player takes his turn. The second player gets a further turn if his shooter knocks a target marble out of the circle or if it knocks an opponent's shooter that has come to rest inside the circle out of the circle.

After his first shot, a player makes subsequent shots from the point where his marble has come to rest, if it is inside the circle. If it lands outside, the player may shoot from any point that is the same distance from the centre as where the marble came to rest. The game continues until all the marbles forming the cross are shot outside the ring. The winner is the player who hits the greatest number of marbles out of the circle.

Jacks

A game of skill and dexterity with its roots in history

This game, under various names, has been played by children all over the world for thousands of years. As Jackstones, Fivestones, Checkstones, Knucklebones, Dibs, Dabs or Snobs, the game has preserved its essential characteristics for centuries. Under all these names the game is played with four or five small stones that are thrown up and caught on the back of the hand or in the palm.

Jackstones have been found in crannogs, or lake dwellings, which indicate the ancient origins of the game. In the Greco-Roman room in the British Museum there is a statue of two boys quarrelling at a game of Tali. In Deptford, London, and in parts of Cornwall and Northamptonshire, the stone that is thrown in the air is called a 'tally', and this provides an interesting piece of evidence to link the spread of the game by the Romans throughout Europe.

The Romans played the game with knucklebones, the small bones found in the knee joints of sheep, and the name Knucklebones survives in many districts.

The game appears to have spread eastwards and westwards around the world because a Japanese version called Tedama (Handballs) is played in the United States under the names of Otadama, or Japanese Jacks.

In all variations the complicated sequence of throws is important, because any player who makes a mistake (dropping or missing all the stones, or not following the sequence correctly) must hand over the stones to the next player.

The basic game is as follows:

Five small stones about the size of a cube of sugar are placed in the palm of the hand, tossed into the air and caught on the back of the hand. These are then tossed into the air again and caught in the palm of the hand.

Following this, four stones are scattered on the ground and the fifth stone is used to throw into the air. While the stone is in the air one stone is picked up and the falling stone is caught in the same hand. The remaining three stones are next picked up in turn.

The four stones are scattered on the ground in sets of two. When the fifth stone is thrown into the air two stones are picked up at a time, with the falling stone being caught in the same hand.

Following this, the four stones are arranged in a group of three and a single stone. Play continues with first the three being picked up and then the single.

Four stones are then placed in a group and the fifth stone tossed into the air—all four stones are picked up at the same time and the falling stone is caught in the same hand.

The five stones are again tossed into the air and caught on the back of the hand. Should any stones fall off they are retrieved by opening the fingers to hold them, then they are tossed into the air and caught along with the others.

With the five stones now in the hand, the game proceeds by throwing up one stone and placing one of the stones in the hand on the ground and catching the falling stone. This is done until four stones are on the ground. The game continues by placing two stones at a time (two throws), three stones and one stone (two throws), then finally four stones (one throw).

There are a number of variations of Jacks.

Magic
Throwing a full hand

This game is played in the same way as One'ers except that instead of throwing up a single stone, all the stones in the hand are thrown up as another stone is picked up.

In *Magic Flycatchers*, which is played like Magic, all stones thrown up must be caught in a snatching or pouncing movement from above. This variation requires great skill.

One'ers
A traditional toss-up

To play One'ers the stones are thrown up and caught on the back of the hand. Any stones falling off are picked up in the following manner: The stones remaining on the back of the hand are tossed into the air and caught in the hollow of the hand. Retaining these in the hand, one stone is thrown into the air and a stone is picked up with the same hand holding the stones—the falling stone is also caught with the same hand. This continues until the stones have been picked up.

Two'ers, Three'ers, Four'ers are variations of One'ers, except that any stones not caught on the back of the hand must be arranged in sets of two, three and four by the hand on which the stones are lying. If the number of stones that fall when the stones are thrown up do not allow the right group to be formed, the player has to drop from the back of his hand

the required number (but no more).
Magic Flycatchers is played in a similar way as One'ers, except that the falling stone is caught by a snatching or pouncing movement from above.

Round the Square
The drill is: Form fours

This game is also known as Four Squares and Fourses. Four stones are placed in a square. The fifth stone is thrown into the air and one stone from the square is picked up. The stone that was picked up now becomes the throwing stone and the first stone is placed in the vacant corner position. This action continues round the square, sometimes clockwise and sometimes anti-clockwise.
Trotting Donkeys is played in the same way as Round the Square, except that the stones are placed in a straight line.

Cradle
Up, up and pick-up

Four stones are placed touching each other in a line. The fifth stone is thrown into the air and one stone at a time must be picked up from the line without the other stones being moved.
In *Chimney,* four flat stones are placed one on top of the other to form a chimney. The fifth stone is tossed into the air and one by one the stones forming the chimney must be picked up without disturbing those remaining.

Arches
The stones go underneath

Four stones are scattered on the ground. The tips of fingers and thumb of the left hand are placed on the ground and fingers are spread to make arches.
The fifth stone is thrown into the air and the stones on the ground are flicked by the little finger of the right hand one by one through the arches until all stones are underneath.
When all stones are underneath, the hand is removed and the fifth stone is tossed into the air and the four stones are picked up together. The falling stone is caught by the same hand.

Downs and Ups
No-bounce, one-bounce two-bounce

A player holds six stones, or jacks, and a ball in his playing hand. He tosses the ball up, scatters the jacks and catches the ball before it bounces. Then the action is reversed. With the jacks already scattered, the ball is tossed, the jacks picked up and the ball caught before it bounces.
In *Eggs in Basket* the player scatters the jacks. Using only one hand, he tosses the ball and picks up one jack. He transfers the jack to his other hand—the basket—and catches the ball on one bounce. In this manner he picks up all the jacks, one by one, by twos, threes, and so on.
In *Crack the Eggs* a player scatters the jacks, then using one hand he tosses the ball up, picks up one jack, taps it on the floor (to 'crack the egg') and catches the ball on one bounce. The action is repeated by ones, twos, threes, and so on.

Yo-Yo Games
They started in the Philippines many years ago

The Yo-Yo, meaning 'come-come', originated as a large, weighty jungle weapon used by Filipino warriors. The Yo-Yo craze began in the United States in 1926, and since then its popularity has gone up and down like the action of the toy itself. According to the *Guinness Book of Records*, the world endurance record is held by an American who played for 120 hours. Another American also goes into the records for completing 20,302 loops in 3 hours.
The Yo-Yo consists of two round pieces of

wood or plastic joined by a short axle. There are two types. The standard type has one end of a piece of string up to 1 metre long embedded in the axle. This allows only one kind of action after the string is wrapped around the axle and the loose end is looped around the player's forefinger. When the Yo-Yo is thrown sharply down or forwards it unwinds, then immediately winds up again, returning to the player's hand.

In a second type, the stunt Yo-Yo, the string is knotted in a loose loop around the axle, permitting numerous variations on the basic action. A stunt Yo-Yo is needed to perform the tricks described here, all of which require considerable practice to master. Once players become proficient in these tricks they can compete among themselves to see who can keep going the longest.

The Sleeper
An easy spinner winner

This is the easiest Yo-Yo trick. With a flick of the wrist, the Yo-Yo is thrown downwards. When it reaches the end of the string, it begins to spin—'sleep'—and the string remains fully extended. When the spinning slows down, the player jerks his wrist up slightly and the Yo-Yo climbs up the string into the player's hand. Players compete to see who can keep a Yo-Yo sleeping for the longest time.

Creeper-Sleeper
Getting a good grounding

The player throws a fast Sleeper. When the Yo-Yo is fully extended on the string, the player lowers his hand close to the ground to allow the Yo-Yo to travel forward. The player then jerks the string sharply upwards, the Yo-Yo returns to his hand and the player repeats the action. The player who can keep this up the longest wins the contest.

Forward Pass
Out it goes, back it comes

The player's arm rests loosely by his side, the palm of his hand facing in. His arm is then brought up sharply in a forward motion and the Yo-Yo is released, sending it out to the end of its string. As it returns the hand is turned palm up to receive it. The player who throws the most forward passes without stopping wins.

Over the Falls
A neat double trick

This combines the Sleeper and the Forward Pass. It begins like the Forward Pass but when the Yo-Yo returns, the player, instead of catching it, turns his hand and lets it fall straight down, where it sleeps. When the sleeping begins to flag, the player brings the Yo-Yo up and repeats the action. The player who performs this double trick the greatest number of times wins.

BALL GAMES TO PLAY IN THE GARDEN

Ball games have been popular since the time of the ancient Greeks and Romans. It is thought that in even earlier times the games had some astrological significance, because of the spherical shape of the ball. They might also have had a religious meaning, implying a battle between good and evil. Whatever the origins, ball games, such as football, rugby, cricket, golf and tennis, are now the most popular sports in the world. The games in this section are far more simple than the duels fought out at Wembley Stadium, Lord's cricket ground or the All-England Lawn Tennis Club at Wimbledon. But for young participants, these games can give as much excitement as a Cup Final.

Catch Ball
One takes on the rest

Two parallel lines are marked about 5 or 7 metres apart, according to the amount of playing space available. All the players but one stand behind one line. The lone player stands behind the other. He is the server.
The server tosses a football or volleyball up with one hand, and hits it with the other, sending it into the group of players. If one of them catches it without a bounce, he becomes the next server. If not, the server continues until he has hit a ball that is caught without bouncing.

Circle Serve
Plenty of bounce, plenty of speed

Players stand in a small circle, about 3 metres in diameter, facing inwards. The player with the football or volleyball points to a player across the circle, bounces the ball once, and serves it to him. This player catches the serve, bounces it once, and serves it to another player.
The action is continued in this manner, with players who fail to serve accurately, or catch the ball, given a penalty point. The player with the least number of penalty points after 10 minutes is the winner.
The serve is normally done with the flat of the hand and an underhand or sidearm movement.

Three Times Round
Sit-down shows who's first

Players divide into two or more teams of equal numbers. Each team forms a circle. One player in each team has a football or volleyball.
He passes the ball, using both hands, to the player on his right. The second player gives it to the third and so on until it has gone completely around the circle. When the ball reaches the first player again, he bounces it on the ground once and calls out 'One time round!' and passes the ball on. This action is repeated by each player, until the ball reaches the first player, who bounces it twice and calls 'Twice round!' The third and last time he bounces the ball three times and calls 'Three times round!' The first team to complete the circle sits on the ground to show it has won.

Stride Ball
Keeping it in the circle

A circle is formed and players take 'stride' position, standing with their feet well apart, touching their neighbours' feet on each side. One player stands in the centre holding a football or volleyball. The centre player tries to throw or roll the ball so that it escapes

outside the circle, either between a player's legs or between two players. If the ball passes above the players' shoulders, the throw does not count.
Players on the edge of the circle must not move their feet but they can use their hands to block the ball or hit it back into the middle.
If the ball goes through a player's feet, that player changes position with the centre player. If the ball goes between two players, the one on the left moves to the centre.

Skittle Race

For teams with accurate eyes

Two teams line up behind a starting line, with another parallel line 7 metres away. Behind the second line, five skittles or plastic bottles are placed about 1 metre apart in front of each of the teams.
The first player in each team rolls a ball trying to knock down a skittle. He then runs up, gets the ball and throws it to the next player in his line and remains behind the skittles to retrieve the ball. The other players take turns bowling, until they have knocked down all the skittles. The first team to knock down its five skittles wins.
In *One Skittle Bowling*, two teams (or individuals) take turns bowling at the same skittle placed about 8 metres away. Each time the skittle is knocked down, that team makes a point. The team with the highest score after 5 minutes, or the first team to reach a set number of hits, wins.

Wide Awake

Caught out by a missed catch

Players stand just over 1 metre apart in a circle, facing inwards. A soft ball is thrown from one player to the next around the circle. If a player makes a throw that is too poorly aimed to be caught or fails to catch a throw he is eliminated. The one who remains in the game the longest is the winner. The game leader must decide which throws are bad and which are good.
The game may also be played by giving any player who makes a bad throw or fails to catch a good one a penalty point. After an agreed period, such as 3 or 4 minutes, the player with the least number of penalties wins.

Count the Passes

The ball moves in fast circles

Two circles are formed with the players standing about 2 metres apart. Each circle has a ball and at a signal begins to pass it in turn from player to player. The purpose of the game is to pass it as many times as possible within a set period, say 2 or 3 minutes. A dropped or missed throw does not count. The game is made exciting by a leader in each circle calling out the score as each pass is made. When the time is up, the winning circle is given a point.

Circle Pass

Variations on a popular theme

Players, spaced 1 metre apart, form a circle about 10 metres in diameter. One player is in the centre holding a volleyball. The centre player passes the ball to any player in the circle. That player catches the ball and passes it back to the centre player, who passes it to another player and so on until each player in the circle has had a turn.
The game may be played as an elimination contest in which those failing to catch the ball drop out, or as a race between two groups in two circles.
In *Circle Volley Bounce*, the centre player calls out the name of a player in the circle, bounces the ball once and serves it to the named player. If the serve is a good one, the called player hits it with his hand to another player whose name he has called. In this way each player tries to hit the ball to someone else. A referee decides when a ball has been

hit out of reach of a called player or when a called player has failed to hit a properly served ball.
When a server makes an error, he drops out and the game resumes with a new server. Eventually only two players remain, and they hit the ball to each other until one makes a mistake. His opponent then becomes the winner and a new round of play can begin.

Bucket Ball
Throw it in and win

A bucket or basket is placed in the centre of a circle of players. The circle can be 5–7 metres in diameter, to suit the age of the players. Each player takes his turn trying to throw the ball into the bucket from his place in the circle. He may try to throw it in directly or on a bounce. If he hits the bucket he gets one point, if he gets the ball in he gets two. After each player has had five chances, the one with the highest score is the winner.
In *Team Bucket Ball*, players form into two, three, or four circles with a bucket and ball for each. The action is the same but the teams compete for the highest score within a set period.

Keep-away Touch Ball
The art of interception

Players form a circle facing inwards and standing about 2 metres apart. One player is in the centre.
The players in the circle pass a ball rapidly from one to the other moving in any direction around or across the circle. Meanwhile, the player in the centre tries to block or catch the ball. When he does, the last person to have handled the ball goes to the centre.

Skittle Guard
In defence of a triangle target

Players form a circle about 8 metres in diameter. One stands in the centre guarding a small triangle of skittles or plastic bottles which are placed about 1 metre apart.
Players on the edge of that circle try to knock the skittles down by throwing, bouncing or rolling a ball. The player in the centre may catch the ball directly and throw it back or block it with his hands. The others can pass the ball around to get an open shot at the target. The winner is the one who protected the skittles for the longest time.

RELAY RACES TO PLAY IN THE GARDEN

Jump-the-Stick
Game with a moving hurdle

The first two players in each team hold a cricket stump, or a stick about 60 centimetres long, by its ends. They move out beyond the line of their team, turn and face them. At a signal, holding the stick close to the ground, they run down each side of their column so that the stick becomes a moving hurdle. Each player in the column must jump over the stick. When the two players with the stick reach the end of the column, the first player lets go of the stick and stands at the back of the column. The second player runs back with the stick to the front of the column and teams up with the third. Together they repeat the action, then the third player teams up with the fourth and so on until all players in the team have run with the stick. The first team to finish is the winner.

Washday Race
Quick work at the clothes-line

A clothes-line is stretched across a turning line about 5 metres away from the starting line. The first player in each team is given a shirt, a pair of shorts, two socks and four clothes-pegs.

At a signal, he hangs each of these articles on the clothes-line. Then he races back and touches the second player who runs up to the clothes-line, takes down the clothing and brings them back to his team. The action is repeated and the team that finishes first wins.

Back-to-Back
Racing—facing both ways

Teams line up in pairs behind the starting line, 7 metres from the turning line.
The first pair in each team stands back-to-back, hooking each other's elbows firmly. At a signal, each first pair race to the turning line, one player moving forwards and the other backwards.
After crossing the turning line and returning to the starting line in the same manner, they are followed by the next pair. The first team to complete the action is the winner.

Three-legged Hobble
Test of timing and team work

Teams divide into pairs who tie themselves together at the ankle, with a belt, a piece of string or a handkerchief.
At a signal, each first pair races to the turning line, about 10 metres away, and back. They touch the second pair in line, who in turn must complete the action. The game continues until the last pair in one team is home.

Wheelbarrows
For young players with push

Each team divides its members into pairs, who form columns on the starting line. A turning line is marked 7 metres from the start.
The first pair in each team takes the wheelbarrow position. One player places his hands on the ground and stretches his legs straight out. The partner stands between the outstretched legs, holding them firmly at the ankle and lifting them to waist height.
At a signal, each first pair races to the turning line, the front player travelling on his hands, and the other guiding him like a wheelbarrow.
At the turning line they reverse positions and race back to the starting line to touch off the next pair, who have been waiting in wheelbarrow position. The game continues until the last pair in one team is home.

Over and Under
A game of highs and lows

Each leading player holds a football or any ball of similar size. The rest of his team lines up behind him. He passes the ball over his head to the player behind, who then passes the ball between his legs to the next player. The action continues in this manner, with the ball passing 'over and under' until it reaches the last player, who runs with the ball to the front of the column and begins the action again.
The game continues until the first player in one team is back in his original position.
There are two variations of this game: *Archball* in which players pass the ball only over their heads and *Tunnelball* in which they pass it between their legs.

Dizzy Turns
With a leaning for laughter

The leading player in each team holds a cricket bat or a tennis racket. Players line up in equal columns behind the starting line, about 10 metres away from the turning line.
At a signal, the first player runs to the turning line, places one end of the bat or racket on the ground and, holding it upright, puts his forehead down on the top of it. In this position the player runs around it three times, then runs back to the starting line. The next player repeats the action.
This game can be very amusing because the action of running around the bat or racket

makes players dizzy, and the trip back from the turning line is usually not as straight as the trip towards it.
The first team to complete the action wins.

Crab Relay
Now we're getting really complicated

Since crab relays are difficult to play, the turning line should be not more than 5 metres from the starting line.
The first player in each column turns his back to the starting line, squats and reaches backwards so that his hands are on the ground. At a signal, the lead players race backwards, on heels and palms, to the turning line. They cross it and return in the same way, touching the next players. Each player in the column repeats the action until the last player in one team is home.

Bunny Hop
Definitely not for rabbits

Teams line up in equal columns. The starting and turning lines are about 5 metres apart. The first player races to the turning line and back in the 'bunny hop' position: squatting, holding his arms around his knees, and jumping along. The first player then touches the next player and the game continues until the last player in one team is home.

Kangaroo Hop
The object must not be dropped

A 'kangaroo' is forced to hop in this relay because he must hold an object, such as a rubber ball, a block of wood or a bean bag, between his knees. The object must be identical for each team.
A turning line is marked 7 metres from the starting line and the teams form into columns. At a signal, the first player places the object between his knees and hops along, feet together, to and from the turning line. The 'kangaroo' may not keep the object in place with his hands. If it falls he must pick it up, place it between his knees, and start again from that spot.
On returning, the first player passes the object to the next player and the game continues until the last player of one team gets home first.

'TAG' GAMES FOR THE GARDEN

These 'touch' or 'tag' games are suitable for playing in the garden. Similar games that require more space can be found on p. 208.

Squirrel in the Tree
But he can be displaced

All the players, except two, form into groups of three. Two members of each group join hands and they become a tree; the third stands inside their arms and is a squirrel. One of the two players left over is a hound, the other is a running squirrel.
At a signal the running squirrel is chased by the hound and seeks safety by ducking under the joined hands of a tree to displace the squirrel already there, who becomes the new runner. When a hound touches a running squirrel their roles reverse.

Stoop Touch
Can it catch 'em bending?

The players are scattered around a play area trying to avoid being touched by the chaser. When a player thinks he is about to be touched he can make himself safe by stooping or crouching on the ground. No player may stoop more than three times. If he does, he becomes the new chaser and all the players are allowed three more stoops.

Streets and Alleys

A most popular game in which it is hard to know which way to turn

At least 15 players—but the more the merrier—are needed to generate the great excitement of this popular chasing game.

Players form three or more parallel lines with at least four players in each line. Each player, with arms extended, holds the hands of his neighbours. The lines are formed so that a player, with arms extended, can reach the extended hand of his opposite number in the next line. CONTINUED ON NEXT PAGE

CONTINUED FROM PREVIOUS PAGE

When the players are facing the front, the aisles between rows are called streets. When they turn to the right and take the hands of their new neighbours the aisles are called alleys (see p. 193).

Three players are not part of the rows: one is the runner, another the chaser and the third, the caller, stands in front of the rows.

As the game begins, all players are facing the front, each holding hands with his neighbours. At a signal, the chaser pursues the runner down the streets. At any time, the caller may shout 'alleys' and the players turn to the right and take the hands of their new neighbours. At this, the runner and chaser must change their direction to run down the new aisles. When the caller shouts 'streets', the players turn forward again and the direction of the chase is once more reversed. Neither the runner nor the chaser may run through or duck under clasped hands.

A round ends when the chaser touches the runner, or after 3 minutes of play. For the next round, the chaser becomes the runner, the runner the caller and the caller replaces a player in the lines, who is the new chaser.

Running Up the Alleys is a simple form of the game. The formation is the same but once the rows are formed they remain the same. There is no caller. When the chaser touches the runner, he becomes the new runner, and the old runner replaces a player in the lines who becomes the new chaser.

Chain Touch
It grows more and more exciting

One player is chosen as the chain-maker and the other players scatter about the play area. The chain-maker chases the others, and when he touches one they join hands to form a two-link chain. Together, they chase the other players, and when a third is touched, he too joins the chain.

The chain grows, but it must stay together. Therefore, only the links on the two ends can make a touch with their free hands.

The last player to remain free wins the game and becomes the chain-maker for the next round.

Exchange Touch
A winner, indoors or out

If the game is played indoors, players sit on chairs in a large circle, if outdoors, they sit on the ground. The chaser stands in the middle.

The chaser calls out the names of any two players, who try to change places with each other while the chaser tries to touch one of them. If he succeeds, that player becomes the chaser and the first chaser takes his place in the circle.

Fox and Chickens
The chickens swing to fox him

All players except one form a single line, each player placing his hands on the waist of the one in front. The leader of the line is the hen and the others are chickens. The remaining player is the fox.

The object of the game is for the fox to touch the last chicken in the line. To prevent this the hen swings the line from side to side and flaps her arms to block the fox. The hen, however, must not hold the fox.

When the fox finally succeeds in touching the last chicken, he joins the end of the line and the hen becomes the new fox.

Steal the Bacon
—And bring home a point

The players divide into two equal teams and are told their numbers. Each team stands on a line, facing each other about 7 metres apart. The numbers of one team line up in reverse order to the other. If, for example, there are 12 players, number 1 in one team is directly

opposite number 6 in the other team, number 2 opposite number 5 and so on.
The 'bacon', a ball or some other suitable object, is in the middle.
The game leader calls out a number and the two race for the bacon. The one who gets it tries to reach his own goal line before he is touched by his opponent. If he makes it, his team wins a point. If he is touched the other side wins a point.
The first team to reach a set number of points, usually 21, wins.

Quoits

It all started with horseshoes

This game began as a pastime for farm workers and others in rural communities who threw horseshoes over an upright stake and scored points according to their skill.
Nowadays it can be played indoors or outdoors, in the playground or on the beach, by people of all ages. The rules can be adjusted to suit the preferences and abilities of the players, and the equipment is easy to improvise. All that is needed is a set of rings and a stake to act as a target. The rings, which should be about 10 millimetres thick and 140 millimetres in diameter, can be of plastic, rubber or rope. Outdoors, the stake, which can be, for example, a cut-down cricket stump, is hammered into the ground. It should be about 350 millimetres high. Indoors, a rubber plunger with a wooden handle, of the sort used to clear blocked sinks, makes an excellent stake. Just push the plunger against the floor and the upright handle makes the target. A throwing line is marked out at a distance from the stake best suited to the strength of the players, ranging from a couple of metres for the very young sportsman to 17 metres for the skilled adult.
Quoits can be a singles or a team game. In each case, the players take turns to stand behind the throwing line and throw a quoit at the stake. A quoit that settles over the stake, a 'ringer', scores three points, a quoit that leans against the stake, a 'leaner', counts two and the quoit closest to the stake counts one.
In singles, each player has six quoits, in a team game each player has two. Each round ends when all the quoits have been thrown and the scores are added up. Rounds continue until one player or a team has reached 21 points.
One variation in scoring which makes the game last longer is to count only the top ringer at the end of each round if, during the round, both teams or players have succeeded in encircling the stake. Some players count only ringers when adding up the score, others ignore quoits which are neither ringers nor leaners.

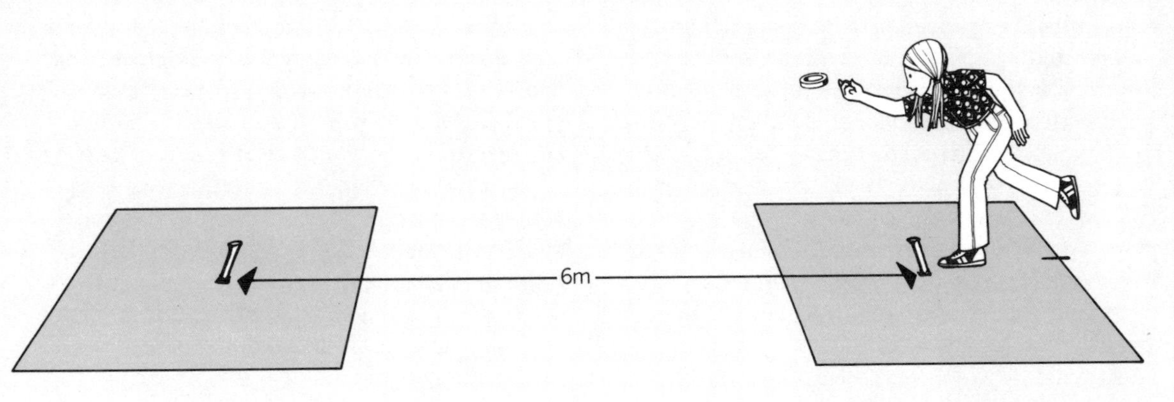

Croquet
Going through the hoop

Croquet is a great family game, either for the old or young. All it entails is hitting balls with a mallet through hoops set out on a grass court. The smoother the grass the better—and the better the players the smoother the grass should be.

The game is said to have originated in France as early as the 13th century, and there is evidence that it had spread to England two centuries later. But it was in the 19th century that a system of rules was first drawn up.

The first English Croquet Championships were held in Evesham, Worcestershire, in 1867. Three years later the championships were transferred to Wimbledon—now world famous for its international tennis tournament, which was then known as the All-England Croquet and Lawn Tennis Club.

In 1871 the first formal layout of the court was finalised. Known as the Hale setting, it used six hoops and two pegs. This layout was used until 1921 when a new arrangement was devised. This was known as the Willis setting, and involved six hoops and one peg. This setting has been used ever since.

The court measures 32 by 25 metres. Boundaries are marked with a white line, if possible, and the court is set out as shown in the diagram. The hoops are made of iron 1·59 centimetres thick. They are stuck in the ground so that they stand 30·5 centimetres high. The inside measurement between the uprights is 9·53 centimetres.

Four balls are used made of compressed cork covered with plastic. Each ball is a different colour: black, blue, red and yellow. They are 9·21 centimetres in diameter, 0·32 centimetres less than the width of the hoops through which they have to pass, a very small margin of error.

The peg is wooden and stands about 45 centimetres out of the ground. The mallets are also made of wood. The head is about 23 centimetres long and can be either square or round.

The game is always played with four balls and always black and blue against red and yellow. If two people are playing they have two each, if four are playing they have one each.

The object of the game is to hit the balls through the hoops around the court and back again in the direction shown in the diagram, finally hitting the peg in the middle. The first player or pair to hit the peg with both balls is the winner. To help keep track of how things are going—during the game the balls are hit all over the place—a set of clips is used, each clip corresponding in colour to one of the balls. These are clipped to the next hoop any ball has to go through—which means that at the start of the game all four will be clipped to the first hoop. They are clipped to the top of the hoops on the way out, to one of the uprights on the way back.

The winner of the toss has either choice of colours or first turn.

Though croquet appears to be a simple game, in practice it is far from that.

Not only have you to play through the hoops in the correct order and finally hit the peg, you also have to keep an eye on how your opponent is getting on—and do all you can to put him off. The rules could fill a small volume—but here is a simplified version for the back garden.

A turn consists of one shot, with two exceptions. When you hit through a hoop you get another shot. When you hit any of the other balls, either yours or your opponent's you get two extra shots. This is called a 'roquet'. One of your extra shots can be used to knock the ball you hit anywhere you want. You do this by placing your ball behind and touching the other one and hitting them in the desired direction. If you want to move the other ball only, put your foot on the top of your ball and when you strike your ball smartly the other flies off while yours stays still. Obviously if the croquet ball is an opponent's you will want to knock it into as awkward a position as possible; if it is your own you will want to knock it into a favourable position.

The other extra shot must be an ordinary shot. You can roquet as many balls as you like during each turn, but only once each before you go through a hoop. Once you go through a hoop and, therefore, get another shot you can roquet them all again if you want. Your turn ends when you fail to go through a hoop or fail to hit another ball.

Any ball hit out of bounds is hit into play again from the point on the line where it went out.

Each team need not play its balls in sequence, in other words it can persevere with the blue, for example, before carrying on with the black. When you have played a ball through the last hoop, you then aim to hit against the peg. You may roquet it against the peg only if the other ball has been played through the last hoop.

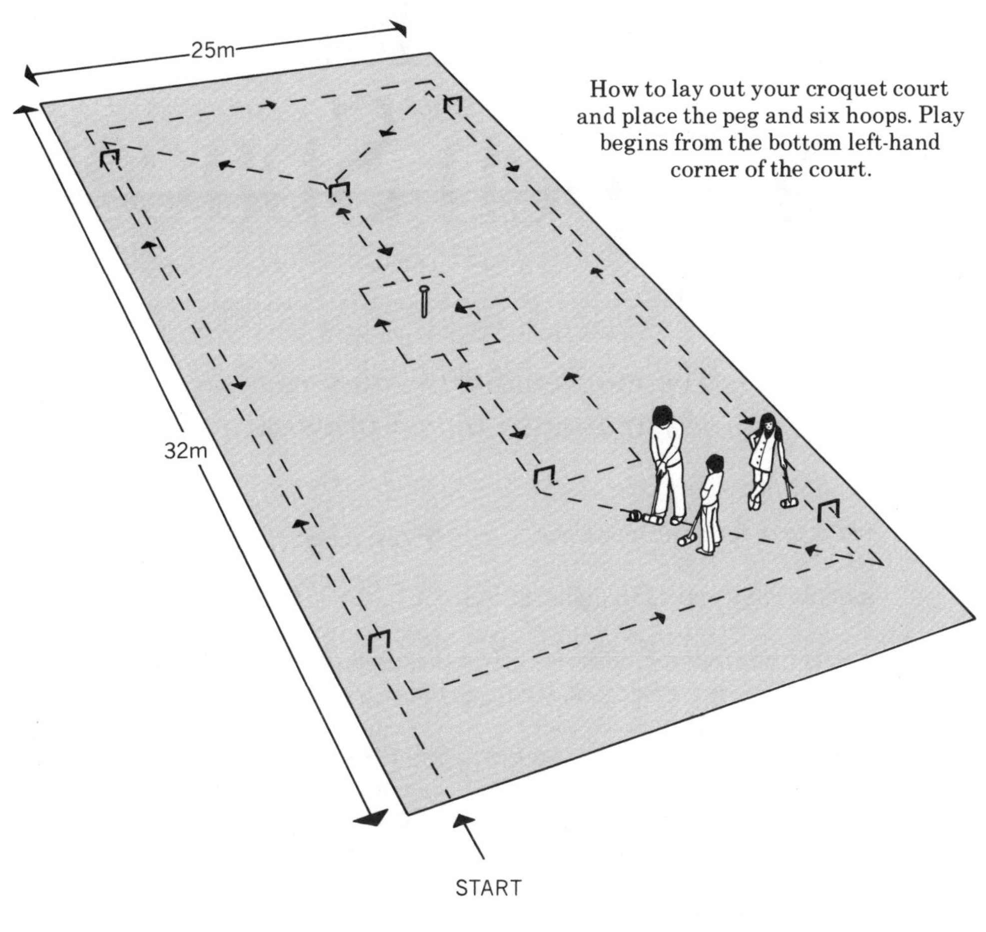

How to lay out your croquet court and place the peg and six hoops. Play begins from the bottom left-hand corner of the court.

Chapter 8

Games for Open Spaces

Games for team and individual rivalry; Ball games; The excitement of relay races; Learning to play Volleyball

It was easy for children in the past to find space to play their games. They played in fields, on the village green or in a town's traffic-free streets. Children today enjoy the same time-proven games, but to find the necessary space they usually have to play them in parks, in playing fields or on a beach.

Many games, popular with generations of children, were originally played in the street. The boundaries in these games were pavement kerbs, house walls that faced on to the street, or else basement area or yard walls. Red Rover and Crusts and Crumbs are examples of these 'pavement' games.

Today's traffic prevents children from playing in the street, but the 'kerbs' and 'walls' of the original games survive as the boundary lines that must be marked on playing fields or beaches before play can begin.

Twenty-one

It's essential to be exact

Players line up at the free-throw line on a basketball court facing the basket. The object of the game is to score exactly 21 points, by making basketball shots in the following way. Each player takes a turn, consisting of three successive throws at the basket.

The first shot is made from the free-throw line, and scores five points, if successful.

The next two shots are made from wherever the ball is recovered. The second basket is worth three points and the third is worth one.

When the first player has taken his three shots, the next player takes a turn, and so on. The game goes on until one player gets 21 points.

If a player makes more than 21 points, his own score goes back to nought and he must start playing again.

A simpler form of this game is *Twenty-one*

Plus, which is scored in exactly the same way except that the winning player is the first to make 21 points or more.

Basketball Five Tries
Every one can count

Players divide into two teams, each standing in single file behind the free-throw line on a basketball court. The first player in line holds a basketball. The last player in each team stands under the basket.
At a signal, the first players in both teams begin to shoot for the basket. They continue from the free-throw line until one of them scores, or until each has had five tries. The players under the basket retrieve the ball and pass it back.
The first player to score wins one point for his team. When this happens—or if both shooters have had five tries without scoring—the first players become retrievers, the second players move up to the free-throw line and the former retrievers go to the rear of the line to wait their turn to shoot. The team with the higher score, after all players have had a turn, wins.
In *Basket Shot Relay*, each player shoots until he scores and then goes to the back of the line. The first team to bring its lead man back to his starting point wins.

Freeze-out
Cold comfort for the losers

Before this game begins players decide the order of shooting, then the first player stands wherever he likes on the basketball court. The first player shoots at the basket until he makes it, then the next player stands in exactly the same spot and must score in the same number of shots or better. If he fails he is frozen out, that is eliminated from the game. If the second player succeeds, the third must throw from the same spot and so on.
Whenever a player is frozen out, the next player has the option of choosing a new position. The winner is the last player to remain in the game.

Centre Ball
Exciting game of chuck and chase

One player, holding the ball, stands in the centre of a circle which has been formed by the other players.
The holder throws the ball to any other player who catches it, moves to the centre, places the ball on the ground and then chases the thrower. The thrower runs through the opening in the circle left by the catcher and runs around the outside until he reaches the opening again, and then back into the circle to touch the ball.
If the catcher touches him before he can touch the ball, the catcher becomes the new thrower and the game proceeds as before.
If the catcher fails to make the touch, the thrower continues in his position until he is caught.
The game leader should not allow one player to be the thrower for too long so that other players may have a chance.

Keep Away
The action is lively but fair

Players are divided into equal teams, scattered over the playing area. Members of one team should wear handkerchiefs tied around one arm for identification.
One team has a ball. At a signal, it is passed from player to player, while the other team tries to intercept it. Scoring is not vital, but the referee may time how long each team can retain control of the ball. The action is very lively, though tripping, holding, pushing or other rough play is not permitted.
If the ball is thrown out of the playing area, the team that last touched it is responsible, and the other team puts it back in play. The game may last from 15 to 20 minutes, depending on the vigour of the players.

Goal

A fast, action-filled team game

Players form two teams which stand facing each other on either side of a centre line and each in front of a goal line. The play area is about 14–15 metres square. Three players from each team, the goalies, stand behind their opponent's goal line. The toss of a coin decides which team has the football.

The team which wins the toss tries to throw the ball over their opponents' heads to their goalies. The opponents try to intercept it, but they may not move over the centre line. The attacking players may not run with the ball, but they may pass it to each other inside their own territory.

One point is scored each time the ball is thrown to a goalie and the goalie catches it. The defending team moves into the attack when it intercepts the ball or retrieves it after a goalie fails to catch it. The game lasts 15 minutes.

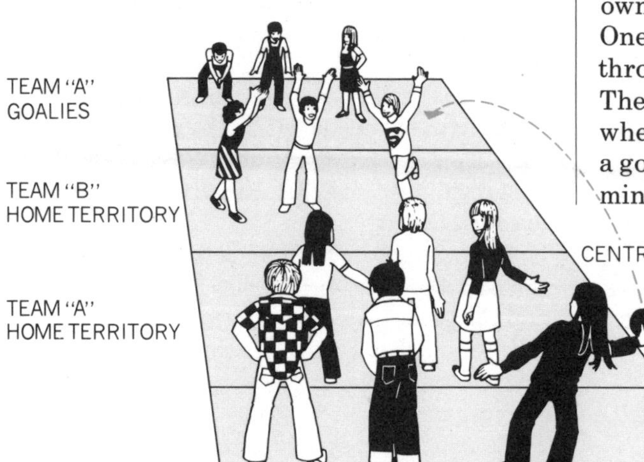

Train Dodge Ball

When the engine is the guard

Four players stand in single file, each with arms around the player in front. This is the train. The player at the head of the line is the engine, the one at the back, the guard's van. All the other players stand around the edge of a circle about 7 metres in diameter. They try to hit the guard's van below the waist with a ball. The engine tries to protect the van by slapping or kicking the ball away, and by swinging the train around.

When the van is hit, the player who threw the ball becomes the engine, the old engine is now the first carriage, the first carriage is the second, the second becomes the van and the old van replaces the new engine in the circle. The engine who protects a van for the longest period is the winner.

Sky-high Ball
Success for safe pairs of hands

Two equal teams are formed, with the players of one team knotting a handkerchief on the arm as identification. Players scatter around a playing area that is about 10 metres square.
A player in the first team throws the ball high in the air within the playing area. If a member of the second team catches it he scores one point for his side. If not, the throwing team scores.
Then a member of the second team throws it and this continues until all the players have had a turn. The team with the greater number of points after 10 minutes wins.

Kick and Catch
Soccer fun for the young

Two equal teams stand behind goal lines set 10–16 metres apart, depending upon the age and kicking ability of the players.
The first player in one team kicks a football from behind the goal line towards the other team's goal line. If the ball crosses the other team's goal line without being caught, one point is scored for the kicker's team. If it fails to go over the goal line, or if it is caught in the air, the opposing team gets one point. After the first player in the kicking team has had a turn, the ball is given to a player in the opposing team to kick. The game continues until all the players have had a turn at kicking the ball. The team with the highest score is the winner.

Soccer Touch
The players are the goal

Players scatter around an area which is at least 8 metres square. Three players are chosen as kickers. They wear handkerchiefs tied around one arm to identify them.
The kickers kick a football or volleyball around the area, trying to hit any of the other players beneath the waist. Any player who is hit becomes a kicker. The game continues until all players but one have been hit. The survivor becomes a kicker for the next game and picks two others to help him. A hit scored above the waist does not count.

Hot Ball
Working together to stay cool

Players stand in a circle, facing inwards. One player has a football in front of him.
The player with the ball calls 'The ball is hot!' He kicks it across the circle, hitting it with the inside of his foot, soccer-style. Other players continue to kick the ball quickly, the idea being that it is so 'hot' that they must get rid of it at once or it will burn them. This goes on, until the ball escapes from the circle. Then a new player begins the action again.
This game is co-operative rather than competitive. All players work together to keep the ball moving inside the circle. Children usually enjoy this game for about 10 minutes.

Free Ball
One by one, then a scramble

One player, the caller, has a football and stands about 10 metres away from the others, who are lined up facing him.
The caller shouts the name of any other player and kicks the ball soccer-style, with the side of the foot, in that player's direction. The called player stops the ball with his foot and returns the kick; another player is called on, and the action is repeated until all have kicked the ball back once.
The caller then shouts 'Free ball!' and kicks the ball in the general direction of the others who scramble to receive it. The player who retrieves the ball holds it over his head to prove his possession. He is the caller for another round of play.
The player who holds the caller's position most often in a 10-minute period wins.

Soccer Keep-away
Possession is the point of it

Two teams scatter over a playing area of about 10 by 13 metres. Members of one team wear handkerchiefs tied around one arm for identification. The purpose of the game is to keep control of the football.

A toss of a coin decides which team will have the ball when the game begins, and its members kick it back and forth among themselves to keep control. Using only feet, heads or bodies, the opposition tries to intercept passes or steal the ball.

A period lasts 7 minutes, and a referee keeps the times that each team has held the ball. The team with the best time wins.

Circle Dodge Ball
Target is the man in the middle

All players, except one chosen as the dodger, stand on or outside the edge of a circle about 8 metres in diameter. The dodger stands in the centre. The players on the edge try to hit the dodger with a ball. They may not move within the circle itself when they throw and a fair hit is below the waist. The player who hits the dodger exchanges roles with him.

Spud
Collect three and you're out

A caller is chosen and the other players are each given a number. The players form a circle and the caller stands in the centre with a ball.

The caller shouts out a number and throws the ball high in the air; the player with that number retrieves it. While the ball is being retrieved all the other players scatter but when the ball has been caught, the catcher calls out 'Spud!'

This is the signal for everyone to stand still and the ball-holder searches out an easy target and throws the ball at him. The target player may duck or swerve to avoid being hit, but may not move his feet.

If the target player is hit, he is penalised with 'one spud' and becomes the new caller. If the target is missed, the player who threw the ball gets the penalty and is the new caller.

A player who is 'spudded' three times is out of the game and the last player in wins.

Elimination Dodge Ball
One by one the players go

Half the players stand in the centre of a circle about 8 metres in diameter formed by the others. Players forming the circle throw a ball and try to hit those in the centre below the waist. When a player is hit, he joins the others in the circle. The last player to be hit wins the game.

Team Dodge Ball
A fast-moving, exciting game

Two teams stand on opposite sides of a centre line dividing the play area. The leader rolls a ball down the centre line and the first player to retrieve it starts the action.

The idea is to eliminate players on the opposite team by hitting them below the waist with the ball. Any player who is hit, or who steps across the centre line, is eliminated from the game. There are two ways to score: the winner is either the team that has the most players left after 3–5 minutes, or the team that manages to eliminate its opponents. If there are enough players and a very large playing area, more than one ball may be used.

In *Bombardment,* the players begin by standing on their own base line, while several balls are placed on the centre line. At a signal, they all run forward to get as many balls as they can and throw them at their opponents. If a player catches the ball, it does not count as a hit. The game goes on until all players on one side have been eliminated.

Free Zone Dodge Ball

As exciting as the others and everyone has a second chance

Two teams stand on opposite sides of a centre line. On each side of the line, about 7 metres behind it, is a goal line. The areas between centre line and goal lines are free zones. The areas behind the goal lines are end zones.
This game differs from most dodge ball events in that players who are hit are not entirely eliminated. They go to the end zone behind the opposition and from there can continue to play should the ball come their way. Therefore, free zone players must protect themselves from the rear as well as the front.
The object of the game is to get as many opponents into one's own end zone as possible.
The game begins with players trying to hit members of the opposing team below the waist with the ball. When a player is hit he goes to the opposing team's end zone and though he may attack from there, should he get the ball, he may not move in front of the goal line.
If a player catches the ball, the thrower goes to the opposition's end zone. If the thrower was already in that zone the catcher can point out any member of the opposing team and send him to the end zone. Should one team lose all its free zone players, the game automatically ends; otherwise it ends after 10 minutes and the winning team is the one with more players remaining in its free zone.
A less complex version of this game is *End Dodge Ball*. Players hit are not eliminated, they go to their own end zone and continue to play from there. They are forced to throw a much greater distance to make a hit and may not pass the ball to a team-mate in the free zone. The game ends after 10 minutes and the team with more players in its free zone wins.

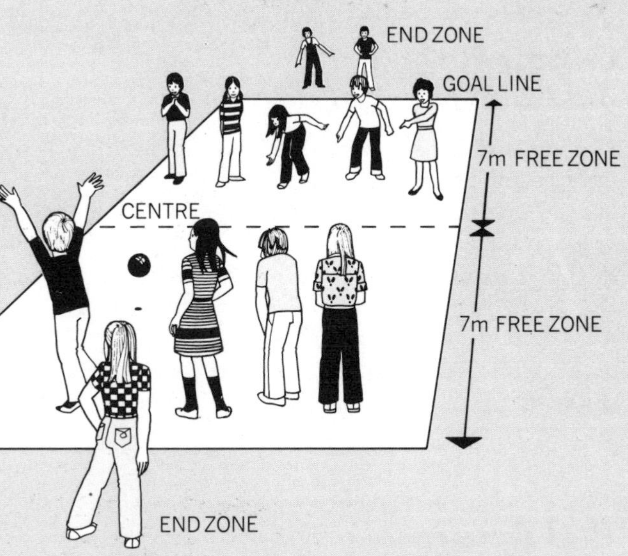

RELAYS FOR THE PLAYGROUND AND BEACH

Relay races have always been among the most popular of games involving, as they do, speed and dexterity, excitement and the team spirit. They are suitable for children of all ages and those described here can be held in the playground or the park, or on a hard beach.
The equipment required is simple. Relay races can be played on any kind of surface as long as it is possible to run on it.
Marking the starting and turning lines is not difficult. Chalk is fine for a cement surface and suitably placed stones will do for grass. Cricket stumps or pieces of stick can also be used.
It is necessary to have someone to act as referee, just to make sure that in the excitement of the moment the rules are kept.
Although the principle is the same, there are many variations of the relay race that can provide hours of excitement and fun, as you will see from the following examples.

Simple Relay
An easy one to start with

The teams line up in equal columns behind the starting line directly opposite the turning line, about 10 metres away.
At a signal, the first player in each column runs to the turning line, touches it with his foot, then runs and touches the second runner, who is now at the front of the column. The second runner repeats the action, touching the third runner as he returns. Each player moves to the back of his column after completing his run. The game continues until all the players are back to their starting positions. The team that achieves this first is the winner.

Couple Hobble
Just a bit more difficult

The rules of this race are similar to Simple Relay except that the teams line up in pairs behind the starting line. Each player places an arm around his partner's waist and lifts the knee of his outside leg as close as possible to the chest, gripping the knee with his free hand. At a signal, each lead pair hops towards the turning line, crosses it, returns and touches the second pair and so on until all the pairs are home.

Ball Return
Fun with fast passes

Players line up in columns behind a starting line. A second line, the throwing line, is marked about 7 metres away, parallel to the starting line. The first player in each team has a ball. At a signal, each first player runs to the throwing line, turns and throws the ball to the next player in the team. That player catches the ball and then runs to join him on the throwing line, turns, throws the ball to the third player, and so on. If a catcher drops the ball, it must be retrieved and the catcher must return to the starting line before running to the throwing line. The first team to move all players to the throwing line wins.

Sack Relay
The best is in the bag

The leading player of each team holds a large 'sack', such as a polythene dustbin liner or a multi-layered paper bag. Players line up in equal columns by the starting line, about 10 metres from the turning line.
At a signal, each leading player climbs into the sack, and holding its open end up around the waist, jumps to the turning line and back to touch the next player and hand over the sack.
The first team to complete the course wins.

By the Heel
The referee must be on his toes

This relay requires a referee to watch out for any cheating. Players line up in equal columns behind the starting line, about 10 metres away from the turning line. At a signal, the first players move towards the turning line walking on their heels. After reaching the turning line the players return on their heels to the starting line and touch off the second players in their respective teams.
Not more than three teams should compete, so that the referee can keep an eye on all contestants, making sure that no toes touch the ground.
A player who commits this foul is sent back to the starting line and must begin again.

Triple Squat
It ends with knees bend

Players squat about 1 metre apart in equal columns. At a signal, the first player in each column stands up, turns to the right and runs clockwise once around the column. Once back

in place, the player does three knees-bends quickly, counting them out loud.
Each player repeats the action, and the first team to complete the course wins.

Soccer Dribble
For budding footballers

This and the following game are good practice for budding footballers trying to improve their skill.
Players line up in equal columns behind the starting line, about 10 metres from the turning line. The first player in each team dribbles a ball, soccer-style, using the side of his foot only, to the turning line and back across the starting line. The ball is brought to the second player who cannot leave his position to get it.
The game continues until the last player of one team brings the ball home.

Circle Relay
With fleetness of foot

Each team forms a circle. One player in each team has a ball.
At a signal, the player with the ball dribbles it with the side of his foot around the outside of the circle and back to the starting place.
The ball is then passed to the player on the right. This player repeats the action.
The game continues until all the players have run. The first team to complete the action wins.

Tug-along
Everyone pulls together

Players divide into teams and each team forms two-player partnerships. Teams line up in double file with partners side by side, behind the starting line about 10 metres from the

Figure-eight
In and out and round about

Three skittles or empty plastic containers are placed on the ground in single file and about 1 metre apart. Players line up in equal columns behind the starting line and about 10 metres from the first skittles. At a signal, the first player in each column runs to the skittles and passes to the right of the first, the left of the second and the right of the third. Then the player weaves back through them in the same manner as if forming a figure-eight with an extra loop. If a skittle is knocked over, the player stops and sets it up in place before returning to the starting line and touching off the next player.
The first team to complete the action wins.

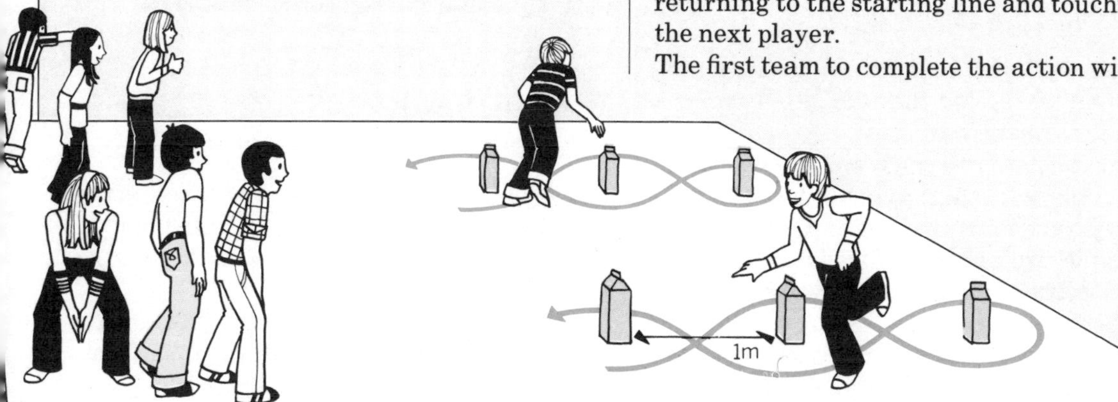

turning line. At a signal, the first pairs in each team join their inside hands and run towards the turning line, one partner pulling the other along.
At the referee's signal, the partners change position; the one in front moving to the rear. During the action, from the turning line and back to the starting line, the referee calls for a position change three or four times. If the partners don't follow the instructions they must return to the starting line to begin their run again. The first team to complete the action wins the relay.

Bounce Ball
For the young and agile

A throwing line is marked about 3 metres from a wall. Players line up in equal columns on a starting line about 10 metres from the wall. Each first player holds a football.
At a signal, the first players run to the throwing line, throw the balls against the wall and catch them on the first bounce. A player who fails to catch the ball first bounce must repeat the action.
The player then runs back to the team and gives the ball to the next player in line. The first team to complete the action wins.

Racing the Ball
A relay with a difference

This relay is unusual because two teams are set different tasks—but they are pitted against each other to finish first.
Players divide into two equal teams. One team forms a circle, with the players standing about 1 metre apart and facing inwards. One player in the circle holds a ball. The other team stands in a straight line facing towards the circle (see diagram).
At a signal the ball is bounced around the circle from player to player, with one bounce between each. If the ball is dropped, it is picked up and the player must return to his

starting place in the circle before passing it on. The ball travels around the circle as many times as there are players in the team. The lead player should call out 'One!' as he receives the ball the first time and keep the score until the final time when he shouts 'Finish!'
At the same starting signal the first player in the line (the opposing team) runs forward and around the circle. Once back in place, he touches the second player who makes his run, and so on through the team. The first team to complete the action is awarded one point. The roles are then reversed and points are awarded until a predetermined score is reached.

Pick-a-back
Game where the burden is shared

Players line up in columns behind the starting line, about 10 metres from the turning line. Each team divides into pairs as matched in size as possible.
The first pair in each team form a pick-a-back and at a signal race to the turning line. There they reverse roles and race back to the starting line. The first team to have all its players complete the action is the winner.

Shuttle

A touching turn of speed

In Shuttle, players form into teams and each team then divides into two equal groups. The team groups line up in columns facing each other behind two parallel lines about 10 metres apart.

The first player in each team runs across to the opposite line and touches the first player there and then moves to the back of that line. The player who was touched sprints to the opposite side, touches the first player in line there and takes a position at the back of that line. This action continues until all players are back in their original positions and the team that completes the relay first wins.

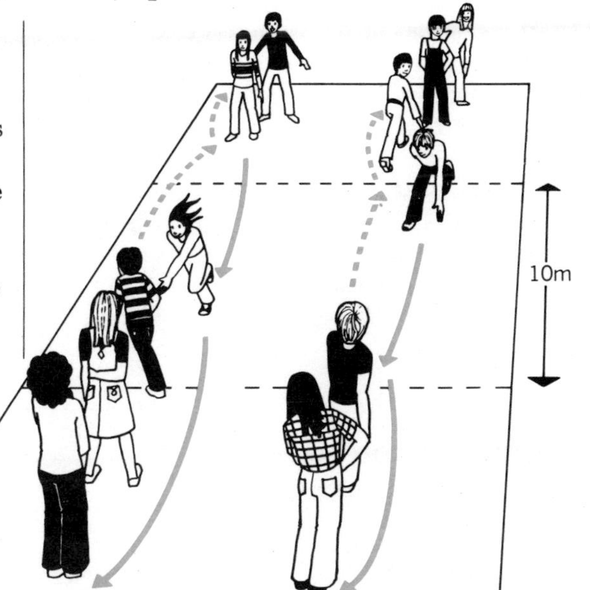

Human Caterpillar

Putting talent on display

This relay is something of a junior gymnastics display. Players line up about 1 metre apart in equal columns behind the starting line. The first player stands with his feet wide apart, the next bends over in a leap-frog position. Positions alternate down each column.

At a signal, the last player in each column either crawls under the legs of the player in front or vaults over, according to the player's posture. He carries on in this manner until he reaches the front of the column. He then takes the alternative posture to the player he has just passed. Then the player now at the back of the column repeats the action, going over or under the players in front of him.

The team that completes the action first—so that all the players are back in their original places—wins.

TOUCH GAMES FOR OPEN SPACES

The excitement for children in the many variations of the game of Touch is being chased. The chaser has the most exasperating task and often rules are made to make his job even more difficult. The aim of the games, therefore, is to avoid being touched or tagged, which means that the touched player must become the chaser. The games in this chapter require some space, such as in a park or a playground or on a beach. Other Touch games for a more restricted space are given on page 192.

Bronco Touch
When a tail becomes a head

All but two players pair up and scatter around the playing area. Each pair becomes a bronco, with one player in front (the head) and the other (the tail) behind, with his arms around his partner's waist. The remaining two players become the runner and the chaser.

The chaser gives the runner a start, then pursues him. If a touch is made, the two exchange roles. At any time, the runner may join a bronco by clasping the waist of the bronco's tail. The tail thus becomes the new head and the old head breaks free to become the new runner.

Broncos may dodge to prevent the runner from joining them, but they may not push a runner away.

Fox and Geese
Both must stay on line

A circle, about 15 metres in diameter, is marked on the ground with four equally spaced spokes radiating from the centre. One player, the fox, stands in the centre and the others, the geese, spread out at random along the spokes and the rim of the circle.

The fox chases the geese along the spokes or the rim. Any goose touched by the fox becomes the fox's helper in running down other geese. The last goose to be caught is the winner and becomes the fox in the next round of play.

Peep Behind the Curtain
Don't be seen on the move

One player stands about 10 metres away from the others with his back towards them. The others, starting from behind a line, try to be first to sneak up and touch him before he sees them. He is allowed to turn round suddenly and try to spot them moving.

When he turns, if he sees a player moving even a hand, he sends that player back behind the line while the rest stay where they are.

The first player to touch the one in front takes his place for the next round.

Have You Seen My Sheep?
Heading for a fast round-up

Players stand in a circle facing outwards with one, the shepherd, outside.

The shepherd asks any player he chooses: 'Have you seen my sheep?' The player answers: 'Describe your sheep.' The shepherd describes someone in the ring and the player shouts: 'Your sheep is . . .' (naming the player described).

The named player races round the outside of the circle trying to get back to his place before being touched by the player who named him. If he succeeds, he becomes the shepherd; if he fails, the toucher becomes the shepherd.

Chinese Touch
Puts the chaser on the spot

This begins as an ordinary game of touch, the difference comes in when someone is touched. He then becomes the chaser—but while he is running after the others he must keep his hand on the spot where he was touched.

Consequently, the aim of the game is to touch players on places such as the ankle or the knee to make it more difficult for them to run.
In *Reverse Chinese Touch* the rules are the same, but all the players have to run backwards.

Last Couple Out
Hand-to-hand struggle

Two equal columns are formed with all players facing the front. The caller stands 3–4 metres in front of the columns with his back turned.
The caller shouts 'Last couple out', and the two players at the rear of the columns run forward and try to touch hands with each other in front of the caller. As soon as he sees them he tries to touch one before the couple can touch hands.
If they succeed they go to the front of their columns and the caller continues.
If they fail, the one touched takes over the caller's role and the old caller replaces him at the front of his column.

Skip Touch
For those who know the ropes

All the players have skipping ropes. They form a large circle facing inwards; one stays outside. The outsider skips around the circle, moving to the right. He touches one of the other players and the two of them have a

Crusts and Crumbs
A good game by any name

This popular chasing game is played throughout the world under different names. In the United States, for example, it is known as Crows and Cranes and it is called various names in different regions of Britain, but the most popular is Crusts and Crumbs.
Players are divided into two groups, one called Crusts and the other Crumbs. They stand about 2 metres apart, facing each other.

Behind each group, about 8 metres away, is a goal line.
When the game leader calls out 'Crumbs' that group turns and runs towards its own goal line with the Crusts in pursuit. Any Crumb touched before crossing the line joins the other side. The game continues until only one group is left.
The leader has a most important part in this game. He should give each group an even chance to catch the other, and he must keep each group on its toes by varying his calls and by drawing out the 'crr' sound so that they don't know what to expect.

skipping race around the circle, the touched player moving to the left. The first to reach the empty place stays there; the other continues the game as the outsider.

If there are not enough skipping ropes, the players can hop instead.

Red Rover

Keep clear of the caller's den

The caller is the most important player in this game. He stands in the middle of the area between the rest of the players who are lined up behind two goal lines about 10 metres apart. An area on one side is the 'caller's den'.

The caller shouts 'Red Rover, Red Rover, send someone over', naming one of the players. The named player tries to reach the opposite goal line without being touched by the caller. If he fails he becomes a prisoner in the caller's den, if he succeeds he stays in his new position. In either case, the caller names another player and the action is repeated.

Then comes the caller's third and final call: 'Red Rover, Red Rover, send all of them over.' All the players race for the opposite lines and the caller touches as many as he can. The touched players go to the caller's den and the caller's score is the number of prisoners he has taken.

All the players get a turn at being caller and the one with the highest score wins.

Two Deep

Running to a standstill

Players form a large circle facing inwards. Two of them, the runner and the chaser, stay outside.

The chaser tries to touch the runner and if he succeeds they change places. The runner may escape by entering the circle and standing in front of another player who then becomes the runner.

Volleyball

A game for all seasons: A game for all ages

This is a popular team sport played by boys and girls of all ages. It can be played outdoors on the beach or in a park or playground, or indoors in a gymnasium.

The standard volleyball court is 20 by 15 metres, and has an overhead clearance of at least 7 metres. A net about 16 metres long and 1 metre deep is strung across the centre of the court; its top is about 3 metres from the ground. The volleyball has a circumference of about 65 centimetres and is made of rubber or a rubber bladder covered with leather.

Each team forms a front line of three players and a rear line of three players. The object of the game is to hit the volleyball from one side to the other over the net. Each team tries to keep the ball from hitting the ground on its side and tries to make it land on the ground in the other team's court. The ball is usually hit with the hand but it may also be struck by any part of the body above the knee. The ball may be touched by no more than three players in a team before it goes over the net and a player is not allowed to hit the ball twice in succession. The ball is served by the player in the rear, right-hand position. He stands behind the base line, tosses the ball up and hits it with the palm of his hand into the opponent's court. If a serve hits the net, even if it goes over, it is a fault and possession goes to the other team. During a volley, a ball that touches the net and goes over continues in play. If a player hits a ball into the net another player in the team may hit it over, provided it has not touched the ground. No player may touch the net or step over the centre line under it.

Only the serving team can score. A player continues to serve as long as his team wins each volley. When the server's team faults, the serve goes to the opposite team. Players in the team that is about to serve move one position in a clockwise direction. The players in the

front line move to the right, or back, and the players in the back line move to the left, or forward. In this way, each time a team receives the service, a new person serves.

The strategy in Volleyball is not for a player to hit every ball that comes to him directly over the net but to hit the ball to another in his team—preferably a player in the front line. In this way, the ball is 'set up' so that the second player can 'spike', or hit it hard, into the opponents' court with a smashing one or two-handed overhead shot. A 'spiking line' is drawn about 2 metres from the net. It does not affect front-line players but the rear-line players may not cross it when trying to smash.

The winning score in Volleyball is usually 15 points. However, a two-point margin is required to win; a game tied at 14-all is continued until one team is ahead by two points.

One-bounce Volleyball

Easier but just as much fun

One-bounce Volleyball is an informal, fun-making version of the serious team game of Volleyball.

It can be played in a large back garden, in a park or on the beach by eight to twelve players.

The equipment needed: a volleyball, or football, and a net about 2 metres high. A net used for back-garden Badminton makes an admirable substitute.

Two teams play on an area about 7 by 13 metres with a centre net.

The first player in the serving team serves the ball by hitting it with the palm of his hand from behind his back line. If it crosses the net, an opposing player lets it bounce once before hitting it back with an open hand. This is kept up until a player fails to return the ball, or hits it out of bounds.

If the serving team wins the exchange, it gets a point and keeps the serve.

If it loses, the opposing team gets no points but receives the ball and has a turn to serve and win points.

The server is given two chances to hit a fair serve.

No player may hit the ball twice to keep it in play.

Only one bounce is allowed before the ball is returned.

The team with the most points after 10 minutes is the winner.

Chapter 9

Fun on the Beach and in the Country

Games to play on a long car journey;
Nature trails and games of observation;
Games on the beach;
Swimming-pool games

A few hours' preparation can mean the success or failure of a holiday at the seaside, in the countryside or at home. If you are going away read this chapter before leaving home so that you have equipment for the games and for nature trailing. Before setting out, put the book in the car. Many of the games suggested in Chapter 7, 'Games for the Garden', and in Chapter 8, 'Games for Open Spaces', can be played at the seaside or in the country.

Long journeys by car can be tedious for a young traveller. The games that follow are designed to make the trip happier for everyone and to encourage junior passengers to take an interest in the passing scene. Make sure, before the journey begins, that you have a plentiful supply of paper and soft crayons. Pencils or ballpoint pens can be dangerous in a car, in the event of a sudden stop.

Pub-sign Tennis

The 'court' is the roadside

This is a car game calling for sharp eyes. There are two players and each selects one side of the road as his tennis court. The front-seat passenger is the umpire. Points are scored as in tennis, 15–love, 30–love, and so on, and they are gained when a player sees a pub sign on his side of the road. The umpire keeps the score as in tennis and announces the winner of each game. If the tennis system of scoring is unfamiliar to some passengers, they can use a simple system of scoring individual points. The first player to reach a total of five points is the winner.

Pub-sign Cricket
You need the legs for it

Pub-sign Cricket is a variation of Pub-sign Tennis. One player is a batsman, the other is a bowler. The batsman scores runs by spotting signs—on either side of the road—with animals or people in the names and adds up the number of legs. The Red Lion, for example, would give a total of four runs, the Green Man a total of two. If the bowler sees a 'legless' sign—The Crown, for example—the batsman is bowled out.

Pairs
Doubles—and two by two

There are two players. One has the numbers 0 1 2 3 4; the other has 5 6 7 8 9. When they see a number-plate with their numbers paired, such as 0–1 or 5–6, or doubled, such as 5–5 or 4–4, and so on, they get a point. The first player to get five points is the winner.

Travelling Zoo
The 30-minute animal hunt

Finding animals for a zoo can keep children amused for 30 minutes or so. A player must point out an object on the roadside the name of which starts with the same letter as the name of an animal. A garage, for example, could be a giraffe or a gorilla or a goat. Once an object has been used it cannot be used again by any player. The referee, having a busy time in the front-passenger seat, keeps the score and a note of the objects used. After, say, 30 minutes, the player with the largest zoo wins.

How far?
The tricky time test

The object is to guess how far the car will travel in 5 minutes. When all the guesses have been noted down the referee times a 5-minute run using a watch and the car's mileometer. Decide beforehand if stops are to count.

Scavenger Hunt
Seeing is winning

This is a game that should be prepared in advance. Make up a list of things that might be seen during the journey and give each child a copy when you want the game to start. Here are a few examples: horse, cow, donkey, barn, bicycle, tractor, plough, helicopter, plane, train, pond, river. The list should contain from 15 to 20 objects. Whenever a player sees one of the objects he calls it out and crosses it off his list. When one player calls out an object, say a donkey, the others cannot cross it off their lists. They have to wait until they see another donkey. The winner is the player who has crossed off most objects in 30 minutes, or whatever time the referee decides.

Animal, Vegetable or Mineral?
Twenty questions is the limit

This is one of the simplest and most popular of parlour games. One player selects an object and the others have to guess what it is, asking him not more than 20 questions. The answer to each question must be either 'yes' or 'no'. Before the game became popular on the radio, the players had to ask Animal? Vegetable? Mineral? perhaps using up three questions. In the radio version, the question-master announced the category, 'It is vegetable', and the questioners took it up from there. Not every object can be classified so simply. A glass of wine, for instance, would be 'vegetable and mineral with animal connections', because

glass is mineral, wine is made from grapes and people drink it.
The most skilful players can make full use of the classification of the object. 'Is the animal connection human?' Yes. 'Is it enjoyable?' Yes. 'Is it food?' No. 'Drink?' Yes, and so on. The first player to guess the object selects the next one and answers the questions. If the object is not guessed in 20 or fewer questions, the same player selects another object.

Number-plate Spelling
Words awheel

Each player writes down a word, each word having the same number of letters. The players watch the number-plates of other cars and whenever they see a letter included in their word they cross it off. The first player to cross out his complete word is the winner.

Number-plate Alphabet
The A to Z of motoring

Each player writes down all the letters of the alphabet and crosses them out as he sees them on number-plates. The winner is the player who crosses out all of the letters, or the most after 10 minutes.

Number-plate Race
Figuring out the winner

Each player writes down the numbers 0 to 9, and when they see them on number-plates they cross them out. The first player to cross out all the numbers is the winner.

FINDING OUT ABOUT NATURE TRAILS

There are about 400 scenic nature trails in Britain where a great variety of wildlife can be seen on a comfortable stroll. The trails can be found in National Parks, Forest Parks, Country Parks, Nature Reserves, in the grounds of National Trust properties and on public and private land.
Many trails are open throughout the year. This enables a child to see the same stretch of countryside changing with the seasons.
Most trails are short (1–5 kilometres) and easy to walk. They are, therefore, suitable for a family morning or afternoon outing. Usually no special clothing is needed, but it is advisable to wear waterproof walking shoes or gum boots after rain.
A knowledge of natural history is not called for since the planners of the trails offer a printed guide, which sometimes includes a map. It is essential to have one of these to follow and understand the trail. In summer, guides can often be obtained at the start of the trail, but the supply may be temporarily exhausted. It is therefore a good idea, whatever the season, to order guides by post beforehand.

Hear, See, Smell
A real eye-opener

This game is played during a nature walk. Each child is given a sheet of paper and a pencil and is asked to make a note of all the different sounds, sights and smells he observes. It is a particularly good game for developing the senses and for helping children to realise just how much is going on in the apparently quiet countryside. They become very much aware of things that often pass unnoticed—such as the sound of a grasshopper, the sight of a spider weaving his web or the smell of wild honeysuckle.
After 15 minutes, or at a suitable spot when everyone is ready for a break, the lists are read out. Each child gets two points for listing things that nobody else has noticed and one point for each shared item.

Country Cribbage
Knowledge is a stone's throw away

Before setting out, each child collects ten small pebbles which he carries in one hand. As the walk proceeds, the leader of the game points out various natural objects one at a time and calls on one of the children to identify them. If the child succeeds he is allowed to throw one of his pebbles away. If he fails, the next child gets a chance. The game continues until someone wins by being empty handed.

Tree Touch
When trunk routes lead to safety

Players divide into two equal teams for this game which introduces a nature study into the traditional game of touch. Each team selects the name of a tree which can be found in the area. For example, one might pick oak, the other beech. The teams line up a few metres apart and the organiser of the game calls out one of the trees they have selected. If he calls out 'Oak!' the members of the oak team must try to touch an oak tree before being themselves touched by a member of the other team. Points may be awarded for each successful touch.

In *Safety Tree*, a more complicated version of the game, there is only one chaser, the rest of the children are runners. In this game, the chaser stands with his back turned to the others who are about 15 metres away from him. The organiser calls out the name of any type of tree that can be found in the area and the children make a dash for one of that type and try to touch it before being touched by the chaser. The first child touched becomes the new chaser.

Memory Ramble
The list comes later

This is a game to be completed after a nature walk. Before starting out, the children are told to make a mental note of everything interesting they see. Then, when the ramble is over they are each given a sheet of paper and a pencil and asked to list the things they have observed. The child with the longest correct list wins.

What am I?
The others will try to tell you

This is a game for one of those welcome rest-stops when everyone is relaxing. One child makes up a list of facts about a familiar animal or bird and reads them out very slowly. The others try to guess what it is. They are allowed only one guess each so they should wait until they are sure before they call out. The first child to call out correctly is the next to make up a list. If they all guess wrongly the child who made up the list gets another turn. An example is on the right.

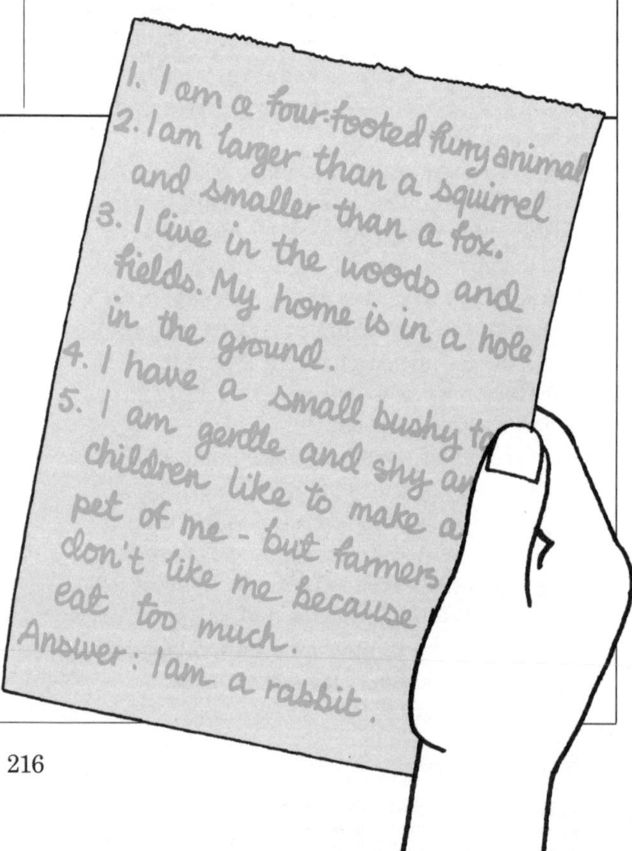

GAMES BY THE SEA

Most of the games that are played in open spaces (see p. 198) can be played on the sands. Here are some more that are best played at the seaside.

Sandcastle Marbles

And see how they run

Build a pyramid-shape sandcastle in damp sand and press out a winding path from the summit to the base, like a helter-skelter. Form a small ridge on the outside, so that marbles do not come off at the first bend.

Two players set their marbles at the top and let them run at the starting signal. The first to reach the bottom wins.

Clock Golf

The time for holiday fun

Sink a bucket in the sand and make a circle about 8 metres in diameter round the bucket. Set 12 pebbles round the circle as points of the clock. Using a sand spade and tennis ball, each player starts at 1 o'clock and tries to get the ball into the bucket. The player with the fewest strokes after playing 12 o'clock wins.

Shadow Touch

A game for a sunny day

This is a game for a bright sunny day since the players must throw distinct shadows. One player is chosen as shadow chaser and the others scatter around the playing area. To make a touch, the chaser must step on the shadow of another player. When the chaser makes a touch he joins the runners and his victim becomes the new chaser.

The chaser has a difficult task, so to make it a little easier, he may at any time call out 'Shadows cross over!' All the runners must then sprint to the edge of the play area farthest from their positions at the time of the call.

MAKING A SPLASH IN THE POOL

There's no end of fun to be had in a swimming pool, and opportunities to enjoy water sports grow every summer as more and more pools are installed in our gardens.

The games that follow make for enjoyable relaxation after the serious and important business of learning to swim.

They can be played either in a home pool or a school swimming bath and some of them can be played by young people who are not yet experienced and fully proficient swimmers. This form of water play builds up their confidence as they happily compete in the shallow end and lets them find out early in life how pleasant water sports can be. They can become expert swimmers later.

None of these games should be played without the supervision of at least one adult and none should be attempted in the sea.

Take the Plunge

And make an early splash

This is a good, simple game to start off with. The children take it in turn to dive in at one end of the pool and glide underwater, arms outstretched in front of them, as far as they can before surfacing. The longest glide wins.

Underwater Touch

Ducking to safety

This is a game to be played in the shallow end so that children who are not particularly good swimmers can join in the fun. One player is the chaser and his job is to try to touch the others in the pool. The others try to keep out of this way, but if they are cornered they can still avoid being touched by ducking under the water. No player can be touched when completely submerged. The first player to be touched becomes the new chaser.

Shark
Jaws in the middle

Only good swimmers should compete in this exciting game. One player is the shark and he lurks in the middle of the pool. The others line up, out of the water, at each side. Their aim is to dive in and swim to the opposite side without being touched by the shark. They may dive in any order and it doesn't matter how many there are in the water at the same time. The first player to be touched becomes the new shark.

There is an amusing variation of this game in which the players try to cross the pool as many times as possible in 5 minutes without being touched by the shark. The player who makes the most crossings before being touched is the new shark.

How Many Ways?
Victory comes at a stroke

This is a splendid opportunity for small swimmers to show off their skill, and the game is played in waist-deep water to make things easy for them. Children take turns to swim a width of the pool using a stroke which has not been used by anyone else.

They draw lots to decide the order in which they go and clearly, in this game, the luck of the draw is most important and the game gets more difficult with each crossing. However, even non-swimmers or almost-non-swimmers can take part. They can wade across forwards or backwards, or hop across or use any method they can think of.

In *Follow the Leader* everyone jumps in the pool and swims around using whatever stroke the organiser calls out. The organiser keeps changing the stroke and swimmers who do not follow his instructions are eliminated. The last swimmer in the pool is the winner.

Water Joust
Who has the most pull in the pool?

Players pair off for this game which is played in the shallow end of the pool. Ideally, they should be paired so that one partner is smaller than the other. The small one climbs on his partner's back and they are ready for the fray. To start the joust, two pairs face each other in the pool; their aim is to unseat the other rider. The riders use one hand to hold on to their 'horse' and they grip each other's free hand. Then they pull and tug until one of them falls into the water.

If there are a number of pairs the game is played as an elimination contest with the winners in each round meeting in the next round until only one pair is left—the winners of the contest.

Pebble Carry
Just a matter of balance

The dog paddle or the side stroke are called for in this game which also needs a steady hand. Two teams line up at one side of the shallow end of the pool, each player holding three pebbles. At a signal the first players swim to the opposite side and back again—but while they do it they must balance their three pebbles on the back of one hand. If a player drops any or all of the pebbles he must swim back, collect three more and start again. The first team to complete the relay successfully is the winner.

Cork Collecting
Chasing the flotsam

Two equal teams line up out of the water at one side of the pool. The organiser throws a basketful of corks into the middle and when they hit the water the players dive in and swim for them. The team which collects the greater number of corks is the winner. If there are not enough young people to make two teams, this can also be played as an individual game.

Hoop Relay
For swift swimmers, smart divers

This is a game which calls for both swimming and diving skill. Two equal teams line up out of the water at one end of the pool and two hoops are floated on the water at an equal distance from them. When the start signal is given, the first players in each side dive in, swim to their hoops, dive through them and swim back to the start where they touch off the next players. The first team home is the winner.

Treasure Diving
Everyone drops like a stone

Children divide into two teams and each team picks a non-playing captain. The captain of one team throws a stone into the water and one member of the opposing team dives to find the 'treasure' and bring it back. The captain who threw the stone times how long it takes the diver to retrieve it. Then the action is reversed, with the captain of the second team tossing the treasure into the water and a member of the first team diving after it. The contest goes on until every member of each team has a turn in the water. The winning team is the one with the shortest total time.

In *Bottle-top Diving*, bottle tops are thrown into the pool and two swimmers at a time try to collect as many as possible before coming up for air.

Umbrella Race
The result is open and shut

Two umbrellas are placed at one side of the pool. Children in two equal teams line up on the opposite side. At a signal, the first player in each team dives in and swims across to the other side, seizes his team's umbrella, opens it and swims back holding the open umbrella over his head. He hands the umbrella to the next player in his team who, in his turn, swims across the pool, closes the umbrella, places it at the side of the pool, swims back and touches off the next player in his team. The game continues until one team has completed the action.

Waterball Carry
This game is a real knees-up

Two teams line up, each in single file at one end of the pool. A plastic beach ball is given to the lead player in each team. At a signal, each lead player places the ball between his knees and jumps into the pool. He swims to the opposite end and back again with the ball between his knees. He then hands the ball to the next player in his team.
Any player who loses the ball must stop and place it back into position before swimming on. The first team home wins.

PARTY TREATS

Recipes for savouries, sweets, cakes and drinks for children of all ages

boxes. Each child has a gaily decorated carton or basket, partly open at the top, with a stapled paper handle. These are their personal boxes of party food which they take into the garden.

Things to avoid

With the very young it is better to avoid chocolate confections if furniture or party dresses are at risk. Fizzy drinks and excited children don't mix. Attractively coloured milk shakes are better.

Don't overload the table with sandwiches, for most children they are fairly run-of-the-mill, and it is better to make and fill small pastry shells, tiny vol-au-vents, and celery and cucumber baskets. Do not think that the guests will invariably enjoy jellies. The only real use for jelly is as the base for a place-name.

On the Big Day

Prepare yourself a light, uncomplicated lunch the evening before or with the minimum of difficulty. But don't forget to have one—or the day will seem endless. Have teacups and saucers, sugar and milk ready on trays, covered with cloths, for mothers to have a cup of tea when collecting their children at the end of the party.

Having decided where you can safely set the table, clear the room and get the table set up as soon as possible. Take any sandwiches, cakes or other food out of the deep freeze.

When do you sit the children down to eat? The most satisfactory time is after the boisterous games. Follow the food with a quieter period—an entertainer, magician or a Punch and Judy show, for example. You and your helpers then have a chance to clear up and will not be left with a mountain of debris when the sounds of battle have died away.

Preparing for a barbecue

If you are giving a summer barbecue party it is a good idea to have a rehearsal with your family beforehand.

Set up the barbecue and have a trial run with the food that you intend to serve. Timing is important. You may be surprised how long it takes to get a barbecue fire going—and how quickly the food will cook. This trial will guide you on the time to start on the day.

A TABLE CENTRE THAT IS DIFFERENT

A table centre that is spectacularly different can be made in the following way:

Level the base of a cabbage by cutting off a slice so that it stands firmly on the table. Cover the cabbage with silver foil. Thread alternate mandarin slices and glacé cherries, or pineapple cubes and dates, on cocktail sticks. Spike the foil-covered cabbage with the decorated sticks, then put to one side.

Red apples and white grapes coated in pink frosting and black grapes coated in green frosting make up the decoration.

Polish some red apples until they shine brightly. Whip an egg white gently to break it up. Take half the quantity of apples and paint a broad band of egg white from the top to the bottom of each apple. Put a plate under the apples and, while the egg white is still wet, liberally shake caster sugar over them. Leave to dry.

Put 50 g. (2 oz.) of caster sugar into the liquidiser. Switch the machine on and drip a few drops of pink or green food colouring into the sugar through the hole in the cover. Switch off as soon as the colouring is incorporated, which will only take a second or two. Dip bunches of white grapes into the egg white and then into the coloured sugar. Allow to dry.

When all the fruits are dry, put them together, adding the unfrosted apples, on a tall stand if possible. If you have not got a purpose-made stand, you could use a large salad bowl fixed firmly on an upturned vase, broad-based jar, or flower pot. Place your fruit-spiked cabbage in the bowl, surround it with the apples and drape the grapes so that they tumble over the edges of the bowl. Finish the centrepiece off by incorporating some slender flowering twigs from your own (or a friend's) garden.

Treats for the Very Young

SAVOURIES AND SNACKS

Cheese Straws

100 g. (4 oz.) basic cheese pastry makes approximately 30 straws

COOKING TIME: *8–10 minutes*

INGREDIENTS:

100 g. (4 oz.) plain flour
50 g. (2 oz.) lard
Pinch of salt
Pinch of Cayenne pepper
2–3 tablespoons of milk
75 g. (3 oz). grated cheese (Cheddar if possible)

Prepare the pastry, folding the grated cheese into the rubbed-in mixture before adding the liquid. Roll out until about 5 mm. ($\frac{1}{4}$ in.) thick. Cut into 5 cm. (2 in.) straws. Place on a greased oven tray and cook in the centre of the oven for approximately 8–10 minutes at 200°C (400°F), gas mark 6.

Pinwheel Sandwiches

Buy small brown and white sliced loaves. Cut off all the crusts. Roll the bread with a wooden rolling pin. This will compact the texture, enabling you to roll it more easily when filled. Butter the slices well to the edges. Put on your filling, which should be at least as thick as the bread itself. Roll the filled slice along the long edge, making sure that you keep the roll fairly tight. At this stage you can pack the rolls close together into a container, putting greaseproof paper between layers, and place in the deep freeze.

Two hours before they are required, remove the rolls from the deep freeze and allow them to thaw at room temperature. Halfway through thawing, cut into five slices (as you would a Swiss roll), and arrange ready for the table. If you have to make the pinwheels on the day of the party, try to chill them well before cutting.

Don't forget name flags, to help the children identify the fillings.

SOME SUGGESTIONS FOR FILLINGS:

Very thin sliced ham topped with a layer of cream cheese
Light cream cheese spread with cucumber relish
Mashed tuna fish to which a few drops of lemon juice have been added

Tomato Boats

Choose firm, medium-size tomatoes. Wash, cut in half and de-seed, leaving them cut side down on kitchen paper. Soften cream cheese with a very little lightly whipped cream and pipe into the tomato halves.

Make the sails by cutting two triangles for each boat from a firm cheese, such as Edam. The mast, which is placed in the middle of the boat, can be made from a very thin slice of celery, or the white part of a spring onion. Press the sails and the mast into the cheese. Chill well.

Hearts and Diamonds Savoury Sandwiches

When making small sandwiches, be as adventurous as you can with the fillings. Use white bread for one side of the sandwich and brown bread for the other. Leave some sandwiches open, and mix the type of bread. A French stick cut at a slight angle makes an interesting shape for various fillings. Use pastry cutters to form as great a variety of shapes as possible, including hearts and diamonds. Crescents are made by overlapping a circular cutter. Diamonds are fashioned by

making a 5 cm. (2 in.) wide strip which is then sliced across at an angle.
Again, don't forget the name flags for identification of fillings.

SOME SUGGESTIONS FOR FILLINGS:

Jam
Egg and cress
Marmite
Sliced or spread cheese
Banana

Other ideas for Savouries

Celery cut into 5 cm. (2 in.) lengths and stuffed with peanut butter.
Hard-boiled eggs, cut in half and stuffed; fillings include mild curry, fish, and tomato sauce mixed with the yolk and piped back into the whites.
Cocktail sausages (the thin types twisted in the centre and cooked before cutting).

BISCUITS AND CAKES

Tiny Iced Eclairs

The following amount of choux pastry makes approximately 36 eclairs, or 20 eclairs and 20 Savoury Choux Buns (see p. 240).

COOKING TIME: *10–15 minutes*

INGREDIENTS:

100 g. (4 oz.) plain flour
75 g. (3 oz.) butter
3 eggs weighing no more than 175 g. (6 oz.)
225 g. (8 oz.) double cream
225 g. (8 oz.) fondant icing
150 ml. ($\frac{1}{4}$ pint) water

Boil the water and butter together. Add the flour and beat until smooth. Draw the pan away from the heat and allow the mixture to cool.
Whisk the eggs and add to the almost cold mixture, beating well. The addition should be done gradually, so that the result is not too soft. Place the mixture into a forcing bag fitted with a plain nozzle, preferably 9 mm. ($\frac{3}{8}$ in.) in diameter, and pipe lengths of not more than 5 cm. (2 in.) on to a baking sheet that has been lightly greased and then dampened under the tap. At this stage, the eclairs can be successfully frozen, if you so wish.
Cook in a pre-heated oven at 190°C (375°F), gas mark 5, for approximately 10–15 minutes, or until firm to the touch; do not remove too soon. Cool on a wire rack.
Whip the cream, flavouring if you wish by adding sugar with a few drops of vanilla or peppermint. Pipe the cream into the cold eclairs.
Gently warm the fondant, colouring one-third pink, one-third green, and leaving one-third white. Coat the eclairs.
Pull the sides of individual paper cake cases apart to make them into boat shapes and lay the eclairs inside.

Tartlets

The recipe makes approximately 24 tartlets.

COOKING TIME: *10–15 minutes*

INGREDIENTS:

225 g. (8 oz.) plain flour
100 g. (4 oz.) butter
100 g. (4 oz.) caster sugar
4 egg yolks
Pinch of salt
Fillings—to choice

Sieve the flour and salt on to your pastry board or table. Make a well in the centre.
Cut the butter into small pieces and place them, with the sugar and egg yolks, in the well.
Mix together, using the fingers of one hand only, until the sugar is thoroughly dissolved and all ingredients are fully blended. Now gradually draw in the surrounding flour and knead together until mixed; do not over-handle. This paste should then be wrapped in greaseproof paper and placed in the

refrigerator for up to 2 hours.
Roll out thinly and line very small tartlet tins. Bake at 190°C (375°F), gas mark 5, for approximately 10–15 minutes blind or filled, depending on your choice of filling or personal preference.
Be bold with decorations. Angelica handles across the tartlets turn them into baskets. Bought orange and lemon slices can be cut into fan shapes to decorate the iced coatings. Flaked chocolate can be lightly sprinkled on lemon curd. Mandarin oranges dipped into boiled apricot jam and left to drain and cool on wire racks make a good topping for black cherry tartlets.

SOME SUGGESTIONS FOR FILLINGS:

Strawberry jam
Lemon curd
Black cherry or apricot pie fillings
Rich fruit

Rich fruit is prepared as follows. Mix 400 g. (14 oz.) dried fruit, including glacé cherries chopped very small, with 100 g. (4 oz.) brown sugar and juice of half a lemon. Melt a knob of butter in a pan. Add the fruit mixture and cook gently until the sugar has dissolved and the fruit is sticky. Allow to cool and spoon into the tartlets. Ice with lemon icing.

Happy-face Biscuits

This quantity makes approximately 24 biscuits.

COOKING TIME: *approximately 10 minutes*

INGREDIENTS:

100 g. (4 oz.) self-raising flour
25 g. (1 oz.) cornflour
100 g. (4 oz.) butter
50 g. (2 oz.) caster sugar
2 drops vanilla

Beat the butter, sugar and vanilla until white. Add the sifted flour and cornflour and mix well. Roll the mixture into balls the size of small walnuts and place them on a lightly greased baking sheet, allowing enough space between

them to spread without touching each other. Flatten each ball with a broad-bladed knife moistened in tepid water.
Cook on the middle shelf of the oven at 190°C (375°F), gas mark 5, for approximately 10 minutes until golden-brown. Remove from the oven and allow to cool slightly before transferring the biscuits from the baking sheet to a wire rack. Pipe happy smiling faces on to the cold biscuits using melted chocolate or icing. You can, alternatively, use piping jelly bought in tubes of various colours.
If you are feeling creative or ambitious, you can pipe an outline of body and arms on one biscuit and an outline of legs on another, so that children can assemble a complete figure by choosing three biscuits of the same piped colour.

Chocolate Bows

COOKING TIME: *approximately 20 minutes*

INGREDIENTS:

50 g. (2 oz.) plain flour
100 g. (4 oz.) sugar
3 egg whites
225 g. (8 oz.) almonds or other nuts
100 g. (4 oz.) plain chocolate
Chopped hazelnuts (or other nuts) for decoration

Melt the chocolate and mix it together with other ingredients, except the hazelnuts, in an

electric mixer. Drop teaspoonfuls of the mixture on to a greased and floured baking sheet.
Flatten each spoonful with the back of a fork and sprinkle with chopped hazelnuts or nibbed (finely chopped) almonds and bake at 170°C (325°F), gas mark 3, then remove from oven. When cool but not set, pinch the sides together to form a bow. Lift from baking sheet when cold.

Orange Crusted Jumbles

The recipe makes approximately 30 jumbles.

COOKING TIME: *10–15 minutes*

INGREDIENTS:

350 g. (12 oz.) self-raising flour
100 g. (4 oz.) butter
100 g. (4 oz.) sugar
1 egg
1 orange
1 tablespoon milk
1 egg white

Grate the rind of the orange and squeeze out the juice. Cream the butter and sugar until white. Add the egg, orange rind and juice. Fold in the sieved flour and use the milk to mix to a firm dough.
Roll out the dough 5 mm. (¼ in.) thick and cut into narrow strips about 15 cm. (6 in.) long. Coil each strip like a flat Catherine wheel. Place the coils on a greased baking sheet, brush with white of egg and sprinkle with nibbed sugar (sugar crystals that are used, for example, to decorate Bath buns). Cook at 230°C (450°F), gas mark 8, for 10–15 minutes.

Walnut Wafers

This quantity makes roughly 30 wafers.

COOKING TIME: *7–10 minutes*

INGREDIENTS:

75 g. (3 oz.) plain flour
50 g. (2 oz.) butter
50 g. (2 oz.) sugar
2 eggs
50 g. (2 oz.) walnuts
Vanilla essence

Cream the butter and sugar until white. Add the eggs and sifted flour alternately, beating well. Chop the walnuts finely and add to the mixture together with a few drops of vanilla essence.
Spoon in small teaspoonfuls on to a greased baking sheet, keeping the drops well apart. Bake at 230°C (450°F), gas mark 8, for 7–10 minutes.
Remove from oven and allow to cool on a wire tray. When quite cold, sandwich the wafers together in pairs with a little coffee butter cream (see p. 231).

Gingerbread Shapes

This quantity makes approximately 24 gingerbread shapes.

COOKING TIME: *10–15 minutes*

INGREDIENTS:

225 g. (8 oz.) plain flour
1 dessertspoon bicarbonate of soda
2 teaspoons ground ginger
½ teaspoon cinnamon
Pinch of salt
50 g. (2 oz.) butter
100 g. (4 oz.) soft brown sugar
3 tablespoons black treacle

Place the butter, sugar and treacle in a

saucepan over a low heat and cook gently until the sugar has dissolved. Allow to cool whilst sifting together the flour, bicarbonate of soda, ginger, cinnamon and salt. Add the dry ingredients to the cooled liquid in the saucepan and mix, using a little top of the milk or evaporated milk to make a stiff dough.
Wrap this dough in greaseproof paper and place in the refrigerator for 30 minutes.
Roll out the dough to a thickness of 5 mm. ($\frac{1}{4}$ in.) on a pastry board sprinkled with caster sugar. Using a gingerbread-man cutter, which is available from most hardware stores, cut 18 shapes and lift them carefully with a palette knife on to a lightly greased baking sheet. Mark eyes, nose and coat buttons with currants. Using shaped cutters, make the remaining pastry into biscuits. Bake at 170°C (325°F), gas mark 3, for 10–15 minutes, or until firm to the touch.

Swiss Roll

COOKING TIME: *10 minutes*

INGREDIENTS:
75 g. (3 oz.) plain flour
Pinch of salt
3 large eggs
75 g. (3 oz.) caster sugar
1 tablespoon hot water
Jam or cream filling

Sift the flour and salt twice into a bowl or on to greaseproof paper. Butter a Swiss-roll tin measuring 30 by 20 cm. (12 by 8 in.), and line with buttered greaseproof or non-stick paper.
Put the eggs and caster sugar in a large bowl over a pan of hot water, and whisk until the mixture is pale and leaves a thick trail.
Remove from the heat, sift half the flour and salt over the egg mixture, and fold it in carefully, using a large metal spoon. Repeat with the remaining flour, and add the hot water. Turn the mixture quickly into the prepared tin, tilting it until evenly covered with the mixture. Bake at once just above the centre of an oven pre-heated to 220°C (425°F), gas mark 7, for about 10 minutes or until well-risen, light golden and springy.
Have ready a sheet of sugar-dredged greaseproof or non-stick paper. Turn the soft cake out on to the paper at once, remove the lining paper and quickly trim off the crisp edges from the sponge with a sharp knife.
Spread with 4–5 tablespoons warm jam, to within 1·5 cm. ($\frac{1}{2}$ in.) of the edges. Roll up the sponge at once from the short side, making the first turn firm, then rolling it lightly. Cool on a wire rack covered with a clean tea towel, and with the join of the sponge underneath.
The Swiss roll may also be spread with a butter-cream filling, just before serving. In this case, do not remove the lining paper, but roll the sponge round it while still warm. When cold, carefully unroll the sponge, then spread with whipped cream or butter cream (see p. 231) and roll up again.
Before serving, dust with caster or sifted icing sugar.

Short Fingers

COOKING TIME: *10–15 minutes*

INGREDIENTS *(for 12 biscuits):*
130 g. (4½ oz.) butter
25 g. (1 oz.) icing sugar
150 g. (5 oz.) plain flour
75 g. (3 oz.) plain cooking chocolate
BUTTER CREAM (see p. 231)

Grease two baking trays. Cream the butter with a wooden spoon until soft, but not oily, then beat in the sifted icing sugar. Stir in the sifted flour. Put the mixture in a forcing bag, fitted with a medium star vegetable nozzle, and pipe it in 5 cm. (2 in.) long fingers, on to the baking trays. Bake just above or in the centre of a pre-heated oven, at 190°C (375°F), gas mark 5, for 10–15 minutes or until pale golden-brown.
Meanwhile, break the chocolate into small pieces and place them in a bowl over hot water until melted.
Leave the baked biscuits to cool completely on a wire rack. When cold, sandwich them in

pairs with the butter cream. Dip one end of each biscuit in the melted chocolate and place them on a rack with the chocolate end protruding over the edge. When the chocolate has set, repeat the procedure with the other ends. Leave the biscuits for about 1½ hours.

Royal Icing

INGREDIENTS:
4 egg whites
800–900 g. (1¾–2 lb.) icing sugar
1 tablespoon lemon juice
2 teaspoons glycerine

Whisk the egg whites in a large bowl until frothy. Stir in the sifted icing sugar, a little at a time, beating thoroughly with a wooden spoon. When half the sugar has been added, beat in the lemon juice. Continue adding more sugar, beating well after each addition until the icing forms soft peaks when pulled up with a wooden spoon. For piping purposes the icing should be slightly firmer. Stir in the glycerine, which keeps the icing soft.
Ideally, leave the icing to rest for 24 hours, covered with polythene, and work it through before using. The above amount is sufficient to coat the top and sides of a 25 cm. (10 in.) wide and 5 cm. (2 in.) deep cake. Leave the coating to set before piping on the decorations. An electric mixer may be used, but care must be taken not to overbeat the icing—a fluffy Royal icing results in a rough surface and will also break when piped.

Cream Horns

COOKING TIME: *10 minutes*

INGREDIENTS *(for 8 horns):*
Half portion flaky pastry (see p. 235)
1 egg
Raspberry or blackcurrant jam
150 ml. (¼ pint) double cream
4 tablespoons single cream
Icing sugar

Roll the prepared pastry out to a strip 61 cm. (24 in.) long and 10 cm. (4 in.) wide. Beat the egg and brush it over the pastry. Cut the pastry into eight ribbons, 61 cm. (24 in.) long and 1·5 cm. (½ in.) wide, using a sharp knife. Wind each pastry strip round a cream horn tin, starting at the tip and with the glazed side of the pastry outside; overlap each turn by about 3 mm. (⅛ in.). As it rises during baking, the pastry should come just short of the metal rim of the horn. Set the moist horns on a baking tray, join downwards.
Bake towards the top of a pre-heated oven at 220°C (425°F), gas mark 7, for 8–10 minutes, until the horns are light golden. Leave to cool for a few minutes, then with one hand grip the rim of each tin with a clean cloth and carefully twist the tin. Hold the pastry lightly in the other hand and ease it off the tin.
Leave the horns to cool completely, then put a teaspoon of jam into the base of each horn. Just before serving, whip the two creams and spoon them into the horns. Dust with icing sugar.

The art of varying Cake Fillings and Toppings

Although a cook can use her own inventiveness to create superb cakes with a variety of fillings and toppings, there is a basic procedure that should be followed.

Always cool a cake thoroughly before filling and icing, and brush off any loose crumbs which would stick to the icing.

Do not put a firm-textured frosting or filling on a soft crumbly surface. For crumbly sponge cakes, use a light cream filling which spreads easily.

Make sure that the top of the cake is completely flat if it is to be iced. The cake can be turned upside down and the underside iced if this is more level.

To sandwich two layers of cake, place one layer, top side down, on a plate or flat surface and spread the filling to the edge. Allow the filling to set for a few minutes, then place the second layer, top side up, on the filling and lightly press the two together.

Before coating a cake with soft icing, put the cake on a wire rack over a plate. Pour the icing over the centre of the plain or filled cake, and gradually work the icing over the top and down the sides with a palette knife.

For a professional touch, spread the icing evenly round the sides of the cake before rolling it in chopped nuts or chocolate vermicelli. Spread the icing evenly over the top of the cake, then pipe on coloured icing in thin lines, 1·5–2 cm. ($\frac{1}{2}$–$\frac{3}{4}$ in.) apart, using a plain writing tube. Before the icing has set, draw lines, at right-angles, over the coloured icing with the blunt edge of a knife blade. Turn the cake 180 degrees and draw the knife between the intersections.

Make butter cream by beating butter in a basin until very soft. Sieve icing sugar and add to the butter while still beating. When the icing is soft, add two or three drops of vanilla essence and beat again.

To coat a cake with butter cream, place the cake on a board and decorate the sides first. Spread the coating evenly round the sides, using a round-bladed knife, then pile more butter cream on top of the cake. Smooth the cream evenly to the edges with a small palette knife, then finish the top with a swirled, latticed or roughed-up pattern, using a fork, knife or confectioner's comb.

The sides may also be covered with butter cream and then decorated. Cover the sides before the top, spreading the cream evenly with a palette knife. Roll the sides carefully in chocolate vermicelli, then spread butter cream or fondant icing over the top.

Piped decorations should be applied after the covering icing has set, but shaped decorations, such as rose buds, should be applied while the icing is still soft.

To make rose buds from coloured Royal Icing (see facing page), fix a small square of waxed paper to an icing nail with a little of the soft icing. Using a plain or star-shaped small nozzle on the icing bag, pipe a centre cone on to the paper, and then pipe on small petal shapes. Work from right to left and overlap the petals slightly until a rose of the required size is formed. Remove the waxed paper, and when the rose bud has set place it on the still soft icing.

IDEAS THAT MAKE A BIRTHDAY CAKE SOMETHING SPECIAL

The following recipe makes a basic plain light cake that can be decorated and modelled just as you choose. You can freeze it without any trouble, and you can cut it without being bothered by crumbs on the surface.

The Basic Cake

COOKING TIME: *1½ hours*

INGREDIENTS:
215 g. (7½ oz.) self-raising flour } *sifted together*
50 g. (2 oz.) cornflour }
175 g. (6 oz.) margarine
175 g. (6 oz.) caster sugar
3 eggs

Line a 15 cm. (6 in.) cake tin with greaseproof paper. Beat the margarine and sugar until white and fluffy. Add the beaten eggs and 1 tablespoon of flour. Fold in the rest of the flour lightly but thoroughly. Bake at 180°C (350°F), gas mark 4, for approximately 1½ hours.

Roundabout Cake

At equal intervals on the underside of a cake board fix coloured ribbons or paper streamers, allowing one ribbon for each place setting. Bake a round cake as above and place it on the prepared board, and ice with white icing. Cut a circle of greaseproof paper the same size as your cake tin, and mark it out in pencil in eight equal segments. Place this pattern carefully on top of your set iced cake. With a pin, prick through the lines marked on the paper, lightly marking out the guides for the decoration of the roundabout. Remove the paper, lightly marking out the guides for the tiny holes to make the top of the roundabout. Cut animal shapes out of stiff card and place them carefully against the sides of the cake, pipe around the outline in coloured icing, and then remove the card and fill in the detail. As an alternative, you can buy animal-shaped biscuit cutters, press them lightly into the sides of the cake, and then mark out the outline and detail in varying coloured icing. Finish the decoration with a circle of candles in the centre of the cake and a tall flag with the name of the birthday child printed on it.

Building a House

Using twice the quantity of ingredients in the basic recipe, make a cake in a 20 cm. (8 in.) square tin, cooking for approximately 2¼ hours or until baked right through. When cold, slice off the top 4 cm. (1½ in.), and cut 2·5 cm. (1 in.) slices off two sides of the cake. From these 2·5 cm. thick slices cut two triangles for the gable ends of the house.

Place the cake, which can be sliced through horizontally and layered with a flavoured butter cream (see p. 231), on a cake board and brush it over with boiled, sieved apricot jam to which a little boiling water has been added (1 tablespoon of water to every 3 tablespoons of jam).

Cut the slice taken from the top of the cake down the middle, and trim the cut edges at an angle so that they fit neatly together to form the ridge of the roof. Coat the roof pieces and gable ends with the hot apricot glaze.

Make up a sugar syrup with 300 ml. (½ pint) of water and 350 g. (12 oz.) of sugar boiled together. Whisk 450 g. (1 lb.) of sieved icing sugar to 65 g. (2½ oz.) of hot sugar syrup to form a water icing. Colour and flavour the icing as you wish. Also adjust its consistency with more sugar syrup if necessary, as you will need a smooth, fairly stiff icing.

Ice the main cake. Fix the roof pieces in place, using sugar syrup along the edges to hold them. Put the two gables in position and keep them steady with cocktail sticks. Ice the roof and gables and allow to set, then remove the sticks. Pipe lines of butter cream or icing around all joints and windows to hide any irregularities. Buy some tiny flower decorations to put on the walls, using angelica for stalks, and pebble the surrounds with small sweets and chocolate drops.

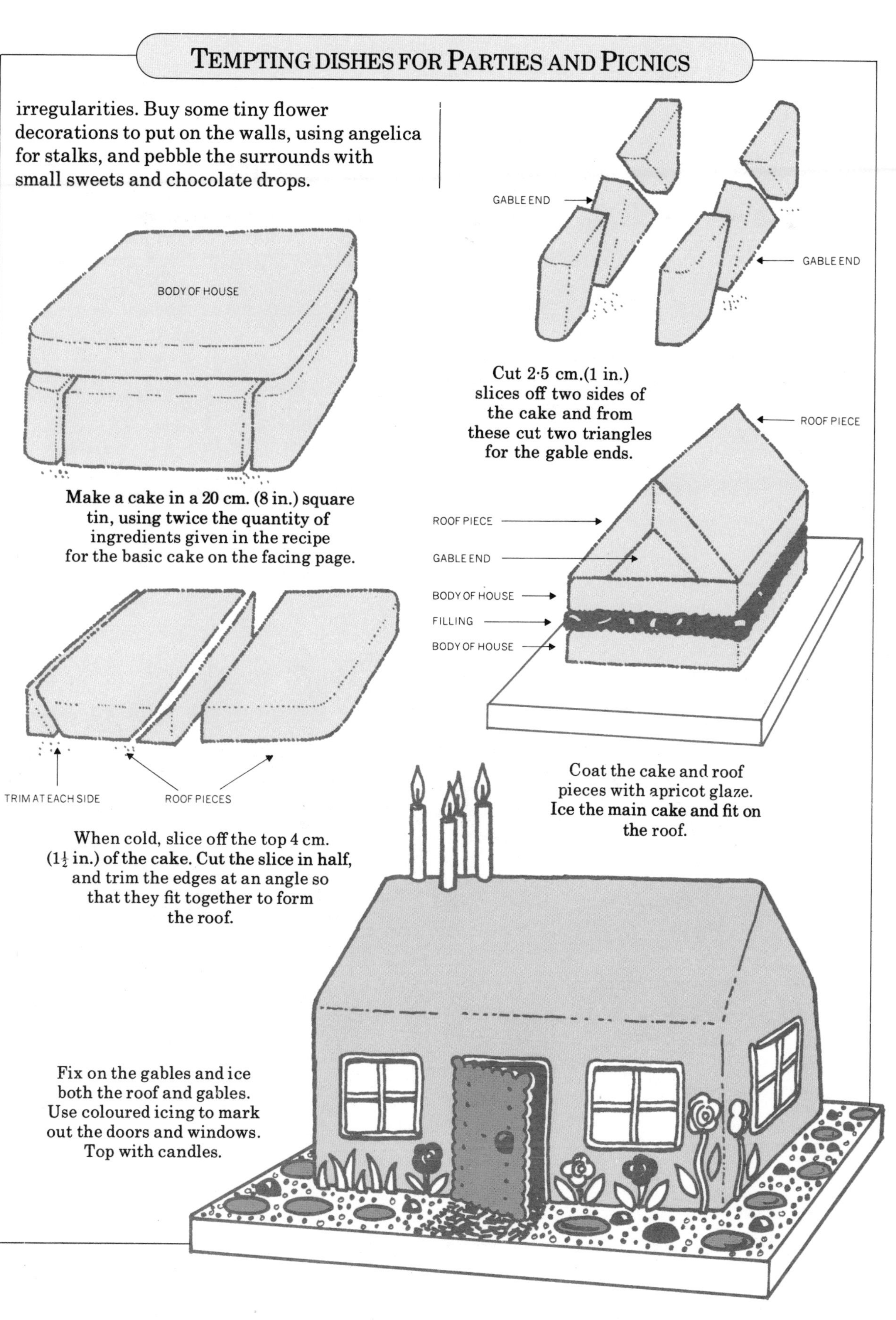

Make a cake in a 20 cm. (8 in.) square tin, using twice the quantity of ingredients given in the recipe for the basic cake on the facing page.

When cold, slice off the top 4 cm. ($1\frac{1}{2}$ in.) of the cake. Cut the slice in half, and trim the edges at an angle so that they fit together to form the roof.

Cut 2·5 cm.(1 in.) slices off two sides of the cake and from these cut two triangles for the gable ends.

Coat the cake and roof pieces with apricot glaze. Ice the main cake and fit on the roof.

Fix on the gables and ice both the roof and gables. Use coloured icing to mark out the doors and windows. Top with candles.

Railway Engine

INGREDIENTS:
225 g. (8 oz.) marzipan
1 mini Swiss roll (bought)
Melted chocolate
Make a cake from the basic recipe using a 900 g. (2 lb.) loaf tin

Turn out and cool. When cold, coat with an apricot glaze. Place on a cake board and fix the bought Swiss roll in place for a funnel. Ice the whole cake with water icing (see Building a House, p. 232), or, as an alternative, pour over melted chocolate, and don't worry at this stage about cleaning up the cake board. Put aside to set.

Roll out the marzipan to a thickness of 5 mm. ($\frac{1}{4}$ in.) and cut six circles with a plain 4 cm. ($1\frac{1}{2}$ in.) cutter. Dip a cocktail stick into melted chocolate or cochineal, and mark out a spiral starting from the centre of each circle and extended to the edge. Alternatively, draw six or seven spokes from the centre of each wheel to the edge.

Clean the cake board and fix the wheels to the engine with cocktail sticks, putting glacé cherries for the wheel hubs. Pipe in a contrasting colour for the windows and door. Put the child's name and age across the front of the engine. Place candles around the board.

How to make Flaky Pastry

This pastry can be used as crusts for savoury pies, sausage rolls and cream horns. It should be made in a cool atmosphere, and it is not advisable to make flaky pastry in hot weather.

INGREDIENTS *for 575 g. (1¼ lb.):*
225 g. (8 oz.) plain flour
½ level teaspoon salt
75 g. (3 oz.) lard
75 g. (3 oz.) butter or margarine
7 tablespoons iced water (approx.)
1 teaspoon lemon juice

Sift the flour and salt into a wide bowl. Work the lard and butter on a plate until evenly blended, and divide it into four equal portions. Rub one portion of the fat into the flour with the fingertips until the mixture resembles breadcrumbs. Add the water and lemon juice and mix the ingredients with a round-bladed knife to a soft, manageable dough. Turn it out on to a lightly floured surface and knead until all cracks have disappeared. Cover the dough with a clean polythene bag and leave it to rest in a cool place for 20 minutes. Keep the fat cool as well.

On a lightly floured surface roll out the dough, about 61 cm. (24 in.) long, 20 cm. (8 in.) wide and 5 mm. (¼ in.) thick. Brush off all surplus flour. Cut another quarter of the fat into small flakes and dot them evenly over two-thirds of the pastry and to within 1·5 cm. (½ in.) of the edges. Fold the unbuttered third of the pastry over the fat and fold the buttered top third down. Turn the dough so that the folded edge points to the left and seal all the edges firmly with the side of the little finger.
Cover the pastry with a polythene bag and leave it to rest again in a cool place for about 20 minutes.
Turn the pastry so that the fold points to the right-hand side. Roll the pastry out as before, cover two-thirds with another quarter of fat, and repeat the folding, sealing and resting as before. Continue with the remaining fat, giving the pastry a half-turn between each rolling. Finally, roll out the pastry to the original rectangle, brush off any surplus flour, fold it up and wrap it loosely in polythene. Leave it to rest in a cool place for at least 30 minutes before shaping. Bake in the centre of a pre-heated oven, at 220°C (425°F), gas mark 7.

How to make Traditional Shortcrust

INGREDIENTS:
225 g. (8 oz.) plain flour
½ level teaspoon salt
50 g. (2 oz.) lard
50 g. (2 oz.) margarine or butter
2–3 tablespoons cold water

Sift the flour and salt into a wide bowl. Cut up the firm fats and rub them into the flour, using the tips of the fingers, until the mixture resembles fine breadcrumbs. Lift the dry mixture well out of the bowl and let it trickle back through the fingers to keep the pastry cool and light. Add the water, sprinkling it evenly over the surface (uneven addition of the water may cause blistering when the pastry is cooked). Mix the dough lightly with a round-bladed knife until it forms large lumps. Gather the dough together with the fingers until it leaves the sides of the bowl clean. Form it into one piece and knead it lightly on a floured surface until firm and free from cracks. Chill for 30 minutes before use.
Roll the pastry out as required, using short, light strokes and rotate the pastry regularly to keep it an even shape.

Puff Pastry

INGREDIENTS:

450 g. (1 lb.) 'strong' bread-making flour
450 g. (1 lb.) butter
300 ml. (½ pint) cold water
Lemon juice
Pinch of salt

Rub 100 g. (4 oz.) of butter into the sieved flour

and salt. Add the water and a few drops of lemon juice and knead well together (this is very important). Cover and leave in a smooth ball in a cool place for 30 minutes.

Work the remaining butter by hand to soften it. Roll out the pastry into a rectangle and dot the butter over the lower half. Fold the top half down and seal the edges. Carefully roll out to approximately 30 by 30 cm. (12 by 12 in.), cover with a cloth, and allow to stand for 5 minutes. Roll out to approximately 61 by 30 cm. (24 by 12 in.), rolling the dough away from you and applying an even pressure all round. Do not let the rolling pin run off the edge as the object is to keep the dough rectangular in shape. Fold the upper and lower ends into the middle, and then fold the upper half on top of the lower half, sealing the edges with your hand. Again, allow the pastry to rest in a cool place for 20 minutes. Now move the pastry rectangle through a quarter turn. The whole of this process is called a 'double turn'. Repeat this operation in exactly the same way three more times. Do not turn the pastry over.

MAKING YOUR OWN PARTY ICE CREAM AND SORBETS

It is as easy to make cream ices and water ices at home as it is to make an egg custard or sugar syrup. Indeed, a basic ice cream is more often than not based on a custard enriched with double cream. The basis of a water ice is a sugar syrup flavoured with fruit juice or purée.

There are, however, some important guidelines to follow.

1 The amount of sugar in the mixture is important—if too much, the ice cream will not freeze, and if too little it will be hard and tasteless. Freezing does, however, take the edge off the sweetness and this must be borne in mind when tasting. In sorbets or water ices it is even more important to have the correct amount of sugar, as the soft yet firm consistency depends on the sugar content.

2 Some recipes recommend milk instead of cream, especially for strong-flavoured ice cream. The milk must be evaporated, not fresh dairy milk.

3 Use maximum freezing power. Whichever method is used for freezing the cream, it has a better texture if frozen quickly. Chill the equipment as well as the ingredients before starting.

4 Once the ice cream is frozen, it should be transferred to a shelf in the refrigerator for a little while before serving. Rock-hard ices are never pleasant and lose much of their flavour.

5 Ice cream may be stored in the freezing compartment of the refrigerator for the length of time indicated by the star rating.

Making ice cream in a refrigerator

Set the dial of the refrigerator at the coldest setting about 1 hour before the ice cream mixture is ready to freeze.

Make up the mixture according to the recipe. Remove the dividers and pour the mixture into ice trays or any other suitable freezing container, such as refrigerator boxes, loaf tins and stainless-steel dishes. Cover the trays or containers with foil or lids and place in the freezing compartment.

To obtain a smooth texture, the ice crystals must be broken down as they form and the ice cream mixture whisked at intervals until part

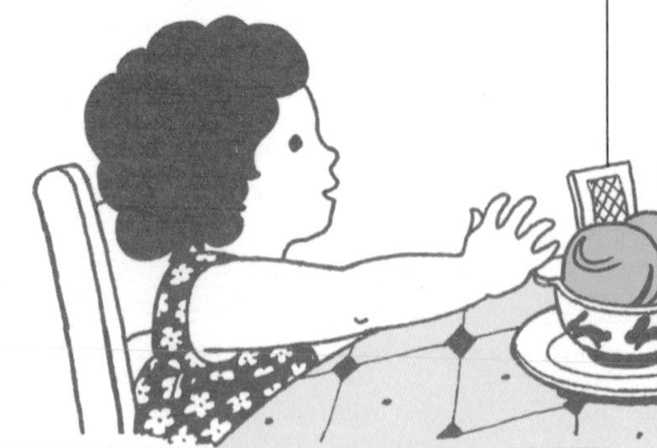

frozen and slushy. Remove the tray from the freezing compartment and scrape the ice crystals, which have formed on the sides and base, towards the centre. Whisk the mixture with a fork until smooth, and return the tray, covered, to the freezing compartment. Thereafter, leave the ice cream undisturbed until it is firm, after 2–3 hours.
Freezing time varies with different refrigerators, but several hours are necessary in every case. When freezing and maturing of the ice cream is completed, return the dial to its normal temperature setting or other food in the refrigerator may be spoilt by exposure to low temperatures.

Making ice cream in a home deep freeze
Set the dial to 'quick-freeze' about 1 hour before the ice cream is ready to be frozen. Prepare the ice cream mixture according to the recipe, place it in a mixing bowl in the deep freeze and leave it until mushy.
Remove the bowl from the deep freeze and whisk the mixture thoroughly with a rotary beater. Pour the ice cream into empty ice-cube trays or rigid polythene containers, and freeze until firm. Set the dial of the deep freeze to its normal temperature. If the ice cream is to be stored for any length of time the container should be sealed or over-wrapped and labelled.

Vanilla Ice Cream

FREEZING TIME: *about 3 hours*

INGREDIENTS *(for 6):*
¼ litre (½ pint) milk
Vanilla pod
1 whole egg
2 egg yolks
75 g. (3 oz.) caster sugar
¼ litre (½ pint) double cream

Bring the milk almost to the boil with the vanilla pod, then leave to infuse off the heat for about 15 minutes. Remove the vanilla pod. Cream the whole egg, yolks and sugar until pale. Stir in the vanilla-flavoured milk and strain this mixture through a sieve into a clean pan. Heat the custard mixture slowly over gentle heat, stirring all the time, until the mixture thickens enough to just coat the back of a wooden spoon. Pour into a bowl and leave to cool.
Whip the cream lightly and fold it carefully and thoroughly into the cooled custard. Spoon into ice-cube trays or a suitable freezing container, cover and set in the freezing

compartment until half-frozen. Whisk the ice cream thoroughly, then freeze until firm.
For a praline ice cream, add 50 g. (2 oz.) crushed praline, nut brittle or toasted hazel nuts to the beaten, half-frozen ice cream before returning it to the freezing compartment.
For coffee ice cream, add 1 tablespoon coffee essence to the cooled custard mixture.
Tinned, drained pineapple, thoroughly crushed, may be added to the ice cream at half-frozen stage.

Granita

A true Italian granita is a fruit (or coffee) flavoured, coarse-textured water ice.

FREEZING TIME: *3–4 hours*

INGREDIENTS *(for 4):*
100 g. (4 oz.) caster sugar
225 ml. (8 fl. oz.) fresh lemon juice
Finely grated rind of 2 lemons

Put the sugar in a pan with ¼ litre (½ pint) of cold water. Bring to the boil over gentle heat until the sugar has dissolved, then continue boiling, without stirring, for 5 minutes.
Remove the syrup from the heat and leave it to cool.
Stir the fruit juice and rind into the cooled syrup and pour the mixture into ice-cube trays, with the dividers left in. Set the trays in the freezer compartment.

Rich Chocolate Ice Cream

FREEZING TIME: *4 hours*

INGREDIENTS *(for 6):*
75 g. (3 oz.) caster sugar
4 egg yolks
½ litre (1 pint) single cream
Vanilla pod
200 g. (7 oz.) plain chocolate

Put the sugar with 6 tablespoons of water in a small pan and heat gently until the sugar is dissolved. Bring to the boil and continue boiling until the sugar has reached the thread stage—about 110°C (230°F). The thread stage is reached when the cooling syrup forms fine threads when dropped from a wooden spoon. Beat the egg yolks in a mixing bowl, then pour in the syrup in a thin stream, whisking all the time.
Put the cream, vanilla pod and chocolate, broken into small pieces, in a pan and cook over low heat until just below boiling point. Remove the vanilla pod and pour the chocolate cream into the egg mixture, whisking until it is thoroughly mixed. Cool and freeze.

Blackcurrant Sorbet

FREEZING TIME: *3–4 hours*

INGREDIENTS *(for 6):*
¼ litre (½ pint) water
100 g. (4 oz.) caster sugar
225 g. (8 oz.) fresh or frozen black currants
1 teaspoon lemon juice
2 egg whites

Put the water in a saucepan together with the sugar. Heat over low heat until the sugar has dissolved, then bring to the boil and boil gently for 10 minutes. Set aside to cool.
Meanwhile, strip and wash the black currants if fresh. Put the fresh or frozen currants, with 2–3 tablespoons of water, in a pan and cook over low heat for 10 minutes. Rub the currants through a sieve and make up the purée with the sugar syrup and extra water to make a total of ½ litre (1 pint). Leave until quite cool. Stir in the lemon juice and pour the mixture into ice-cube trays or a shallow freezing container. Place in the freezing compartment or the deep freeze until nearly firm.
Whisk the egg whites until stiff, but not dry. Turn the frozen mixture into a chilled bowl, break it down thoroughly with a fork, and carefully fold in the egg whites. Return the sorbet mixture to its container and freeze until firm.

COLD AND HOT DRINKS

Lemonade

Scrub six juicy lemons. Cut them up into small cubes leaving on the skin. Place in a saucepan and add 1·7 litres (3 pints) of cold water and 175 g. (6 oz.) of sugar. Bring to the boil and simmer for 20 minutes. Remove from heat and leave covered until cold. Strain into a clean jug, pressing the fruit lightly with a wooden spoon. Add ice cubes.
This is a good drink with tonic water or by itself, diluted to taste. Add slices of fresh orange, if desired, or more sugar if you prefer.

Cold Milk Shakes

Add commercial flavouring, or 1 teaspoon of coffee essence or powder with sugar to taste, to very cold milk. Stir or whisk briskly. Try serving a small scoop of ice cream in milk shakes. Make a small cut in a thin slice of fresh orange and place it on the edge of the glass.

Hot Milk Shakes

Make hot drinks in exactly the same way as cold milk shakes, but be careful not to allow the milk to boil. If you have a large party, heat the milk beforehand and keep it hot in Thermos flasks or insulated containers. Make up the drinks when you are ready. Melted chocolate whisked into hot milk is delicious. To add interest for children, whip an egg white lightly and dip the rim of the drinking glasses into the egg white and then quickly into caster sugar. The sugar can be tinted by the addition of a few drops of red or green food colouring. Stand the glasses upright and allow the frosting to dry before filling with liquid.

Treats for Older Children

COLD DISHES

Bacon and Onion Squares

The ingredients make approximately 30 pieces.

COOKING TIME: *approximately 15 minutes*

INGREDIENTS:
225 g. (8 oz.) plain flour
100 g. (4 oz.) lard
175 g. (6 oz.) bacon scraps
Pinch of salt
1 large onion
1 egg
Poppy seeds or Cayenne pepper

Make a shortcrust pastry (see p. 235). Wrap the pastry in greaseproof paper and leave in the refrigerator for 30 minutes. Meanwhile, chop the bacon and onion into very small pieces. Fry the bacon; add the onion and cook until transparent. Remove from pan and allow to cool.

Take out the pastry and roll evenly to a thickness of 5 mm. ($\frac{1}{4}$ in.). Scatter half the mixture over the middle third of the pastry and fold the top third down over it. Put the remaining half of the mixture on the folded part and draw up the bottom third of the pastry to cover it. You should now have three layers of pastry and two of mixture.
Give the pastry a half turn and roll lightly with a well-floured rolling pin. Make sure the filling is not sticking by keeping the pastry board or table lightly floured. Fold the pastry again by turning the top third down and drawing the bottom third up. This ensures an even distribution of the mixture. Now roll out evenly again to a thickness of 5 mm., and place on to a greased baking sheet. Before putting into the oven, mark out 4 cm. ($1\frac{1}{2}$ in.) squares and brush over with beaten egg. Sprinkle half the squares with poppy seeds or Cayenne.

Cook at 190°C (375°F), gas mark 5, for approximately 15 minutes or until deep golden-brown. The cooking time depends on how thinly you rolled out the mixture.
NOTE: Placing the pastry as a whole on to the baking sheet saves time, but if you find the large piece too awkward to handle, cut the squares out on your pastry board and lift them individually with a palette knife on to the baking sheet.

Prawn Puffs

Either buy 450 g. (1 lb.) of puff pastry or make it (see p. 235).

INGREDIENTS:
50 g. (2 oz.) plain flour
50 g. (2 oz.) margarine
1 medium-size onion
2 cloves
600 ml. (1 pint) milk
225 g. (8 oz.) prawns
50 g. (2 oz.) finely grated Cheddar cheese
¼ teaspoon each of mustard, salt and pepper

Make a basic white sauce as follows:
Melt the margarine and with a wooden spoon stir in the flour until the mixture leaves the sides of the pan. Do not allow the mixture to become browned. Warm the milk and gradually stir it in. Cook until boiling. Add the onion studded with cloves and allow the sauce to simmer over a very low heat for 30 minutes.
Remove and discard the onion. Cover the sauce with damp greaseproof paper to prevent a skin forming. Put the prawns and grated cheese into a dish and spoon enough of the sauce on to them to make a fairly stiff mixture. Season with mustard, salt and pepper.
Now roll out the puff pastry to a thickness of 5 mm. (¼ in.). Using a 6·5 cm. (2½ in.) cutter, cut out as many circles as possible. Dampen the edges of half the pastry circles, put a heaped teaspoon of the prawn and cheese mixture on to the centre of each, and cover with the remaining circles. Seal each of the rounds well, fluting the edges with a fork. Make a tiny slit on top of each puff with a knife, and brush with beaten egg. Bake in a hot oven at 220–230°C (425–450°F), gas mark 7–8, for approximately 10–15 minutes. These are very good either hot or cold.

Savoury Choux Buns

COOKING TIME: *10 minutes*

INGREDIENTS:
Choux pastry (for recipe see p. 226)
6 eggs
1 tablespoon of cream or mayonnaise
1 teaspoon of curry paste (or powder)
Lemon juice
Salt and pepper

Make the choux pastry and pipe small bulbs about the size of a walnut on to a damp baking sheet. Cook at 190°C (375°F), gas mark 5, for approximately 10 minutes until they have risen golden and firm. Cool on a wire rack.
Boil the eggs for 10 minutes. Plunge them into cold water and shell at once. Immerse the shelled eggs in cold water for 5 minutes.
Remove the yolks to a clean basin and beat them well with the cream or mayonnaise. Add the curry paste, a little lemon juice, and salt and pepper. The consistency should be very smooth, with a well-flavoured taste. If the texture is too stiff, due to over-cooking the yolks, add more cream.
Scrape the mixture into a piping bag, fitted with a small plain nozzle, and pipe it into the choux buns through any existing holes, or through small holes made underneath. Put plenty of the mixture into each bun, and arrange on a dish alternately with Savoury Barquettes and Prawn Puffs.

Savoury Barquettes

Barquette moulds are available from many hardware stores. As an alternative, you can use your own small tart moulds, but the difference in shape is almost as important as the difference in flavour between savoury and sweet. It is therefore worth making the effort

to get the real thing. For adults, barquettes are also useful for hors d'oeuvre and cocktail snacks. The moulds are usually sold in sets of four. In this recipe the barquette shells can be stored, so you can re-use the moulds and cook only a few at a time if you wish.
The ingredients should make approximately 24 barquette shells.

COOKING TIME: *approximately 15 minutes*

INGREDIENTS:
250 g. (9 oz.) plain flour
75 g. (3 oz.) margarine
75 g. (3 oz.) lard
175 g. (6 oz.) cheese
Pinch each of salt, pepper and nutmeg

Beat the margarine and lard together. Grate the cheese finely, add it to the fats, and beat well until smooth. Add the sieved flour and spices gradually. When the mixture clings together and leaves the sides of the bowl, knead lightly. Wrap in greaseproof paper and leave in a cool place to rest for 30 minutes. Roll out the paste to a thickness of 5 mm. (¼ in.). Line the barquette moulds and prick the bases with a fork. Bake at 200°C (400°F), gas mark 6, for approximately 15 minutes or until golden. Allow to cool completely. When cold store in an airtight tin. The shells will keep crisp for 3 or 4 days.

SOME SUGGESTIONS FOR FILLINGS:
Chopped sauté mushrooms mixed with chopped hard-boiled eggs
Flaked fish in mayonnaise with a dash of Cayenne pepper
Cream cheese and pineapple
Diced chicken and lightly cooked frozen mixed vegetables, bound with salad cream
Cottage cheese and grated onion sprinkled with paprika

HOT DISHES

Whitebait Pick-up

COOKING TIME: *approximately 15 minutes*

INGREDIENTS:
450 g. (1 lb.) fresh or frozen whitebait
Seasoned flour
2 eggs
100 g. (4 oz.) fine oatmeal
Paprika
Corn oil

Wash the whitebait in a colander under cold running water. Drain well and pat dry with a clean cloth. Toss in seasoned flour, then pass first through beaten egg, then through the oatmeal.
Heat the corn oil, which should not fill more than one-third of the depth of the pan. When the oil is just below smoking point, drop in one of the fish. It should immediately rise sizzling to the surface. Cook for 1 minute and remove. Cook all the fish, a few at a time, in the same way. Sprinkle paprika liberally on a sheet of greaseproof paper and shuffle the cooked fish through. Then place the fish on a wire rack until cold. The cooked whitebait should be piled up like crisps for the children to pick up and eat.

Savoury Plaits

This recipe makes approximately 12 portions.

COOKING TIME: *approximately 35–40 minutes*

INGREDIENTS:
450 g. (1 lb.) plain flour
225 g. (8 oz.) cooking fat
1 level teaspoon salt
6 tablespoons cold water
450 g. (1 lb.) sausage meat
1 large onion
½ packet stuffing
Lemon juice
2 dessertspoons cold water
1 egg

Make short pastry using the flour, fat, salt and 6 tablespoons of cold water (see p. 235). When

thoroughly mixed, leave in a ball in a cool place to rest. For the filling, chop the onion finely, and mix well with the sausage meat, stuffing, lemon juice, and 2 dessertspoons of cold water.
Roll the pastry into two rectangles measuring approximately 30 by 23 cm. (12 by 9 in.).
Place half the filling down the centre third of each rectangle. Slash the sides of the pastry diagonally on each side of the filling in 1·5 cm. ($\frac{1}{2}$ in.) strips. Fold the pastry strips alternately from each side across the filling to form a plait.
Place the finished plaits on a lightly greased baking sheet, brush with beaten egg and cook in the centre of a pre-heated oven at 200°C (400°F), gas mark 6, for approximately 35–40 minutes.

Spaghetti Sauce

COOKING TIME: *approximately 1 hour*

INGREDIENTS:
2 large onions
50 g. (2 oz.) dripping
Plain flour
1 large tin of tomato juice
2 bay leaves
Clove of garlic
Salt and pepper
Optional additions: meat or mushrooms

Chop the two large onions finely and cook gently in the dripping until transparent. Add enough flour to the pan to absorb the fat and cook for 2 minutes. Remove from heat and add the tomato juice.
Replace on heat and bring to the boil, stirring constantly. Reduce the heat, add the two bay leaves and garlic clove, and allow to simmer for approximately 45 minutes. Remove the bay leaves and garlic, and adjust the seasoning to taste.
Any small amounts of meat, such as salami or cooked or uncooked chicken or minced meat, and mushrooms can be added to the onions while frying to make this into an excellent sauce. It will be memorable if a small amount of cream is stirred in just before serving.

Fish Goujons

INGREDIENTS:

Fish
Plain flour
Salt and pepper
Beaten egg
Breadcrumbs

Goujons can be made from any filleted white fish such as plaice, sole or even skate, if you have the patience to remove the fish from between the pliable bones in the wings.
After filleting, cut the fish in strips 8 cm. by 5 mm. (3 by $\frac{1}{4}$ in.) and pass them through the seasoned flour, beaten egg and breadcrumbs, in that order.
Deep-fry in oil and serve in small bowls lined with paper napkins and wedges of lemon.
The recipe may sound expensive, but you will be surprised how many strips you can get from a few fillets, and be delighted by the tempting curly golden heap that results. Your children, too, will love their fish done this way.

Vol-au-vents

You have to be an exceptional cook to improve on vol-au-vent cases that can be bought deep frozen and uncooked. The secret of success with these is to place them on greased and dampened baking sheets, and to allow them to stand at room temperature for 30 minutes.
Brush with milk. Do not put more than one tray in the oven at a time, otherwise the cases on the lower shelf will not rise evenly. Bake at 200°C (400°F), gas mark 6, for 15–20 minutes, or until crisp and light brown.

SOME SUGGESTIONS FOR FILLINGS:
Sweet corn and bacon (chopped small and fried)
Cottage cheese and sweet chutney
Diced chicken in mayonnaise
Prawns in cream with a dash of tomato purée
Curried egg (mix salad cream, curry powder, salt and pepper and chopped hard-boiled eggs)

Sausage Rolls

COOKING TIME: *30 minutes*

INGREDIENTS *(for 18 rolls):*
1 portion flaky pastry (see p. 235)
450 g. (1 lb.) sausage meat
Plain flour
1 egg

Cut the prepared rough flaky pastry, 45 by 15 cm. (18 by 6 in.), into two strips each 8 cm. (3 in.) wide. Divide the sausage meat in half, shape it into two long rolls to fit the pastry strips, and coat the meat lightly with flour.
Lay the sausage meat in the centre of the pastry strips, brush the edges with beaten egg and fold the pastry over. Seal the two long edges firmly.
Brush the two pastry lengths with beaten egg and cut them into 5 cm. (2 in.) long pieces. Score the top of the pastry lightly with the point of a knife. Set the sausage rolls on greased baking trays and bake just above the centre of a pre-heated oven at 220°C (425°F), gas mark 7, for 25–30 minutes or until golden-brown and puffed.

CAKES AND PUDDINGS

Chequerboard

Make a large shallow cake and trim it to a reasonably accurate square. Seal it by brushing all over with a hot apricot glaze (see Building a House, p. 232). Place on a cake board and cover completely with white glacé icing.
Buy white and pink marshmallows and white and pink peppermints. Using a sharp knife dipped in hot water cut through each marshmallow and, with the cut side downwards, place them side by side over the entire surface of the cake, alternating pink with white. At two ends place pink peppermints on the white marshmallows and white peppermints on the pink marshmallows of the two back rows. Tie a ribbon round the chequerboard.

A Hedgehog Birthday Cake

Make a cake using twice the ingredients given in the basic recipe (see p. 232). Bake in a deep cake tin. When cold, cut the cake with a sharp knife into an oval shape. The shape can be obtained by making the outline of an oval jelly mould or pie dish on a piece of greaseproof paper, and cutting along the pencilled line. Place the oval paper on top of the cake and cut downwards, carefully working round your pattern.
Choose the end of the cake that is to be the face and head, and shape it to a point by cutting a wedge shaped piece from either side. Now cut away the cake gradually to make a gently rounded back and slope the head down towards the pointed nose. Brush with hot apricot glaze (see p. 232) and leave to cool. When cold, stand the cake on a wire rack and pour over enough chocolate icing to cover it completely. When set, place the hedgehog on a cake board and pour a second coat of chocolate icing over it. As soon as this second coat has cooled, take a box of orange-flavoured chocolate matchsticks, cut them in half to form the quills, and push the cut ends into the back and sides of the animal. They should be close together, and should slant backwards away from the face, leaving the front slope to the nose clear. Put in two sweets for eyes, and use a circular liquorice allsort covered in hundreds and thousands as a splendid nose. Clean the cake board round the base of the cake, and pipe greetings on the board.

Football Pitch

Make a cake from the basic recipe in a large, shallow sponge tin. If you haven't got a tin of this kind you can bake a square cake, cut it horizontally, and place the two halves side by side to form a long pitch. Place it on a cake board, and brush over completely with hot

apricot glaze (see Building a House, p. 232). Leave to cool.
Mix enough white icing, with a very little green colouring, to cover the cake completely. Pipe in the pitch line markings in white (see diagram). Brush the pitch surround with sugar syrup and sprinkle it with chocolate strands. Make the goalposts out of one or two white straws, gluing the cross-bar to the uprights before gently pressing the posts into the cake.

Buy little footballer figures at a stationer's or a large store and place them on the field. The ball can be a round sweet.
Use candles to make the corner flags. The birthday name can be piped on the sides of the cake.

Lemon Meringue Pie

COOKING TIME: *40 minutes*

INGREDIENTS *(for 6):*

100 g. (4 oz.) shortcrust pastry (see p. 235)
1 large thin-skinned lemon
2–3 level tablespoons granulated sugar
2 level tablespoons cornflour
2 eggs
15 g. (½ oz.) unsalted butter
100 g. (4 oz.) caster sugar

Roll out the pastry and line a 21.5 cm. (8½ in.) pie plate or an 18 cm. (7 in.) flan ring. Bake the pastry case blind in the centre of a pre-heated oven at 200°C (400°F), gas mark 6, for about 15 minutes or until the pastry is crisp and golden. When cold, remove the pastry from the pie plate or ease away the flan ring.
Meanwhile, peel the rind from the lemon in thin slivers, carefully omitting all white pith. Squeeze the juice from the lemon and set it aside. Put the lemon peel, granulated sugar

and $\frac{1}{4}$ litre ($\frac{1}{2}$ pint) of water in a pan; cook over low heat until the sugar has dissolved, then bring this syrup to the boil. Remove the pan from the heat. Blend the cornflour in a bowl with 3 tablespoons lemon juice, then pour in the syrup through a strainer, stirring thoroughly. Separate the eggs, and beat in the egg yolks, one at a time, together with the butter. The mixture should be thick enough to coat the back of a wooden spoon; otherwise return it to the pan and cook for a few minutes without boiling. Spoon the lemon mixture into the cooked pastry case, set on a baking tray. Whisk the egg whites until stiff, then add half the caster sugar and continue whisking until the meringue holds its shape and stands in soft peaks. Fold in all but 1 teaspoon of the remaining sugar, using a metal spoon.
Pile the meringue over the lemon filling; spread it from the edge towards the centre, making sure that the meringue joins the pastry edge to prevent the meringue 'weeping'.
Sprinkle the meringue with the remaining sugar. Reduce the heat to 150°C (300°F), gas mark 2, and bake the pie in the centre of the oven for 20–30 minutes, or until the meringue is crisp. Serve the pie warm, rather than hot or cold.

Pineapple Butterflies

The ingredients should make approximately 24 biscuits.

COOKING TIME: *approximately 15 minutes*

INGREDIENTS:

350 g. (12 oz.) plain flour
225 g. (8 oz.) margarine
100 g. (4 oz.) caster sugar
Tin of pineapple rings
Pinch of salt
Cornflour
Chocolate vermicelli

Sieve the flour and salt. Mix in the margarine and sugar. Work all together making a smooth paste. Flour the pastry board lightly with cornflour. Roll the paste carefully to a thickness of 5 mm. ($\frac{1}{4}$ in.). Cut into circles with a 5 cm. (2 in.) plain cutter. Place on a lightly greased baking sheet and prick each biscuit with a fork. Bake at 190°C (375°F), gas mark 5, for about 15 minutes. The biscuits should be very pale. Cool on a wire rack.
Drain the pineapple rings on a double thickness of kitchen paper. Meanwhile, make up a packet of proprietary topping.
Cover each biscuit with the topping. Cut the pineapple rings in pieces and place two at 45 degree angles on each biscuit, making a pair of wings. Put 25 g. (1 oz.) of chocolate vermicelli in the creased fold of a small sheet of greaseproof paper, and carefully shake out a line between the wings, to form the body of the butterfly.

Strawberry Cream Sponge

COOKING TIME: *15 minutes*

INGREDIENTS:
75 g. (3 oz.) plain flour
Pinch of salt
3 eggs
75 g. (3 oz.) caster sugar
Strawberry jam
150 ml. ($\frac{1}{4}$ pint) double or whipping cream
Caster or icing sugar for dusting

Butter and dust with flour and sugar two 18 cm. (7 in.) straight-sided sandwich tins.
Sift the flour with the salt twice into a bowl or on to a sheet of greaseproof paper. Place a deep mixing bowl over a pan of hot water, break the eggs into the bowl and gradually whisk in the sugar. Continue whisking until the mixture is pale, and thick enough to leave a trail. Carefully fold in the sifted flour and salt. Divide the mixture equally between the two tins, putting any scrapings from the bowl at the side of the tins, not in the middle. Bake just above the centre of an oven, pre-heated to 190°C (375°F), gas mark 5, for about 15 minutes or until pale brown and springy to the touch.
Carefully ease away the edges of the baked cakes with a palette knife, and cool on a wire rack.

When cold, spread the bases of both sponges with a thin layer of jam, cover one sponge with whipped cream and place the other cake, jam downwards, on top. Press lightly together and dust with caster or sifted icing sugar. Chill until serving.

Chocolate Layer Cake

COOKING TIME: *30 minutes*

INGREDIENTS:
100 g. (4 oz.) butter or margarine
100 g. (4 oz.) caster sugar
2 large eggs
2 level tablespoons cocoa
100 g. (4 oz.) self-raising flour
Pinch of salt

INGREDIENTS FOR FILLING:
40 g. (1½ oz.) butter or margarine
75 g. (3 oz.) icing sugar
2 teaspoons coffee essence
1 tablespoon top of the milk

Grease a straight-sided 20 cm. (8 in.) wide sandwich tin and line with paper, cutting the band of paper to come 1·5 cm. (½ in.) above the rim. Grease the paper lining.
Beat the butter until soft, then add the sugar and cream the mixture until light and fluffy. Beat the eggs before beating them into the mixture, a little at a time. In a small bowl or cup, blend the cocoa with enough cold water to make a paste. Lightly beat this into the creamed mixture, alternately with the sifted flour and salt. Turn the cake mixture into the prepared tin, level the surface and bake in the centre of a pre-heated oven at 180°C (350°F), gas mark 4, for about 30 minutes or until well risen and spongy to the touch.
Meanwhile, make the filling. Beat the butter until soft and creamy, sift the icing sugar and add a little at a time. Stir in the coffee essence and milk.
Turn the cake on to a wire rack, and remove the lining paper. Cut the cold cake in half horizontally, and spread the bottom half with the filling; place the top in position and lightly press the two halves together. Dust the top with sifted icing sugar. Using the back of a knife blade, draw a lattice pattern across the sugar.

Rum Truffles

This recipe provides about 24 pieces.

INGREDIENTS:
175 g. (6 oz.) cake crumbs
175 g. (6 oz.) caster sugar
175 g. (6 oz.) ground peanuts
4 tablespoons grated dark chocolate
2 egg yolks
2 tablespoons rum or 1 tablespoon rum essence
2 tablespoons finely grated orange peel

When making the Birthday Cake (see p. 232) you may have pieces which were cut away when making a basic shape, such as the house. If so, use these pieces, or alternatively trifle sponge cakes. Crumb the cake and mix with the sugar, peanuts and chocolate. Beat in the egg yolks, rum essence and orange peel.
Shape heaped teaspoons of the mixture into balls and roll in additional finely grated chocolate. These truffles will keep fresh for up to seven days in a plastic container at the bottom of the refrigerator.

Lemon Delight

The ingredients make approximately 24 slices.

INGREDIENTS:
16 individual trifle sponges
225 g. (8 oz.) butter
350 g. (12 oz.) caster sugar
8 eggs
2 large tins mandarin oranges
Rind and juice of 2 large lemons
Fresh cream or lemon icing (for decoration)

Cut each of the trifle sponges twice horizontally to give three thin layers of sponge. Cream the butter and sugar together until white. Separate the eggs and beat the yolks into the mixture with the lemon rind and juice. Whip the whites until stiff, then fold into the lemon mixture.

Line two bread tins with greaseproof paper and put in alternate layers of sponge and lemon mixture until the tins are half filled. Then put in a layer of mandarin orange slices Continue with alternate layers of sponge and lemon mixture, finishing with sponge. Cover the tins with foil and freeze for 24 hours. Turn out of the tins on to a plate or board and decorate as you wish with either lightly whipped cream or lemon icing, using a few orange slices. Cut into slices as you would a loaf.

Tipsy Trifle

INGREDIENTS:

6–8 individual trifle sponges
1 packet ratafia biscuits
450 ml. (¾ pint) thick custard
Red jam
300 ml. (½ pint) cream (double or single), or 150 ml. (¼ pint) cream and 1 packet pink and white marshmallows
Sweet sherry or fruit juice
Glacé cherries and angelica

Cut the sponge cakes in half horizontally, spread with jam, and put the halves back together. Put the sponges in a glass dish. Sprinkle with the sherry or fruit juice and allow to soak in well. Scatter the ratafia biscuits on the sponges and mix together, adding a few chopped glacé cherries. Make the custard, allow it to cool, beat in 150 ml. (¼ pint) of lightly whipped cream. Pour the custard at once over the sponge base and leave for 2 hours in a cool place. Finish the top either in a pattern of alternating pink and white marshmallows with a few glacé cherries and leaves of angelica, or with 150 ml. of whipped cream spread over the top and decorated with crushed ratafia biscuits around the edge of the dish, and a bunch of glacé cherries and angelica leaves in the centre.

Coffee Meringues

The recipe will provide approximately 30 meringues.

INGREDIENTS:

275 g. (10 oz.) caster sugar
5 egg whites
2 teaspoons coffee essence
300 ml. (½ pint) sweetened coffee-flavoured cream

Make sure none of your utensils has the slightest trace of grease—scald them before use.
Whisk the egg whites until stiff. Add the coffee essence and continue whisking. Add 175 g. (6 oz.) of sugar, whisking all the time. Continue to whisk until the mixture is very stiff. Stir in the remaining sugar gently but thoroughly. Pipe on to an oven sheet lined with waxed paper, using a piping bag and nozzles or two spoons. You can be adventurous with the shapes—cigars, crescents and fans, as well as the usual shells.
Bake at 140°C (275°F), gas mark 1, for 30 minutes. Leave the oven door open slightly to allow any steam to escape. Remove the meringues from the oven when they are sufficiently set to be lifted from the sheet. Carefully press in the base to make a hollow for the cream filling. Leave in a warm dry place until required. Put the meringues together with piped coffee-flavoured cream.

PREPARING A BARBECUE

Collect together all the equipment you will need. Long-handled forks, carving forks, long-handled kitchen spoons, tongs, a sharp knife and chopping board, oven gloves, cotton or linen (not plastic) aprons, and a large pot for holding all the utensils. You will also need paper napkins, paper plates, cutlery, seasonings and sauces, and a bottle opener. Use firelighters to get the charcoal going at least 45 minutes before you start cooking.

Stuffed Baked Potatoes

INGREDIENTS:
Potatoes
Grated cheese (any kind)
Tuna fish
Bay leaves

After scrubbing well, pre-bake the potatoes in their skins. Cut them lengthways and carefully remove the flesh. Mash the potato and divide equally into separate basins. In one of the basins mix in an equal quantity of grated cheese; in the other an equal quantity of tuna fish. Season both mixtures well, and replace in the potato jackets. One half of each potato will now contain cheese mixture, and one half fish mixture. Place a bay leaf between the two halves, wrap each potato in foil and re-heat in the oven at 190°C (375°F), gas mark 5, for approximately 20 minutes, or place on the barbecue. Remove bay leaf before eating.

Baked Potatoes

Pre-bake potatoes in the oven, then finish cooking them on the grill in foil wraps. Cook for 10 minutes before serving.
For a filling, chop mixed herbs (fresh if possible) and pound them with 225 g. (8 oz.) butter. Roll this on damp greaseproof paper, place in the refrigerator, and cut into slices when well chilled. Put slices inside baked potatoes or on top of chops.

Hot Flavoured Bread Rolls

Cut a French loaf in slices, taking care that each slice goes only two-thirds of the way through the loaf. Spread one of the following fillings between each slice, wrap the loaf in silver foil and bake in the oven at 200°C (400°F), gas mark 6, for approximately 15 minutes.

SOME SUGGESTIONS FOR FILLINGS:
100 g. (4 oz.) butter, 1 tablespoon chopped parsley, 1 clove crushed garlic, salt
100 g. (4 oz.) butter, 25 g. (1 oz.) grated Parmesan cheese, 1 tablespoon French mustard, a little grated onion
50 g. (2 oz.) butter, 1 tin sardines, 1 tablespoon lemon juice

Hamburgers with Pepper Sauce

COOKING TIME: *up to 2 hours for the sauce*

INGREDIENTS:
Hamburgers
40 g. (1½ oz.) plain flour
25 g. (1 oz.) dripping
600 ml. (1 pint) beef stock
15 g. (½ oz.) tomato purée
Large carrot
Medium-size onion
Lemon juice
6 crushed peppercorns

The hamburgers should preferably be of medium thickness. Brush them before grilling with melted butter or oil. Use tongs for turning. Baste to avoid the meat drying out. To make the pepper sauce (which can be prepared in advance), melt the dripping, add carrot and onion roughly chopped, and brown slightly. Add the flour and cook gently, stirring continuously. When the flour has taken on a golden colour, remove from the heat, and cool slightly. Add the tomato purée

and the boiling stock.
Return to the heat and bring to the boil. Reduce the heat and simmer for approximately 2 hours, stirring from time to time. Just before using, add lemon juice to taste and the crushed peppercorns. Sieve into a hot jug, or for outside use, into an insulated container.

Beef Bungs

INGREDIENTS:

450 g. (1 lb.) best minced beef
1 large onion
1 teaspoon mixed herbs
100 g. (4 oz.) fresh white breadcrumbs
2 juniper berries
2 dessertspoons Madeira wine (or cream)

Pound all the ingredients together very thoroughly until smooth. Add the Madeira (or cream) and pound again. Mould the mixture into shapes as follows. Scoop up a dessertspoonful and hold in one hand. Take up a second dessertspoon and, keeping both spoons horizontal all the time (that is with the bowls downwards), scoop the mixture out of one spoon into the other, repeating the process. Cook the bungs on foil or a baking sheet, brushing them with oil as they cook.

Barbecue Snack

This super snack, prepared earlier in the day, can be eaten while waiting for the first of the barbecued meats to cook.

INGREDIENTS:
4 medium-size potatoes
2 onions
8 eggs
25 g. (1 oz.) butter
25 g. (1 oz.) cooking oil
2 tablespoons cold water
Salt and pepper

Peel and dice potatoes, chop onions finely. Fry together in a knob of butter until almost cooked, then remove from pan.

Beat the eggs and cold water; add salt and pepper. Put the butter and cooking oil into a large frying pan and heat until the butter is melted. Add the egg mixture and reduce the heat to a medium flame. When the bottom of the omelette is just setting, scatter the cooked potato and onion evenly into the pan.
Continue cooking until the filled omelette is firm. You may have to set the top of the omelette by placing it under the grill, but try not to brown it too much.
Allow the omelette to become quite cold, then cut into 4 cm. ($1\frac{1}{2}$ in.) squares and impale them on cocktail sticks, or place them on small biscuits or squares of toast.

Chicken Drumsticks

INGREDIENTS:

Chicken drumsticks
100 g. (4 oz.) butter
Tarragon
Rosemary
Salt
Black pepper
1 cup white wine (optional)

Chop the tarragon and rosemary finely. Mix with 100 g. (4 oz.) butter and pound together until a thick green cream is obtained. Cover the chicken drumsticks with this green butter, season with salt and pepper, and wrap in squares of kitchen foil. Barbecue for approximately 25 minutes.

Other barbecue items

Don't forget that hamburgers, chops, sausages, liver and bacon are not the only things one can barbecue. Fish can be grilled in exactly the same way, except that the grill must be very hot and brushed with oil. The fish itself should be basted during cooking with oil in which bruised herbs have been allowed to stand. Fruit and vegetables (apples, mushrooms, tomatoes) can also be threaded on skewers with cubes of meat, and grilled.

TASTY TREATS FOR A PICNIC

Careful planning will turn a picnic from a snatched sandwich outing into a memorable family event.

Provide blankets or rugs for the children to sit on and prepare food on trays packed into boxes. It's relatively easy to ensure that food is not spoiled by crushing, if you choose sensibly and cover it with foil or other protective material.

To keep food cool, use a camping cool box, if you have one or can borrow one. As an alternative, line a cardboard box with pieces of polystyrene packing. Stores often throw away this material, or you might save it from the case in which your television set or washing machine was delivered. Such a box effectively keeps food and drinks cool for some hours. Make sure that food you intend to keep cold is well chilled before packing.

Individual Quiches

The quantities will provide approximately 16 quiches.

INGREDIENTS:

175 g. (6 oz.) fats (preferably half butter and half lard)
175 g. (6 oz.) finely grated cheese
250 g. (9 oz.) plain flour
Pinch of salt

Loose-bottomed 11·5 cm. (4½ in.) flan tins, available in hardware stores, help to make quiches attractive and easier to produce. Alternatively, you can use Yorkshire pudding tins or tart tins, although these are small for quiches.

To make the pastry, beat the fats and cheese together. Gradually add sifted flour and salt, and work together to form a firm, smooth pastry. Wrap in greaseproof paper and cool well for 30 minutes.

Roll out to a thickness of 5 mm. (¼ in.) on a floured sheet. Cut out to fit your baking tins. Prick the pastry, and cook at 200°C (400°F), gas mark 6, for 10 minutes. Remove from the oven and fill with any of the fillings or custard. To make the custard, add two well-beaten eggs, salt and pepper to 300 ml. (½ pint) of milk. Replace in the oven and cook at 200°C for a further 10 minutes. Reduce the heat to 180°C (350°F), gas mark 4, and cook for a further 10–15 minutes.

SOME SUGGESTIONS FOR FILLINGS:

Bacon and onion chopped finely and gently fried
Tuna fish
Sweet corn and ham
Chicken and asparagus

Cheese Tartlets

The recipe makes approximately 30 tartlets. Make the pastry as for the individual quiches and line tartlet tins. Prick the pastry and cook at 200°C (400°F), gas mark 6, for 10 minutes.

INGREDIENTS FOR FILLING:

225 g. (8 oz.) cream cheese
2 eggs
150 ml. (¼ pint) single cream
1 garlic clove, crushed
¼ teaspoon nutmeg
1 tablespoon parsley
Salt and pepper

Beat the eggs into the cheese. Gradually add the cream and all the other ingredients. Pour carefully into the part-baked pastry cases and return to the oven for a further 15 minutes at 200°C (400°F), gas mark 6, reducing heat to 180°C (350°F), gas mark 4, for the final 5 minutes.

Savoury Eggs

Boil eggs for 10 minutes. Plunge into cold water, shell and cut in half lengthways. Take out the yolks and mix with an equal quantity of a proprietary sandwich spread and a good pinch of Cayenne pepper. Put the mixture into the whites and place the two halves together. Cut a French stick loaf into 5 cm. (2 in.) thick slices. Scoop out some of the bread in the middle of each slice, making a small bowl shape. Butter the slices well and put them in the oven for 15 minutes at 180°C (350°F), gas mark 4. They should then be golden and crisp. Remove from the oven and allow to cool. When cold put the filled egg in the hollow.

Chopped Salad

INGREDIENTS:
6 sticks of celery
100 g. (4 oz.) walnuts
3 red dessert apples (washed and polished)
Salt
Lemon juice
Mandarin segments
Salad cream
2 teaspoons curry paste (optional)

Chop all the ingredients very small. Add a few drops of lemon juice and mix with salad cream.

Chicken 'n' Rice

The recipe makes enough for about 12 children.

INGREDIENTS:
Chicken
350 g. (12 oz.) patna rice
4 tomatoes
50 g. (2 oz.) raisins
Chives or spring onions
Mayonnaise

Roast the chicken. Allow to cool, take off all the meat and cut into bite-size pieces. Skin the tomatoes by making small cuts in the stalk end, plunging into boiling water for 3 minutes, and immersing in cold water. The skin will then curl off easily. Cut each tomato in half, and gently squeeze out the seeds. Chop the tomato flesh.
Cook the patna rice in salted water and refresh under the cold tap. Shake free from water and dry in a cool oven for a few minutes. Swell the raisins in a colander over boiling water for 15 minutes. Chop a few chives or the green of spring onions very finely.
Mix all the ingredients together, adjust the seasoning and add just enough mayonnaise to bind the mixture lightly together. Stand in a cool place for at least 2 hours. Pack in a cool box with a well-fitting lid.

Fruited Gold Salad

INGREDIENTS:
225 g. (8 oz.) grated raw carrot
100 g. (4 oz.) salted peanuts
100 g. (4 oz.) raisins
1 small can of pineapple pieces
Mayonnaise
Salt
Lemon juice

Chop the peanuts finely. Add to the raisins and grated carrot. Drain the pineapple pieces, dry on kitchen paper, mix with other ingredients. Just before serving, pour on only enough mayonnaise to bind the salad together. Add salt, pepper and lemon juice to taste.

Swift Paté

INGREDIENTS:
225 g. (8 oz.) liver sausage
225 g. (8 oz.) cream cheese
1 teaspoon Worcestershire sauce
½ teaspoon curry powder
1 tablespoon double cream
1 tablespoon brandy
1 tablespoon melted butter
Salt and pepper

Mix all the ingredients together, beating well with the melted butter. Place in a dish, smooth the surface and seal with the melted butter.

Index

For easy reference, subject areas given extended treatment are listed in *italic type*. Specific games are in roman type

Q

R

S

T

U

V

W

X

Y

CONTRIBUTORS
The Publishers wish to express their gratitude for major contributions by the following people:

DOUGLAS ST. P. BARNARD
PATRICIA BURNSTONE
MAURICE DAY
HARRY GOLOMBEK
GORDON MESSAGE

ARTISTS:
KATE SIMUNEK
GRAHAM PERCY

PHOTOGRAPHY:
ROBERT GOLDEN (PARTY TREATS)
SPECTRUM COLOUR LIBRARY (INDOOR GAMES AND OUTDOOR GAMES)

A NUMBER OF GAMES IN THIS BOOK HAVE BEEN ADAPTED FROM THE READER'S DIGEST BOOK OF 1000 FAMILY GAMES, PUBLISHED BY THE READER'S DIGEST ASSOCIATION, INC. OF PLEASANTVILLE, NEW YORK, U.S.A.

FAMILY GAMES AND PARTY TREATS
was edited and designed by
The Reader's Digest Association Limited, London

Printed and bound in Great Britain by
Waterlow Ltd, Dunstable